T0089953

The Ballad of Bob Dylan

"A portrait that explodes the semihostile cliché of much unauthorized biography. New interviews and photographs add depth to an account distinguished by a fine sensitivity to all aspects of Dylan's art, from the personal to the music's history, but Epstein also manages to put across a significant amount of biographical detail. . . . Well-written, perceptive, and concise, Epstein's book never goes far from the music in which Dylan's apparent contradictions dissolve."

— Tim Martin, *The Telegraph* (London)

"In *The Ballad of Bob Dylan*, Daniel Mark Epstein does what few have been able to do at all, much less this well: capture that spirit, and in so doing, somehow manage to get closer to the essence of an American icon." — Dave Moyer, *New York Journal of Books*

"The broad picture that emerges, both of the man and his work, is coherent and convincing. . . . Epstein is a musician and poet as well as an acclaimed biographer, and his appreciation of Dylan's art is subtle and multilayered. . . . Epstein's thoughtful examination of Dylan's life and work . . . will send you back to his music with your ears reopened and your mind refreshed."

— Simon Griffith, *Mail on Sunday* (UK) (4 out of 5 stars)

"A galvanizing interpretation of Dylan's many masks and achievements. . . . Illuminates the complex symbiosis between Dylan's theatricalized personas and ever-evolving art."

— *Booklist*

"[Epstein] cleverly pits the young Mr. Dylan's self-styled orphan-hobo persona against the real-life son of middle-class Jewish parents from Hibbing, Minn. . . . Mr. Epstein, an accomplished poet and biographer, is one of the better stylists to tackle the Dylan story. . . . A musician himself, Mr. Epstein is particularly good on tunings and chord progressions, on where Mr. Dylan's capo is placed in each song and the sound his harmonica makes clicking into its holder." — David Yezzi, *Wall Street Journal*

"Brilliant—that Daniel Mark Epstein is both a poet and a biographer stands him in good stead in this penetrating, compassionate (but utterly clear-eyed), beautifully written portrait of Bob Dylan as an artist and a man. Among the very best writing about Dylan, ever." — James Kaplan, author of *Frank: The Voice*

"Raptly observant." — *Publishers Weekly*

"A vivid portrait of the visionary artist. . . . If you like Keith Richards's *Life*, then read *The Ballad of Bob Dylan*." — *US Weekly*

"What sets Epstein's book apart is its accessibility. . . . Epstein is refreshingly direct and approachable, and while the author, also a folk musician, makes much of his extensive quotes from Dylan's lyrics, it is his own clear, emotional enthusiasm that carries the tale." — Rob Fitzpatrick, *Sunday Times* (London)

"Even he [Dylan] might approve of the mission that inspires the most recent crop of writing about him: to 'celebrate the impossibility of pinning down Bob Dylan.' . . . Above all, that means exploring the desire for change that drove Dylan from the start and still consumes him in his latest period, as Daniel Mark Epstein understands in his biography." — John Dickerson, *Slate*

"Epstein is not essentially a hagiographer, and . . . he remains essentially clear-eyed about his subject's achievements and failings. The Dylan that emerges in these pages is by turns ambitious, seductive, single-minded, generous, cruel, witty, kind, gnomic, blunt, and charismatic. . . . The accumulation of detail gives texture to Epstein's depiction of Dylan as a performer, which in turn buttresses his often perceptive analysis of the songs, both as texts and as performed works. . . . Epstein has a knack for sharp, indelibly etched character sketches. . . . Epstein's skills as an interviewer serve up a few unforgettable passages."

— Webster Younce, *National Review*

"[*The Ballad of Bob Dylan*] begins with an account of a solo Dylan concert the author attended on Dec. 14, 1963. It's a beautiful thing, how [Epstein] brings this evening back to life."

— Jim Windolf, *New York Times Book Review*

"Plenty of good works explore Dylan's massive musical corpus, but Epstein surpasses them in exploring Dylan's personal relationships. . . . Bob Dylan needs a poet, not a biographer. . . . Epstein is the poet Dylan deserves."

— W. Scott Poole, *PopMatters*

"Epstein is at his best dealing with his subject's Minnesota boyhood, embrace of folk music, and meteoric early-'60s ascent; fresh recollections from Nora Guthrie, daughter of Dylan's role model Woody Guthrie, highlight the early going. Likewise, later chapters on the making of the important albums *Time Out of Mind* (1997) and *Love and Theft* (2001) benefit from revealing interviews with session men like drummer David Kemper and the late keyboardist-raconteur Jim Dickinson."   — *Kirkus Reviews*

"Intense and intimate. . . . A satisfyingly clear portrait emerges from the shadows, ever sharpening the focus on the most cleverly elusive artist in the age of media saturation. . . . Happily, the book is laced through with Dylan's lyrics. While many of these are now taken for granted as part of the vernacular, Epstein makes you appreciate anew just how many memorable words have flowed out of just one man."

— John Belknap, *Jewish Chronicle* (London)

"As a near-contemporary of Dylan, Epstein is in a better position than most to show how the meaning of an artist's work, and the nature of that work's effect on its audience, evolves over the long haul. An unabashed fan, Epstein is still no sentimentalist."

— Ian McGillis, *Montreal Gazette*

"[Epstein] astutely notes Dylan's evolution from wisecracking '60s child to wizened grandfather—a transformation that both humanizes and dignifies its subject."

— John Lewis, *Baltimore* magazine

The Ballad of Bob Dylan

Also by Daniel Mark Epstein

POETRY

No Vacancies in Hell

The Follies

Young Men's Gold

The Book of Fortune

Spirits

The Boy in the Well

The Traveler's Calendar

The Glass House

PROSE

Lincoln's Men

The Lincolns: Portrait of a Marriage

Lincoln and Whitman: Parallel Lives in Civil War Washington

Star of Wonder

Love's Compass

Sister Aimee: The Life of Aimee Semple McPherson

Nat King Cole

*What My Lips Have Kissed: The Loves and
Love Poems of Edna St. Vincent Millay*

PLAYS

Jenny and the Phoenix

The Midnight Visitor

The Leading Lady

TRANSLATIONS

The Trinummus of Plautus

The Bacchae of Euripides

Also by Daniel Mark Epstein

POETRY

No Enemies But Time

The Follies

Young Men's Gold

The Book of Fortune

Spirits

The Boy in the Well

The Traveler's Calendar

The Glass House

PROSE

Lincoln's Men

The Lincolns: Portrait of a Marriage

Lincoln and Whitman: Parallel Lives in Civil War Washington

Star of Wonder

Lucid Company

Sister Aimee: The Life of Aimee Semple McPherson

Nat King Cole

What My Lips Have Kissed: The Loves and Love Poems of Edna St. Vincent Millay

PLAYS

Jenny and the Phoenix

The Midnight Visitor

The Leading Lady

TRANSLATIONS

The Trinummus of Plautus

The Bacchae of Euripides

The Ballad of
BOB DYLAN

A Portrait

Daniel Mark Epstein

HARPER ● PERENNIAL

NEW YORK • LONDON • TORONTO • SYDNEY • NEW DELHI • AUCKLAND

HARPER ● PERENNIAL

A hardcover edition of this book was published in 2011 by HarperCollins Publishers.

THE BALLAD OF BOB DYLAN. Copyright © 2011 Daniel Mark Epstein. All rights reserved. Printed in the United States of America. No part of this book may be used or reproduced in any manner whatsoever without written permission except in the case of brief quotations embodied in critical articles and reviews. For information, address HarperCollins Publishers, 195 Broadway, New York, NY 10007.

HarperCollins books may be purchased for educational, business, or sales promotional use. For information, please e-mail the Special Markets Department at SPsales@harpercollins.com.

An extension of this copyright page appears on pages 489–96.

FIRST HARPER PERENNIAL EDITION PUBLISHED 2012.

Designed by Leah Carlson-Stanisic

Library of Congress Cataloging-in-Publication Data has been applied for.

ISBN 978-0-06-180733-6(pbk.)

21   OV/LSC   10 9 8 7 6 5 4 3

For Mike Seeger

Contents

Contents

The Ballad of Bob Dylan

Washington, D.C., 1963

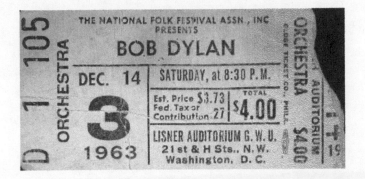

❉ CHAPTER 1 ❉

Lisner Auditorium, December 14, 1963

The frail-looking young man with tousled brown hair entered the auditorium from stage left, strumming his guitar while people were still getting settled in their seats.

A triple row of folding chairs had been hastily arranged in a semi-circle upstage behind the performer's spot to handle the last-minute overflow. Now these latecomers were sitting down, applauding as he passed them. He wore a pale blue work shirt, blue jeans, and boots. It was as if he had come from some distance and had been singing all the while to himself and whatever group he could gather on street corners and in storefronts, his entrance was so casual and unheralded.

He moved toward his spot center stage next to the waist-high wooden stool. On the round seat was a clutter of shiny Marine Band harmonicas. Scarcely acknowledging the applause, mildly embarrassed by it, he lurched toward his place onstage wearing a steel harmonica holder around his neck that made him look like a wild creature in harness, blinking at the floodlights, hunching his shoulders to adjust the guitar strap that held the Gibson Special acoustic high on his slender body.

He was in our midst before we knew it and already performing. He stood and strummed. The houselights dimmed but remained on. The applause that began from the spectators behind him was warm but brief because we did not wish to interrupt the singer or miss any of his words. He sounded the simple melody on the mouth harp. The song he chose to sing first was unfamiliar but it was an invitation promising familiarity, like so many old ballads where the bard invites folks to gather round so he can tell them a tale: *Come all ye fair and tender maidens*, or *Come all ye bold highway men*.

There were fifteen hundred seats in the sold-out Lisner Auditorium of George Washington University that night in December, and fewer than half of those were taken by college students. The steeply banked rows were filled with the faithful members of the Washington folk music community. The concert in fact had not been sponsored by the university but by the National Folk Festival, founded in the 1930s with the support of Eleanor Roosevelt and the novelist Zora Neale Hurston. Men in goatees or full beards, wearing plaid lumberjack shirts, dungarees, and horn-rimmed glasses, sat shoulder to shoulder with long-haired women in peasant blouses with ban-the-bomb buttons; scholarly types in tweed or corduroy jackets with leather elbow patches; a few middle-aged beatniks in black turtlenecks. There was more philosophy than conscious style, in boots and sandals, a rejection of button-down fashion and shoelaces that cut across generations during the Cold War.

My sister, Linda Ellen, age thirteen, was probably the youngest person in the building. My best friend, Jimmy Smith, and I had just turned fifteen and could not legally drive so my mother, thirty-seven, had driven us from the Hyattsville, Maryland, suburbs down Connecticut Avenue to the edge of campus, Twenty-first and H streets, N.W., to hear Bob Dylan in concert. She had purchased our seats in advance at the box office—she always got the best—and so now we sat in the center of the fifth row, close to the lip of the stage apron, a few feet above and not ten yards away from Bob Dylan. When he finally stopped blinking and opened his eyes to the audience we could see how blue they were.

We heard the guitar first, a powerful sound that was percussive, modal, and clarion. He was strumming a full G chord with a flat pick in moderate tempo, 3/4 time. What made it distinctive and commanding was the force of the first stroke of the measure, and that the guitarist had added a high D on the second string to make a perfect fourth with the G next to it. That was the trick, the special magic that transformed the chord from a simple major triad to a mystical, ancient strain, Celtic perhaps, medieval or Native American, a mood transcending time.

Come gather 'round people, wherever you roam
And admit that the waters around you have grown
And accept it that soon you'll be drenched to the bone.

This was a call to the barricades if not to arms. It was a reveille, a wake-up to the living and dead and the half dead that *the times are changing.* The composer had been clever enough to write the tune in waltz time so that no one drunk or sober would ever march to it. (He'd write a drunken march someday—all in good time.) The song as performed and phrased had an incantatory voodoo power to alert, transfix, caution, and alarm us; stanza by stanza it singled us out: writers and critics, senators and congressmen (just around the corner here), mothers and fathers (my mother sat at attention), each being warned in turn that there would be hell to pay if they did not "heed the call." The well-traveled road will not be viable, he was telling us, the old order is fading, the wheel of change is spinning, the battle is already raging, and if it hasn't rattled your windows yet it will soon.

Your sons and your daughters are beyond your command. . . .

Invoking the Old Testament prophets as well as the Gospels (Mark 10:31, "Many that are first will be last"), a singer born in the year the Japanese attacked Pearl Harbor was proclaiming to my mother and everyone her age and older that there was a generation gap—and the phrase had not yet been coined—and anyone who dared to stall or stand in the way of reform would be hurt. I am not sure what my mother thought of this opening salvo of the concert. After all, she had purchased the tickets, and driven us to the brick-and-limestone theater from West Hyattsville in her green Nash sedan. I suppose we were all more or less startled. But there was something about the young man's simultaneous authority and humility that was disarming—the biblical, archaic tone, the passionate plea for everyone to join the movement, not to stand in the way but to heed the call, lend a hand.

Bob Dylan had been in the capital for the great civil rights March on Washington back in late August 1963. On the steps of the Lincoln Memorial he and Joan Baez had performed his songs "Blowin' in the Wind" and "Only a Pawn in Their Game." The duet as well as the romance between the beautiful folksingers received considerable notice in the press that year, although he was not a celebrity. His songs were far more famous than he was.

In the autumn he had played three recitals: Carnegie Hall in New York, Jordan Hall in Boston, and the University Regent Theatre in Syracuse, New York. After John F. Kennedy was assassinated on November 22, Dylan had appeared only twice in concert, in Princeton and Newark, New Jersey. Now this concert at the Lisner Auditorium would be his sole appearance before Christmas. The only publicity was a small poster showing the singer playing guitar and harmonica on the left side of a split format with his name and the concert specifics printed on the right, and tiny display ads in the amusement sections of the *Washington Post* and the *Evening Star*. The tickets, $4.00 for orchestra and $3.50 for the parterre, could be purchased at the Willard Hotel, Learmont Records in Georgetown, and at the YMCA in Alexandria, Virginia.

As of Friday night, seats had still been available. It was evidence of the rapid momentum of Dylan's reputation that by the time we got to the auditorium the show was sold out and the management was unfolding chairs onstage to seat the late arrivals.

How did Jim, Linda, and I happen to be there, in these seats purchased weeks in advance, three minors in a crowd of adults mostly in their twenties and thirties? Jim and I were folksingers, card-carrying members of the Washington Folk Music Guild. We attended concerts, open-mike events, sing-outs, and hootenannies all over the city. We heard fiddling contests in gymnasiums and barns, fretless banjo masters in church basements, and barefoot blues pickers and jug bands in abandoned houses. We heard old Mississippi John Hurt at Ontario Place, Judy Collins and Donal Leace at the Cellar Door, and Carolyn Hester, Paul Clayton, and Josh White at the Showboat Lounge. We saw Harry Belafonte at the Carter Barron Amphitheatre. Elizabeth Cotten, the former housekeeper of Pete and Mike Seeger's parents, who wrote "Freight Train" and played the guitar upside down and left-handed, still lived in town. She was in her mid-sixties. We used to go and visit Miss Libba in her little row house at 625 Fifth Street, N.E. She played for us, sitting in the front parlor, and taught us songs like "Ain't Got No Honey Baby Now"; she would teach us as much of her picking style as we could learn by screwing our heads around until our necks were stiff. Then she would serve sugar cookies.

Mike Seeger, in his twenties, grew up in the area, and we saw quite a lot of him, too. Mike played guitar, banjo, autoharp, jew's harp, fiddle, and harmonica—often a couple of these instruments at once. He encouraged us to do the same. John Fahey, the legendary guitarist, had graduated from our high school a few years ahead of us. Recently we had gone to hear Joan Baez and Pete Seeger at the Uline Arena; it was there, in the 7,000-seat coliseum, that we first heard Bob Dylan's apocalyptic song "A Hard Rain's A-Gonna Fall" performed after a glowing introduction by Pete himself, the polestar of folk music. He announced that a young poet had arrived on the scene with some important things to tell us.

We already knew that. The first time I heard Bob Dylan's name was in 1961 at a hootenanny near the University of Maryland, College Park, outdoors at the Duck Pond on Adelphi Road. There was a very skillful, tall blond guitarist in a Hawaiian shirt and sandals who had attracted a group of admirers by playing a rendition of the Reverend Gary Davis's "Cocaine Blues." As part of his patter between verses he told us, "This is the way Bobbie Dylan does it," and then played a figure with some hammered-on notes on the fretboard. But he pronounced the name *Die-lyn*, "this is the way Bobbie *Die-lyn* plays it." The guitarist had just come down from New York, where he had heard Dylan playing in some Greenwich Village club; Dylan's reputation was growing so rapidly his name—or at least the proper pronunciation—couldn't keep up. The blond guitarist whose name I can't remember spoke Dylan's name with such forceful admiration I never forgot it. I made a mental note to look out for this Bobbi Dylan because he must be a man worth listening to.

That was the late summer of 1961, just before Dylan played Gerde's Folk City in Manhattan as a warm-up act for the Greenbriar Boys, a bluegrass ensemble. Robert Shelton wrote it up in the *New York Times* on September 29, 1961, praising Dylan so extravagantly that the twenty-year-old folksinger would never again know what it was *not* to be known, to be recognized in certain circles, admired and envied.

A bright new face in folk music is appearing at Gerde's Folk City. Although only 20 years old, Bob Dylan is one of the most distinctive stylists to play in a Manhattan cabaret in months. . . . Resembling a cross between a choir boy and a beatnik, Mr. Dylan has a cherubic look and a mop of tousled hair he partly covers with a Huck Finn black corduroy cap. His clothes may need a bit of tailoring, but when he works his guitar, harmonica or piano and composes new songs faster than he can remember them, there is no doubt that he is bursting at the seams with talent.

Six months later I was grazing the record bins in our local music store, the small folk section, and I saw the face that Shelton described in the newspaper review. It was the face of a boy who appeared to be about my age, with wide-set eyes, soft cheeks and chin, and a perfectly formed mouth, his curls pressed under the black cap, wearing a sheepskin coat, hands laced around the upright neck of a Martin guitar. There was something sly about him. He was a choir boy with a grenade in his pocket.

I read the liner notes, which included Shelton's review, and put the album back in the bin. There was only one copy, but I did not buy it that day. I returned several times to look at the portrait of the sly, calm-looking boy, and reread the liner notes before I had saved the two dollars to purchase the LP. That was in April 1962. I bought one of only five thousand copies of the album titled *Bob Dylan*. Produced by the prescient John Hammond, the record sold so poorly his colleagues at Columbia Records called it—and the artist he had signed—"Hammond's Folly."

I had never heard Bob Dylan's voice, or heard him play until that day in the spring of 1962 when I dropped the vinyl onto the turntable of a Westinghouse portable record player in the privacy of my bedroom. My expectations were high, and the experience was not altogether pleasant. This must be an acquired taste, I thought, like cigarette smoking or whiskey. It seemed unnatural to me that such a young man should sound, or try to sound, like an old man. I liked the choppy, wailing harmonica on the fast Jesse Fuller number "You're No Good." Dylan had learned some things from the blind blues harpist Sonny Terry. But the way he shrieked the refrain, "You give me the blues, I guess you're satisfied / You give me the blues, I want to lay down and die," made my skin crawl. His voice was all over the place.

The singer began to settle into his skin—so it seemed—in the second cut of the album, a Woody Guthrie–inspired "talkin' blues" called "Talkin' New York," which was described in the liner notes as "a diary note set to music."

> *Ramblin' outa the wild West,*
> *Leavin' the towns I love the best,*
> *Thought I'd seen some ups and downs,*
> *'Til I come into New York town.*
> *People goin' down to the ground,*
> *Buildings goin' up to the sky.*

This was good poetry, the play on "ups and downs," and Dylan was speaking in a natural voice, although perhaps the western accent was somewhat exaggerated. The wandering minstrel told of his arrival in New York in the freezing cold, his landing downtown in Greenwich Village, his first job in a coffeehouse playing harmonica for small change, joining the musicians' union and paying his dues. He quoted a famous line from the master of the talkin' blues, Woody Guthrie, who wrote in "Pretty Boy Floyd" that "some rob you with a six-gun, some with a fountain pen." Now, toward the end of the song that owed so much to Guthrie, Dylan quoted the verse "some people rob you with a fountain pen," adding that it did not take long to understand Woody's meaning: there are those who don't have much food on their table, "But they got a lot of forks and knives / And they gotta cut somethin'." This was poetry sure enough, lines as memorable as Guthrie's own. Had Dylan been robbed, by the club owners or the musicians' union? Had he himself robbed Woody Guthrie with his fountain pen, swiping his verse form and style in order to put food on the table?

By the time I got to the third track, the familiar song "In My Time of Dyin'" by Blind Willie Johnson, I had begun to settle into this world of sounds. Dylan's slide guitar on the haunting blues was mesmerizing, and his voice had the right tone for the subject.

In my time of dyin'
Don't want nobody to moan.
All I want you to do
Is just take my body home.

His voice followed the lead of the slide guitar, high and low. The song has a range of more than an octave, and a driving rhythm. He was playing a role, the role of an old blues master; somehow he managed to inhabit it persuasively.

The traditional folk tunes on the record were not unpleasant but very eccentric in their rendering. I had heard Mike Seeger perform "Man of Constant Sorrow" many times with his autoharp, simply and sadly; I had heard Judy Collins sing "Maid of Constant Sorrow" with a brilliant guitar accompaniment. Dylan's version was an athletic exhibition; he meant to show us how long he could hold the first note of the chorus. "I . . . am a man of constant sorrow . . . I . . . 'm goin' back to Colorado . . ." and then the harmonica would imitate the voice, wailing the first note for several measures, until one could imagine the player turning blue for lack of air. "Pretty Peggy-O" was a brash spoof on the earnest folk performances of the classic "Fennario," full of whoops and hollers and acrobatic harmonica passages. There was a soulful "House of the Rising Sun," a song Odetta sang, with an intriguing descending progression of bass notes on the guitar; there was a humble and tender tribute to Woody Guthrie, the only other original composition on the record.

Hey, hey, Woody Guthrie, I wrote you a song
'Bout a funny ol' world that's a-comin' along.
Seems sick an' it's hungry, it's tired and it's torn,
It looks like it's a-dyin' and it's hardly been born.

He sang this homage in 3/4 time, strumming the simple three-chord accompaniment to a tune Guthrie himself used for his "1913 Massacre," a tune that was already three hundred years old when

Guthrie cribbed it from "The Soldier and the Lady," a sixteenth-century ballad.

The track that knocked me out was "Baby Let Me Follow You Down," a bright, up-tempo rendition of "Mama, Let Me Lay It on You," a song that bluesmen knew from a 1930s recording of blind Reverend Gary Davis. But Dylan's chording, finger-picking style, and harmonica accompaniment were unique, precise, altogether perfect while maintaining a natural spontaneity. The song came with a little introductory patter, as the guitarist was picking out the melody line.

This was the first glimpse I had of the real person behind the voice that had morphed through so many roles in the course of half an hour: "I first heard this from Ric Von Schmidt. He lives in Cambridge. Ric's a blues guitar player. I met him one day in the green pastures of Harvard University." Dylan's midwestern speaking voice was natural and pleasant, full of humor—the joke was on the folk music purists. Musicologists like Alan Lomax went out into the fields of rural America to bring back the authentic treasures of the American songbook. Meanwhile, younger folk like the painter/bluesman Eric Von Schmidt and his protégé Bob Dylan were doing their collecting in the greenswards and city parks of Boston and New York.

An act of generosity to the older blues artist Von Schmidt, Dylan's acknowledgment is a little misleading. Dylan had transformed "Baby Let Me Follow You Down" and made it his own. "House of the Rising Sun," on the other hand, he had stolen, latchkey, walls, and rafters, from the playing of his best friend Dave Van Ronk. Van Ronk forgave him but never quite got over the theft of an arrangement he meant to record himself.

I discovered the Dylan album in April 1962, and by the end of the year had learned to play most of the songs on it, with harmonica. The guitar riffs and the harmonica accompaniments were not too difficult to copy, but the singing was impossible. Dylan was doing things with his voice (or had done things to it) that no one in their right mind would want to emulate. My father, whose favorite singers were Nat King Cole and Frank Sinatra, said that it was the most god-awful racket he had ever heard in his life. My mother, more curious and broad-minded, was the one who first exclaimed over how peculiar it was that such a young man should choose to sound like an old man, but she was intrigued, sharing my interest in the tradition of blues and folk music Bob Dylan represented.

About the same time I purchased his record, Bob Dylan wrote the song "Blowin' in the Wind." He later claimed that he wrote it in twenty minutes prior to a Monday night hootenanny at Gerde's Folk City, at the corner of West Fourth and Mercer streets, in Greenwich Village. Arriving at the club with the song in his head, he sang it to folksinger Gil Turner and taught him the chord changes. Turner taped the lyrics to the microphone and premiered the song at the hootenanny, wasting no time in getting the piece from the composer to the public. The stout, kindly Turner was also a founding editor of *Broadside*. In May we read "Blowin' in the Wind" in the pages of that groundbreaking magazine.

In September 1962 Dylan wrote "A Hard Rain's A-Gonna Fall" in a boiler room and a sitting room, spaces under and over the Village Gate coffeehouse, where he first performed the epic. We did not hear it until Pete Seeger played the Washington Coliseum early in 1963, the night Joan Baez sang "Blowin' in the Wind." From April 24, 1962, until April 24, 1963, Dylan was in and out of Columbia Studio A on Fifty-fourth Street in New York on eight different dates, recording more than thirty songs. Thirteen of these would make up *The Freewheelin' Bob Dylan*, which came out in late May 1963. During that time he wrote more than a hundred songs. He said he was afraid to go to sleep at night for fear he would miss one.

We bought the record as soon as we could get it, and so did a lot of other people. My uncle, a World War II hero, a teacher who read Walt Whitman and Hart Crane and had an amazing collection of blues and folk albums—78-rpm records of Leadbelly and Sonny Terry, Woody Guthrie, the Carter Family, and the Golden Gate Quartet—was the first person in my family to own Dylan's second album. This veteran, whose opinion I valued above all others, gravely pronounced that Bob Dylan was the real thing, a genuine poet, prophet, and folksinger.

The Freewheelin' Bob Dylan, with its cover picture of the poet and his adoring girlfriend Suze Rotolo linked arm in arm on a snowy street, its enchanting melodies and lyric poetry, was far more approachable than the first album. When the popular folk trio Peter, Paul and Mary released "Blowin' in the Wind" in July of that year as a single, and it shot toward the top of the *Billboard* charts, many people became curious about the folksinger who had written the enigmatic anthem. Nearly as many were even more curious about the "prophet" who had written the apocalyptic "Hard Rain" during the year of the Cuban Missile Crisis.

Yet even after his triumphant performance at the Newport Folk Festival that summer, Dylan did not have so many fans in Washington that he could easily sell out a medium-size recital hall. My other friends, who would kill for seats to see the jazz musicians John Coltrane, Charles Mingus, or Thelonious Monk, were not particularly interested in going along with us. So my mother and sister and I, and my best friend, sat in the fifth row, surrounded by strangers, listening to Bob Dylan.

That night at Lisner Auditorium the applause erupted as soon as the last harmonica blast and triple-time guitar strokes signaled the end of "The Times They Are A-Changin'." It was as much for the prophet's message as for the song itself. No one in that place wanted to find himself on the wrong side of the argument for change.

He smiled warmly, looking up at us, squinting from the lights, turning his back to bow to the people clapping behind him. Pulling the harmonica rack over his head, he set it on the stool as the applause faded and the hall grew silent in anticipation. He began retuning the guitar, the low E string down to D. Dylan would have little to say to us between songs. Now he just said this is a *true* song and launched into the rapids of the "Ballad of Hollis Brown," a song in D minor, in driving 2/4 time that *sounded* familiar though we had never heard it, a relentless horror story of a man in such desperate poverty he cannot bear the sight of his hungry children.

> *Your baby's eyes look crazy*
> *They're a-tuggin' at your sleeve (repeat)*
>
> *You walk the floor and wonder why*
> *With every breath you breathe*

Hollis Brown looks for work and money, sees the rats eating his flour and his mare die of disease; he prays to God for a friend to save him. At last, when Brown's wife's screams are stabbing him, his well is dry, and his grass has turned black, he spends his last dollar. On shotgun shells. This was the Book of Job seen through the lens of Hitchcock and in the mood of Edgar Allan Poe, as Dylan built the suspense and volume to a climax. He had cast the tale in the second person, so that the "you" who was Hollis Brown eventually became every member of the audience.

> *There's seven breezes a-blowin'*
> *All around the cabin door. . . . (repeat)*
>
> *Seven shots ring out*
> *Like the ocean's pounding roar.*

When the deed is done the song is all but over—no moral or commentary apart from the chilling observation that there are seven people dead on that farm and somewhere, faraway, another seven would be born. And then the double-time strumming that signaled the end of the song, an uneasy silence in the auditorium, and finally the rippling and swelling of applause.

I don't believe that any of us was prepared for the questions raised by that bleak South Dakota landscape, the harsh "Ballad of Hollis Brown." But now we stood warned and ought to be ready for anything. Another performer with Dylan's range of themes might have gone for comic relief but he was not ready to let us off the hook. In March the Cuban boxer Sugar Ramos had knocked out the featherweight champion Davey Moore in the tenth round of the title fight in Dodger Stadium; Moore fell into a coma and died. Weeks later Dylan premiered a song in the form of "Who Killed Cock Robin" called "Who Killed Davey Moore?"

Now he retuned the guitar to the standard E tuning, fastened a capo on the third fret, and shouted out the question *Who killed Davey Moore?* at the high end of his vocal range. Everybody knew of the killing; the Vatican had called for an end of boxing; newspaper columnists debated the question. Dylan's song was printed in the July 1963 issue of *Broadside* magazine. The poet poses the question, as a refrain, to the referee, the crowd, the manager, the gamblers who bet on the fight, the sportswriters, and finally Ramos himself, the fighter "whose fist / Laid him low in a cloud of mist." Everybody has an alibi, and the singer articulates the half-dozen apologies, all sincere, all credible. The crowd? They just went to see a good fight: "We didn't mean for him t'meet his death / We just meant to see some sweat. . . ." The fighter's manager? He claims he had no prior knowledge of the medical condition that doomed Moore. The gambler protests he bet on the boxer to *win*; the sportswriter says not to blame boxing—football is just as dangerous.

Fist fighting is here to stay
It's just the old American way.

The most poignant response comes from the Cuban pugilist in the final stanza, who admits that it is true that he hit Moore, and that he was paid to do it.

Don't say "murder," don't say "kill."
It was destiny, it was God's will.

And that's the last word excepting the chorus, posing the question again, as coldly and heartlessly as any Elizabethan tragedian. No simple moral to be learned here, either.

The audience clapped louder than ever, although it is difficult to say why. The tune was not pretty. Some may have thought they were hailing a protest against the barbaric spectacle, the blood sport that claimed Moore's life. And yet the song had broken down the social components of boxing, defending the human interests one by one. What we were applauding in fact was the vision of that tragedy from every human angle except for the feelings of the boxer's wife and children. There was pathos, but no one in particular to blame. The social fabric is fatally flawed and all of us are complicit in the crimes of the social contract: war, boxing, starving children, legalized discrimination. We were applauding the poet's stark presentation of the problem.

Fifteen minutes of the concert had passed and all three of the songs had been songs of protest, challenges in varying degrees of intensity. Now Dylan turned down the volume, softened his attack, smiling, picking out a delicate figure on the strings, double thumbing, anticipating the downbeat of the moderate 2/4 ballad. "This is called 'Boots of Spanish Leather,'" he said, bashfully. Dylan blinked a good deal, as if his eyes were light-sensitive, or as if he struggled to control his emotions. "All it is, is . . . is a . . . kind of . . . when you can't get what you *want* you have to settle for less kind of song."

This romantic ballad, already familiar to me in 1963, had caused me a memorable astonishment when I learned that Bob Dylan had written it in the middle of the twentieth century, in my lifetime.

Oh, I'm sailin' away my own true love,
I'm sailin' away in the morning.
Is there something I can send you from across the sea,
From the place that I'll be landing.

The nine quatrains capture a dialogue between lovers, one depart-
ing. Although the melody never changes, stanza to stanza, the singer
subtly distinguishes the voices. The woman is taking her leave, her
voice ever-so-slightly stronger as she asks, again and again, if there
is anything of silver or gold from the mountains or the coast of
Spain that she might send her lover to assuage the pain of their long
separation, to ease the passage of time. No, he answers, and again,
no. He just wants her to return to him unspoiled. If he had the stars
of the night, or the diamonds of the ocean (where diamonds are
rare), he would forsake them, if he could, for one kiss from her. He
wants nothing more.

Oh, how can, how can you ask me again,
It only brings me sorrow.
The same thing I want from you today,
I would want again tomorrow.

In the manner of all ancient ballads this one proceeds without a
musical bridge, but that quatrain above marked a transition in narrative time.

The woman's ship weighs anchor, and the last three stanzas are
the words of the man left behind, yearning. He hears from her, on
a lonesome day, that she does not know when she might return. He
writes to her that, in that case, her heart is no longer with him but
with the life ahead of her. With his heartfelt blessing and a warning
to heed stormy weather, he lets her go. This gentle, mutual farewell
could only come with time. Only now is he able to request the material gift that he had forsworn earlier. He mentions this in the final
line almost as an afterthought, yet it is climactic because we have

been wondering about it from the first, the song's announced title. It is striking because he has withheld the words for the previous eight stanzas. In the woman's physical presence, the notion of a material gift was repugnant. Now that they have let each other go he can accept her offer: he asks for the "Spanish boots of Spanish leather" that will carry him on his journey into the future.

This song brought down the house. It put everyone at ease. More than any other this lyric had revealed the singer's vulnerability, and by now there was hardly a man, woman, or child in the space who was not captivated by Bob Dylan.

I have mentioned the fact that this song, perhaps above all others, surprised me because I could scarcely believe that the young man standing before me had written it. I cannot recall now when I first heard "Boots of Spanish Leather" (like "Sweet Betsy from Pike" or "I've Been Workin' on the Railroad"), although I feel certain it was not from his lips.

The piece had been published in the summer 1963 issue of *Sing Out!* but I did not immediately read it there. Since Dylan began performing the song early that year it had spread virally from hand to hand and ear to ear, like a nineteenth-century broadside ballad. There may have been twenty folksingers like Gil Turner and Carol Hedin moving from city to city performing "Boots of Spanish Leather" with or without identifying the source. There was not a line in the lyric that marked it as contemporary; there were many lines that sounded timeless, like stones worn smooth in a riverbed from centuries of water coursing over them. The lovers in the ballad, their plight and their yearning, were as authentic as any in fact or fiction—at least since lovers have had a choice in their destiny. In short, the song sounded like it had been around for generations because it had all the qualities of a song that would be around forever.

Taped to the waist of Dylan's guitar was a scrap of paper with a set list. Looking down at the list, at one point, he remarked that he had written several hundred songs. He mentioned this not proudly but rather as if it were an embarrassment of riches; sometimes, he admitted, he couldn't recall all the words. "Boots of Spanish Leather" provided a needed mood change from high drama to romance. Now Dylan fumbled comically with the harmonica rack. The lights onstage never varied, yet the performer signaled a shift of mood as sharply as if the atmosphere had changed from blue to gold.

He launched into the bright 2/4 time of the talkin' blues, blasting away on the mouth harp a full sixteen measures before speaking.

> *Well, I was feelin' sad and kinda blue*
> *I didn't know what I was a gonna do*
> *Them communists was comin' around,*
> *They was in the air, they was in the ground. . . .*

So far this evening the poet had played a half-dozen roles, including a fiery prophet, a fight referee, a sportswriter, a gambler, a boxer, and two yearning lovers—all with deep conviction. Now he would play the buffoon, a new member of the ultraconservative John Birch Society. They were a favorite target of left-leaning folkies since the late 1950s when the "Birchers" cheered the witch hunt of the McCarthy era. During the Cold War, Joe McCarthy's Senate committee had warranted that many entertainers, including Pete Seeger and Woody Guthrie, were blacklisted for their beliefs.

Though we had heard about this "Talkin' John Birch Paranoid Blues," we had never heard anyone play it, and the song showed us a side of the folksinger we had not known—Dylan the humorist. Inhabiting the paranoid psyche of the John Bircher, he wrinkled his brow in mock seriousness as his character joins the society, gets his special membership card. He rushes home to commence the hunt for reds in his TV set, gets a 110-volt shock for his trouble—blames the *Hootenanny* television program. He accuses the mailman, who punches him out, and then he wonders about poor Betsy Ross, who sewed *red stripes* in the American flag! At last he decides to stay at home and investigate himself.

Dylan's comic timing was spot-on. He used the harmonica the way George Burns, the stand-up comedian, used his cigar, to mark a punch line at the end of a story, hiding his smile behind it, then pulling a straight face so that we could do the laughing. As the story ended the applause was raucous, shot through with cheers and whistling.

Dylan hastily fastened the capo to the third fret of the guitar and silenced the audience with his pensive strumming. He spread out a languorous, loose 3/4 rhythm and began singing after a few measures.

Lay down your weary tune, lay down,
Lay down the song you strum,
And rest yourself 'neath the strength of strings
No voice can hope to hum.

He sang this song mostly with his eyes closed or half closed as if he were in a trance. The melody was familiar, a variation of the lovely Scottish tune "The Water Is Wide." Hymnlike, back and forth the song moved from stanza to chorus, like sea waves lapping the shore.

On the beach at dawn the singer feels the morning breeze, sees the wild ocean, and hears the waves crashing. All of these sights and sounds in nature he compares to instruments in an orchestra: a trumpet, a drum, an organ, cymbals. Perhaps this was the most curious song of all. Traveling on the chassis of an old melody, the words, theme, and structure were strange—unlike any folk song. This was not a love song (though there was a reference to leaves that clung to a loved one's breast) or a protest song, although the chorus did seem to ask the singer to put aside a particular tune in favor of a more cosmic muse. There was no drama of gamblers, murderers, shipwrecks, or star-crossed lovers. There was nobody at home here but the singer, contemplating nature and his song. It was like a Wordsworth ode, or a Wallace Stevens poem set to a Scottish air.

The manner of Bob Dylan's performance, his strumming, metrically ambiguous, searching; his trancelike state, and the rambling length of the composition suggested a raga-like improvisation.

> *I stood unwound beneath the skies*
> *And clouds unbound by laws.*
> *The cryin' rain like a trumpet sang*
> *And asked for no applause.*

When at last he came to the end, he got a long and steady ovation for this rhapsody. No cheering or whistling, just admiring, sustained applause, as if he had made a bouquet of roses appear and vanish in the air, or lifted the lid off his guitar and produced a phoenix. We were convinced that Bob Dylan had invented this poem on the spot tonight for the crowd that had come to see him.

However spontaneous the individual performances appeared, the overall structure of the concert must have been carefully considered. "Blowin' in the Wind" came next—the familiar song following the unfamiliar. By now this "anthem of the protest movement" could be heard on any jukebox, in covers by Peter, Paul and Mary, Chad Mitchell, or Bobby Darin. Even people with no interest in folk music knew the words—standard fare at hootenannies, peace vigils, campfire sings, and civil rights marches. Dylan sang slowly and emphatically, trumpeting the tune on the harmonica between stanzas.

After the final notes on the mouth harp and the firm triple-time strum that ended most of his flat-picked songs, came the ovation. Dylan quickly returned to the moderate 3/4 time of "Lay Down Your Weary Tune" and the same dreamy mood. Someone behind us stifled a cough. Again Dylan was singing about a singer, watching a beautiful woman move in and out of the shadows of the audience, a woman enraptured by his words.

> *My eyes danced a circle*
> *Across her clear outline*
> *With her head tilted sideways*
> *She called me again*
> *As the tune drifted out*
> *She breathed hard through the echo*
> *But the song it was long*
> *And it was far to the end*

The melody was like "Song to Woody" on his first album, simple and traditional, three chords. Now he used the tune to create a more complex rapport with the audience. Each of us was like that woman, wanting a personal connection with the singer beyond the barrier of the stage lights. Sensing that fervor the singer looks down, pretending that "of all the eyes out there" he can see none. Still this woman's attention is magnetic, and he wants to move toward her. But—as the refrain reminds us at each stanza's end—"the song was too long." Upon this refrain he works gentle and humorous variations: first, he'd just *begun*; then there was *more*; it was far to the *end*; it must get *done*. At last when he finishes and puts down his guitar he goes looking for the mystery girl but she and her shade have vanished. So he jumps back onstage, picks up his guitar, and plays the next song.

The "Eternal Circle," Dylan called it, the timeless story of the emotional loop between the singer and the audience, feeding on each other, one locked in the light, the other in the darkness of the theater, no one ever completely satisfied. The greater the performance, the more yearning there must be on both sides. Singing for an audience is a courtship, a seduction; now and then a musician will single out someone in the crowd, a pretty face, serenade her, and then run off with her after the encores. It has been known to happen. But the story Dylan told in "Eternal Circle" is a more accurate allegory of what transpires, song after song, night after night on the circuit. The audience is not an individual to be known, possessed, satisfied, but instead a creature with many faces that must always be left wanting more. The singer, onstage, is not really himself but a hero the audience has created in its excitement.

At some point during the first set Dylan turned his back on us so that he could face the forty or fifty people who were seated behind him. He made some funny remark about how much some folks had paid to see the back of him, then turned the microphone around and started strumming and blowing his harmonica. He sang an entire talkin' blues to the cluster of people upstage, and we were as delighted as they were for the act of generosity. It was in keeping with the gentle and generous spirit that animated the performance all evening.

I believe the last song he sang before his break was a gloomy ballad about a boys' reformatory, called "The Walls of Red Wing." Sung in the words of an inmate, the song tells of the trials and abuses suffered by boys between the ages of twelve and seventeen, "Thrown in like bandits / And cast off like criminals" within cast-iron gates, where smiling guards wield clubs, waiting to catch a boy behind a wood piling and dust him up.

Was Bob Dylan a former inmate of the infamous Red Wing reformatory in Minnesota? He did not tell us, and so there was one more question that added to the singer's mystique.

When he had sung the last verses, he bowed for the applause and ducked as he pulled the leather guitar strap over his head. Smiling sheepishly he nodded to us, holding the guitar by the neck, then turned and bowed to the people behind him. Suddenly he was gone, offstage through the curtains where he had come from more than an hour before; an apparition, leaving behind him the ghosts of a dozen vivid characters his songs had conjured before us.

CHAPTER 2

The Night Bob Dylan
Rescued My Sister

The big headlines of the day came from Hollywood: The FBI had
arrested a house painter, a vacuum cleaner salesman, and a boxer
in connection with the kidnapping of Frank Sinatra, Jr. The feds
recovered most of the $240,000 in ransom money, and the nineteen-
year-old boy was frightened but unharmed. "Thank God it's over,"
said Frank Sinatra, Sr.

The international reports were ominous Cold War debris, persistent dark clouds on the horizon: "United States–Cambodian relations hit a low point yesterday with Cambodian Prince Norodom
Sihanouk openly hoping for a quick break in the two countries' dip-
lomatic relations." We had recalled our ambassador. The rift arose
from our alliance with South Vietnam and Thailand, the prince's
mortal enemies. A Cambodian government broadcast had called for
a celebration of the death of President John F. Kennedy as well as
the recent deaths of Sihanouk's enemies, Thai premier Sarit Thana-
rat and the president of South Vietnam, Ngo Dinh Diem. We demanded "clarification."

In London, top sources revealed that discussions of a "multilateral nuclear force" would get little attention from the North Atlantic Treaty Organization (NATO) council. Flora Lewis, foreign correspondent for the *Post*, commented: "the problem is how the Western World is to be organized now that it has emerged from the post-war period. . . . The disasters of war and the fears of cold war released a new force on the international scene, an urge to build new institutions which would give protection against the old ways of anarchy among nations." West Germany and the United States were going ahead with plans to launch a nuclear test ship. Britain and France wanted nothing to do with this test ship. The British asked NATO to issue a declaration of unilateral nonaggression.

U.S. secretary of state Dean Rusk had arrived in Paris the night before to confer with President Charles de Gaulle, carrying a message from President Lyndon Johnson to the NATO meeting. Defense Secretary Robert S. McNamara accompanied him. This would be the first meeting of the Big Four—America, England, France, and West Germany—since the assassination of President Kennedy.

In other news, Iraq's president, Abdel Salam Aref, warned that the Arab states would declare war on Israel if the Jews proceeded with their plan to divert water from the Jordan River. The Jordan was fed by tributaries originating in Lebanon, Syria, and Jordan, even though the biblical Sea of Galilee—from which Israeli engineers planned to pipe water to the Negev Desert—fell within Israel's borders as demarcated in 1948.

President Aref declared that Iraq's relations with America "will be affected more by Washington's policies than by the change of personalities in the White House. If America continues to follow a peaceful course, relations will be good, but if it supports Zionists, they will be very bad." The world community was shaken by the Kennedy assassination three weeks earlier and sought to define alliances, friends, and foes. Even the Vatican was stirred, contemplating a new doctrine that would lift the alleged responsibility of the Jews for the death of Christ. Aref and other Arab leaders like Gamal Abdel Nasser pretended to ignore the Vatican's strategy but it made them uneasy. It was hard enough to fight the Jews when Christendom saw them with Christ's blood on their hands. Absolved of two thousand years of guilt, the chosen people might find new alliances.

Drew Pearson, the journalist who wrote the "Washington Merry-Go-Round" for the *Post*'s feature section, devoted his column to the tension between J. Edgar Hoover, the sixty-nine-year-old director of the FBI, and Chief Justice Earl Warren, who was heading the commission to investigate the tragedy in Dallas. Hoover wanted to steal a march on the commission by publishing his report on the assassination immediately. "What the public doesn't realize," wrote Pearson, "is that for the first time since the days of Warren Harding the FBI itself is under investigation. The FBI is not accustomed to being investigated. It is accustomed to do the investigating itself and has become one of the most powerful and feared agencies of the Government. Most newspapermen," Pearson added, "and most congressmen do not criticize the FBI." LBJ understood the problem when he picked the Presidential Commission. Either the FBI had failed in Dallas or they had not been cooperating with the Secret Service there. It was well known that FBI agents had interviewed Lee Harvey Oswald a week before the murder, knew of his Cuban and Russian connections and his mental instability, and yet did not report him to the Secret Service. So he fixed the scope on his rifle and took up his position high in the Texas School Book Depository as Kennedy's entourage passed below his window.

Blues singer Dinah Washington ("What a Difference a Day Makes") had been found dead of an overdose in her Detroit home at age thirty-nine, a probable suicide. The Dow Jones Industrial Average reached 760, near its all-time high.

The Metropolitan Police Department reported progress in rooting out elements of segregation among police officers in the District of Columbia, long after having banned discrimination in squad car assignments and foot patrol teams.

All of these topics — the Kennedy assassination, integration, the multilateral nuclear force, the Sinatras, Dinah Washington—hovered in the air of the lobby as several hundred people stood talking, smoking, sipping from hip flasks, and waiting for the lights to dim and rise again to signal that Bob Dylan would be returning. Yet the characters that he had produced for us, Hollis Brown, the fight manager for Davey Moore, the sad lovers separated by a lonesome ocean, seemed as real as anything in the newspaper. We talked about the songs, strange and familiar, that he had sung, we quoted from the funny verses of "Talkin' John Birch," wondered aloud if he had *really* written "Boots of Spanish Leather." Was he improvising the lyric poetry of "Lay Down Your Weary Tune" in the trancelike moment during which we had just heard it? As much as we had loved the first set, we longed to hear certain songs we had heard about from other singers—the song about Medgar Evers, the fallen civil rights leader, and the one about our own Hattie Carroll of Maryland, the poor barmaid who had died after being struck by a wealthy patron at a high-society dinner in Baltimore.

The lights dimmed and came up again, dimmed and brightened. We made our way back to our seats, front and center of the hall.

This time the singer and his guitar did not rush onstage and start so impetuously. Dylan took his time approaching his spot on the stage as the audience members were taking their seats. He shook hands with some of the people who reached out to him, seeming to have a word or two for all who approached him. He fastened the capo on the third fret of his guitar. When at last everyone was settled he began strumming meditatively, flat-picking slowly in 3/4 time the sad notes of the A minor chord. He explained to us that this was a song about the mining towns in Virginia, and that he had written it in a woman's voice.

Then the performer began his set, as he had before, with a call for all of us friends to gather around so he could tell us a tale. At one time, the heroine recalls, the iron pits produced enough ore to provide plenty of work. But now, as anyone could see from the windows filled with cardboard and the men sitting idle on the benches, the town is nearly abandoned. This is like a picture from an album of Walker Evans, who photographed the shacks and drawn faces of Appalachian miners and dirt farmers during the Great Depression.

Having set the scene, the woman goes back to the beginning of her story, to the death of her mother when she was a girl, and the day her brother failed to come home—just like her father years before. She does not tell us that her menfolk died in the mine, nor does she speak of abandonment. The pathos of Dylan's narrative does not come from the woman's complaints; it arises from her stoicism and understatement, the sadness between the lines underscored by the dirgelike movement from the A minor chord to the leading G major, then resolving, again and again, to the melancholy minor chord.

In the spring she quits school to marry one John Thomas—a young miner. They enjoy a few good years together, when there is always food for the lunch bucket. Then suddenly, with three children to feed, he finds his work cut to half a day's shift. Soon the mine shuts down altogether. A corporate officer comes to explain that the ore is no longer worth digging. It can be bought cheaper in South America, where men labor for pennies, so the gates of the mine are locked and the red iron "rots."

And the room smelled heavy from drinking.
Where the sad silent song
Made the hour twice as long
As I waited for the sun to go sinking.

I lived by the window
As he talked to himself. . . .

The silence of unspoken despair builds to the breaking point and then, one morning, she wakes up and her husband is gone, the bed is bare, and she is left alone with her children.

Still she shuns self-pity, and will not complain. In the final strophe she simply marks the passage of time: Autumn is coming, the earth grows cold, and one by one the town stores are folding. The singer wails:

My children will go as soon as they grow
For there ain't nothing here now to hold them.

The effect of this naturalistic story, the stark details, the cruelty of the woman's life and her courage in the face of it, was unnerving. I looked over at my mother. She was sitting on my left, and I saw tears in her eyes. As the applause came she was wiping her cheeks with the back of her hand. She had grown up in the farming and fishing village of Vienna, Maryland, on the Eastern Shore during the Great Depression. She had known women like the one who had just passed before us in Bob Dylan's song.

A bearded man behind us said to his companion, "He's so real, I can hardly believe it."

Dylan adjusted the capo to the second fret and twisted the tuning engines. Lowering the sixth string to a drop-D tuning, he strummed. A thrill went through me because I felt I knew what was coming. No one but Dylan could make quite this sound on a guitar, opening its full range like the stops on an organ.

"A Hard Rain's A-Gonna Fall," he said softly, and the audience, in suspense, applauded. "Means something's gonna happen." And he flat-picked in steady 3/4 time, coming down hard on the bass notes. The guitar sounded huge.

We knew it well, since his recording of the song had come out on *The Freewheelin' Bob Dylan* in the spring. This song, above all others, marked Dylan as a poet in the tradition of Walt Whitman and Hart

Crane—this postsymbolist travelogue through an imaginary land-scape that figured forth the hopes and fears of a generation.

He had adopted the question and response form of the seven-teenth-century Child ballad "Lord Randal."

O where ha you been Lord Randal, my son?
And where ha you been, my handsome young man?

In Dylan's song Lord Randal becomes "my blue-eyed son," and my handsome young man becomes "my darling young one." Each of the five long stanzas begins with a question: Where have you been? What did you see, hear? Who did you meet? And finally, What will you do now? The answers come in strings of anaphoric images set in a repeated melodic phrase.

I've stumbled on the side of twelve misty mountains,
I've walked and I've crawled on six crooked highways.

There are five answers in the first stanza, seven in the second, eight in the third, six in the fourth, and twelve answers in the final stanza, some rhyming, some not, avoiding monotony, forcing attention upon the imagery. Each of those replies begins with the G chord that climbs to a ringing A major before returning to the bass-heavy drone of the tonic D. While the literary structure resembles "Lord Randal," the musical composition is original. The chorus at the end of each stanza repeats the song title, building upon it phrase by phrase in rising chords. "It's a hard, well it's a hard," before exploding into the fifth repetition of the phrase at the song's highest pitch, the full title: *A Hard RAIN'S A-Gonna Fall;* and he holds on to that high D on the word *rain* as if the note contained the code that must carry him through the imagery of the next stanza.

What did you see?

I saw a newborn baby with wild wolves all around it,
I saw a highway of diamonds with nobody on it.

He sees a black branch dripping blood, men with bleeding hammers, and children bearing guns and swords—all horrific emblems of war.

Who did you meet?

I met a young child beside a dead pony,
I met a white man who walked a black dog

He meets a woman whose body is on fire, a girl who gives him a rainbow, a man wounded in love and another wounded with hatred. Each of the answers rises on the single step from G to A and resolves to the root D chord, again and again until the chorus comes booming, *It's a hard rain . . . is gonna fall.*

And at the beginning of the last stanza the Great Questioner, who must be the poet's mother, his father, or his God, asks him the ultimate question: What will you do now? Having stood on the shores of dead oceans, moved thousands of miles in the mouth of a graveyard; having heard the roll of a wave that could drown the world, and thousands of people whispering and no one listening, what will you do now with the grim evidence of your senses? Here Bob Dylan drew out the measure for dramatic effect, strumming a bar extra before singing the answer.

Suitably the last stanza is the longest and richest, as it proclaims the poet's passionate resolve to go out into the world again before that rain starts to fall, heedless of danger, into the depths of the darkest forest, where the people are empty-handed, where poison is flooding the water.

Where hunger is ugly, where the souls are forgotten
Where black is the color, where none is the number

There, at ground zero of the cataclysm of human suffering he means to abide, and bear witness, and think it and tell it, and speak out the truth until "all souls can see it." He ends the stanza with a rich couplet that is both messianic and humorous: like Jesus he will stand on the sea—until he starts sinking; but he'll know his song well before he starts singing. Having heard this song of fifty-seven verses and nearly eleven minutes' duration, the last line of the closing stanza made us smile. This was not only a tour de force of post-symbolist imagery, it was also a considerable feat of memory.

After the chorus and the flat-picking of the final, high notes, the applause that pealed and resonated through the auditorium was partly in admiration and somewhat an expression of relief, as if we had watched a tightrope walker on a high wire above our heads. We were grateful that he had gone on that frightening journey, and relieved that he had come home alive if somewhat dazed and perhaps wounded from the ordeal.

He had done, in those minutes, exactly what he said he would do, gone to hell and returned to tell the tale. The event was illuminating—promising further illumination upon reflection—and thoroughly cathartic, a tragedy in a jewel box.

Dylan tuned up the guitar to the natural E tuning and fit a G harmonica into the spring of the clicking neck rack. A humorous talkin' blues was on the way as comic relief, a black comedy, suitably, "Talkin' World War III Blues." The yarn starts with a trip to the psychiatrist's to tell the doctor a crazy dream, about walking through the city after a nuclear firestorm. He walks deserted streets, lighting his cigarette on a parking meter along the way. He rings the bell at a fallout shelter—begging for a string bean—and is greeted with a shotgun blast. On a corner he sees somebody, hails him as a fellow survivor, and the stranger screams and runs off, fearing that Dylan might be communist. Lonely, he calls up the lady who announces the time on the phone; she tells him that when he hears the sound it will be three o'clock. "She said that for over an hour / And I hung up." It was black humor about a threat that had hung over our lives since we were children practicing air raid drills in school, cowering under our wooden desks.

The psychiatrist interrupts him to say he's been having the same sort of dream, only slightly different. "I dreamt," said the doctor, "that the only person left after the war was me. I didn't see you around." This is the point where Dylan raised the bar for the humble talkin' blues with its cracker-barrel punch lines, creating a moment of transhistorical, metaphysical insight. Time has passed, he tells us, and now everyone is having this dream of walking through the streets of a ruined city, alone. Mangling a well-known American aphorism, that you can fool some of the people all of the time, and all of the people some of the time, *but you can't fool all of the people all of the time,* Dylan rolled his eyes back in his head as if searching for the words:

Some of the people can be all right part of the time,
But all of the people can't be right all of the time

And he says he believes that Abraham Lincoln said that (which Lincoln, in fact, did *not*). However:

I'll let you be in my dreams if I can be in yours.
I said that.

Dylan really *did* say that, covering the final phrase of the song with the blast of his mouth harp. And what he said, a play on the children's routine "I'll show you mine if you show me yours," would remain in our heads long after the words wrongly attributed to Abraham Lincoln had faded away. No doubt we had appeared in Bob Dylan's dream long ago, like the shadowy girl in the "Eternal Circle," the creature with many faces beyond the footlights. And now he would appear in our dreams. He had made the prophecy, and we sealed the pact with our applause.

He reached for another harmonica in the clattering pile to replace the one in his neck rack. Finger-picking a lovely, bouncing tune, he said, "This is a song I wrote one time . . . in order to make me feel better at other times." Then he played the entire melody of "Don't Think Twice, It's All Right," thirty-two measures in 2/4 time, on the harmonica—the most lyrical, precise harp playing of the evening. We knew the song well from recordings by Peter, Paul and Mary and Joan Baez. Many singers sentimentalized the lyrics, but Dylan captured both the sweetness and the anger involved in the love affair gone wrong.

I ain't sayin' you treated me unkind
You could have done better but I don't mind
You just kinda wasted my precious time
But don't think twice, it's all right.

For the next forty-five minutes he would sing the songs we had come for, the antiwar "With God on Our Side," the angry dirge "Masters of War," which pursued the D minor chord through eight voodoo stanzas describing and cursing the leaders of the military-industrial complex. "Masters of War" was relentless, unforgiving. No turn-the-other-cheek, passive resistance here—it was youthful rancor worthy of the crimes.

And I hope that you die
And your death'll come soon
I will follow your casket
In the pale afternoon

With a furious flourish of strumming Dylan backed away from the microphone as the audience roared and cheered its approval.

Quickly retuning the guitar, he played a G chord. The next song, rendered without prologue or apology, was as intense—although considerably more subtle—as the jeremiad that went before. In mid-June, Medgar Evers, a field secretary for the NAACP, had been assassinated near the door of his home in Jackson, Mississippi. In early July Dylan went down to Greenwood, Mississippi, with Pete Seeger, Theodore Bikel, a *New York Times* reporter, and a film crew to sing in support of a voter registration drive. He arrived with this new song in his head.

A bullet from the back of a bush took Medgar Evers' blood
A finger fired the trigger to his name.

You didn't have to know much about poetry to know how well alliteration had served those lines. Blood never sounded redder or a trigger finger more lethal. Dylan's enunciation of the plosive consonants made the words leap into three dimensions.

When he sang the bitter song in Greenwood the cameras rolled. The *New York Times* reporter wrote, obtusely, that "the refrain of the song [also the title] was that the man who shot Mr. Evers didn't know what he was doing and should be forgiven, 'he's only a pawn in their game.'" Some of us had seen Bob Dylan singing the song on television. More had heard him perform it at the Newport Folk Festival in July and at the Lincoln Memorial in late August. Before Dylan spat out the second line of the song here in Lisner Auditorium, the audience was already clapping.

Amazing how quickly a song, as yet unrecorded, had become famous in certain circles—in a matter of weeks—because it answered an urgent need. Half a dozen songwriters, including Nina Simone, Bob Gibson, and Phil Ochs, had taken a stab at this subject, but everybody was hearing and learning Dylan's, not because he was more famous or more insistent, but because Dylan's lyric soared above the righteous indignation that needed no poet to express it. He gave us an aerial view of the political power plant that had generated a genocidal hatred in the South. He nearly shouted the first lines of each stanza.

A South politician preaches to the poor white man,
"You got more than the blacks, don't complain.
You're better than them, you were born with white skin," they explain
And the Negro's name
Is used it is plain
For the politician's gain

The guitarist struck at the instrument like a drum, underscoring the end-rhyme words, slashing chords opening each stanza. Dylan had a way of baring his teeth on the rhyme words as he sang in anger, a canine ferocity. The repetitive structure of the short verses was hammerlike, antilyrical, intended to mimic the machinelike behavior of the underclass whites: six or seven of these rhymed couplets would pile up before Dylan would cry out the chorus lines of absolution. *The poor white man's not to blame, He's only a pawn in their game.*

He cried out on the highest pitch of the song the word *pawn* and held the note a full measure before letting it go. The song was just as grim as "Masters of War" but had a certain grace in its complexity, its intersection of dimensions, like a cubist painting. No one was getting out of that song with their innocence or self-righteousness intact—at least no one of us in this white audience. Three miles from this spot Abraham Lincoln had issued the Emancipation Proclamation one hundred years ago. Still Negroes were being ambushed in the South, and the government by the people and for the people, the politicians we had elected, was at the root of this bloody tree.

When the chess pieces had been put away the show was nearly over. Dylan had been playing his heart out for more than two hours and he began to look weary, as if he had gone through all the real experiences he had played for us. I had the feeling that he wasn't playacting. I think that most of this audience understood that no human being could do this for very long. He stripped off the capo, retuned the guitar, and locked a G harmonica into the neck rack. The Goliaths of our time had been exposed and cross-examined, cursed and flailed: masters of war, corrupt politicians, greedy mine owners, masked executioners.

Recalling the cruel Goliaths of the past and the crueler ones of our present day, Dylan spoke hopefully. One day, two thousand years hence, people might look back and rejoice that our enemies too had been slain like those of old. He began the upbeat strumming of the G major, blowing a wide chord on the mouth harp, introducing the cheerful melody.

> *Oh the time will come up*
> *When the winds will stop*
> *And the breeze will cease to be breathin'*
> *Like stillness of the wind*
> *'Fore the hurricane begins,*
> *The hour when the ship comes in.*

It is a joyful allegory: the rough surprise landing of the ship of our dreams, manned with wise men and high-principled rebels who will not take no for an answer. The seas make way for the bow, laughing fish swim out of its path, the hovering seagulls smile upon the vessel, the rocks on the shore stand proudly awaiting the deliverers. The Goliaths shake in their boots, raising their hands,

> *Sayin we'll meet all your demands*
> *But we'll shout from the bow your days are numbered.*

After the pageant of horrors we had seen that night—infanticide, suicide, starvation, assassination, genocide, nuclear war—this fantasy of triumph provided a much-needed uplift, a hopeful if not altogether happy ending. It was no more than prophecy, but we were all aboard. With such a captain to show us the way, if the wind and seas were favorable surely we must succeed.

Now he was really tired, blinking at the lights and the onrushing tide of applause and cheering. He took off his guitar and held it at his side. He thanked us, again and again, nodding right and left, stepping back and bowing. He stooped slightly. For a while he had been larger than life. He really was small, maybe five foot seven, and you could see that, now that the people behind him were standing up to honor him, he was a little taller than the women and shorter than most of the men. The pale blue of his work shirt set off the blue of his eyes.

We were not about to let him go without an encore, so he strapped on the guitar again and began strumming, slowly, searchingly, in 3/4 time. He played a haunting melody on the harmonica, the Irish tune some of us knew from the Clancy Brothers recording "The Parting Glass." We thought he might sing that air, although thus far he had sung no songs but his own. In fact he had borrowed the Irish tune and made his own song of it, a composition that he called the "Restless Farewell." The five strophaic stanzas, resembling the ten-verse stanzas of W. B. Yeats's poem "All Souls' Night," comprise one of Dylan's finest lyric poems, autobiographical and heartfelt.

Oh ev'ry foe that ever I faced,
The cause was there before we came.
And ev'ry cause that ever I fought,
I fought it full without regret or shame.
But the dark does die
As the curtain is drawn and somebody's eyes
Must meet the dawn. . . .

Marking the end of the song, the end of the performance, the end indeed of a very long year that had nearly defined him as a folksinger, he cast his lot with Rhett Butler/Clark Gable in the closing moments of *Gone with the Wind*. A false clock, he told us, had been trying to measure his time and disgrace him. He felt covered in the dust of rumors. And yet . . . and yet: trusting in his own resources, a straight arrow with a slick point, he knew he could pierce through all the dirt and dust. He would take his stand, faithful to himself,

And bid farewell and not give a damn.

He blew a final coda on the mouth harp, bringing his song and the concert to a close. There was a moment of silence. As the applause rose in the auditorium so did all of us to send him off. He ducked his head under the guitar strap, lowered the harmonica rack, and bowed, left and right. He kissed his left hand to us, once, twice, bowed a final low bow, smiling, and walked off the stage. The people behind him turned their heads to watch him go.

We kept on clapping but Dylan did not return and we hardly expected it. He seemed to have given us every ounce of his strength. My mother said to me: "I hope to God that nothing happens to him."

My thirteen-year-old sister (who later became an investigative reporter for the *New York Post*) wanted to go and get Bob Dylan's autograph. She would always find her way backstage after a play or concert, or wait at the stage door for the stars to emerge; her pen and program were ready in case she got lucky, which was most of the time. She led all of us from our row up the side aisle, then out a door under the red exit sign to the right of the stage.

When we got outside it was cold but the rain had stopped. We were in a small crowd of people, fewer than a hundred folks waiting for the star to come out. It was not a pushing, hysterical mob. This was a post-Elvis, pre-Beatles folk audience, enthusiastic but polite, and it seemed likely that the singer who had been so warm and personable onstage would pause to sign autographs and greet his admirers. Up the street a blue Ford station wagon was idling, with its lights and windshield wipers on.

A swarthy, broad-shouldered man came out of the stage door carrying a guitar case. Bob Dylan, bare-headed, in a suede jacket, followed him. Another man, slender and with a Vandyke beard, followed close behind the singer. They moved swiftly in the direction of the station wagon and the people made way for them. Every few steps he paused. Smiling, he held out a hand with a ballpoint pen in it, scribbling on whatever people held out to him. He shook hands with this one and that one, said hello. We couldn't get near him.

My mother lost sight of my sister when Bob Dylan was about twenty feet away from us. The crowd was not huge but it was big enough that a child could get lost in it, no joke in the city. My mother became frightened and started calling out, "Linda! Linda!" My sister didn't answer. Now Bob Dylan was out of sight, somewhere near the blue station wagon, which by now was surrounded by people, chattering, laughing. My mother pushed forward shouting my sister's name at the top of her voice.

Then, over all the hubbub and shouting came a voice just loud enough to be heard. "Ma'am!" Bob Dylan called, in our direction. "Ma'am?" We moved toward the voice and people let us pass. At last we could see Dylan standing near the car, behind the glare of the headlights. He had his right arm around my sister's shoulders, and he was signing autographs with his left hand as he leaned against the door. He seemed to recognize my mother as soon as he saw her.

"It's all right, ma'am," he called out. *"I've got her."*

He signed my sister's autograph book. He signed the little green spiral notebook in which I had scribbled notes about the performance.

He waved to everyone, got into the backseat of the blue station wagon, and it rolled away.

CHAPTER 3

The Pauper and the Prince

Once upon a time there was a boy who landed in an orphanage in Gallup, New Mexico, in the early 1940s. Part Sioux Indian, part Irish-English-Welsh-Okie, he had been abandoned as an infant. He was left in swaddling clothes on the back steps of somebody's house and this Good Samaritan delivered the boy to the orphanage, whence he was received into a foster home.

They called the boy Bob Dylan.

As it turned out, the foster parents were unsatisfactory, so as soon as the boy was old enough to run away he did. When the police caught up with him they sent him back to the orphanage, where he stayed until another family took him in. That family included an uncle who was a riverboat gambler and another who was a second-story burglar. He ran away again, and so on, until the third or fourth foster family, in Fargo, North Dakota, threw him out—or just gave up pursuing him.

Little Bobby joined the carnival when he was thirteen, greased the Ferris wheel, drove tent stakes for the sideshow. He traveled all over the West and Southwest playing piano for the carnival dancers. The boy learned guitar from an old man named Wigglefoot in New Mexico, the style of blues bottleneck slide guitar that he first played with a butcher knife fretting the strings. Wigglefoot was missing teeth and had a patch on one eye like a pirate. The boy sang in the carnival tent on a stage next to the bearded lady.

When he ran away from the carnival he worked on a ranch grooming horses and shoveling manure. Bob Dylan shoveled a lot of manure. Then when he grew some he operated heavy machinery, steam shovels and forklifts from the mining country of Duluth to the Texas border towns, places like Laredo, Brownsville, and Eagle Pass. He hopped freight trains. His hair and his fingernails grew long. He loved the feel of the wind in his hair. Nobody ever told him to brush his teeth or take a bath. Everywhere he went he played guitar and sang whether people liked it or not. He learned from the old singers. When he was fifteen he met black Mance Lipscomb in Navasota, Texas, before Mance was rediscovered in a log cabin there, where he had been working as a sharecropper. Mance was slender and wore a fedora. He recorded on the Arhoolie label. He must have known a thousand songs and taught the boy most of them, songs like "Baby Please Don't Go" and "Corrina Corrina," "Jack of Spades" and "Sugar Babe."

Sugar babe I'm tired of you
Ain't your honey but the way you do
Sugar babe, it's all over now. . . .

In a Detroit coffeehouse the orphan was performing and couldn't find the kitchen knife he used to play slide guitar so he pulled out a switchblade, clicked it open onstage, and half the audience fled in terror. In Chicago he learned to play harmonica from Little Walter Jacobs of Muddy Waters's band. In Nashville he played with Gene Vincent on an album that was never released. In Denver at age eighteen he met Jesse Fuller, who taught him "San Francisco Bay Blues" and other songs.

Somewhere in Minnesota he played piano awhile in Bobby Vee's band. In Carmel, California, he met Woody Guthrie, who was on the road with Ramblin' Jack Elliott and banjo picker Billy Faier. He fell in love with Woody Guthrie. When he heard Woody was sick in a hospital in New York, the boy hopped a freight train, his guitar slung neck down over his back, and rode the blinds to New York City in January 1961.

About the same time that infant was born and abandoned in New Mexico a boy child was born to Abraham and Beatty Zimmerman at St. Mary's Hospital, Duluth, Minnesota. They named the child, their first, Robert Allen Zimmerman. It was hot in New Mexico, but cool that day in Duluth, May 24, 1941. And chilly the day the child was circumcised and the mohel at the bris pronounced his name in Hebrew, Shabtai Zisel Ben Avraham. This was no hothouse flower but a sturdy, hearty perennial rooted high in the hill country west of Lake Superior.

It was mining country, the Mesabi Range, rich in iron ore. The Ojibwa (Chippewa) Indians looked at the long range of hills lying along the northern horizon and called it Mesabi, the sleeping giant, somehow prophesizing that one day the peaceful pine and birch forests would give way to fire-breathing mine shafts and smoking chimneys. White men would come and wake up the giant but first they would have to endure the cold. Those settlers who were hardy enough to make it through the long winters—Finnish immigrants, Slavs, Poles, a few Russian Jews—put down roots deep in the mineral-rich soil and stayed planted there.

Robert Zimmerman's father was the son of Jewish immigrants from Odessa, a Ukrainian port city on the Black Sea. They arrived in Duluth in the first decade of the twentieth century, fleeing a pogrom. Robert's mother, Beatrice, came from a family of Lithuanian Jews who settled in the nearby town of Hibbing, Minnesota, in the same decade. Her father owned a clothing store there; her grandfather Benjamin H. Edelstein owned and operated several movie theaters. There were not a great many Jews in that part of the world, so the young ones sought one another out in courting. Pretty Beatty Stone, eighteen, met Abe Zimmerman, a charming, well-built violin player of twenty-one, at a New Year's party in Duluth in 1933. They were married in June at her parents' home in Hibbing.

In the depths of the Great Depression Abe worked his way up to middle management at Standard Oil, yet the frugal newlyweds lived with Abe's mother in Duluth. They saved their money. Not until Beatty was pregnant did they move into their own home, a two-bedroom apartment in a clapboard house with a verandah on a hill above the town and the lake. In that apartment, under the high-pitched roof, Bobby took his first steps.

In February 1946, his brother, David, was born. In the same year Abe Zimmerman fell victim to the polio virus epidemic. Parents prayed that their children would be spared from the "infantile paralysis" that struck randomly and without mercy, but adults were not immune to the cruel sword of the disease. After a week in the hospital Abe was bedridden and housebound for six months while the fever ran its course. He lost his job. It was a defining moment in the life of the young family. He would never regain his natural stride or move without pain, and he had been a lithe, vigorous man. If he was not embittered he was chastened, stunned into a stoical realism more austere and humorless than the worldview of others who weathered the hard times. There was no treatment in those days but bed rest, fluids, and aspirin for the pain and fever. They massaged the patient's limbs to try to straighten them. As the eldest son in the family, six-year-old Bobby would no doubt have seen service as a mother's helper.

A year later, convalescing, out of work, Abe Zimmerman looked to his extended family for support: his wife's family and his two older brothers, who lived in Hibbing. The brothers, Maurice and Paul, took Abe into partnership in their company, Micka Electric. The men were electricians who worked out of a Fifth Avenue storefront that sold refrigerators and washing machines. They drove a truck around town, wiring houses and delivering kitchen appliances while Abe stayed behind to mind the store. For a while Beatty and Abe and the boys lived with her mother, Florence Stone, recently widowed, in her apartment on Third Avenue.

When they had saved enough money the Zimmermans moved into their own home, a two-story corner house of pale stucco on Seventh Avenue with seven rooms, a basement, and two garages. One garage they rented to the baker. As the bread truck came and went the sweet smell of warm dough wafted through the two windows of the room at the back of the house Bob shared with his little brother. The half-dozen houses in the middle-class neighborhood called the Fairview Addition were well spaced, with neat lawns and clipped bushes. Children ran across the yards in good weather, and in and out of one another's houses, slamming the screen doors, mostly Catholic and Lutheran children; the Zimmermans were the only Jews. Beatty was outgoing and sociable, and opened her heart and home to her neighbors, so her boys had many friends. They enrolled in the little Alice Elementary school, and six years later went to Hibbing High School, a palatial redbrick building with marble steps and columns, two blocks away.

His childhood and early youth were unremarkable. The boy was remarkable and some people sensed it, but the childhood was typical of middle-class Jewish experience in most of America during World War II and the decade after. The young parents were devoted, constant, sober, and diligent. They were considerate of each other and the children, worked hard to provide for and educate them, and were grateful to God for the fortune that allowed them to thrive in a country where their freedom was guaranteed. In Europe their relatives had been penned up, decimated, buried alive. Next to God, family was paramount, life taught the Zimmermans. Family loyalty was indispensable. Where would they be now without it?

Even the dispositions of Beatty and Abraham Zimmerman answer to a paradigm, a personal archetype of the midcentury nuclear family. Mother was adoring, affectionate—telepathic in responding to the child's desires, hopes, and fears. Her love was unmistakably unconditional. Father was distant, a being apart, with one foot in another world. He seemed not to understand the child, although he certainly cared; one could be sure of it because of his expectations. He was rarely satisfied. Beatty, like the sound of her name, was all sunshine, beaming, an endless source of a stream of words that nourished the children. If Bob sang she was the first to applaud, and if he wrote a poem for her, it was the best she had ever seen. Abraham was dark, taciturn, descending from a mountain with laws, and quick to judge. Such love is also precious but the value resides partly in its inaccessibility, the distance one must travel to achieve it.

The archetypes are merely that: rough sketches of a complex family portrait. Beatty Zimmerman did not spoil her child or indulge him often, or he would not have behaved as well as he did. He was a good boy. There were rules in the home: do your chores, brush your teeth, be gentle with your brother and polite to everyone; but Abe later said he told his boys, "Do things for us because you like us, not because you are afraid of us." Abe had a dry wit but held his peace. After a day's work he would solve the crossword puzzle, avoiding small talk whenever possible.

Abe sometimes spoiled his son with gifts: soon after his sixteenth birthday a pink Ford convertible, then a Harley-Davidson motorcycle. If there was schoolwork to be done it was probably mother who assumed the role of taskmaster and critic, as father was otherwise engaged, in the sale of refrigerators and davenports, in paying the bills. But when the little boy was too shy to attend his first day of school, nothing would do but that father would lead him by the hand to the classroom and see that he was settled before waving goodbye. For all of mother's kindness and comfort, it was father who provided protection against the mysterious world outside.

The child was remarkable, and the first person to notice this was his mother, who said to him, "You should have been a girl, you're so beautiful." In those days no harm could have been intended by such a gushing comment, as boys were not supposed to be so beautiful as this boy was, with his wide-set blue eyes and golden curls, the angelic round face. Beatty would not have made this comment to the child while he could understand it. The quote comes from a friend who interviewed Beatty forty years after she festooned Bob's hair with ribbons and posed the fifteen-month-old baby for the camera. Physical beauty was a precious commodity not to be squandered upon Jewish males of the species who had other attractions. With luck and the natural friction of experience he might outgrow it.

Beauty comes and goes, particularly in children, but certain qualities of character declare themselves early and remain constant. He was wonderfully receptive. Before the age of four Bobby Zimmerman's blue eyes expressed an unchildlike empathy for the people around him, a quality that often anticipates the precocious command of language—more common in girls than boys. Proud Abe would take the two-year-old to the office to show him off. By the age of three, when Bobby toddled into the office of Standard Oil the secretaries would put aside their papers. They would gather around as this little boy, sitting on his father's desk, spoke well-balanced sentences into the Dictaphone and sang verses of songs. When he was done talking and singing his father would play the record back to him, and the child would laugh and clap, amazed by the sound of his own voice.

He was a good boy, but he was willful, stubborn even. Invited to sing, at an aunt's wedding, or a public Mother's Day celebration, he would gladly oblige—but then he would perform only after exacting a pledge of complete silence and attention from the crowd. The five-year-old would stamp his foot, scowling until the chatter ended; then he would begin his song, "Ac-Cen-Tchu-Ate the Positive."

The Johnny Mercer/Harold Arlen song became popular when Mercer recorded it in 1944. Mercer had been inspired by a Father Divine sermon in which the black ex-convict enjoined his following:

"You got to ac-cen-tchu-ate the positive, and eliminate the negative," and by no means "mess with Mr. In-Between." The message of moral uplift was fit for Americans at the end of World War II, an attitude that would inspire a generation of empire builders, schoolteachers, and the popular philosophy of Norman Vincent Peale. This was Bobby's song—not "Would You Like to Swing on a Star," or Cole Porter's "Don't Fence Me In"—instead, the future anthem of the Power of Positive Thinking, a song that used the Old Testament figures Noah and Jonah as role models. The child learned it from the radio.

He was a good boy for the most part, who loved his mother, and his father somewhat less, and tolerated his younger brother. In the way of older brothers the world over he struggled with the desire to torment little David and resisted temptation most of the time. Robert Shelton tells of the boys tussling on the carpet, Bob pinning David to the floor by his greater weight and might, and sitting astride the wailing boy until somebody pulled him off. This is not the sort of story one usually hears about young Bobby.

"People would laugh with delight at hearing him sing," Abe recalled. "He was, I would say, a very lovable, a very unusual child. People would go out of their way to handle him, to talk with him."

As someone who took in more than others, he developed a response to people that played upon their deficiency. Did they not know what he knew? Or hear what he heard? How delightful! What fun to play in that field! The human mind cannot see far beyond a paradox: beyond that lies God's country and no-man's-land. A person who learns this can drive people around him crazy who don't know it, by conjuring up the paradox and then running away from it, laughing. *The world must be finite in space and time: but there is an equally good argument that it is infinite. "I am lying." Is the boy who says he is lying telling the truth, or not?* A few children learn this very early—the boundaries of human knowledge. They can lead a friend or an enemy to the edge of the unknown and then step back, leaving them befuddled, teetering on the precipice. This is not a cheap trick. It is a peculiar human endowment, an instinctive feel for metaphysical terrain, like an acrobat's innate sense of balance.

Bobby made friends easily in that postwar melting pot of Poles, Finns, Czechs, and Russian Jews. Beatty did not keep a kosher house with two sets of dishes or make the boys wear tzitzit under their shirts; the family did not regularly attend the synagogue. But then hardly anyone did in Minnesota.

They saw to it that Bob had a tutor to teach him his Hebrew letters so that on the appointed day of his Bar Mitzvah in May 1954 he would stand up to read his Torah portion in the clapboard synagogue on Second Avenue. Afterward there was a grand reception at the Androy Hotel and many people attended, relatives from Hibbing and Duluth, and friends and business associates who were not Jewish. Being a Jew in Hibbing in the 1950s distinguished a child somewhat but it was not like being black or crippled with polio. There were a few clubs that Jews were restricted from joining. But they had their own clubs, B'nai B'rith, Hadassah, American Zionists, and summer camps where they bonded. Soon after his Bar Mitzvah Bob began attending the Jewish Camp Herzl in Wisconsin. During summers there he met Harriet Zisson and Judy Rubin. He met musician Larry Kegan, and Louis Kemp, son of the seafood tycoon, both of whom would become lifelong friends.

As a student Robert Zimmerman did little to distinguish himself after his display of verbal precocity in the early grades. He read and conversed fluently. His IQ was only a few points above average— perhaps the dreamy child could not focus on standardized tests— and his grades matched, C plus, which in the days before grade inflation was above average. He did what schoolwork was required and no more. His parents bought a Gulbransen spinet piano, but Bob mostly ignored his piano teacher, preferring to pick out tunes on his own. He would not bother to read music.

The time he might have spent learning scales or improving his grade-point average he passed in reading Classic Comic Books and literature of his own choosing, drawing pictures, and listening to the radio. There was a big wooden console in the living room where the family would gather to hear radio theater like *Amos 'n' Andy*, *The Lone Ranger*, and *The Shadow*. The local stations played the songs of the Hit Parade, songs by Johnny Mercer and Hoagy Carmichael, songs like "What's the Use of Dreamin'" and "In the Cool, Cool, Cool of the Evening": songs sung by the Ames Brothers, Jo Stafford, Patti Page, and Rosemary Clooney, like "How Much Is That Doggy in the Window" and "The Naughty Lady of Shady Lane" and the sultry "Come On-a My House." One of his favorite singers was Hank Williams, who nearly always had a song on the Hit Parade, tunes like "Cold, Cold Heart," "Jambalaya," and "Your Cheatin' Heart." This was hillbilly music that everyone liked. The local station WMFG also played a few polkas for the audience in Hibbing, whirling tunes with accordion, fiddle, and guitar.

Soon Bob had his own desktop radio upstairs in his bedroom. The radio of choice in those days was a Zenith of brown Bakelite the size of a toaster, and the owner of Micka Electric could order them wholesale. The Zenith had a large dial that looked like a golden compass. At night the boy lay in the bed under the covers and turned the dial. Outside it was twenty degrees below zero. The radio glowed in the dark and was warm to the touch from the faint buzzing of the amber vacuum tubes. This medium and the voices and music it transported defined the adolescent psyche. His ear was extraordinary, almost as if he had been born blind. Where others heard a phrase he heard a paragraph; where some heard a theme he heard a fugue. He could hear long distances in space and time.

Maybe the gift was compensatory. By the time someone discovered that Zimmerman could not read the blackboard, his myopia had reorganized his senses, aggrandizing his hearing. Fitted for spectacles he was too vain or absentminded to wear them, or he had grown fond of the iridescent haze, the impressionistic blur of edges and horizons that surrounds the nearsighted.

He became an audiodidact, one who learns mainly through his ears rather than his eyes, from the sound of voices rather than words on a page.

Beyond the golden glow of the radio dial, a boy on the edge of dreams could envision all of America, all of history, and glimpse something of the future. The static between clear stations bespoke mysterious distances and journeys, highways, prairies, railroads, and mountains and cities beyond. Late at night he could reel in a clear-channel station from Little Rock, Arkansas, KTHS, which licensed Frank Page's show *No-Name Jive*. "Gatemouth" Page hosted a program of rhythm and blues, singers like Howlin' Wolf, Muddy Waters, John Lee Hooker, Bill Haley, and Little Richard. That was the sound of the future. Little Richard, who sang "Long Tall Sally" and "Tutti Frutti," had a gospel streak; he used to say that his music was "the healing music that makes the dumb and deaf hear and talk." It made Bob Zimmerman leap out of bed in the morning, run to the piano, and imitate those sounds he had heard the night before. He rented a cheap guitar and purchased *Manoloff's Spanish Guitar Method Book* so he could learn the chords.

With or without his eyeglasses Bob could see well enough to enjoy the movies on the wide screen at Hibbing theaters like the Lybba, which was owned by his mother's family and named for his great-grandmother. He saw John Ford westerns like *Stagecoach* and *The Searchers* with John Wayne; he saw *The Blackboard Jungle*, a melodrama about teenage angst in a New York high school, with rock-and-roll music by Bill Haley; he watched movies like *On the Waterfront* with Marlon Brando, and *Mister Roberts* with Jimmy Cagney. He particularly admired the brooding, handsome figure of James Dean in *East of Eden* and *Rebel Without a Cause*. In the autumn of 1955, not long after Dean died in an auto crash, *Rebel* premiered at the State Theatre. Half the teenage boys in America saw themselves in the movie's hero, the outsider whose toughness and courage can't conceal his vulnerability as he fights to get by in a hostile world—parents who don't understand him, a gang of bullies in a new high school, girls who tease him, always just out of reach. With his slicked-back hair, tight jeans, and zipper jacket, James Dean—along with Elvis and Marlon Brando—appeared in the mirror of every adolescent male of Zimmerman's generation, to be mimicked, burlesqued, or rejected.

A youth studying his image in the glass tries on expressions, hairstyles. He wrinkles his brow, he pouts, discovering his face.

The teenage years are a period of individuation, healthy narcissism. Rarely in America has a generation wanted so much to define itself as what its parents were not, as in 1955. The process did not begin or end in front of the mirror; it fed upon music, books, and politics that parents disliked. But the outward expression was a fashion statement. Bob Zimmerman got a leather zipper jacket, blue jeans, and boots with half-moon tap heels. He wore his hair long and slicked back, like Elvis, or in a tall pompadour, like Little Richard. He struck certain attitudes and poses in the bedroom, and had his brother David photograph him with the Polaroid camera so he could quickly see the results. Self-consciousness, for this youngster, would soon be transformed into a power to project his state of mind. He would look into the mirror until—like James Dean—he became a mirror himself.

It was much easier to figure out how one would look to the world than how one would sound. For the sake of appearance two or three role models would suffice, but for the sake of music there were a hundred examples and models, a thousand, from Hank Williams and Johnny Ray to Little Richard and Elvis Presley.

To sort these things out it helps to have like-minded friends, and Bob had plenty. He was popular with the girls, who had their opinions. And there were boys in town who shared his passion for blues and rock and roll; they would gather in the Zimmermans' house for jam sessions. After some false starts he formed a band with guitar player Monte Edwardson and drummer Le Roy Hoikkala. In 1958 they performed at a variety show, the annual Jacket Jamboree, on the stage of their magnificent high school auditorium. Bob, at the black Steinway piano, sang "Rock and Roll Is Here to Stay" at the top of his lungs, pounding the keys and shriek-singing in imitation of Little Richard. He played with such abandon that he broke the piano, but they went on with the show. Beneath the high cut-glass chandeliers the crowd laughed and clapped and hooted, loving the spectacle of little Zimmy the greaser, with his hair piled up on top of his head, aping the Negro rhythm-and-blues singer.

One gig led to another. The Golden Chords played at a dance at the National Guard armory, and at the Chamber of Commerce's Winter Frolics. They even appeared on a television show, the *Polka Hour* in Duluth, before going their separate ways to play solo, or with other musicians. Bob Zimmerman may not have been the best teenage musician in Minnesota but he was probably the most obstinate. He formed several bands that got away from him. "When I put together my early bands," he later recalled, "usually some other singer who was short of one would take it away. . . ." At first he didn't understand. Then he realized it was not because they were better singers than he was but because they had connections, "an open door to gigs where there was real money . . . someone up the ladder in the chamber of commerce or town council." Money was the root of the problem. "It got so that I almost always expected to lose my band and it didn't even shock me anymore if it happened."

He kept organizing bands because he was determined to play for an audience. This was perhaps the most striking characteristic of the teenage Zimmerman, his determination, his blind ambition to become a performer and make his name known beyond the hill-bound confines of Hibbing and Duluth. Beatty recalled how often Bob told his grandmother, "Grandma, someday I'm going to be very famous. You are never going to have to worry about anything." Although they were no longer in need, there must have been a troubling memory of need.

Bob practiced long hours on the piano and guitar. He memorized the songs he learned from the radio and his growing record collection: songs of Hank Williams, Hank Thompson, Chuck Berry, Buddy Holly, Carl Perkins, Elvis Presley, Johnny Cash, Gene Vincent, and the Everly Brothers. He played along with the records. The name he had been given did not have the ring of fame so he would have to re-create it, as he had redesigned his clothing, hair, and expressions—the better to travel in the world beyond the glowing dial of the radio. He tried the name Elston Gunn for a spell and then Robert Allyn, but after reading some poems by Dylan Thomas he changed it fatally to Bob Dylan. That was the beginning of the love-hate relationship between the Oklahoma Orphan and the Jew from Duluth.

Parallel to his ambition to make his name as a musician was a more occult and private desire to write poetry. A handsome young English teacher with the unlikely name of Boniface J. Rolfzen was one of the few who held his attention at Hibbing High School. For two years Zimmerman sat in the front row of Rolfzen's class, third seat from the door, transfixed by the teacher's lively readings from Donne and Shakespeare. Bob spent quiet hours in his bedroom writing poems. This caused his parents graver concern than the public display of the musical talents that were probably a harmless phase he would outgrow, like pimples. The poetry looked like a more serious threat to the boy's future. He might become really good at it.

So on this subject his parents stood firm: "You can't go on and on and on and sit and dream and write poems," his mother told him. "I was afraid he would end up being a poet! Do you know the kind of poet I mean?" Beatty shuddered, reliving the Jewish mother's worst nightmare. "One that had no ambition, and wrote only for himself . . . Here we would be at the back of him with a pitchfork.

"When he was planning to go to college, I would say: 'Bobby, why don't you take something useful?' He said: 'I'll take something in science, literature, and art for a year and then I will see what I want to do.' I told him: 'Don't keep writing poetry, please don't. Go to school and do something constructive. . . .'"

On January 31, 1959, Bob drove to Duluth to hear his idol, Buddy Holly, play a concert with guitarist Link Wray at the Duluth Armory. He sat in the front row and looked Buddy Holly in the eye, and the star looked back at him. Holly was only five years older than Zimmerman, skinny and intense, his eyes buggy behind horn-rimmed glasses. He was brilliant, the quintessential rockabilly star who wrote his own sweet songs: "Peggy Sue," "That'll Be the Day," "Rave On," and "Every Day." Three days later he was killed when a small plane carrying him and two other singers crashed near Clear Lake, Iowa.

Folk music was in the air, the voices of Harry Belafonte, the Kingston Trio, and Jimmie Driftwood; songs like "Scarlet Ribbons" and "Tom Dooley" and "The Battle of New Orleans" were on the radio and the jukeboxes. It was nothing like the driving rhythms of rock and roll, but for a young poet the old songs had a lyric intensity and melodic variety that could reach further and deeper, back in time and forward into dramas to come. He began learning the folk repertoire and discovered he could memorize long narrative ballads like "Barbara Allen" and "Frankie and Albert" that unfolded in a dozen or more stanzas after hearing them a few times—as if the verses were already known to him and he was simply recollecting them.

In his high school yearbook, senior year, he wrote that his ambition was to go and join Little Richard, but this was not the sort of thing that was expected of him. He had promised his parents he would go to college. Dutifully Robert Zimmerman went off to the University of Minnesota in Minneapolis in September of that year. "When Bob came down here in 1959, he looked pretty, fair-skinned, fair-haired, absolutely beardless. His eyes were vaguely popping, and his cheeks a bit too full," recalled Harry Weber, a classicist and roommate of blues musician John Koerner. "Dr. Dan Pugh, a psychiatrist, was fascinated by Dylan's looks. 'A very interesting endocrine system,'

Dr. Pugh said," referring to the complex of glands that regulate hormones, moods, and metabolism.

He lived in the only "single" room in the Jewish fraternity house, Sigma Alpha Mu, where he abided and was tolerated by his fraternity brothers. They found him strange, remote—a boy with an alias. He tried to study. His attention to the books and class attendance was fitful, sufficient to earn him passing grades at best and appease his parents, who were supporting him in the ill-fitting role.

But as the year went by so did any hope or pretense of academic commitment. School began to interfere with his musical education, which was advancing briskly in Dinkytown, a bohemian neighborhood adjacent to the college campus. There was Peine's bookstore, a movie theater, the Purple Onion Pizza Parlor, Bridgeman's ice cream parlor, and the East Hennepin Bar. In coffeehouses students and hipsters read Beat poetry, argued politics, played guitars, bongos, and banjos.

About a year before Bob enrolled in the university, Dave Lee opened the Ten O'Clock Scholar in a storefront on Fourteenth Avenue between Fourth and Fifth streets. This was the gathering place for the best folk musicians in the area, including the white blues guitarists John Koerner and his friend Dave Ray, and harmonica player Tony Glover. There was banjo player Jon Pankake, who had collected hundreds of rare recordings, and a long-haired, gaunt singer and poet named Dave Morton. Morton had actually heard the legendary Huddie Ledbetter (Leadbelly) play live in 1948; he wrote topical songs about race relations and politics, à la Woody Guthrie. Morton introduced Bob to the wry intellectual Dave Whitaker, who knew the Beat writers and poets personally—Allen Ginsberg, William Burroughs, and Gregory Corso—and told tales of his travels and adventures on the Left Bank of Paris, North Beach in San Francisco, and New York's Greenwich Village, all the power spots of the literary subculture.

There in the long room with wooden tables and benches and the coffee bar, the budding folksinger found his teachers and his first audience. Dylan was self-conscious, intense—a youth who struck poses. He would stand in the doorway with his legs wide apart, his thumb hooked in his belt. Single-minded, passionate about the music, in 1960 he spent more time in the Ten O'Clock Scholar and the flats of Morton, Whitaker, and Pankake than he spent in classrooms or the library. From Koerner, Ray, and Glover he learned blues progressions, from Morton old folk ballads, from Whitaker poetry and as much philosophy as his restless mind could tolerate.

He spent hours in Pankake's apartment listening to records: Woody Guthrie, Woody's disciple Ramblin' Jack Elliott, the Carter Family, the Weavers, Leadbelly, Sonny Terry, the Clancy Brothers, John Jacob Niles, Odetta, Paul Clayton, Burl Ives, and a hundred dead and forgotten singers. He practiced the guitar. He begged, borrowed, and stole recordings, memorizing songs. He created in his head a collection more fantastic than any that existed in acetate or vinyl because the songs were all alive and connected, instantly available whole or in snatches, perpetually mutating, dividing, and combining in the poet's imagination. People called him a sponge; he called himself "a musical expeditionary," for whom the rights of property were provisional. He allegedly stole Jon Pankake's records of Ramblin' Jack Elliott and the magical six-disc *Anthology of American Folk Music* that Harry Smith had compiled in 1952. The *Anthology* was a precious source for the 1920s and '30s recordings of blues singers like Furry Lewis, Mississippi John Hurt, and Blind Lemon Jefferson, and old-time players like Clarence Ashley, Bascom Lamar Lunsford, and Doc Boggs.

At the Ten O'Clock Scholar and in other bohemian dens of Minneapolis in 1960, Robert Zimmerman at last came face-to-face with that itinerant orphan Bob Dylan, and the one character would soon make way for the other. Woody Guthrie had something to do with that fatal encounter. It was the power not only of Woody's songs but of his picaresque autobiography *Bound for Glory*, with its hobo heroes crossing America on freight trains, free spirits singing the pleasures and virtues of a life in motion where good-hearted men play by their own rules.

Woody was a rebel poet, a prophet, labor organizer, and the voice of the downtrodden farmers and migrant workers of the 1930s. There was not much more to his politics than sympathy for the working man and a hatred of greed, prejudice, and fascism. A romantic hero, Guthrie became a figurehead for disaffected Marxists/anarchists of the 1940s and '50s whose politics remained emotional, inchoate. Out of *Bound for Glory,* Jack Kerouac's *On the Road* was born.

Listening to the twelve double-sided 78 recordings of Guthrie in a friend's apartment for hour after hour, Zimmerman was transported, transformed. "It made me want to gasp. It was like the land parted," Bob Dylan recalled, years later. The songs could not be categorized, but "they had the infinite sweep of humanity in them. . . . For me it was an epiphany, like some heavy anchor had just plunged into the waters of the harbor." He listened all afternoon to Guthrie, mesmerized, feeling like he had found "some essence of self-command . . . feeling more like myself than ever before." He decided he would sing no songs but Guthrie's for a while. Woody's writings became a lens through which Dylan's vision was suddenly clarified.

He even noted that Woody, as a young man, looked a bit like his own father in his younger days. Although Guthrie had never laid eyes on Dylan, Dylan thought he heard him saying, "I'll be going away, but I'm leaving this job in your hands. I know I can count on you."

In May Bob Dylan made his first serious recording on a reel-to-reel tape, set up in Karen Wallace's apartment in St. Paul. He poured out a cornucopia of tunes imbued with the accents of Hank Williams and the spirit of Woody Guthrie, twenty-seven songs beginning with young Paul Clayton's recent hit, "Gotta Travel On." He sang American chestnuts like "Rock a Bye My Sara Jane," "Take This Hammer," and "Nine Hundred Miles"; he sang bloody Child ballads such as "The Two Sisters."

There were two sisters, they went playing
With a hey down down, a downy
To see their father's ship come sailin' in
With a hi down down, a downy
And when they come to the ocean's brim
With a hey down, a hi down
The elder did push the younger one in.

He sang "Go Down You Murderers," by British singer Ewan Mac-Coll, and "Go Away from My Window," which had been adapted from traditional sources by the spectral, falsetto singer John Jacob Niles, who wore a white robe and his hair down to his shoulders. But mostly he sang songs of Woody Guthrie: "This Land Is Your Land," "Pastures of Plenty," "The Great Historical Bum." He even sang one song of his own making called "One-eyed Jacks."

Won't you dig my grave
With a silver spade?
And forget my name.
I'm twenty years old. [He was nineteen.]
Can't you see my crying,
Can't you see my dying,
I'll never reach twenty-one. . . .

It was a death notice for the boy who had been born Zimmerman in Duluth. Bob Dylan ended the St. Paul tape as he had begun, with a Woody Guthrie song, "Columbus Stockade Blues"; Guthrie linked the past to the future, somewhere out west where Dylan the mythic orphan had been born and abandoned.

Following in the footsteps of Woody Guthrie and Guthrie's heir Jack Kerouac, Bob Dylan headed west that summer. With his guitar strapped to his back, a small suitcase, and a few dollars in his pocket, he stuck his thumb in the air somewhere east of Fargo where the foster family had thrown him out and hitchhiked to Denver, Colorado. There was a lively folk music scene in Denver, and Dylan had been told to look up a black singer named Walt Conley. He was the manager of the Satire, a club that booked funny acts like the Smothers Brothers, and the folk group the Brothers Four. Conley had a small house on East Seventeenth Avenue.

Dylan slept on Conley's floor while Tommy Smothers slept on the couch. Conley let the vagabond play a set or two at the Satire, sharing the bill with the Smothers Brothers, but they didn't much like Dylan's unpolished performance or his unconvincing Oklahoma accent. Neither did the audience in Denver, so soon he was gone. Conley referred him to Sophia St. John in nearby Central City, a former gold rush town that kept its gingerbread Victorian hotels, clapboard general store, and saloons; tourists could pan for gold nearby and pass their leisure time in the ambience of a John Ford western. St. John managed a club she called the Gilded Garter. Judy Collins had been singing there and now St. John wanted another folksinger, so she hired Bob Dylan.

The Gilded Garter was a rowdy joint with swinging doors, waitresses in low-cut dresses, and a big bar with mustachioed bartender in vest and sleeve garters, a beveled mirror reflecting rows of beer glasses behind him. Blue-eyed Judy Collins, who looked like a high-fashion model and sang like an angel, might have gotten the drunken crowd's attention. But Bob Dylan, with his mournful Child ballads and rugged country blues guitar, could scarcely be heard on the stage. He moved to the piano and banged on it for a while but got little more respect over there. After a bad week in the frontier town he returned to Denver, broke.

This time Walt Conley would not let him stay at his house. Somehow Dylan scraped together enough money to rent a room in a cheap hotel next door to the Exodus, then the hottest folk club in the city. Leon Bibb, a black Broadway baritone turned folksinger, was playing at the Exodus for three days on his way through town. During the next few weeks Dylan could hear Bibb and Judy Collins, banjo player Dave Hamil, and the great blues guitarist and singer Jesse Fuller, author of the "San Francisco Bay Blues," which was a mainstay of the folk repertoire. Fuller played guitar and harmonica at once, using the steel harmonica rack around his neck. Getting to know Jesse Fuller and learning songs from him in after-hours sessions at Conley's and Dave Hamil's house was perhaps more important than anything else Bob Dylan accomplished that summer—apart from establishing some authentic Wild West credentials.

The Denver adventure ended prematurely and awkwardly. It seems that the musical expeditionary, desperate for a few dollars, "borrowed" several records from Dave Hamil's collection while he was out. Some were folk albums one might have borrowed to study and return, in all innocence; others were pop albums and Broadway show tunes of no use to the folksinger apart from their value in hock for a few dollars. In the wee hours of the morning Hamil and Conley surprised Bob Dylan in his hotel room. When the police arrived the missing records were found scattered in the alley three stories beneath Dyan's hotel window. No one pressed charges.

"I was kicked out of Denver," he told a friend, "for robbing a cat's house."

Upon his return to Minneapolis for the autumn semester of 1960 there was little left of the college student but his formal enrollment at the university and some guilt that his family was sponsoring the charade. Churning with nervous energy, he couldn't keep still. Something was going on metabolically, a burst of hormones or the effect of coffee and cigarettes. He talked fast, nonstop, when he wasn't listening. When sitting he bounced his leg, pumping it up and down in time to some inaudible rhythm. Standing, he marched in place, knees high. He improved his singing and his guitar playing, as well as his Chaplinesque stage presence. Rolf Cahn, a respected guitar teacher who knew the scene, informed the concert producer Lynn Kastner that Bob Dylan was decidedly the most talented folk performer in the Twin Cities area. The summer in Denver had paid off.

Soon after, the black folksinger Odetta, who already had two hit records with Vanguard, was passing through town; somewhere she heard Dylan perform, and she agreed with Rolf Cahn. Odetta told Dylan yes indeed he had great potential. Around the same time John Koerner recalled a "turning point. He'd been listening to just about everything, all kinds of styles, and writing all kinds of styles. Then he heard Jesse Fuller and Woody Guthrie. And he started going off with the Guthrie thing, and a direction kind of sprang up."

He performed Guthrie's songs with fanatical devotion, particularly the talkin' blues—like "Talkin' Merchant Marine," "Talkin' Columbia," and "Talkin' Inflation Blues"—recording them on his girlfriend's tape recorder. He began talking like Woody Guthrie when he was not recording or performing, droppin' end consonants, and dressin' like Guthrie in the pictures he'd seen of the dust-bowl balladeer on record albums, the hobo minstrel. Dylan held the guitar high on his chest, head cocked, cigarette dangling from his lips. He told a girlfriend, Gretel Hoffman, that he was "building a character." Tony Glover recalled that Dylan "said it was an act, but only for about two days." After that, he admitted, "It was me."

Dylan was not the first young man to develop this obsession. Ten years earlier a Jewish boy named Elliott Charles Adnopoz, born in Brooklyn in 1931, had a similar feeling for Woody Guthrie. He met up with Guthrie in New York in 1951 and became his friend and star pupil. As Ramblin' Jack Elliott, Adnopoz traveled the country with Guthrie, Cisco Houston, Pete Seeger, and others, absorbing Guthrie's songs, his plain flat-picking style, and his sense of humor. In 1955, at the age of twenty-four, Ramblin' Jack struck out on his own, sailing to England, where he made three albums that established his reputation in Europe and the United States as one of the premier folksingers of his generation. Bob Dylan studied the recordings of Woody Guthrie's disciple Jack Elliott with enormous interest.

Guthrie was something more and less than a legend, a flesh-and-blood balladeer born in Okemah, Oklahoma, in 1912, and dying now in a New Jersey hospital of Huntington's disease. When Dylan learned of Guthrie's fate he told his friends he was going to see him. "Bob would get drunk," Dave Morton recalled, "and call Guthrie on the phone. . . . Bob told Guthrie that he was coming out to see him."

That was his promise and his plan, drunk or sober. Dylan practiced Woody's songs night and day, honing his act. He played at the Bastille in Minneapolis for five dollars a night, the Purple Onion in St. Paul for six dollars. He shared a second-floor apartment on Fifteenth Street in Minneapolis with two friends until the landlord evicted them, in the December cold, for disturbing the peace with their music and shenanigans.

At the end of the first semester, in December 1960, he went home to tell his parents he was leaving college to become a folksinger, a transition he had actually made about a year earlier. Abe and Beatty Zimmerman were unenthusiastic but forbearing. "He wanted to be a folksinger, an entertainer," Abe recalled. "We couldn't see it, but we felt he was entitled to the chance. It's his life after all, and we didn't want to stand in the way." They struck a bargain: "He could have one year to do as he pleased, and if at the end of that year we were not satisfied with his progress, he'd go back to school." A year from December 1960. The date is significant because Bob Zimmerman—what was left of him at age nineteen—was a dutiful son. He had most of a calendar year to satisfy Abe with his progress.

The meter was running, and Bob Dylan would not waste a minute of time the next year or the year following. He had a girlfriend in Dinkytown named Bonnie Beecher, but there was not much else holding him back.

Although his inner eye was fixed on New Jersey and New York, the pilgrimage to visit Woody Guthrie and the storming of the folk clubs in Greenwich Village, the troubadour was not quite ready. He needed to work on his music and even more on his history. Bob Dylan would not go directly from the stucco home of Abe Zimmerman in Hibbing to the hub of the folk music scene around Washington Square, because the route did not suit the legend. After stopping in the Twin Cities to bid farewell to his friends he hitchhiked to Chicago, four hundred miles through a blizzard. Arriving just before Christmas he looked up Kevin Krown, a young folksinger he had met in Colorado. Dylan seemed aimless in Chicago, staying a few days with Krown, playing in college dorms, coffeehouses, and student apartments, and sleeping on couches wherever he passed out. In a blues club he heard Muddy Waters and his harmonica player Little Walter. The folk scene in Chicago centered on the Gate of Horn, a club way out of Dylan's league, in the basement of the Rice Hotel. The joint was managed by a thirty-four-year-old graduate of Roosevelt University named Albert Grossman, whose degree was in economics. Grossman also managed Odetta, who played there when she was in town.

Skittish, drifting, Dylan headed back home in early January, toward Minneapolis. Midway, hitchhiking on Route 12, he stopped to rest in Madison, Wisconsin, the state capital and home of the state university. Walking along a street in the biting cold, his guitar strapped on his back, he stopped a college student named Paul Breines. "I'm passing through on my way to New York," said Dylan, who had been traveling *away* from New York. "Do you know where I can stay for a while?"

The student invited him to a party at his house. One party led to another in the warren of student flats and folk clubs in bohemian Madison. The music scene was not as high-powered as in Chicago but there was a firm fan base for folk and a few good players, including eighteen-year-old Danny Kalb, a precocious blues guitarist who knew Dave Van Ronk, and Marshall Brickman and banjo player Eric Weissberg, who sang together as the Tarriers. Pete Seeger passed through town, and Dylan saw him there for the first time at a university concert picketed by members of the American Legion, who considered Seeger a communist. At the heart of Seeger's repertoire in those days were songs of Woody Guthrie and Huddie Ledbetter. The performance made a strong impression on the nineteen-year-old Bob Dylan.

Half a dozen students later recalled identical impressions of Dylan during his brief stay in Madison. He would appear at a party and say, "I'm Bob Dylan, I'm sort of bumming around the country. What would you like me to sing?" Then he would perform a Woody Guthrie song, with a harsh voice and slipshod guitar technique. He would start playing and keep singing until the party broke up around him. "Between songs he would talk a lot about himself. He said he'd been bumming around, had met singers, met country people. He said he stopped with this country family somewhere. 'Simple folk,' he said. They took him in . . . said he had left home, and something about his parents . . . lower class, unpleasant people. But he gave out very little specifics. It was all very vague."

Jennifer Warren, who put him up for a while in her apartment there, remembers his single-mindedness. "All he ever did was play his songs and talk about Woody. His whole thing was he was going to New York so he could sit by Woody's bedside because Woody was dying." He also told her that he was going to "make it" in show business in New York. This notion held special significance for Warren, a native New Yorker whose family had been prominent in the Yiddish theater. *He's going to be eaten alive*, she thought. Dylan told her he had been to Texas to visit the grave of Blind Lemon Jefferson, author of the classic "See That My Grave Is Kept Clean," who froze to death in a Chicago snowstorm in 1929; he said he had learned bottleneck guitar from Big Joe Williams, the Chicago bluesman who played a nine-string guitar. He was building a character. Dylan said he was going to make it big: like Woody Guthrie and Hank Williams, like Elvis.

❊ CHAPTER 4 ❊

Spiritual Homing Pigeon

Bob Dylan and his older relation Robert Zimmerman have always had "an extreme sense of destiny," as he once told a reporter. From the time he was a boy in Hibbing, dreaming of cities whose names and stories reached him via the radio, he was drawn to New York, "the city that would come to shape my destiny." And when he learned that the legendary Woody Guthrie was languishing in a hospital somewhere near New York, the idol and the metropolis combined in his imagination like a king and a kingdom, Guthrie and New York, a single destination, an emblem of the future.

Nora Guthrie was a little girl of eleven when Bob Dylan came knocking on the door of her family's apartment in the borough of Queens that winter, early in 1961. He looked like he had been sleeping in the same clothes for days. He was asking for Woody Guthrie, and Nora told the young man that her father wasn't home. In fact he spent his weekdays at the Greystone Park Psychiatric Hospital in Morristown, New Jersey. Her parents were divorced, and her mother, Marjorie, had remarried, but she was still devoted to Woody, and cared for him in Queens on weekends and holidays. At the moment Nora's mother was not at home, either, and so Nora's babysitter closed the door on him. But Dylan knocked, again and again, and said he had no place to stay. Finally Nora's older brother, Arlo, let him come in.

Nora came to consider Bob Dylan as part of her family. "We were brought up with many people around us we called aunt, uncle, cousin, brother, even though they weren't blood, so you just want to start with that premise. When I say family, I'm not at all talking about blood family; I'm talking about my sense of community, a nest where I hatched." So Pete Seeger was family, uncles Leadbelly and Sonny Terry were family, sister Odetta was family. "These are people who were always around, or around enough when I was growing up, they were considered part of our tribe. We're very tribal. There's a lot of people in that mix, like Ramblin' Jack Elliott, who lived with us when I was little, took care of me when I was a year old.

"So people came and went and connected with my family in varying strong, profound ways. They would be strangers and then they would come in the door and either my mom or dad would say 'why don't you stay awhile' or they'd say 'I don't have anyplace to stay' and then they'd end up living with us for a year or six months or ten weeks, whatever it was. And so, as children see it, these folks become family because they're in your house sleeping on the couch and so your emotional impression is they're family so there's a lot of people I include in that." Her parents were always taking people in, especially young people. "Maybe they got kicked out of their own homes or they didn't feel like they belonged where they were born and they would come to our house. And my mother was really good—someone who really inspired people to become themselves. So. She was very nurturing."

Marjorie, Woody's second wife, lived with her three children, Arlo, Joady, and Nora, on Eighty-fifth Street in Queens. She taught dance in Brooklyn to support the family while Guthrie was in the hospital. "She was encouraging to these individual kids who would come. And she'd say, 'Keep writing like that and keep doing what you're doing and it's okay . . . and don't let anyone stop you. . . .' She was an inspiring person and so in that sense again she was *mothering*, and my dad was *fathering*, and to us kids, they were brothering and sistering, you know, that's what we were doing. That's what I mean by family. And I include Bob [Dylan] in my sense of family as one of those kids who showed up at our door, because I guess he didn't feel like he belonged where he was born or even belonged to his name and he needed a place where it was okay—for someone to say, 'It's okay, make up your own, be who you are.'"

That was the atmosphere in the Guthrie home, and the moment Dylan walked through the door he could feel it.

Nora, who grew up among musical legends, has set the bar quite high for greatness in that field; she was more impressed with Dylan the person than Dylan the singer. "He's written some great songs, I'm sure. But his relationship with my dad, I believe, was completely sincere and from the heart and completely helpful. I think he added something."

The Woody Guthrie whom Dylan met in 1960 was not very communicative. With advanced symptoms of Huntington's chorea, he had been housed in Greystone Hospital on weekdays since 1956, and by 1960 he had mostly lost control of his muscle functions. As Nora Guthrie recalled, "Although a lot of these people would come to the house to visit Dad on Sundays there was a certain point when my mom said this was embarrassing my dad. He doesn't want to see all of this dirty laundry being hung out. Then she really started limiting visitors; she didn't want all the fans coming and seeing him. Because he was *horrible* looking, absolutely horrible.

"But I remember thinking: Dylan was okay with him. He didn't judge Woody based on what he looked like. The visuals of Huntington's disease, it's hard to take in. He had no control over his arms or his legs, they would just move around in jagged and erratic movements." In those days there was no effective medication, not even a clear diagnosis for Huntington's. Guthrie was placed in a psychiatric ward because they didn't know what else to do with him. He had no control over his bowels or his bladder. "He couldn't get the food to his mouth so the food would go here, the food would go there.

He was in a ward with fifty patients. And they didn't clean up after you." Once a week Marjorie would bring him home and put him in the bathtub.

"But even so," Nora recalled, sadly, "even with clean clothes . . . he was emaciated. He looked like he'd come out of a concentration camp because he was so thin; he couldn't eat and my mother would stuff him with high-calorie food that would last a week, like a chocolate cake, three quarts of milk, five hot dogs, high-calorie stuff because when you're moving all the time you're just burning off calories. He would come home and you'd see the bones all over his body.

"My mother was very sensitive to people looking at Woody and I think somehow I sensed that she trusted Bob and that he wouldn't judge my father or be completely blown away by it in a bad way. Some people would come expecting to see someone that maybe looked more like Pete Seeger, like a healthy, uplifted folksinger who was . . . sick. But not as scary. You couldn't imagine what you were going to witness when you opened the door. And either Bob pretended that he was very composed or he really was more composed than others. And that could only be attributed to some inner connection that they had."

As Dylan got to know the young folksingers in the Village he would invite them to come with him to see Woody. He brought people like Tony Glover and John Paul Hammond, or "Jeep," who had a car and would drive them. Nora remembers hearing a story from Tony Glover that revealed a lot about Dylan's unusual understanding of Woody.

"My mom had created clothing for him that would be easy for him to put on by himself," Nora said. In the fifties Marjorie tore apart all the tops of Woody's pants and put elastic waists in them so he could just pull them on. Elastic waists were pretty much unheard-of until the seventies, but she wanted to make it easier for him to manage. "Elasticized pants, large buttons—and so he was dressed a little . . . oddly. And then he had these big work boots? They were the tan, leather work boots that you slip on. No shoelaces to tie. So she had work boots for him and elasticized khakis that were easy to wash and clean, very well thought through."

She would put his cigarette pack in the boot. "They were easy for him to get. He couldn't get cigarettes from jackets or things like that. Anyway, Woody was trying to light a cigarette, and so here's this guy whose hand is flying all over the place, and he's holding this lighter, and everyone is saying, 'Oh! I'll light it for you,' and Dylan kind of smacked them all down and said, 'No he wants to do it himself.' And they just let him. And then he *did*. And he looked at them all with satisfaction, as if to say, *You see! I can still light my cigarette!*

"It's little things like that that make you know that Bob was there for Woody as opposed to being there for himself." Bob understood that it was a matter of dignity.

In Woody Guthrie and his family Dylan indeed found his destiny. He was, in Nora's words, "a homing pigeon. He's a spiritual homing pigeon. He knew right where to fly and land and nest and sit. *I get it!*" she said. "And then he went out, and did it." Nora has always thought of this earthly contact as transpiring on a cosmic, mystical level. "It's not on a trivial level. It ticks some people off that he doesn't go to parties where you celebrate and say, 'Yes, I'm going to honor Woody, and blah, blah.' People get ticked about that. But I don't think that's their relationship." She mentions some other songwriters who claim a connection with her father, but says it's just not the same thing. "It's really different. This is a soul that flew home, looked at his spiritual family—of sorts, and I don't know how else to express it—and said *I get it*. And then he went off and became a great songwriter. Because he was affirmed for the moment, just took a second, or a day or two just to say, *Okay, I get it.*"

Nora's maternal grandmother, the well-known Yiddish poet Aliza Greenblatt, lived across the street from the Guthries in Brooklyn, and in the 1940s she collaborated with Woody on a number of Yiddish songs. In Grandma Aliza's apartment there was a picture, a watercolor of this little Jewish boy, pre-adolescent, with the *payess*, the long ear-ringlet hair worn by Hasidic Jews in the shtetl. "Just a portrait of a boy, I don't know who it is. I've always loved that little drawing." When Aliza passed away she left Nora the portrait and it now hangs on her wall. "And every time I look at it, I think, oh, that's Bob! I don't know *why*, I don't know what's goin' on in my brain. But as long as I've known him, I always look at that picture and I say that's him from another life . . . to me he's the same spirit, either literally they were the same kid in another life, or there's something about this round, innocent face that I first knew, when he first came to the house. It was other-worldly. He didn't look like he'd quite landed. . . .

"He's a very unusual being, he really is, in my mind, and so that's why I don't judge him on the same terms as everybody else. I'm not making him a god or anything, but he's very otherworldly and he's come to do what he has to do and in his somewhat seemingly detached way—which is appropriate as far as I'm concerned—and leave, and he will have left us these incredible songs, like my dad did."

Nora Guthrie admires Dylan's courage in living his life the way he wants to, "whether anyone else *understands* that or not, or looks at him and says, 'That's not you.' No one else knows that. Only he knows that. And that kind of freedom to create your life, try this, try that, express your life; who cares if anyone likes it, left or right or center? *That* kind of complete freedom is what my family was all about. I think he's very much an experimentalist, looking into himself all the time, saying what do *I* want to do now. And that's awfully brave. He's experimenting with his own soul. That's incredible, I think. I mean, he's taken *chances*, with his soul."

In the company of two college students, Bob Dylan drove from Madison, Wisconsin, to New York City in a four-door Chevrolet, a 1957 Impala, arriving in the knee-deep snow on January 24, 1961.

"I was there to find singers," he recalled, "the ones I'd heard on record—Dave Van Ronk, Peggy Seeger . . . The New Lost City Ramblers, Reverend Gary Davis and a bunch of others—most of all to find Woody Guthrie." Someone had told him to ask for a singer named Fred Neil, who emceed the daytime acts at the Café Wha?, a subterranean club on the corner of MacDougal and Minetta streets. Neil auditioned Dylan and invited him on the spot to play harmonica with him during his sets.

It was not difficult for the newcomer to find food and lodging among the good-hearted folksingers of New York. He had lots of invitations. To say that young Bob Dylan was charming hardly does justice to the strange magnetism that soon charged his stage performances. Diminutive, beardless, he looked younger than nineteen. His looks, the wide-set blue eyes, the perfect, androgynous mouth, the triangle of brow and chin, were, as Nora Guthrie recalls, "otherworldly." Ramblin' Jack Elliott, who knew James Dean before meeting Dylan, said that no one but Dylan ever had the kind of magnetism of the late James Dean. At breakfast in a noisy diner in Fell's Point, Baltimore, I asked Jack what he meant by that. In his best ironic cowboy drawl, Ramblin' Jack replied: "Well . . . they were both *cute*. You know what I mean by cute?" Jack managed to say the word with a clever blend of contempt and admiration. "They were cute and they were happy. Now in Bob's case it wasn't so much a grinning, beatific kind of happy as it was the pleasure of keeping everybody guessing about what he was up to. That kind of happy." A sort of cat-that's-swallowed-the-canary kind of happiness.

Ramblin' Jack, one of the folksingers Dylan had come to New York to see, first met the boy he would soon call his "son" (just as he himself had been called "Woody's son") in a grim ward of the massive Greystone Hospital, where Dylan had gone to pay his respects. He continued to visit Guthrie once a week for most of that year. Dave Van Ronk, who first saw Dylan onstage at the Café Wha?, recalled, in his memoirs, Dylan's stage presence as well as his unique devotion to Guthrie, whom they all revered. At twenty-five, Van Ronk, a gentle, broad-shouldered bluesman with a gruff voice and a wolfish aspect, was a pillar of the folk revival although he had not yet cut a record. He made it his business to check out every new folksinger who came to town, so very soon after Dylan's arrival Van Ronk went to see him at the Café.

When Van Ronk and his friends arrived, Fred Neil was onstage performing. And sitting next to Neil, playing the mouth harp, Van Ronk recalls "was the scruffiest-looking fugitive from a cornfield I do believe I had ever seen." Amused by Dylan's anarchic harmonica style, Van Ronk recalled, "there was a gung ho, Dada quality to it that cracked me up." He liked it in spite of himself. Then Fred Neil gave over the stage to Bob Dylan, who played a few numbers solo. Van Ronk remembered the songs were Woody Guthrie tunes and "his singing had the same take-no-prisoners delivery as his harmonica playing. We were impressed."

When the newcomer had taken his bows, Fred Neil introduced him to the veterans. Van Ronk put out his hand to receive, for the first time, Dylan's "famous dead-fish handshake," and the whole gang adjourned to the Kettle of Fish, a bar nearby between Third and Bleecker streets, for a nightcap.

Van Ronk was struck by Dylan's nervous energy. When they played chess, Dylan's knees knocked up against the table so "it was like being at a séance." He sat on the edge of his seat, jiggling. Van Ronk said he could never pin Dylan down on anything; he had so many different stories about himself he couldn't keep them straight. Van Ronk surmised that his new friend's thinking was "so convoluted that he simply does not know how to level," because Dylan was so preoccupied with the effect he was having on whoever was listening to him.

But that was only part of the picture. There was something quite real and valuable underlying the doubletalk. Van Ronk recalls in particular Dylan's genuine devotion to Woody Guthrie. "I have heard him say . . . that he came to New York to 'make it' but that's bullshit. When he came to New York, *there was no great folk music scene.*" This is a significant fact, often overlooked in the chronology. Dylan arrived in New York in January 1961, when no folksinger living there was making much money, including the Mayor of MacDougal Street, Van Ronk himself. What Dylan confided to him, and what Van Ronk always believed, is that Dylan came to New York above all to be in the paternal presence of Woody Guthrie. It was a romantic, adolescent obsession that—as sometimes transpires—turned out to be the prescient choice because it plugged him into the power source and center of a musical heritage. Back and forth in time the energy of American folklore surged through the wasted body and unconquerable spirit of Woody Guthrie.

Woody's illness had advanced to an appalling stage that made him difficult to approach. According to Van Ronk, "Bobby went out to the hospital and, by dint of some jiving and tap dancing, managed to get himself into his presence, and he sang for Woody, and he really did manage to develop a rapport with him." And Van Ronk believed this was what inspired Dylan to write his first songs. "He wrote 'Song to Woody' specifically to sing in the hospital. He was writing for Woody, to amuse him, to entertain him." Dylan wanted the master's approval but this was not his main purpose. "We all admired Woody and considered him a legend," Van Ronk concluded, "but none of us was trucking out to see him and play for him. In that regard Dylan was as stand-up a cat as I have ever known, and it was a decent and impressive beginning for anybody's career."

The rocket trajectory of that career over the next two and a half years—unlike any ascent in the annals of American entertainment—has been documented in dozens of books and films, each trying to capture or account for the utter strangeness of it.

In a community of ambitious and gifted performers Bob Dylan was distinguished at first by his apparent lack of musical skills and glamour. He could not sing as well as Fred Neil, Tom Paxton, Paul Clayton, Richie Havens, or Jack Elliott. He was not as handsome as Ramblin' Jack with his square-jawed cowboy grin and calico neck-

erchief, or the fine-featured Mark Spoelstra, the twelve-string guitar wizard. As a guitarist Dylan couldn't hold a candle to Spoelstra,
Dave Van Ronk, Danny Kalb, or Eric Von Schmidt. He dressed like
a rag picker, in baggy Goodwill castoffs; his tousled grooming and
rank hygiene were modeled upon post-Huntington's Guthrie. His
harmonica playing was interesting—peculiar, characterized by full-
chord blasts on the exhale rather than the sinuous reed-bending up-
drafts typical of blues harp players. In this he was no match for his
friends Tony Glover or young Johnny Hammond, and would never
be in the same league with his models Sonny Terry, Sonny Boy Wil-
liamson, and Little Walter Jacobs; but in a field without much competition his harmonica got his foot in the door. He had notoriously
strong lungs, a sign of health lacking in the rest of his appearance.
He was welcome to play behind Van Ronk, Fred Neil, and Ramblin'
Jack. His first professional recording gig was playing harmonica on
the title track of Harry Belafonte's album *Midnight Special.*

Most of the club managers did not want to hire him during his
first months in New York. "He was too raw," Van Ronk recalled.
Some would not even let him perform for free; he was the kind
of act you would bring on near closing time to clear a room. What
he had going for him was a unique personal intensity anyone could
perceive with four out of five senses at least: he played and sang
loud, his appearance was outlandish and pungent, he had a story too
colorful to be true, he rattled the furniture in a still room, and so on.
He came from Woody Guthrie's cell with the aura and aroma of the
legend. There was that personal intensity of the body and spirit, and
then there was this immense capacity for hard work, coupled with
an excellent memory.

He spent many hours with Van Ronk—a man widely known
for his kindness and honesty. Van Ronk was not only a great music teacher, he also knew history, literature, and politics. He called
Dylan "unteachable." The boy watched Van Ronk's hands on the
guitar strings, but when the older man would demonstrate a chord,
or a finger-picking technique, Dylan would glaze over or look the

other way, pretending not to pay attention. "He had to reinvent the wheel all the time." A lot of people tried to instruct Dylan in the art of finger-picking, but he insisted on figuring it out for himself. Finger-picking is a major milestone for a folk guitarist, an essential and tricky technique for accompanying the more lyrical songs of the repertoire. During his first year in New York, Dylan developed the rudimentary skills of a rhythm guitarist with a specialty in Guthrie-style flat-picking. It wasn't until 1962 that he learned the "double-thumbing" style of finger-picking that separates the bass accompaniment from the treble melody.

The first recorded evidence of Dylan's progress with finger-picking is a tape made on December 22, 1961, at a friend's apartment in Minneapolis. He played a haunting variation on the traditional "Nine Hundred Miles" in an open-E tuning (so as not to be distracted by fingering in the left hand while attempting unfamiliar maneuvers with his right) and he effectively alternates bass and treble notes to achieve a fair approximation of a five-string banjo tune. With the exception of "Baby Let Me Follow You Down"—which is unsystematically "picked" but not double-thumbed—there is no finger-picking on Dylan's first album. It is all hard-driving rhythmic flat-picking (strumming with a flat pick). Not until his performance in New York's Town Hall theater, in April 1963, was Dylan fully in control of the subtle double-thumbing style that would grace such songs as "Tomorrow Is a Long Time" and "Boots of Spanish Leather."

The point is that finger-picking, a basic skill of folk and blues guitar playing, did not come easily to Bob Dylan, maybe because he was left-handed. He had to work very hard to learn it while concealing the effort. When he finally succeeded, his style was wholly his own and nearly inimitable. I spoke to Milt Okun, an arranger who wrote careful musical transcriptions for Dylan's early music. Okun is proud that his transcriptions are more accurate than those of others, "who didn't quite get the specificity that Bobby did with his harmonic changes. What was most interesting in his music were the changes in harmony—on just the accompaniment. They were not typical. They weren't even what you would expect given that melody. That's what was nice about his playing: it sounded simple but there was always a little spice, something different. He is one of the most interesting guitarists. The technique wasn't brilliant but it is rich. The harmony is rich and textured."

Like the guitar playing, Dylan's singing was a supreme act of will. At a primitive level the young man's voice was a cry for attention similar to his shouting and screaming rock and roll on the high school stage; on an artistic level it was a sound of alarm: *I have something important to say and you need to pay attention.* There is little more you can say about that voice once you have said that he made the most of what God had given him, and it could have sounded only the way it did. Dylan's sound was all over the place at first, bouncing off walls and buildings. The voice came from somewhere far back in time and stayed with you whether you liked it or not, a holy terror and completely his own creation. He would never have to worry about anyone claiming credit for his style of singing.

Van Ronk and his wife Terri Thal's apartment on Waverly Place near Washington Square was one of several places Dylan lived during his first year in New York. He also stayed with various friends of the Guthries: Bob and Sidsel Gleason in New Jersey, Eve and "Mac" McKenzie, who lived on East Twenty-eighth. He had little money and many people who wanted to take care of him. Turn a nineteen-year-old folksinger loose in New York City in 1961 and he's going to find plenty of places to sleep. Between stays with families, various young women took him in.

He did not stay long enough anywhere to wear out his welcome. For a while, when he was studying Ramblin' Jack Elliott's every guitar lick, voice inflection, and stage mannerism, he moved into a third-floor room down the hall from Jack's at the Hotel Earle on MacDougal and Waverly. In his memoir, *Chronicles,* Dylan writes of staying with someone he calls Ray Gooch and his girlfriend Chloe Kiel on the top floor of a rangy building on Vestry Street below

Canal and near the Hudson River. Dylan says Ray was a machinist and Chloe a hat-check girl at the Egyptian Gardens nightclub. "I probably stayed at Vestry Street off and on longer than anywhere." He probably did not because Gooch and Kiel appear to have existed only in the pages of Dylan's memoir, a beautiful confection of a book that never allows truth to get in the way of a good story, or history to interfere with the revelation of the most significant truths.

He devotes eighty pages, an entire section of *Chronicles*, to the details of that fantastic apartment on Vestry Street and his reflections there, calling it "The Lost Land." Using the apartment as a stage set, in that luminous theater he delivers the most revealing monologues about his twenty-year-old character and his education, his coming of age in old New York.

Music was only a part of the process, the most important part of the picture puzzle; without the other pieces the picture dissolves. Wandering through the incredible, preposterous labyrinth of Gooch's library, like Alistair Cooke or Russell Baker, Dylan provides a breezy commentary upon the historical and literary landmarks of his youth. Here is everything a biographer would want to know about a subject's intellectual predilections and foundations. He begins and ends not with poetry but with history. "I was born in the spring of 1941. The Second World War was already raging in Europe, and America would soon be in it."

Anyone born then could feel the end of an old world and the start of a new one. The great leaders of the time, Roosevelt, Churchill, Stalin, Hitler, these were "towering figures that the world would never see the likes of again," resolute, autonomous—men who acted without regard to riches, love, or approval, "all presiding over the destiny of mankind and reducing the world to rubble."

He describes one of the defining terrors of our childhood—the air raid drills of the 1950s, when we were trained to scurry under our school desks and hide our heads when the sirens blew. The Russians (whom our parents had fought alongside only a few years earlier) might be dropping atom bombs on us at any time and we must be prepared. "Living under a cloud of fear like this," he recalls, "robs a child of his spirit. It's one thing to be afraid when someone's holding a shotgun on you, but it's another thing to be afraid of something that's just not quite real." Real or not, a lot of people took the threat seriously, and their children felt it. Even though our history teachers would tell us the communists could not destroy America with bombs alone (they would have to destroy the Constitution itself), when the sirens screamed you ducked under your desk anyway, and prayed for mercy.

"The threat of annihilation was a scary thing. We didn't know what we did to anybody to make them so mad." Dylan's tone here is poignant, freezing childhood wonderment and innocent terror in a single black-and-white frame. It is also a time bomb of generational pathos calculated to produce a sublimation defense reaction. We would presently do so many things to make people mad that we would never have to wonder about that part of it again.

Dylan the tour guide blithely moves on, saying it's all over now, it's New York City, 1961, communists or no communists. He has read somewhere that the Age of Enlightenment ended with World War II, but this meant little to him because he was still in it. With a nod to the bookshelves he mentions Voltaire, Rousseau, Locke, Montesquieu, the visionaries of the Enlightenment. He regards them as old friends, optimists who believe with more and less irony in humankind's potential for improvement. He turns the radio on, hoping for food for thought, but all he hears is pabulum, "and not the real Jekyll and Hyde themes of the times." Kerouac, Ginsberg, and Corso were writing about a new consciousness, the angels and demons of the Cold War era, but their street ideology had not made it onto 45-rpm records or the radio.

From what little he knew of history he discerned a fatal pattern, he recalls, echoing the Beat writers' prophet Oswald Spengler. Cultures are born and develop, grow to maturity, then decay and die. Dylan had no idea what stage America was in, and there was nobody yet who could tell him.

The branch of history that most interested the young man was military history, strategy, and the philosophy of war. He read Tacitus and Machiavelli's *The Prince*. He mentions *Fox's Book of Martyrs* and the nineteenth-century novelists Balzac, Hugo, Dickens; Ovid's *Metamorphosis* and Freud's *Beyond the Pleasure Principle*, the old and new proponents of shape-shifting. He thumbs through Freud, puts the volume back on the shelf, and never looks at it again. He remembers the power of William Faulkner's novels and the curious works of Albertus Magnus, the alchemist and bishop who made a peace between science and religion. But in his opinion Albertus is "lightweight compared to Thucydides."

Thucydides is his guiding light. None of the great writers, poets, or philosophers can hold a candle to Thucydides (circa 460–400 B.C.), the Athenian historian. He had failed as a general but in exile wrote his groundbreaking history of the Peloponnesian War. He taught us to understand events—wars, plagues, the building of cities—in terms of cause and effect and the expression of human nature, motives in individuals and groups. Thucydides' view of the world would influence "historicist" and process philosophers from Machiavelli and Hegel to Nietzsche and Marx. The storytelling alone gave him goose bumps. Beyond this he observes that "it talks about how human nature is always the enemy of anything superior." H. L. Mencken had said the same thing, echoing Nietzsche, that jealousy of the superior man is a constant corrosive element in society.

"Thucydides writes about how words in his time have changed from their ordinary meaning, how actions and opinions can be altered in the blink of an eye." The way Dylan saw it, this was just as true in 1961 as in 400 B.C.

Dylan flatters books by admitting he has read them: a biography of Robert E. Lee, who had grown up without a father and made something of himself anyway; biographies of Thaddeus Stevens, the Radical Republican, and Teddy Roosevelt, who backed down J. P. Morgan, "a deity figure who owned most of the United States at the time. Roosevelt backed him down and threatened to throw him in jail." These were characters that could have stepped out of folk songs. Dylan read *The White Goddess* by Robert Graves, although "invoking the poetic muse was something I didn't know about yet. Didn't know enough to start trouble with it anyway." He read Honoré de Balzac, from whom he learned that sheer materialism can lead to sheer madness, as well as one of the most precious secrets of life: *Hoard your energy.*

Whether or not Dylan actually read all of these books during his first years in New York is not as important as his discussion of them. Learning is not linear and sometimes we understand an idea long before we read about it. At some point in his life he probably did read the texts as carefully as he claims, and he is offering, in the Vestry Street library, a timeless catalog of influences and interests. He was searching for the education he had skipped over. As a child he had told his father that he hated the study of history, and he refused to get a good grade in the subject. Now, along with his Byron and Shelley, Longfellow and Poe, he read his history. It was a natural progression from Thucydides to biographies of Alexander the Great, Simón Bolívar, and Frederick the Great, King of Prussia, who was also a fair composer. And right there in Prussia, the military nerve center of the Enlightenment, Dylan discovered Frederick's countryman Carl von Clausewitz (1780–1831), Thucydides' intellectual heir.

"They called Clausewitz the premier philosopher of war . . . he talks a lot about how to maneuver into position where the other side can see there's no fighting chance. . . ." Like Thucydides, Clausewitz considers the "psychological and accidental factors on the battlefield—the weather, air currents" and how these affect the outcome.

Dylan admits to a long-standing fascination with the art of war. Like Poe, like Robert E. Lee, Dylan once wanted to go to West Point, dreaming of becoming a general with his own army. What was the password that would open the door for him? His father explained to Bob that a Jew without connections, without a "De" or a "Von" before his surname, such as Clausewitz boasted, had little hope of attending West Point. The want of connections and credentials upset him, made him feel disenfranchised.

The student of Clausewitz shifts focus from his resentment over West Point to the battlefield of the music business. He recalls how impossible it had been to keep a band together without family connections to get gigs where there was real money. Dylan never forgot this frustration. "It went to the very root of things, gave unfair advantage to some and left others squeezed out. How could somebody ever reach the world this way?" Before he was twenty-one Bob Dylan had experienced the dark side of realpolitik, the principle illuminated in Thucydides, Machiavelli, and Clausewitz. Dylan would perform solo until the day he could afford to pay his bandmates enough money to keep them.

Having offered his own teenage band experience as illustration, he returns to the library on Vestry Street, paging through the Prussian prophet of war Clausewitz. "When he claims that politics has taken the place of morality and politics is brute force, he's not playing. . . . Don't give me that dance that God is with us. . . . There isn't any moral order. . . . It's not there to transgress. It's either high ground or low ground." Bob Dylan will not turn to Karl Marx to defend his right to a fair share in the capitalist pie; he will not seek refuge in the apologetic dreamworld of Sigmund Freud or the fatalism of astrologers. In espousing Clausewitz and realpolitik, Dylan is forthright about his deepest beliefs, his old-fashioned Yankee pragmatism. Life in the early 1960s looked to him like a battlefield. If anyone was to survive in the melee, succeed or excel, it would be the man who was the smartest general, the bravest soldier. "If you think you're a dreamer, you can read this stuff and realize you're not even capable of dreaming. Dreaming is dangerous."

Dylan writes that the other regular tenant of the Vestry Street apartment is his friend the gaunt folksinger Paul Clayton. Long-necked, with a Lincolnesque beard, Clayton was a delicate flower—a dreamer and an idealist if ever there was one. Ten years older than Dylan, Clayton had already made fifteen record albums before the two men met in New York. Morbidly sensitive, the aristocratic-looking singer suffered from bouts of depression. He was a first-class folklorist, a rare purist who had made a name for himself and a modest living performing folk music. The month Dylan arrived in New York, Clayton even had a hit record, "Gotta Travel On," recorded by country singer Billy Grammer on the Monument label. "Paul didn't get much benefit from it," said Bob Yellin, a friend who played banjo with Clayton. "Paul was not a businessman. . . ." The germ of "Gotta Travel On" came from W. C. Handy's "Harlem Blues" and Clayton had paranoid fantasies that eighty-four-year-old Handy, on his deathbed, would sue him for plagiarism.

Clayton idolized Dylan (some say he was in love with him) and taught him dozens of traditional songs. He taught Dylan a song of his, "Who's Gonna Buy You Ribbons When I'm Gone," based on an old tune titled "Call Me Old Black Dog"; Dylan promptly re-wrote the song and called it "Don't Think Twice, It's All Right." It soon made him a million dollars. The songwriters' publishers sued each other—which in no way dampened the friendship. Dylan retained the rights to his composition, and Clayton swooned deeper and deeper into the tides of substance abuse and depression. A few years later he was found dead by his own hand, in the bathtub of his apartment, fully dressed. He had submerged himself in the bath-water and held a live electrical cord to his chest.

❋ CHAPTER 5 ❋

Finding His Voice

The upshot of Dylan's broad course of study by day and his nightly submersion in the rivers and caves of folk music was the desire to write his own songs. He had heard Mike Seeger play the old music with such perfect innate conviction it was a revelation. He talks a lot about Mike in his memoirs.

Mike, in his full-cut white shirts with their silver sleeve bands, kept a straight face that Dylan said "radiated telepathy." He had mastered all the old-time styles, Delta blues, dance reels, gospel, ragtime, a cappella ballads, valley hollers. Dylan realized that no matter how hard he tried he would never catch up. The intonations and insights he was struggling so hard to learn were bred in Seeger's bones. Dylan realized that some things cannot be taught, and he admitted he "might have to change my inner thought patterns."

Up until then, he confessed, he "didn't have too much of a concrete identity." Now he had a feeling of destiny and his consciousness had begun to change and grow. One thing was clear to him: if he was to write good folk songs he would need a new guide or pattern, a working philosophy that would suit him over the long haul. Listening to Paul Clayton and Ray Gooch, both southerners, converse until the wee hours of the morning, discussing "dogs, and fishing and forest fires—love and monarchies, and the Civil War," he recalled Ray saying that New York had won the war, and "the wrong side had lost." This phrase haunted and troubled him.

He was on the verge of an epiphany. Curious about this War Between the States, he took the conversation to his guru, Dave Van Ronk. Dylan asked Van Ronk if the conflict over states' rights had caused the war. Good-naturedly the older man listened and reflected, declaring that the Civil War was fought to free the slaves, and make no mistake about it. Then Van Ronk waxed philosophical: "Look, my man, even if those elite Southern barons would have freed their captives, it wouldn't have done them any good. We still would have gone down there and annihilated them, invaded them for their land. It's called imperialism." The comment brought Karl Marx to mind, and the conflict between an agrarian and an industrial economy; this raised the ghost of Thucydides.

It was beginning to dawn on Bob Dylan that the American language itself might be responsible for—or at least involved in—the hopes, fears, and dreams that brought about the catastrophe of the War Between the States. Where did this lead him? To the marble halls of the New York Public Library, an upstairs reading room where he started poring over newspapers from the 1850s through the 1860s. He says that he wasn't as interested in the conflicts as he was fascinated by the language of the times. Of course he couldn't absorb one without the other. He scrolled microfilm through the glowing projector until his back ached and his eyes blurred over.

What he found in the newspapers was not a different world but the same America, somehow more focused and insistent. Slavery was an urgent matter, but so were child labor, crime, the temperance movement, and religious revivals. In the South, plantation owners are accused of selling their own children. There are riots in the northern cities and bank failures. The southern planters "run their plantations like city-states." With their monopoly on the stores, the sawmills, the livestock as well as the farms, the southerners reminded Dylan of the Roman plutocracy. He had the creepy feeling that the very newspapers might go up in flames, in a fury of apocalyptic judgment.

He marvels over the fact that people united by geography and ideals could become enemies—that there is hardly any remnant of the neoclassic virtues of chivalry, honesty, and honor. Appalled by the fate of the women and children, "unprotected and left to fend for themselves as victims of the elements," he feels "the suffering is endless, and the punishment is going to be forever." He compares the America of the Civil War period to Christ, crucified and resurrected. The truth of that event "would be the all-encompassing template behind everything that I would write."

Within a year of making these discoveries Bob Dylan would become one of the finest epic poets of the 1960s. Epic: a poem containing history. Some of the songs had a measurable impact on events, in a way that art rarely does.

Van Ronk's wife, Terri Thal, worked as a booking agent for Dave and a few friends. After Dylan had been playing basket houses (clubs where they pass a basket for tips) and hootenannies for three months, the Van Ronks convinced the manager of Gerde's Folk City, Mike Porco, to offer the promising folksinger a regular spot on the bill. Porco, a tough, kindly Italian American, took a liking to Dylan. He helped him get his union card, advanced him money for his dues; because Dylan was underage and claimed to be an orphan, Porco signed the papers as the musician's legal guardian.

In April 1961 Dylan opened for the tremendous bluesman John Lee Hooker on the evening program at Gerde's, playing his "Song to Woody" and Guthrie songs such as "Pastures of Plenty" and "Talkin' Columbia." He played traditional tunes like "Gypsy Davy" (a Paul Clayton favorite) and "House of the Rising Sun," which he had learned from Dave Van Ronk. Watching the deep-grooving Hooker and sharing the stage with him was a big break and a confidence builder for the young singer.

In the same month he played his first paid concert, for the New York University folk society; and at a well-attended "hoot night" at Gerde's he took his turn onstage with Doc Watson, Dave Van Ronk, Gil Turner (editor of *Broadside*), Mark Spoelstra, and the dazzling Joan Baez. He had never met Baez before, but revered her as Queen of the Folksingers. In his memoirs he recalls that she sang with a voice that was divinely inspired; not only that, she was a superb guitarist, in a class by herself, "far off and unattainable." After the show, at 2 A.M., he followed Joan and her younger sister Mimi into the street so he could play them his "Song to Woody." Joan Baez was not yet captivated, but the meeting was still memorable to her. She later described how funny he looked onstage, "bouncing from foot to foot as he played, he seemed dwarfed by the guitar. . . . His cheeks were still softened with an undignified amount of baby fat. . . . He was absurd, new, and grubby beyond words. . . ." She saw immediately that he was exceptional and had the power to move an audience, "but he had only just begun to touch me."

Dylan was making the right connections. One of his companions and collaborators from the early days in New York was the handsome, dark-eyed singer and guitarist Harry Peter "Happy" Traum, who remained, providentially, a longtime friend. Recalling Dylan's entrance on the scene, Traum has never gotten over the uniqueness of that social phenomenon. It was like a magic trick.

"I've never seen anything like it in my life. From the day he arrived in the city it was like nobody could talk about anything else. It was Bobby this and Bobby that, where was Bobby, what was he going to do next. Have you seen Bobby? No matter what he did or what he didn't do, people were just obsessed with the guy. It wasn't just about the music, although that got more interesting as time went on. It was this kid, and people were always talking about what he did, good, bad, funny, outrageous. No conversation could go on for more than five minutes without his name coming up."

This was also true—or soon would be—in places as far-flung

as Washington, D.C., where Dylan played at the Showboat Lounge with Paul Clayton in September; and in Cambridge, Massachusetts, where he met Eric Von Schmidt. He also played in Boston, where he met the novelist/musician Richard Fariña and his wife, Carolyn Hester, the quickly rising folk star. The ripples of notoriety spread from the points of impact in concentric circles to the far shores of the folk music world.

By the late spring his style of performing had developed an eccentric charm that Terri Thal described as Chaplinesque. "He had that funny pathetic little boy style about him." She recalled one night when he was onstage for about forty-five minutes, and he kept falling off the stage, pretending to be drunk. At first everybody believed he was drunk. "It took us a long time to figure out that when he fell off the stage it was timed, a planned thing, he was falling off within the context of the song, and it was hilarious." He would pretend he couldn't get his guitar in tune, and talk to it, pleading and cursing under his breath, peering now and then out of the corners of his eyes at the audience. He neglected to cut the ends of his strings so he could point to them sprouting from the tuning engines and quip, "This guitar needs a haircut."

His baggy pockets were filled with harmonicas. He would pull out one after another, examining one nearsightedly before tossing it onto the table muttering "Where is that F Harmonica" or E flat, cursing the elusive instrument, bringing out another and another, all wrong.

Van Ronk agreed that Dylan—while no great wit in casual conversation—was one of the funniest people he had ever watched onstage. "He never stood still, and he had all these nervous mannerisms and gestures." If this was stage fright, he used it to advantage. "There would be a one-liner, a mutter, a mumble, another one-liner, a slam at the guitar." Van Ronk considered Dylan's sense of timing "uncanny." He recalled one night when Dylan was playing a harmonica chorus that consisted of a single note. As he went on strumming the chord progression, now and then he would blow the note.

Soon "you were completely caught up in trying to figure out where the next note was coming. And you were always wrong. By the end of the chorus, he had all of us doubled over laughing, with one note on the harmonica."

When Dylan sang he had another kind of unique timing, and the precise word for it is *phrasing*. This has everything to do with where the words fall in relation to the melody and very little to do with the beauty or power of the voice. Phrasing is the essence of musical storytelling and Dylan had an incomparable gift for it.

In May he returned briefly to Minnesota for his twentieth birthday. Presumably he visited his parents and brother on the occasion. Eager to show off his new skills he played twenty-five songs in the apartment of his old girlfriend, Bonnie Beecher, in Minneapolis. Tony Glover recorded the session for posterity. Paul Nelson and Jon Pankake, the editors of a folk music quarterly, heard the informal session, and everyone was impressed with Dylan's progress. "It contained all the elements of the new perfected performing style that has made him the most original performer in folk music," Nelson observed.

If he had hoped that his New York success would rekindle his romance with Bonnie Beecher, he was disappointed. In the four months he had been away she had moved on. With a heavy heart he went back to New York in the spring more determined than ever to hold up his end of the bargain he had made with his parents in December. Now he had seven months left to satisfy them with his headway in the entertainment world—or return to school. "I did everything fast," he recalled. "Thought fast, ate fast, talked fast and walked fast. I even sang my songs fast."

A number of fortunate elements—artistic, intellectual, and social—had fallen into place for Bob Dylan by the summer of 1961. He was a vigorous, intriguing performer; he had discovered his "new template" in newspapers of the 1860s; and he had made valuable contacts. A lot of people were eager to help him. There was only one piece of the puzzle that remained to complete the picture.

He had not yet fallen in love.

As a boy growing up in Hibbing and Minneapolis he had had plenty of girlfriends. There had been lots of girls who loved him, for a while at least, and he had known crushes, flirtations, and infatuations, too many to name here. The most recent was Bonnie Jean Beecher, a pretty long-haired blond who studied acting at the University of Minnesota. She had disappointed him. Dylan had not yet known the transformative experience of falling in love with a soul mate—the mingling of eros and psyche that inspired the Song of Solomon, Dante and Beatrice, and Romeo and Juliet. There is delicate work that no poet can do without that inspiration that renders everything else in life so precious.

He was probably looking for it in the summer of 1961 when he met seventeen-year-old Suze Rotolo of Queens. The occasion was an all-day hootenanny at Manhattan's Riverside Church, broadcast live on July 29 on WRVR-FM radio. Dylan shared the stage with Van Ronk, Reverend Gary Davis, Danny Kalb, Tom Paxton, Victoria Spivey, the Greenbriar Boys, Cynthia Gooding, and Ramblin' Jack Elliott. Ironically, Dylan closed the program with Jack Elliott in a rollicking spoof of the teenage love songs popular at the time.

> *You said you'd ask me*
> *To the senior prom*
> *Found out I had acne*
> *Now you won't ask me*
> *To the senior prom*
> *Doo-wah, doo-wah & etc. . . .*

Ironic, given the fact that he was about to meet the love of his life, who was prom-age, and Dylan wasn't much older himself.

Backstage he was chatting with dark-haired Carla Rotolo, an assistant to the folklorist Alan Lomax, and Carla introduced Dylan to her younger sister Suze (pronounced Susie). Fortunately we now have Suze Rotolo's account of that meeting, and the whole love story beautifully told (in *A Freewheelin' Time*, 2008), to complement Dylan's memories of Suze in *Chronicles* (2004). Between the two of them they paint a vivid and moving picture of this important chapter in their lives.

Dylan remembers that from the minute he saw her he couldn't look away from her. "She was the most erotic thing I had ever seen." Although she was Italian American she had golden-brown hair and fair skin. Just looking at her made him dizzy.

For her part, Rotolo recalls that no matter where she turned, Dylan was there nearby. She thought him peculiar, old-fashioned looking but appealing in a diamond-in-the-rough way. His clothing was rumpled, and he was wearing his black corduroy hat. He reminded her of Harpo Marx, friendly and "impish" but remarkably intense. They started flirting early in the day, she recalls, and "didn't stop until the day was done. He was funny, engaging, intense, and he was persistent." Those were the words that defined him throughout the years she knew him. Only the order of the words would change from time to time.

Suze Rotolo described herself as a red-diaper baby—the child of active members of the American Communist Party. Her father was a studio painter and factory worker who became a union organizer; her mother wrote for *L'Unità*, a communist newspaper. They were so poor that at times the children had to go and live with relatives near Boston. The girls were raised without religion, in a home full of good books, records, and the radio—no television. "Outsider status was inevitable," she recalled.

On Sundays she and her sister would take the train to Washington Square Park to listen to the folksingers play and the poets recite their works around the fountain and in the shadow of the stone arch. Going to folk concerts at Town Hall and Carnegie Hall they saw Pete Seeger, the Clancy Brothers, and John Jacob Niles. The sisters attended political study classes at the Ethical Culture Society on West Sixty-fourth Street and the summer Camp Kinderland, a socialist Jewish retreat upstate.

She was attending the public high school in Queens in 1958 when her father died suddenly. Her mother, overwhelmed with grief, unable to cope any other way, drank heavily. When Suze graduated in 1960, at the age of sixteen, her prospects were not bright. Although she was an avid reader she had not excelled in the classroom, and in those days it was not assumed that a woman would go on to college as a matter of course. She had enjoyed her drama classes, escaping into her stage roles, becoming someone else; she also liked designing scenery. She had a gift for drawing.

In the fall of 1960 most of Suze's friends went off to college; she took a job in a convenience store. "I thought about what a loser I was and how scary things were at home," she later wrote. Her older sister left home, went to live in Greenwich Village. Her mother worked part-time for an ear doctor, but her drinking was still out of control, so Suze recalls that she was virtually "without parental guidance" after her father's death. This state of affairs was hardly liberating; she was more fearful and tentative than most young women because she had no one to rely on, nobody to protect her.

She found a job at the Book-of-the-Month Club downtown on Hudson Street. Soon she was living with an aunt and cousin uptown during the week, and staying with her sister Carla or friends in the Village on weekends. A plan to move to Italy with her mother in April 1961 fell through after a car crash seriously injured both of them. Her mother's kneecap was crushed, and Suze sustained a severe whiplash and lacerations to her right eyelid and brow that required thirty stitches; this injury imperiled the nerves and muscles that open and close the eye.

Recovering from the auto accident, Suze stayed with Carla for a while on Perry Street before accepting an offer to house-sit for a couple who were going abroad. Their apartment was on Waverly Place—east of Washington Square—in the heart of Greenwich Village. Then for months she worked for the puppet maker Peter

Schumann, soon to be renowned for his Bread and Puppet Theater. When their work creating the puppets was over, she got a job in the New York City office of the Congress of Racial Equality (CORE) in downtown Manhattan, across from City Hall. CORE was vibrant in the spring of 1961, as its Freedom Riders challenged racism in Alabama, staging protests at segregated restaurants and public facilities. When a busload of Freedom Riders was beaten with lead pipes at a bus station lunch counter, "the civil rights movement had gone to another level," Rotolo recalled. The New York office of CORE was the nerve center of the movement's media presence, and Suze Rotolo was one of a small staff organizing fund-raising events and keeping track of donations.

In the summertime while she was working for CORE, on a Saturday morning in July, Suze Rotolo drove uptown with her sister Carla and Pete Karman, a reporter for the *New York Mirror* who was covering the twelve-hour hootenanny at Riverside Church.

When the concert was over, the singer Annie Bird invited a few of the folksingers to her apartment for a party. "By then," Rotolo recalled, "Bob and I were pretty much glued to each other. When we needed a lift, it was for us as a couple, plus his guitar. Our private little world was taking shape." The party went on all night as the musicians—the young guitarist Bruce Langhorne, the rawboned bluegrass tenor John Herald, and Dylan—were playing, singing, cutting up. At four in the morning Pete Karman drove them home, dropping Dylan at Eve and Mac McKenzie's loft on East Twenty-eighth Street, where he slept on the couch. (This may be the book-lined apartment that the Ray Gooch figment is based upon.)

After that night, Dylan recalls, he couldn't get Suze out of his mind. "I felt like I was in love for the first time in my life." He could sense her physical presence even when he was miles away from her. Since she felt the same, it didn't take long for them to meet up again, at Gerde's or other watering holes in the Village. It really was a village in those days, a place where you could hardly avoid someone you knew. When she wasn't working they would get together for long walks and conversation. She took him to see Picasso's *Guernica* at the Museum of Modern Art. Sitting in the sculpture garden they talked, of art, philosophy, and poetry, as she recalls, "and the horrors and injustices of the world—very earnest we were." But they also made each other laugh. Dylan remembers that they became almost inseparable; apart from his work, spending time with Suze seemed to be his life's purpose. "Maybe we were spiritual soul mates."

This is a heartfelt conjecture, written forty years after the fact. He has confessed that during his first months in New York he was in need of quite a few things—including a concrete identity. And writing of that same period, Rotolo says of herself, "I felt fragmented; I had no mirror to see myself in a context." He was just twenty years of age and she was four months shy of eighteen. They may have been wise beyond their years but they were still adolescents—more children than adults—"two kids bouncing around together, two innocent children falling in love," said one anonymous observer. Seeing them in a crowd yet in their own little world, people teasingly called them Hansel and Gretel. Bob Dylan had always stood apart, figuratively, from the crowd. Now, evidently, a girl had joined him in that unique isolation.

The thing that attracted Bob Dylan to the girl at first was her luminous beauty, that rare splendor that emanates from a deeper and more sustainable light source. Susan Elizabeth Rotolo, born under the sign of Scorpio, was a multifaceted Muse. Not to give the unsuspecting, doe-eyed youngster too much credit, Suze probably had seven out of nine of the legendary goddesses on her side (Cleo, Erato, Calliope, et al.) when she materialized in Dylan's life in the summer of 1961. Within six months he had written "The Death of Emmett Till" about the joy-ride murder of a black teenager by whites in Mississippi, and "Let Me Die in My Footsteps," a protest against fallout shelters. Within nine months he had composed "Blowin' in the Wind."

And then the floodgates opened.

What makes a mortal woman a Muse, apart from a man's excitement in her presence? A skeptic might judge every case on its own merits: one man's muse is another man's washerwoman. Nonetheless, quite uncommon sense seems to be at work in the lives of Petrarch, Dante, Yeats, and Bob Dylan when we consider the characters of Laura, Beatrice, Maud Gonne, and Suze Rotolo. The pattern has survived the Victorian era but now seems almost quaint. In the case of Rotolo, as with the other women, there was an innate wisdom combined with an extraordinary receptivity. Dylan spoke and she listened, and the conversation flowed through her and returned to him purified, refined. He found himself saying things to her that he had never said to anyone else, thoughts and ideas he did not even know he had. He called her the "true fortuneteller of my soul." She believed in him so passionately she could see his future. Of course she in turn would speak and he would listen, but it was Suze who was doing the inspiring, Bob who would write the poems.

The late journalist Robert Shelton (1926–95), who spent a lot of time with Suze Rotolo and Bob Dylan, admitted that he had a hard time—at least at first—getting a sense of her spirit. "She seemed overshadowed by Dylan when she was with him. Although I sensed her keen artistic perception, she generally did not assert herself in those early years." Still, Shelton well understood that "she had a power over Bob." To her vexation, Shelton pressured her to put Dylan's needs before her own, looking out for the poet, unaware at the time that Rotolo was, in his words, "grasping for her own identity in the whirlpool of his needs." For a long time she would put his needs first, inspiring him; when at last she turned the tables she would still inspire him, but in a very different way.

By coincidence or divine intervention, after Dylan met Suze Rotolo things began to happen in his career rapidly and with sensational consequences—like a fairy tale, or a yarn from the *Arabian Nights*. The boy from the north country told tall tales about his past but nothing was so strange as the truth about the present, New York in 1961.

Carolyn Hester was a dark-haired, delicate-featured singer-guitarist from Texas. Impressed by Dylan's harmonica playing, Hester invited him to work with her on the album she was making for Columbia Records. The producer was the incomparable John Hammond, a talent scout with preternatural instincts, the man who had discovered—or first recorded—guitarist Charlie Christian, Billie Holiday, Count Basie, pianist Meade Lux Lewis, and sax player Lester Young. Hammond had longed to record Robert Johnson in the 1930s, but the hapless genius had been murdered before he could take the call. A scion of the Vanderbilt family, Hammond eventually became a vice president of the NAACP.

On September 14, Hester invited Dylan to her apartment on West Tenth Street to rehearse, along with guitarist Bruce Langhorne and bassist Bill Lee. The young harmonica player served up a virtuoso accompaniment to "Come Back Baby" that nearly stole the show from Hester, at one point holding a note with one breath for eight measures, an entire stanza. Houdini himself would have been impressed. Watching that afternoon was John Hammond, who was so fascinated by the blues harp player that he asked Dylan if he would like to come to the studio and cut some demos.

Eleven days later Dylan began a two-week residency at Gerde's Folk City, opening for the Greenbriar Boys (John Herald on guitar, banjoist Bob Yellin, mandolin player Ralph Rinzler), a bluegrass group. That night, a Monday, Robert Shelton of the *New York Times* was in the audience. His rave review of Bob Dylan (quoted in the first pages of this book) appeared in the newspaper on a Friday. It was the shot heard round the world—the folk music world at least—and no one in that competitive and incestuous community would ever quite get over it. Dylan carried the column folded up in the hip pocket of his jeans, to show people, as if it hadn't already been plastered on the figurative walls of the city and wasn't already blowing through the alleys and wrapping fish from Harlem to Battery Park.

The review was the answer to a prayer. He carried it along with his harmonicas on the subway to Columbia's Studio A, in midtown. There he played behind Carolyn Hester on "Come Back Baby," "Swing and Turn Jubilee," and the exuberant "I'll Fly Away." The tall, aristocratic-looking man in the glass control booth, with the close-cropped hair and the bow tie, had read the newspaper. John Hammond agreed with the reviewer—the kid was bursting with talent. When the session was over he asked Dylan to step into the booth. Hammond said he would like him to record for Columbia, and Dylan said he would like that, too. His heart leapt. Even more than the review in the *Times*, "it seemed too good to be true." Every singer in New York wanted a record contract: Tom Paxton, Mark Spoelstra—even Jack Elliott had none at the moment. For the scruffy Dylan to get a contract with a major label, *the* major label, was not only the best thing that could happen to his career, the fact was inconceivable. At least it was inconceivable to everybody but the prescient Hammond, who was in a position to make dreams come true, and Suze Rotolo, who had a lover's clairvoyance about Dylan's future. Perhaps the crucial turn of luck had been the alchemy between the lovers that made him feel he could do anything.

Dylan began to pay more attention to his appearance. For months Van Ronk had been teasing him about the way he looked, his baby fat, his motley oversize clothing. Van Ronk said that a folksinger had to maintain an image, a persona for the public that was both "authentic" and hip. Bob began to lose weight. Carla Rotolo said: "He was very fussy about his clothes. . . . He would always ask if he looked right, jiggling with his dungarees. 'Are they tight enough? Is the shirt OK?'" Suze recalls: "Much time was spent in front of the mirror trying on one wrinkled article of clothing after another, until it all came together to look as if Bob had just gotten up and thrown something on." Folksingers were beginning to have influence, and they wanted to make the most of it; this meant looking, as well as sounding, "authentic."

On October 26, 1961, Dylan signed the Columbia contract John Hammond set before him. Soon after that he began looking for an apartment, a place he could live with Suze. She was not yet eighteen (the legal age for cohabitation), so that would have to wait a few weeks. Meanwhile, he would be busy preparing for his first major recital, in a venue as unlikely as Columbia's Studio A: a space uptown on Fifty-seventh Street and Seventh Avenue—Carnegie Hall.

One of Dylan's staunchest supporters was Israel Goodman Young, founder of the Folklore Center on MacDougal Street, a glorified music store with a cozy back room where musicians and kibitzers sat around a potbellied stove trading stories and songs. Antique musical instruments, fiddles and mandolins, zithers and panpipes, and nineteenth-century prints hung on the walls.

Izzy, in his early thirties, was a kindly, well-read New Yorker with a thick Brooklyn accent and a terrific sense of humor. He loved the folk music revival and its potential to advance his liberal political agenda, yet he took nothing too seriously, including the rivalry and posing of the musicians who wandered through the aisles of his shop. Everybody was welcome, and all were subject to Izzy's good-natured advice and teasing. After the Shelton review appeared in the *Times*, Young heard the shrewd agent Albert Grossman declare that he "thought Dylan could make it." Grossman had been quietly working on Dylan's behalf, greasing the wheels, spreading money around where it might help, in view of getting Dylan's name on a management contract. When it came to Dylan's potential, Izzy agreed with Grossman, who talked him into promoting a concert at Carnegie Chapter Hall, a performance space on the fifth floor of the Carnegie Hall building.

So Izzy shelled out $75 to rent the two-hundred-seat hall and another $35 for printed programs, with the understanding that Grossman would help deliver an audience at $2 per ticket. "He never even showed up himself," Izzy recalled. "He didn't come to the concert. Suze came, and Bob's friends, but no Grossman."

The concert on November 4, 1961, was a failure. About fifty

people showed up, and Dylan's playing was lackluster, imitative of Jack Elliott, curiously uninspired, as if he were disheartened by the meager attendance. Nonetheless, he had played Carnegie Hall—a level of it—two weeks before his recording session for Columbia, and whatever luster the public recital may have lacked he more than made up for in his explosive recording debut.

Suze went with him to the studio and sat nearby as he played. This was an auspicious occasion, her birthday, November 20, as he made his first album. She later recalled, "I watched Bob as he sang and saw his focus, his loyalty to the work at hand, the art he was making." She found his intensity paradoxical, his confidence mixed with uncertainty from moment to moment as he performed. After he was done he was eager to know what she thought.

Soon after Christmas they moved into a fourth-floor walk-up apartment at 161 West Fourth Street, above a furniture store and a restaurant just west of Sixth Avenue. Her mother did not approve, as Dylan recalled. She thought he was shiftless, "nameless," and would never have the means to take care of anyone, including himself. Furthermore—Dylan believed—Mary Rotolo, deep down, loathed him for reasons he couldn't quite explain.

Actually, it wasn't that Dylan was "nameless" but that his name was assumed; Mrs. Rotolo sensed this shadiness, which made her distrust him. His dissembling about his name change and his history caused the first serious rift between the lovers as one night Suze discovered—not from Bob's lips but from the draft card that fell out of his pocket when he was drunk—his name was Zimmerman. They were so intimate, she recalled, "yet I felt insecure in not being able to trust him completely." She never could, and his "facility for not telling the truth" eventually undermined the romance.

Not telling the truth, as playful and harmless as it may seem at first, does take a toll. As Dylan's reputation grew, interviewers and press agents asked more probing questions, not out of idle or mean curiosity but because that is their job. At the callow age when he spun the yarn of his orphan hobo past he had no inkling of the magnitude of his real future, the extent to which he would be called to account. Suze believed that hiding his true origins made Dylan "paranoid." He lived in constant fear of being exposed.

Happy Traum recalled that Bob and Suze "had invited Jane and me to go over and have dinner at their apartment over on West Fourth Street, just off Sixth Avenue, and we ran into him at the grocery store—there was a little deli nearby. He was picking up some things in the grocery to bring back home. And he laughed, and said something like 'Don't tell anybody you saw me buying groceries.' We laughed and didn't think anything of it. But you had the feeling he was thinking about his image: What am I going to look like, what is my appearance. How do people see me?"

Dylan was self-conscious, painfully aware of how his every move might affect his career. Suze helped provide the emotional stability he needed in order to grow as an artist and as a man. Much has been made of Rotolo's influence on Dylan's politics and his education in the arts. She was well read and passionate about great literature; as an artist's daughter and an aspiring artist she had a natural feeling for painting and sculpture. They strolled along the corridors of the museums, discussing the old masters and the new: Rembrandt and El Greco, Picasso, Bonnard, and Red Grooms. Dylan began to draw. And around the time they moved in together she left her job at CORE to accept theater work, designing and building sets for off-Broadway productions. In this role she introduced the songwriter to the dramatic works of LeRoi Jones, Jack Gelber, and Brendan Behan; to the Living Theatre's seminal work *The Brig*; and to Antonin Artaud's theories in *The Theater of Cruelty*.

Of all this museum- and theatergoing, Bertolt Brecht's compositions in a review called *Brecht on Brecht* probably had the greatest influence on Dylan that year. Suze was working on the review at the Circle in the Square, so he listened to live performances of Brecht's songs over and over: "Wedding Song," "The World Is Mean," and the demonic "Pirate Jenny," sung by the growling rogues, hookers, and pickpockets of Brecht's nightmare Epic Theater. Later he described the effect of those "herky-jerky—weird visions" upon his own songwriting. The precise point of view of the narrator, that scorching intensity of the speaker, made Brecht's lyrics unforgettable—that, and the equally precise characterization of the audience. Dylan's grasp of the dramatic roles of the speaker and the listener empowered him to compose songs that were like miniature Elizabethan plays or Jamesian novels. Of that period in his development he later recalled that the kind of song he wished to sing did not exist yet; that was not exactly true. In Brecht there was something like what he wanted, "a song that transcended the information in it" by forcefully deploying the dramatic elements.

If Suze had not led him to Sheridan Square and the little theater where he listened to "Pirate Jenny," Dylan believed he might never have written "The Lonesome Death of Hattie Carroll" or "Only a Pawn in Their Game." This may or may not be so. If Rotolo had never set foot in a theater, I suspect her lover still would have found his way to the alchemy of the dramatic lyric, to "Hattie Carroll" as well as "Mr. Tambourine Man" and "A Hard Rain's A-Gonna Fall." The spirit of Suze Rotolo herself worked the miracle in those years. She believed in his gifts, and in loving her he found everything in life more precious. He began writing love songs and songs of protest against injustice at about the same time, in the spring of 1962.

That year, 1962, was Dylan's pivotal year artistically, just as 1963 was his annus mirabilis in career terms. Because Suze Rotolo was the person closest to him during those years, some of her impressions of him are worth repeating.

While he was very good company, entertaining and considerate for the most part, he had a singular ability to fade out without warning, in plain sight, as if someone had thrown a switch. Loving him, she did not allow this to trouble her too much. She said that she admired Dylan's ability to go deep within himself, to lose himself so completely in the music or thoughts in his head that nothing in the real world—neither Suze nor a roomful of chattering people— could divide his attention. She would watch him slip away from her, mentally, and then return. Other men have been known for this sort of woolgathering, or catatonia, notably Socrates of Athens and Abe Lincoln of Illinois—not to suggest any further resemblance among these luminaries. These public figures all packed an invisible curtain behind which they could confer with a daemon or muse when the need arose. This was an essential part of the working apparatus, like a magician's folding screen.

Another facet of Dylan's character, noted by more and less reliable witnesses over many years, is an irreducible part of the portrait: "He was not known for his generosity." Rotolo mentions this in connection with his windfall success after the Columbia recording contract, when he might have shown a "drinks on me" hospitality in a bar. His tightfistedness was deep rooted and cannot be blamed on childhood privation, fleeting indigence, or fear of pauperism in the future. It is a personality trait like wit or impatience that may explain other things but cannot itself be explained.

After the release of his first album on March 19, 1962, and an ongoing engagement at Gerde's that spring, Dylan had more money than he had ever seen before. Money attracts money, and in May he also had a manager, a heavyset Chicago hustler with horn-rimmed glasses and a ponytail. Albert Grossman, thirty-six, was aptly named, a man of voracious appetites for fine food, vintage wine, beautiful women, and folk songs, with a sharp eye on the bottom line, the big payday. He was the fat kid in school who ate your lunch. His face was an Attic mask of carnality. Albert looked and acted ten years older than he was. By the time he was thirty the former economics major owned the Gate of Horn nightclub in Chicago. He went on to manage the careers of folksinger Bob Gibson, bluesman John Lee Hooker, and the monumental Odetta, before packaging Peter, Paul and Mary for the big time. Grossman, with Boston promoter George Wein, founded the Newport Folk Festival in 1959. That year he informed Robert Shelton that "the American public is like Sleeping Beauty waiting to be kissed awake by the prince of folk music." Shelton wisecracked that Grossman not only kissed the lass but climbed right into bed with her. A student of the psychologist Bruno Bettelheim, Grossman was familiar with the ideas that infused Bettelheim's book *The Uses of Enchantment.*

Grossman believed that what was good for him was good for his clients. If he prospered so would they. Reversing the honorable custom in show business—the Sol Hurok, Harold Leventhal, Carlos Gastel principle that what is good for the client is good for the agent—shocked some players and intrigued others. He reeked of cash and garlic and "palm oil." Joan Baez wouldn't go near him, although he offered her literally anything in the world—diamonds, movie stars, palaces, and eternal life—to sign with him. Grossman charged outrageous percentage fees but also promised colossal gross receipts and then delivered. Bored with the controversy between the folk purists who denied that the music could be popular and the folk entertainers who insisted that it must, Albert Grossman went after musicians he liked who also had the potential to appeal to a mass audience. There is no formula for this, going forward, and to Grossman's credit he loved and understood the music he sold. And like John Hammond, he had uncanny instincts for talent.

Dylan's fateful alliance with Grossman, in its way, was as revealing as his connection with Suze Rotolo. Grossman stalked him from one end of the Village to the other, from his stage-side table at Gerde's to late-night parties in fancy lofts overlooking the bright lights of Manhattan, flashing his bankroll and his sardonic smile, saying exactly the right things about the young man's talent and his future. Dylan ran from Grossman until he caught him.

On April 9, 1962, in the year of the Cuban Missile Crisis and the racial riots at the University of Mississippi, Dylan wrote "Blowin' in the Wind" for a hootenanny at Gerde's Folk City. Before that, in February, he wrote "Talkin' John Birch Paranoid Blues" and "Let Me Die in My Footsteps." In June, Suze Rotolo left New York to study in Perugia, Italy, without clear plans to return, and soon after that Dylan wrote "Tomorrow Is a Long Time," the first of his great love songs. It was also his first tune to employ a delicate finger-picking style that provided an obligato to the melody.

> *If today was not an endless highway,*
> *If tonight was not a crooked trail,*
> *If tomorrow wasn't such a long time,*
> *Then lonesome would mean nothing to you at all.*

The song's melody, wholly original, the plain but bold imagery and skillful use of near rhyme signal a breakthrough in the song-writer's process. He never recorded the piece for a studio album, although it would become part of the repertoire for folk and pop performers from Joan Baez and Judy Collins to Elvis Presley and Rod Stewart. It was almost too pretty for the young rebel to claim it so he left the lyric to others to sing, mostly women. A few months later he would write "Don't Think Twice, It's All Right," based on a folk song he first heard in a version by Paul Clayton, a love song with an edge of irony and anger that better suited his temperament in that year that Rotolo left him behind.

In early September, Tom Paxton, the round-faced twenty-four-year-old songwriter and singer from Oklahoma, found Dylan tapping at a typewriter in a hot, smoky room above the Gaslight Café. The Gaslight, a small, dim club with stained-glass lamps suspended over round oak tables, was a former coal cellar in a tenement building on MacDougal Street. According to Paxton, the co-owner Clarence Hood kept a room upstairs where the performers and their friends hung out and played cards all night. "Kind of like a store-room, and we had a rotating penny ante poker game going there. We rigged up a speaker so we could hear the show. . . . When whoever was preceding you started his first song, you would cash out of the game, get your guitar, and go down and get ready. . . ." The poet/

comedian Hugh Romney (later known as Wavy Gravy) brought in a portable typewriter and paper in case inspiration should strike one of the poets or songwriters. Now and again it did.

"I came down early one night from work," Paxton recalled, "and Bob was just putting the finishing touches on this three- or four-page, five-page magnum opus. And I said 'What's that?' And he said, 'Look at this. Tell me what you think of this.' So I read it and I said, 'Wow, I love the imagery . . . it's really Lord Randal is what it is.' And he said, 'What do you think I should do with it?'"

"Lord Randal" is an ancient Anglo-Scottish ballad about a fellow who goes to visit his wicked lady friend and then patiently answers his mother's anxious questions about the encounter. Paxton advised Dylan to put a tune to his version. "If you send it in to some quarterly or something, they would publish it and that would be the end of it." But if Dylan put it to music, "You would have a song." Simple enough, Paxton's conclusion, and the rest is history, significant cultural history. A reliable source, Paxton was the only young folk musician in New York, before Dylan, who was performing mostly songs of his own composition. So he was, logically, the rare friend whose suggestion Dylan might follow in such a matter.

"The next night [at the Gaslight] he got up and sang what he had showed me the night before, and it was called 'A Hard Rain's A-Gonna Fall.' And now when I hear it, and it goes into the eighth minute or whatever it is, I think, What did I do? What could I have been thinking?" Paxton, forty-seven years later, laughs heartily. "I'm just kidding. I think it's a wonderful piece of work."

Paxton does not mean to take undue credit. He understands, as we do, that the imperishable song would have found its way to the guitar eventually, even if Paxton had been in China during its creation. Dylan himself once claimed that the whole composition of "Hard Rain" unfolded in the boiler room cellar of the Village Gate, Chip Monck's quarters next to the Greenwich Hotel, and never mentions Paxton's advice, although he speaks highly of him elsewhere. The value of this story, corroborated by others, is in the reminder that none of the worthy songwriters of the period was working in isolation—Paxton, Seeger, Ochs, Eric Andersen, Dylan. Paxton says that they regarded Dylan as "first among equals" (that ancient egalitarian paradox). Hearing one another's best lyrics made all of them want to write better songs.

"Hard Rain" is unlike any song that had ever been written. The poet's study of Brecht, Civil War newspapers, Rimbaud, Picasso's *Guernica*, and the ballad tradition had culminated in an artsong, a cri de coeur that effaced the durable stanza and chorus structures like a great river flooding the countryside. It is three times as long as most contemporary songs and rhymes erratically. When the poet Allen Ginsberg first heard the composition he wept tears of bitter joy: joy because he knew then that the true spirit of Walt Whitman had survived a hundred years intact; bitterness because the singer stood witness to an apocalypse.

Other artistic successes of that year include "The Ballad of Donald White," about a murderer who begged to be jailed because "he couldn't find no room in life" and who ends up killing again because the prison has no room for him. Gil Turner, an editor at *Broadside,* called it the first song to apply principles of Freudian psychology, "the ideas of people being afraid of life," to a folk song. The same month Dylan wrote "Hard Rain" he also composed the Brechtian "Ballad of Hollis Brown" to the tune of the traditional "Pretty Polly." In October he wrote the tragic "John Brown" about a soldier who returns from battle so mutilated his mother cannot recognize him. Altogether Dylan wrote more than thirty songs in 1962, most of them after Suze Rotolo left him alone in Manhattan. Three of them suffice to illustrate his new mastery: "Blowin' in the Wind," "Don't Think Twice, It's All Right," and "Hard Rain's A-Gonna Fall"—an anthem for the peace and civil rights movements; a durable love song; and a visionary epic of apocalypse and redemption.

If Bob Dylan had wandered off into Mexico before Christmas of

1962 and vanished, like Ambrose Bierce did in 1914, we would still remember him.

As so rarely happens, Dylan's artistic breakthrough that year was followed by an annus mirabilis every bit as wondrous in career terms as the previous year had been creatively. Between July and December 1962 he had recorded the songs for his next album, *The Freewheelin' Bob Dylan*, in Studio A. On the strength of those songs, released in May 1963, he was taken up as a cause célèbre, a spokesman, an enfant terrible, and a meal ticket by persons as various as Albert Grossman, Joan Baez, Artie Mogull of music publisher Witmark Music, countless newspaper editors and scribblers, TV and radio hosts, and the public—not necessarily in that order.

His response to all this attention was idiosyncratic and provocative. On May 12, 1963, he was scheduled to perform the caustic "Talkin' John Birch Paranoid Blues" on Ed Sullivan's CBS variety show. "I just had it in my mind to do that particular song," he recalled. "I'd rehearsed it, and it went down well. And I knew everybody back home would be watching me on *The Ed Sullivan Show*. . . . It was a dream come true just to be on that stage. Everybody knew that." At the last minute the censors got nervous that the Birchers might bring a libel action; they insisted Dylan sing something less controversial—maybe a Clancy Brothers song? So Bob Dylan packed up his guitar and walked off the set, turning his back on the supreme showcase for an entertainer in those days, and branding himself as a rebel who would march to his own drummer.

He lost fifteen pounds. His bone structure declared itself. Joan Baez fell madly in love with him a few weeks before his twenty-second birthday in May of that year. She began introducing him at her sold-out stadium-size concerts, to the dismay of many who had paid to see her solo. This raised his profile. For months she continued to push him forward at her recitals until he no longer needed her patronage. The two carried on a highly publicized romance as the

King and Queen of Folk Music that inevitably disheartened Suze Rotolo, who had returned to take up residence with Dylan in mid-January but moved out of his apartment in late August.

From coast to coast—from Baez's house in Carmel to Albert Grossman's estate in Woodstock, New York, to Manhattan and around again—Dylan moved back and forth between the two women without their consent or understanding, loving both in different ways, inspired, writing love songs like "One Too Many Mornings," "Farewell," "Mama You Been on My Mind," "I'll Keep It with Mine," and "Love Is Just a Four-Letter Word."

I said goodbye unnoticed
Pushed towards things in my own games
Drifting in and out of lifetimes
Unmentionable by name
Searching for my double, looking for
Complete evaporation to the core
Though I tried and failed at finding any door. . . .

Peter, Paul and Mary, the trio that Albert Grossman had hand-picked and groomed for commercial success, had a blockbuster hit with "Blowin' in the Wind" in July 1963. The record was edging toward the top of the *Billboard* chart just in time for the Newport Folk Festival. Many who remember the festival that year describe it as a virtual coronation of Bob Dylan as the prince of folksingers, heir apparent to the legendary Pete Seeger. With Baez at his side singing his song (which had become everyone's song) "With God on Our Side," the twenty-two-year-old was treated like royalty, with as much deference and reverence as any man could summon in that sentimental, left-leaning community. In public he affected a charming, shuffling, blushing humility, gracefully offsetting the adoration.

Backstage—to the amusement of some and the horror of others—he practiced cracking a twenty-foot bullwhip, cutting the air over the lawn of Freebody Park, making little explosions as the leather tip broke the speed of sound. For a little while he was in command.

The young man we saw in concert at the Lisner Auditorium in December 1963 had been through hell since the summer.

Soon after Suze Rotolo moved out of their apartment she found out that she was pregnant. In those days abortion was illegal and therefore perilous; it was difficult and usually expensive to find a competent doctor who would perform the procedure in a clinical space. Both lovers were confused about what to do, both wanting and not wanting the baby. She later recalled that she was feeling confined, and having a child would only increase that feeling of suffocation. After much soul-searching they chose to end the pregnancy.

The procedure went as well as it could, with no medical complications, yet it left them both exhausted and despondent. They had begun the process of going their separate ways, but the breaking up would take six months and occasion many painful scenes. One night at her sister's apartment on Avenue B, her emotional turmoil came to a crisis. "I was a mess of whirling, wordless, and no longer containable sounds." She had realized there was no future for the two of them. Dylan later reached the same conclusion: "It had to end. She took one turn in the road and I took another."

It was a road of roundabouts and switchbacks. He spent most of September and October with Joan Baez in California before returning to New York, where he had recording dates on the twenty-third and twenty-fourth. He saw as much of Rotolo as she would allow. In the accounts of these affairs—Dylan's, Rotolo's, and Baez's—there is no assignment of blame. One might think, from reading Baez's memoir, that the famous woman did not know of Rotolo's existence. Suze was well aware of Dylan's connection with Baez, but Suze knew that her bond with the poet had unraveled on its own, a casualty of their youth, her insecurity, his dishonesty, and the heat of his sudden fame that burned both of them. He had begged her to marry him. She was not suited for the role of a star's spouse, one to live quietly in his shadow.

"I did not want to be a string on Bob Dylan's guitar."

While there was anguish in his love life, there was also trouble in the development of his public image, a construction he had over-prepared. The pose was compelling, but it had a short shelf life. On October 25, Andrea Svedberg interviewed Dylan for a forthcoming article in *Newsweek*. That was the day before his sold-out Carnegie Hall concert, which was—in that year of triumphs—the most visible landing on the public staircase of success. He had definitely fulfilled his promise to his parents to succeed as an entertainer. So he invited them to see him play the most prestigious venue in the Big Apple.

Dylan had told Svedberg of *Newsweek* that he did not know his parents, and had not been in touch with them for years. So the reporter was delighted to discover afterward that Mr. and Mrs. Zimmerman had come to the concert; their son had put them up in a motel on Eighth Avenue. For background she telephoned Dylan's brother in Minnesota, and David Zimmerman was forthright with her in conversation, mentioning that his inscrutable brother had recently visited the family in Hibbing. The reporter was very pleased to learn all of these new things about the folksinger who had his finger on the pulse of his generation, because he had told her (in an accent unlike his brother's) a sadder story of abandonment and alienation.

The article that came out in *Newsweek* on November 4, 1963, was not the puff piece that Albert Grossman and publicist Billy James had hoped for. It was Dylan's worst nightmare, an exposé of the middle-class Jewish boy with a hobo costume and a fake accent who manipulated the media and had gone so far as to deny "that Bob Dylan was ever Bobby Zimmerman." The speeding locomotive of Dylan's career had been derailed. In a niche of show business where "authenticity" greatly mattered to the audience, Bob Dylan had been exposed as a mountebank. He was stunned. Then he was as furious as if the truth itself had been a lie and now liars were ganging up on him. He scolded his managers and everyone who had talked to the woman from *Newsweek*. This was the beginning of a stormy, adversarial relationship with the mainstream media.

It would take him a year or more to recover from the collision between Bob Dylan and Bob Zimmerman; he would do so by remaking his art and his image so completely that the fiction he created in 1961 would matter as little to the public as it had to his friends in New York. As Van Ronk put it, "All of us were reinventing ourselves to some extent, and if this guy wanted to carry it a step or two further, who were we to quibble?" When the folksingers discovered that Dylan's oral history was a clever fiction, it didn't much affect their opinion of him. Shape-shifting was part of a tradition one could trace to Jack Elliott, Marilyn Monroe, Al Jolson, and countless actors and singers who made up stories about themselves.

Meanwhile, Dylan was mortified, having been caught in a lie. As a poet he was perhaps more sensitive about this than your average liar. Van Ronk—who, with Suze Rotolo, helped him to nurse his pride through that embarrassing time—believed that Dylan never really understood that "nobody cared who you had been before you hit town," and now that the jig was up, the young performer did not yet gather that soon nobody would care what he had *said* about who he was before he hit town. Bad press is the price of doing business. Happy Traum recalls that "we all thought he was this urchin, a carney from New Mexico; we bought into it, that he was this guy from the Southwest, a Woody Guthrie–type hobo, a whole romanticized version of what we all thought was a real folk hero." And Traum didn't know the truth until he read it in *Newsweek*. "We were kind of amused and surprised. I don't think it bothered us that much. It was kind of funny to think that he was a Jewish kid from . . . Minnesota." The character had served him well: Dylan, Van Ronk, Jack Elliott, Happy Traum were all showmen. None of them thought any less of a man because he had assumed an identity in a world of theatrical illusion.

Not three weeks after the *Newsweek* article rained on Dylan's parade, President John F. Kennedy was assassinated in Dallas. Private sorrows were caught up in a tide of grief that swept America like nothing since the death of Franklin D. Roosevelt eighteen years earlier. Bob and Suze watched the TV news at the apartment on Avenue B. For the generation born in the 1940s it was the crucial event in their history. Dylan's friend the songwriter Eric Andersen recalls how Kennedy had inspired an unparalleled optimism and idealism in the people who marched for civil rights and world peace. "The whole movement was kind of protected by the shadow under the span of Kennedy's wing, you know, his presidential authority—a false sense of protection maybe. Because after he died, it immediately splintered into, like, the Black Panthers, the civil rights movement became splintered, the war movement became exposed. People were also getting drafted. When Kennedy was there, this wasn't really happening. Under that protective wing of Kennedy, it had looked like a whole new world."

Andersen, one of the big four singer-songwriters of the Greenwich Village scene (along with Dylan, Ochs, and Paxton), believes that folk music provided the sound track for the pageantry of the early sixties. "Young people growing up during those times were ready for change . . . spearheading this was the singer-songwriter movement." And Dylan was at the cutting edge of it. "The whole thing burst apart when Kennedy got killed," Andersen continues. "Violence was as American as cherry pie. . . . This sort of cozy little womblike existence as a singer-songwriter—things changed. The Beatles came over. The crystal cracked or something. Bob was my draft adviser, he and Jimmy Kweskin [of jug band fame]."

What did he suggest?

"Well, this is funny. We basically had no protection because we weren't in school [for an educational deferment] and no psychiatrist to say 'he's unfit for service.' When time comes for the physical exam you're on your own. You had to go in and do the greatest performance of your life to get out. Or get cuffed and sent over."

"And so?"

"Well, Bob, he was advising that I take—he said, 'Take mescaline, take mescaline.'"

The dramatic change in mood that Eric Andersen has described did not occur at once but during the period of a year of American history, 1964; and Bob Dylan had responded—emotionally and artistically—a few weeks or months earlier than most people. This is not to say that he was intentionally leading the movement but it is understandable that many people would think so. His timing was supernatural. He wrote "The Times They Are A-Changin'" a month and a half before Kennedy's death (just as he had composed "Hard Rain" a month and a half *before* the Cuban Missile Crisis). In Washington on December 14 we were probably the third concert audience ever to hear that anthem of the 1960s student revolution, "The Times They Are A-Changin'." And there was no one among us on that date who really knew what it portended—the tragedy of Vietnam, the race riots of 1967—however deeply we may have been moved by the ominous warning of the song itself.

As wonderful as that performance was, as commanding and moving as Bob Dylan made it, perhaps the most amazing thing about the concert in Lisner Auditorium is that it went forward as scheduled. The events of the past four months had saddened and demoralized the singer. Some people in the audience may have known that. The events of the past twenty-four hours—we would learn soon enough—had nearly traumatized him.

He had been drinking heavily. On the evening of December 13, 1963, Bob Dylan approached the Americana Hotel at Seventh Avenue and Fifty-second Street in Manhattan. He entered the splendid lobby with a mixture of arrogance and tipsy embarrassment—an evil brew. Add to those a pinch of political naïveté.

The Emergency Civil Liberties Committee had invited him to a

6:30 dinner in the grand ballroom of the posh new hotel where they were celebrating the 172nd anniversary of the Bill of Rights. Dylan was to be honored with the yearly award for distinguished service in the cause of civil liberties. The previous winner of the Tom Paine Award had been the British philosopher and pacifist Lord Bertrand Russell. While Dylan was not a humble man, even at twenty-two, he may have recognized that he was a little out of his element if not out of his league. The exposé in *Newsweek* was fresh in everybody's mind. He was the youngest man in the room with the exception of a busboy or two; the old men and women seated at the tables were wearing suits and ties, fine dresses, jewelry and furs.

That night he wore blue jeans, a jacket of thin suede, and an open-collar sport shirt over a black T-shirt; he was slightly better dressed than his friends who he said had been turned away at the door. This scene was not what he expected, but then it is hard to say just what he expected. The ECLC was a task force of Old Left attorneys, authors, labor organizers, and fellow travelers who, like the American Civil Liberties Union, raised money primarily to defend citizens whose rights were threatened by the government or big business. The difference between the two organizations is that the ACLU demanded a pledge from its members that they were not members of the Communist Party, while the ECLC did not. There were some fire-breathing communists in the ranks of the ECLC and many others who approved of them. So the organization stood resolutely to the left of the more moderate, forward-looking ACLU.

Dylan sat at the high table with men wearing suits and boutonnieres, chairman Corliss Lamont, author James Baldwin, radio personality John Henry Faulk, who bravely crusaded against the blacklisters, and director Clark Foreman, who would present him with the award, the framed portrait of Tom Paine himself. Dylan drank more and more to calm his nerves. He pushed the food around his plate. He needed a cigarette. Peering out at the 1,400 people who had gathered to honor Tom Paine and Bob Dylan and themselves, he wanted to bolt. He later recalled, "I looked down from the platform and saw a bunch of people who had nothing to do with my kind of politics. I looked down and got scared."

Despite the efforts of Dave Van Ronk and Suze Rotolo—and perhaps because of them—Dylan's understanding of politics in 1963 was tenuous. It was as naïve and spotty as his understanding of human nature was profound. He knew the hearts of men and women and he had begun to comprehend the dynamics of people in groups (the boxing world, the mining corporations, the class warfare that killed Medgar Evers), social forces, the effects of power, money, and influence. But practical politics—the gritty, indispensable science of guiding or influencing the government— was beyond him.

Dylan was one of many Americans grieving for Kennedy while fretting over our conflicts with Cuba, from the Bay of Pigs invasion to the Cuban Missile Crisis and the ongoing ban on travel to the island. The assassin Lee Harvey Oswald had once helped distribute pamphlets for the Fair Play for Cuba Committee in New Orleans. Suze Rotolo stood firmly against the travel ban, believing it violated our civil liberties, and so did Dylan. He considered himself a friend of Phillip Luce, who led a group of students to Cuba in protest. It seemed like a simple issue, cut and dried, and if Oswald had been deranged in other respects, at least he desired fair play for Cuba. Some people believed that if our government had not created the Bay of Pigs disaster, Oswald might not have shot the president.

So the man who was about to receive the Tom Paine Award had an opinion or two about Cuba. And he had other ideas about social dynamics that were so finely tuned they had enabled him to write the protest songs for which he was being honored. "Only a Pawn in Their Game" and "Who Killed Davey Moore?" demonstrate that acts of violence and injustice result not from depraved individuals but from group behavior, passive and active cooperation. We are all responsible, we are more or less guilty; there is a bit of the assassin in all of us. This is not a political idea. It is a philosophical and religious belief useful to dramatic poets like Brecht, Shakespeare, and Robert Browning and a few saints and martyrs.

Another thing Dylan had on his mind so soon after the *Newsweek* debacle was the possibility that he was being set up, that he was being used. The ECLC had chosen him because he was in the spotlight: in the arena where the committee desired influence Dylan was already a bankable name, the voice of a generation of disaffected youngsters. The committee would profit from gathering him to their cause. While Dylan knew little about the political principles and history of the group, he knew they were the "Old Left" and unembarrassed by their communist connections. A man does not need political sophistication to suspect he is being used, and Dylan was savvy enough to know he had gotten himself into a bind.

The recipient of the Tom Paine Award rose to his feet, reluctantly and unsteadily, to address the crowd in the ballroom. "I haven't got any guitar, I can talk, though. I want to thank you for the Tom Paine award in behalf of everybody that went down to Cuba." He might have stopped right there, and sat down—that much would have seemed peculiar enough, the gratuitous mention of Cuba. They would have clapped and gone home contented. But the speaker warmed to his subject, which was a paean to the youthful protesters of the travel ban, and the glories of youth itself. This led him to consider the impertinence of old age. "You people should be at the beach. . . . It is not an old people's world. . . . Old people when their hair grows out [when they lose it] *they* should go out." They laughed at that, uneasily, giving the guest of honor the benefit of one joke at their expense.

But then he went on to say that the same old people had no real understanding of race, and were obsessed with black and white, and red and yellow, while he himself was color-blind. From this omniscient perch he rambled into an account of strange gifts that people bring the star backstage: the keys to a general's trunk, a Nazi leader's tie clip, a fallout shelter sign, all stolen *for him*, all somehow conveying the message that "there's no black and white, left and right to me anymore. . . . I'm trying to go up without thinking about anything trivial such as politics." At that point he probably *still* might have taken his seat without too much bad feeling, having succeeded in distancing himself from the ECLC and whatever political point of view he thought it represented.

Unfortunately, he was not finished talking. "I want to accept this award . . . in my name but I'm not really accepting it in my name and I'm not accepting it in any kind of group's name, any Negro group or any other kind of group." Then he offered another hundred words on Negroes not being Negroes, friends being friends, friends not wearing suits, and "uncompromisable" support and praise on "behalf of Phillip Luce who led the group to Cuba which all people should go down to Cuba. I don't see why anybody can't go to Cuba." Dylan was preaching to the choir. Did he think that the left-leaning members of the ECLC admired the U.S. policy toward Cuba? Or advocated racism? He might have sat down then and they still would have applauded, forgiving the flushed youth for his heartfelt if not very well-considered sentiments. But the train was headed down a slope and the brakeman was nodding.

"I got to admit that the man who shot the President Kennedy, Lee Oswald, I don't know exactly where—what he thought he was doing, but I got to admit honestly that I too—I saw some of myself in him. I don't think I could go that far. But I got to stand up and say I saw things that he felt, in me . . . not to go that far and shoot." Somebody may have kicked him, under the table. The president had been killed only three weeks before. The audience of old liberals, who had sat patiently and politely while Dylan made jokes at their expense, began to hiss and boo when he took sides against the martyr. At that point Clark Foreman and Corliss Lamont were ready with "the hook" if Dylan went on much longer.

"You can boo but booing's got nothing to do with it. It's just a—I just uh—I've got to tell you man, it's Bill of Rights is Free Speech—" He summarily accepted the award on behalf of James Foreman of the Students Nonviolent Coordinating Committee and the protesters against the travel ban, and sat down in a squall of hissing, scattered applause, and boos.

Dylan had said of Lee Harvey Oswald, *I saw some of myself in him.* That was probably true, in the particular case, and in the abstract. Dylan and Oswald saw eye to eye on the travel ban as a violation of human rights. And everything in Dylan's training as a dramatic poet had taught him to identify with both the victim and perpetrator of a crime. If there were half a dozen people in the ballroom who understood this—and the late James Baldwin should be counted among them—it made only a splash in the ocean of outrage and disgust. In that time and place there is almost nothing Dylan could have said that would have been more offensive.

In ten minutes on the night of Friday the thirteenth he had defined his political position for the rest of his life.

Sometime the next day, hungover, remorseful, Dylan packed up his guitar and suitcase and was driven to Washington, D.C., in the blue Ford station wagon. That night he gave one of the greatest concerts of his career for an audience of 1,500.

PART II

Madison Square Garden, 1974

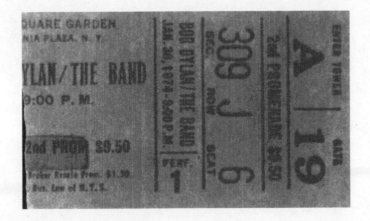

CHAPTER 6

New York, 1974

Madison Square Garden, a colossal, cavernous arena built on top of Pennsylvania Station, seats 20,344 spectators. On the night of January 30, 1974, the bowl was filling up, sold out for Bob Dylan and the Band.

As we approached the coliseum, clutching our tickets, it was cloudy and cool, in the upper thirties. We passed shorn Hare Krishna singers in their robes, motley jugglers, and souvenir hawkers. Not only were all of the seats sold, but for every person in the Garden at Thirty-fourth Street and Seventh Avenue there were five people somewhere who wanted a seat. It was a scalper's heaven: $9.50 seats going for $50 to $75 to see Bob Dylan in concert in Manhattan for the first time since October 1965.

He had not done a solo concert here since his motorcycle accident in July 1966. He quit touring at the height of his box office appeal—a thing unheard-of. Now at the age of thirty-two he would be doing forty big shows in twenty-one cities, a comeback tour of North America predicted to gross $5 million, a record for this sort of entertainment. In the Garden two nights earlier Muhammad Ali earned $72,000 per minute in winning a twelve-round decision over Joe Frazier, $2.6 million for a night's work in the same space, but that included the take from closed-circuit TV viewers all over the country. Buying a ticket to see Dylan, a more elusive legend, was a lot harder.

My sister had become a reporter for the *New York Post*, so she had been able to score a couple of seats thirty rows from the stage.

The stage was enormous and so was the sound equipment. Before the multicolored spotlights hit the setup it looked like Stonehenge on a moonless night. The immense black amplifiers and looming speakers would play havoc with the sight lines. A very large man would have looked small on that stage, and Bob Dylan, dressed in black trousers and a black sport coat with a cloth belt in back cinching his waist, looked tiny. He entered from the left behind lead guitarist Robbie Robertson and singer/pianist Richard Manuel, after the raw-boned Levon Helm had taken up his post at the drum kit and hulking Garth Hudson sat down at the keyboard. Rick Danko strapped on his bass.

The audience was on their feet, applauding, shouting to welcome Bob Dylan home. My sister—who had a keen eye for famous faces—noted that up ahead of us were seated Jack Nicholson and Bette Midler, John Lennon and Yoko Ono, James Taylor and Carly Simon, Paul Simon, Mary Travers (of Peter, Paul and Mary), Dick Cavett, and Judy Collins. I was pleased to hear that Dylan had provided tickets for my friend Nora Guthrie and her mother, Marjorie, Woody's widow. Mike Porco, who had given Dylan his first important job at Gerde's, was there, and so was Happy Traum, with his friend the poet Allen Ginsberg. All had come to welcome the troubadour home. Although Dylan was now living in Los Angeles, he told a journalist it was only temporary—New York would always be home to him.

Without wasting breath on greetings or homecoming sentiments the Band hit the ground running behind Robertson's driving guitar introduction to the rocker "Most Likely You'll Go Your Way (and I'll Go Mine)," played at breakneck speed.

You say you love me
And you're thinkin' of me,
But you know you could be wrong. . . .

Indeed, anyone who thought they were thinking of Bob Dylan was likely to be wrong. His voice was deeper than we remembered it and less melodic, more declamatory. He growled and shouted the words defiantly, "upsinging" the word *wrong*, delivering it several steps above the expected note so that it sounded like speech instead of song.

I'm just gonna let you pass,
Yes, and I'll go last
Then time will tell who fell
And who's been left behind
When you go your way and I go mine.

This was not only thrilling, it was deeply affecting: thrilling to hear the man's voice live again after eleven years, affecting because the song tells of parting, separation, and change. Dylan was making no secret of his rancor over the past, and now at the age of twenty-five I could understand lyrics that had meant little to me when I heard them at seventeen. Poetry grows with you. This song had been written for *Blonde on Blonde* (1966), the brilliant, manic rock album released two months before Dylan's motorcycle accident and subsequent retirement. He would say the song was "probably written after some disappointing relationship where, you know, I was lucky to have escaped without a broken nose." The comment neatly applies to Dylan's relationship with the public in America, Europe, and Australia. Folk purists called him Judas. Rock fans were puzzled by the density of his lyrics, the length of the songs, and the fact that you couldn't dance to most of them. From the time he played the electric guitar at the Newport Folk Festival on July 25, 1965, until the date of his accident, July 29, 1966, the folksinger/rock star had fought a pitched battle on two fronts against an audience that couldn't decide from one day to the next whether to love him or hate him.

Now he had returned to New York in triumph, to a love fest. George Vecsey, covering the tour and filing long reports in the *New York Times*, interviewed a young man in Uniondale, Long Island, at a concert two nights earlier. "This is a pilgrimage," he said. "I ought to be crawling on my knees." The zeal is curious when you consider that the object of all this adoration was only thirty-two years of age and hardly invited it.

Vecsey and other journalists (including two more for the *Times*) were intrigued that most of the audience appeared to be twenty-one and under. "This was somewhat of a surprise to those who had predicted that the 'older generation' of Dylan fans would leave their young children with a babysitter and go see their hero of another decade." The audience for popular music is fast-moving and fickle. This 1974 tour was the first sign that Dylan's work could attract a second generation of fans and the evidence was overwhelming. "His personal following as a performer," wrote Grace Lichtenstein of the *Times*, "was until now limited to aficionados, not to a mass audience in the style of Elvis Presley or the Beatles." Twelve years after "Blowin' in the Wind" he at last had the mass audience. Frank Sinatra was envious. Woody Allen was mystified. "His appeal is finally as great as his significance," said David Geffen, under whose label, Asylum Records, Dylan's new album, *Planet Waves*, had been released.

"Mr. Dylan evoked cheers in Madison Square Garden that matched those to greet any championship team here," wrote George Vecsey. "Two young men danced arm-in-arm down the front aisle; a young girl handed Mr. Dylan a bouquet of flowers that he accepted straight-faced." Before he was quite done with "Most Likely You Go Your Way" the crowd rose to give him a standing ovation. When he was finished singing that song, Bob Dylan, "the figure in black, never changing his expression, said almost grimly: 'An honor to be here,' and many of his fans screamed."

He had given us reason to believe he would never be singing in this place.

Those who followed Bob Dylan's career from 1963 until 1966 did so at a great distance or at their own peril. You might not know this from the numerous books and films that have focused on these years, the period of apotheosis that holds him in suspension in American memory. Some portray him as the pied piper leading a drunken parade coast to coast, or a wisecracking host overseeing a madcap party.

The books and films were released years after the fact and convey only a corner of the reality. His was a niche act whose influence was out of all proportion to his popularity. Grossman's management of his offbeat client was masterful, maximizing the potential at every turn. Dylan's following of aficionados was fragmented and consisted mainly of upper-middle-class intellectuals—teenagers included. If one looks at the album sales and concert receipts before the 1970s it is obvious that—as David Geffen would say—his appeal had not caught up with his significance.

Nonetheless, he was riding a rocket and there was never room for more than two or three people astride it at any one time—Albert Grossman, Joan Baez, Allen Ginsberg, friends like Paul Clayton and Bob Neuwirth the gadfly painter and folksinger, Victor Maymudes the factotum bodyguard, and Sara Lownds, Dylan's future wife. Suze Rotolo perceived an element of "paranoia" in her lover's personality from the beginning. Perhaps the word she uses is too strong, but as Dylan's fame burgeoned in 1964 his personal defenses mounted in direct proportion and in peculiar ways. He was—as Lady Caroline Lamb said of Lord Byron—mad, bad, and dangerous to know. John Sebastian, who turned down an invitation to join Dylan's band, then said, "You can't get too close to Dylan. He burns with such a bright flame you can get burned."

Under the pressure of celebrity, what began as shyness and insecurity in the twenty-one-year-old quickly generated a system of elaborate coping mechanisms, some personal, some organizational. Suze Rotolo recalls that fame came so suddenly to Dylan at twenty-one, and hit him so hard, that we ought to give him credit "for learning how to survive fame with all its pressures and responsibilities." It began at Newport with a bullwhip that spoke loud and clear: stand back, you beasts with fangs and claws; the defense soon evolved into a company of bodyguards, confidants, and court jesters that moved with him, what Clausewitz might call a phalanx that protected him from the public and controlled access to friends and business associates. Paranoia, Rotolo concludes, became a survival mechanism. "Either people wanted to devour him or they offered themselves up for him to consume."

Some wit referred to Dylan's phalanx as "The Mind Guard." This was clever and true enough: the mind needed guarding. It was precious and vulnerable, and better a flawed and corrupt mind guard than no guard at all.

The company included Bobby Neuwirth, Victor Maymudes, Geno Foreman, Albert Maher, folksingers Paul Clayton and David Cohen, and often Albert Grossman, especially when Dylan was performing. Robert Neuwirth, born in Akron, Ohio, in 1939, was the ringleader and master of revels. Handsome, quick-witted, and ruthless, he could cut someone to shreds with a well-timed insult or put-down, and then rescue them with a puckish smile. Dylan met him at a folk festival in 1961. Neuwirth was going to art school in Boston and playing banjo at night in the clubs. In *Chronicles* Dylan recalls, with admiration, Neuwirth's penchant for provocation and the fact that neither conscience nor etiquette could keep him from doing as he pleased. "He was in a mad revolt against something." What it was, no one knows. With his gift for sarcasm and invective, he could keep almost anyone off balance. Neuwirth was a fine gatekeeper and would help Dylan to judge from day to day who was in and who was out of the charmed circle. It was a kangaroo court, arbitrary and heartless.

Neuwirth's idea of a good time was to gain someone's confidence, discover an intimate grief or insecurity, and then pounce and regale the company with it. Dylan would chime in. This was "all in fun," of course, but it was high school meanness glorified by Artaud's *Theater of Cruelty*. If you'd lost your sweetheart, your job, or your dog, that was good fuel for a round of drinks at the Kettle of Fish. This sort of Rabelaisian raillery was Neuwirth's greatest gift, although he had one other talent. He could diffuse rancor, so he might live to torment someone else. This Robin Goodfellow served at the King's pleasure.

"A sort of hierarchy was established of knights of the round table, princes of the blood," Van Ronk (who would have nothing to do with it) recalls, "all paying court to the emperor with the long, bushy hair. And because of who he was, that became a pretty nasty scene." After Neuwirth in rank came a lanky, lantern-jawed, hook-nosed road manager named Victor Maymudes, who did most of the driving. Maymudes had started the first coffeehouse in Los Angeles, the Unicorn, then he became Odetta's producer. Born in 1935, the son of left-wing activists, Victor was "the village philosopher," the quiet one who did not need to speak to be understood. Centered, discreet, he was Dylan's opponent in chess, pocket billiards, and the game of Go, very good at these games but never more than a match for the boss.

After Victor came the bodyguards, tall Geno Foreman with the scraggly brown beard, and the intense Albert Maher, a leftist-anarchist who had led students to Cuba during the travel ban. A Harvard graduate, he was the son of a Texas millionaire. Geno was the wayward son of Clark Foreman, the celebrated civil liberties attorney whom Dylan had offended at the ECLC dinner in 1963. Joan Baez considered Clark Foreman a surrogate father, and Geno a brother. Dylan met Geno when he was performing in Boston in 1961, a competent guitarist perhaps better known for his drug peddling, as "the man who introduced marijuana to the state of Massachusetts."

All of the mind guard carried walking sticks, just as they affected dark glasses, as a fashion statement and for intimidation. Geno carried a wicked-looking shillelagh carved from a tree root, fit to knock a man's brains loose with a stroke. Foreman had given Dylan the bullwhip he brandished at Newport in 1963, and soon after, Dylan put aside the bullwhip and hired Geno to protect him from overzealous fans.

That was the loyal inner circle of a coterie that included Albert Grossman, the manager who wrote the checks and made the bookings, and came and went as he pleased. With an estate in Woodstock and an apartment in New York he frequently played host to this troupe. He encouraged their clannish attitude and manners, believing that the star needed protection, as well as extraordinary care and feeding. Grossman was passionate about the music and committed to the best of the best as long as it made the cash register ring. As the goose that laid the golden eggs, Bob Dylan must have whatever it took—for the time being—to keep him happy and productive.

The half-life of a pop star is brief and lucrative. Managers are eager to please. Dylan was not as intemperate as Billie Holiday nor as avaricious as Benny Goodman; neither was he as lecherous as Errol Flynn. He was not a glutton, like Elvis. But he did require a peculiar mixture of privacy and company, candor and flattery that is difficult to cultivate. Happy Traum got the impression that "Albert started building this wall around Bob, this protective coating that you had to be—you had to have the right key to get in and it was really locked off." This began, Traum says, "right around the time of 'Mr. Tambourine Man' and when Bob started to really get beyond the little folky Greenwich Village scene, and started getting an adoring audience. Suddenly he became inaccessible. . . . It was bodyguards . . . like a wall around him. And then it became an entourage, the guys . . . who were in that inner circle, and it was them looking out at the people trying to get in. And it was not a pretty sight."

Grossman, one of the most successful managers in the annals of American entertainment, neatly divided the world of men into two camps: the friends of his clients and his client's enemies. You were one or you were the other, and if you had not recently proven your loyalty you stood under suspicion. Rotolo recalls that Grossman, Dylan, and Neuwirth all had a rare talent for staring; a stare from any of them could lower the temperature in a room by thirty degrees and bring conversation to a standstill. Fat Albert, with or without his Cuban cigar, his glass of Château Lafite, his hand about to flash his bankroll or put it away, had one of the great stares of all time. Dylan's was pretty good ("the thousand-mile gaze") but Albert's was professional, the consummation of years of exertion and furious distrust. People interpreted his stare in many ways but it really meant one thing: what can you possibly say or do to prove to me *that you are with us and not against us?* Because the question arose from a source of overwhelming power it usually had the effect of silencing the recipient, and flash-freezing most everybody else in the room.

No one knows how much of Dylan's social policy was influenced by Albert Grossman, not to mention his understanding of business. Grossman advised him to change his name officially, which he did in August 1962. There are some who believe that Dylan's mind guard, with its strict hierarchies and snobbism, the sunglasses and sarcasm, and even Dylan's growing reluctance to smile for the camera, was all theater directed by Grossman—compelling theater, no doubt about it, the angry young man and his mystique; that role enshrined Dylan as the coolest of the cool entertainers of the high sixties. There is no arguing with success. Grossman was successful before he signed Bob Dylan. The manager was fifteen years older than his naïve, impulsive client, and had vast experience in the cutthroat music business. Dylan—who had somehow internalized Clausewitz's military model—had the good sense to follow a master tactician's advice.

Even more likely is that Dylan and Grossman were of one mind in the early 1960s: they wanted to make the finest music conceivable while reaching the largest possible audience (and making the most money). And it is fair to say that this was a fitting partnership. Either man would have sold his soul to the devil—or at least would have sold the *other's* soul to the devil—in order to achieve success. John Cohen, the brilliant singer and photographer (who formed the New Lost City Ramblers with Mike Seeger), put the matter succinctly: "I don't think Albert manipulated Bob, because Bob was weirder than Albert." Dylan told a friend in the 1960s: "If it wasn't for Albert, I could be on the Bowery now. Albert's the greatest manager that ever lived in the whole century of the world." That is strong testimony that Dylan took direction from Grossman even if he was not "manipulated." Maybe Grossman's advice to the younger man was that the world out there is brutal despite the folksingers' rigmarole about peace and love; and for a man in Dylan's position the best defense would be a good offense.

By 1964 Dylan found himself at the pole of a magnetic field. "Mr. Tambourine Man," "It Ain't Me, Babe," and his other love songs had reached an audience beyond the folk crowd and touched a chord that the early songs had not. Strangers who had been affected by his songs approached him as a personal friend or a guru, pouring out their hearts and life stories to him.

A member of his inner circle, the late folksinger David Cohen, said that "his power, his mystique, just affected people in crazy ways." Simply from hearing the records, Cohen said, one got the feeling "This guy *knows*, this guy *feels*, and you want to be with him." Rosemary Gerrette, an Australian actress who had a brief fling with Dylan, said, "He was Christ revisited." Eric Andersen, bringing it down to earth after a friendship of forty years, declares, "He's got the heaviest vibes I've ever felt on anyone," an intriguing notion that comes up time and again in interviews with friends and associates.

Pleased with his growing fame, Bob Dylan was not happy that he had so little control over the consequences. "It scared him," according to Dave Van Ronk. "He never trusted anybody in his life. Now there were a lot *more* people grabbing at him, to mistrust." Twenty-three years old, restless, adventurous, he couldn't very well stay at home hiding. "The *scene* had to be made because he was the number-one star. My role was like protection," said David Cohen, one of the phalanx who accompanied Dylan on his rambles.

They would saunter into a club like Max's Kansas City, surrounding Dylan, and take over a table. The wild-haired star sat down with his back to the room and Neuwirth would sit across from him surveying the crowd while somebody went for drinks. The loud voices fell to whispering. In a matter of minutes friends, acquaintances, and strangers would edge toward the table, famous performers like Phil Ochs, Eric Andersen, Tom Paxton, the Rolling Stones' Brian Jones, groupies and autograph hounds.

Tension mounted as the crowd's energy generated a wicked electricity between Dylan and Neuwirth. Somebody would come too close, or be lured in, and the games would begin. "Neuwirth was just egging it on, and doing a lot of it himself," Eric Andersen recalls. But Dylan was almost as skillful in the "mental gymnastics" that tested loyalties and banished the unwelcome and the uncool. "Dylan was very hostile, a mean cat, cruel to people," said David Cohen—quick to add that all of this could be explained by the fact that the poet's privacy was being invaded. People asked him too many questions about the meaning of life, and "it was just too heavy for him, being the center of attention."

The anecdotes that have come down to us describing the Village circus in the mid-sixties are disturbing and not easily explained away.

Brian Jones, the gifted, exquisitely sensitive English guitarist who founded the Rolling Stones, idolized Bob Dylan. Jones was tiny, an inch shorter than his hero, blond-haired, blue-eyed, and androgynous looking, sporting frilly Edwardian blouses and bright scarves. He was notoriously volatile, needy, and drug dependent. By and by Neuwirth led him toward the table where the maestro was holding court.

Neuwirth welcomed the celebrated singer and multi-instrumentalist who had taught Mick Jagger how to play harmonica. Dylan bared his teeth. First of all he declared that the Stones were a joke—they could not be taken seriously. Now everyone could laugh at that, true or not, because the comment cost nothing, drew no blood. But then he explained to Jones that he had no talent and that the band, joke that it was, ought to replace him with someone who could sing. This made Jones unhappy, after he had been so happy to see Dylan in the bar. The Englishman swept his flowing hair out of his eyes, which were tearing up as Dylan went into detail about Jones's musical handicaps. Jones began to cry. Now the whole mob could see his weakness; it was a terrible sight, the flowing locks, the lacy sleeves, the weeping—just the wrong image for a group called the "Rolling Stones," Dylan concluded. He may have been right; Jones did not seem to be long for the Rolling Stones, or this world, for that matter. A couple of years later he was found dead at the bottom of a swimming pool. Some say that Dylan paid for Jones's lavish coffin.

Phil Ochs, as unstable as Brian Jones, not only worshipped Dylan as an artist, he adored him, as did Paul Clayton, and knew two sides of him. "One on one" Dylan could be kind and considerate; in a group—to keep people at bay, perhaps—he turned sadistic. Ochs, Dylan's age, and a very talented songwriter, a peer of Paxton, Andersen, and Len Chandler, was a glutton for punishment at the round table, a human punching bag who would serve for a few laughs until someone new came along. Ochs, like Paxton and Andersen, represented the competition—insofar as there was any—for the fame and fortune that came from folk music. And Dylan, in company, mercilessly berated Ochs, his lyrics, his diction, his nasal singing style.

"You oughta find a new line of work, Ochs. You're not doin' very much in this one." When someone asked Dylan to lay off Ochs for a while, he was surprised and angry. "What do you want me to talk about? I buy your wine, I try to be your friend. What do you want me to talk about? The rats in the sewers? Or the sunrise over the Hudson?"

Andersen recalled that people were so in awe of Dylan, almost no one would stand up to him. One night he invited Phil Ochs and David Cohen to his apartment to hear his new single, "Can You Please Crawl Out Your Window." He said he wanted their opinions. Cohen said the song was great and Ochs said it was just okay. Phil's was the wrong answer and so Bob played the single again to give him a second chance. This time Phil confessed he didn't really like it. Bob insisted on knowing exactly what he meant by that, so Phil explained that the song was not as good as Dylan's old stuff, and "speaking commercially I don't think it will sell," all of which happened to be true.

Dylan brooded over this for a while. Then the men left his apartment and slid into a limousine bound for an uptown nightclub.

When they had gone a few blocks up Sixth Avenue, Dylan suddenly exploded, calling for the driver to pull over. When the car rolled to a stop at the curb Bob Dylan told Phil Ochs to get out. "Get out here, Ochs. Get out! You're not a folksinger. You're just a journalist." Ochs got out and walked away but not forever; Dylan would entertain the depressive songwriter a few more times during the next decade before Ochs hanged himself.

Even a paragon of friendship and magnanimity like Dave Van Ronk was not spared. One night Dylan was drinking with the gang at the Kettle of Fish when he was suddenly moved to advise Van Ronk about how to manage his career. It was patronizing nonsense, "but by that point," Van Ronk recalls, "he had gotten used to everybody applauding any idea that came into his head." The Mayor of MacDougal Street sat and listened, politely. But he knew that Dylan was trying to provoke him.

"Why don't you give up blues?" Dylan asked the renowned bluesman, from whom he had learned fine points of the art. "You do that, and I'll produce an album on you; you can make a fortune," he continued, fatuously, evoking smirks and chuckles from the audience that had gathered around. Dylan was no producer. This was a hurtful suggestion, because as fine a musician as Van Ronk was, he had little luck making records, and less luck selling them.

At last, with the dignity that never deserted him, Van Ronk pushed his chair back from the table and stood up.

"Dylan, if you're so rich, how come you ain't smart?" And he walked out of the bar.

Such scenes would be of less interest if they didn't coincide with a dazzling productivity. The set list we heard in Madison Square Garden in 1974 came as close to a greatest hits program as Dylan would ever perform, and ten of eighteen songs came from the songwriter's pitiless period, 1964–66. They are branded, savagely tattooed: "It Ain't Me, Babe," "Ballad of a Thin Man," "It's Alright, Ma (I'm Only Bleeding)." These and others are poems full of strife, rancor, and vengeance.

> *You see me on the street*
> *You always act surprised*
> *You say, "How are you?" "Good luck"*
> *But you don't mean it*
>
> *When you know as well as me*
> *You'd rather see me paralyzed*
> *Why don't you just come out once*
> *And scream it*
>
> (FROM *"Positively 4th Street"*)

> *He sits in your room, his tomb, with a fist full of tacks*
> *Preoccupied with his vengeance*
> *Cursing the dead that can't answer him back*
> *I'm sure that he has no intentions*

Of looking your way, unless it's to say
That he needs you to test his inventions.

(FROM *"Can You Please Crawl Out Your Window"*)

The sixty or more songs Dylan wrote and sang in those years are full of remarkable poetry. But the attitude of the speaker is as cold, predatory, and aggressive as the younger Dylan had been magnanimous and vulnerable. It is a tonal difference of night and day.

The folksinger has gobbled up his companions in the Kettle of Fish; a lone barracuda peers out of the glass bowl in confusion and fury.

Of teaching your tears, and saying it's too say
That he needs you to trust her intentions.
("from 'Gene You Prince Carry O' / 'You'll index")

The sixty or more songs Dylan wrote and sang in those years are full of remarkable poetry. But the attitude of the speaker is as cold, predatory, and aggressive as the younger Dylan had been magnanimous and vulnerable. It is a tonal difference of night and day.

The folksinger has gobbled up his companions in the Kettle of Fish; a lone barracuda peers out of the glass bowl in confusion and fury.

CHAPTER 7

A Sea Change

In art, as in life, Bob Dylan changed so dramatically between 1963 and 1964, from the affectionate performance at Lisner Auditorium to the bitter recordings of the album *Another Side of Bob Dylan*—songs like "It Ain't Me, Babe" and "Ballad in Plain D" (a melodramatic narrative of the breakup with Rotolo)—the transformation begs for some explanation.

Was it losing the love of his life, which finally occurred in March 1964? Did the pressure of fame disillusion and then embitter him? Was it bad company, or something metabolic, bad medicine or hormones? Was it the fact that power corrupts, and that the emotional power Dylan gathered was more corrosive than any other?

There are as many answers as there are witnesses to the bizarre scenes in bars, cafés, and hotel rooms through which Dylan and his phalanx rambled in the mid-sixties. Two whose memories are reliable are Eric Andersen and his friend the filmmaker Donn Alan Pennebaker, the wizard godfather of cinema verité who captured Neuwirth's tormenting of Joan Baez and Dylan's humiliation of a *Time* magazine reporter in the documentary *Dont Look Back*. At eighty-two Pennebaker is still active and his memory of the sixties razor sharp. He saw much more of Dylan and Neuwirth than he filmed and they made a formidable impression.

I visited "Penny," as his friends call him, in the basement office of a row house near Broadway on Ninety-first Street on a chilly day before Christmas. A jolly, portly man with bushy eyebrows, Pennebaker leaned back in his chair against a foggy window and held forth in long, quotable sentences. He has been everywhere and known everybody: Norman Mailer, John F. Kennedy, Jimi Hendrix, John Lennon, Marlon Brando (his cousin), James Carville—the list seems endless. He is still friends with Neuwirth, and had seen him at an art opening two days before.

Sometimes when Penny is talking his eyes half close and he leans back, looking up at you and you just know he is time-traveling, looking straight back into the past like an ongoing movie he has not quite finished filming.

Penny first met Dylan and Neuwirth in the Cedar Tavern, at 82 University Place in the Village, in March 1965. They got together to discuss the possibility of making a documentary of Dylan's forthcoming tour of England. "Neuwirth was the provocateur of the group," Pennebaker observed. "You have two guys who stick together; one of them sets things in motion and the other watches. Dylan was the watcher. And also, I could feel right away he was from the Middle West, which is where I came from. I grew up in Chicago and I had a sense of the Middle West that I cherished. New York was a wonderful Disneyland kind of place to go. Anybody who came from the Middle West, right away I thought of them as a person I knew. Neuwirth—I never had any idea where he came from."

I told Pennebaker that Neuwirth was from Akron, Ohio.

"He didn't reflect any place," Penny declared. In those days, he recalls, there were culture "junkies" in America who would attach themselves to the music or art scene and become conversant in their subject, and "they were just there. And Bob Neuwirth was kind of that way. I didn't know he was an artist. I didn't even know he was a musician. He was just very hip, *very* hip. Right away I could see that to keep up with *that* you had to be someplace that I wasn't. The idea that if you said *anything*, you had to be prepared to follow it up with whatever came of it. I never played that game. I didn't know enough to even *think* about doing it."

Neuwirth was adept at the mind game and thereby kept Dylan amused, according to Pennebaker. Dylan "on the other hand was interesting to me right off because not only was he a watcher, but I could see he was naïve in ways that were surprising to me. I assumed that everybody I knew had been through the same educational process I had. Maybe they hadn't all read Thomas Mann but they would have read Fitzgerald, Hesse; they would have read the things we thought were our cultural endowment."

The Cedar Tavern was nearly empty that night. But there was a woman sitting alone in the back of the bar. "And right away," Pennebaker recalled, "he asked me, 'Is that the woman from *The Threepenny Opera*, Lotte Lenya, the woman who married Brecht? Is that Lotte Lenya?'" Dylan was starstruck. Now, it just so happened that Pennebaker knew exactly who Lotte Lenya was, and that the woman in the Cedar Tavern was not Lenya, but this was a moment of illumination into Dylan's character. "I just thought: this is a guy who has opened certain windows but also hadn't opened a lot of other ones. He would say things that I was amazed he didn't know about. And I thought, *that* is an interesting person, that—to be where he is, in the firmament. You know, people taking him seriously enough to send him to England, for whatever it was." That was the moment, the filmmaker says, when he "really was wedded to the project."

He has talked about watching Dylan go through the trouble of becoming more and more famous—how difficult it is to imagine that. A normal person has "no idea what the stresses are and what the downside is." I asked him to elaborate.

"People pulling at you. Using hits of friendship to get at you— to describe a sort of loyalty people need when they travel in small groups. Everybody has to subscribe to a kind of loyalty bond; when somebody comes in and insults one of them, everybody has to respond." Pennebaker emphasized that this was the essence of the *group*, the mind guard, an unusual intimacy. "Normally people keep out of this sort of thing by not knowing their neighbors and not knowing the people around them most of the time. They aren't called upon to take up the lance."

Pennebaker believes that the move from Minnesota to New York caused a trauma almost, a stress reaction that the young artist in his excitement scarcely acknowledged. "I figured that Bob had grown up in a place that treated him fairly gently. The people around were probably the kind of people I had known in Chicago—not high-speed people. They were gentle people. Later, when I heard Bob's 'Girl from the North Country' I realized it was for somebody he had lost, who was that gentle kind of person."

Well, if you go when the snowflakes storm
When the rivers freeze and summer ends
Please see if she's wearing a coat so warm
To keep her from the howlin' winds.

Perceptively, Pennebaker realized that Dylan's love song is more than a valedictory to a lost girlfriend; it is a farewell to a gentler, kinder community and the kindly part of himself that flourished there. "And now the people he was dealing with were hard because they expected something. When you're just growing up with people, [at home] they don't expect anything of you. You know? They just hang out with you."

Eric Andersen agrees with Pennebaker that Bob Neuwirth was an important bridge between an old way of life for Dylan and the new path. Andersen says of Neuwirth, "He was kind of like Bob's Yoko Ono. I think he exposed Dylan to different things that he wouldn't normally have looked at. . . . The overwhelming quality I find in Dylan is his curiosity. Maybe it could kill a cat but it can't kill him. That's the beauty . . . that makes him so different." Neuwirth could "expose him to more contemporary worlds because he was in the art scene."

Andersen introduced Bob Neuwirth to Edie Sedgwick, an eccentric actress who starred in Andy Warhol's films; Neuwirth introduced Edie to Dylan. Andersen made a film with Warhol. "Andy was a pop icon. The scene was bigger than just the Village. It was bigger than just concerts with Joan Baez. Bob Dylan was from the Midwest and there were still a *lot* of new things for him to see. Neuwirth was trying to expose him to different things, and they also hung out a lot, so his cynical attitude probably spilled into Bob [Dylan]."

Dylan himself has said that in 1964 and 1965 his consciousness was changing significantly. The crowd at the Newport Folk Festival in 1964 was dismayed that he played songs like "It Ain't Me, Babe" and "Mr. Tambourine Man" instead of the Brechtian dramas of social protest. Dylan's shifting focus, Andersen believes, had a lot to do with the change in the collective consciousness of the period. He refers again to the splintering effect of JFK's assassination. "Remember, things had gotten fragmented. When Johnson came in, the winds were shifting, you might say, politically. So I think he [Dylan] got fragmented, too. The glass developed a crack, and it became a prismatic effect."

> Then take me disappearin' through the smoke rings of my mind
> Down the foggy ruins of time, far past the frozen leaves,
> The haunted frightened trees, out to the windy beach,
> Far from the twisted reach of crazy sorrow.
> Yes, to dance beneath the diamond sky with one hand waving free
> Silhouetted by the sea, circled by the circus sands
> With all memory and fate driven deep beneath the waves
> Let me forget about today until tomorrow.
>
> (FROM *"Mr. Tambourine Man,"* 1964)

"His writing became more interior as he rocketed to fame. This midwestern kid from Minnesota. My parents are from the Midwest and he talks just like my mom! And the kind of expressions he was using, he just projected this idea of a sensibility that was pure, untouchable at first. But then he really took off, with the music, because he saw it as an engine of change. He could go from folk music to what he really loved the best, R&B, rock and roll. . . ."

When D. A. Pennebaker was filming Dylan, Baez, Grossman, and Dylan's phalanx on tour in England in late April 1965, he was not really aware he was capturing this "shift in consciousness" that was affecting Bob Dylan's art and his behavior. "I was after a different bear, I think," Penny says, perhaps referring to the bearlike Albert Grossman and the businessman's campaign to conquer Britain and make Bob Dylan an international star. Those were strange times for an American poet to venture abroad. Washington had recently announced its policy of bombing North Vietnam, and there had been major student demonstrations against the war in the capital on April 17. British rock and roll ruled the scene, the Rolling Stones' "Satisfaction" and the Beatles' "Yesterday" were buzzing on the jukeboxes. Pennebaker wanted to see how Bob Dylan would go over in Merry Olde England, and what Dylan's company would make of their reception.

First of all, Pennebaker was struck by how little Dylan seemed to care about the camera. "What was on his mind was overcoming any concerns he had about being witnessed in such a personal way. Which would bother some people. Some people it didn't. It didn't bother [John] Kennedy. Never bothered James Carville. They were too arrogant and didn't give a shit, really. Kennedy never gave a shit what I did. I could film him doing things that were completely embarrassing and he wouldn't even think about it. You got used to that." Dylan was like that. "You think *these people are mountaintops*, you just shoot them, they don't even know you are there."

"Dylan was kind of abstracted," Pennebaker recalls. "I didn't know that he'd just finished a tour with Joan." Dylan had finished more than a tour with Joan Baez; he had finished a love affair that had been going on and off for two years, since the Monterey Folk Festival in May 1963. Now he wanted to break it off or allow the romance to mellow into friendship, but Baez was too much in love with him and wouldn't let go. "No one told me that," says Penne-baker. "I had to figure everything out myself, nobody told me any-thing except Albert. He would say, 'We're going to see the Beatles tonight. You know who the Beatles are?' 'Yes.' But I didn't know much about Bob. Albert kind of let me find out for myself."

Bob Dylan had admired Joan Baez from a distance long before they met, in passing, at Gerde's Folk City in 1961. He had seen her the year before on a CBS television special with Josh White, Cisco Houston, and Lightnin' Hopkins. He couldn't take his eyes off her. He thought that she was darkly beautiful, with her long, straight hair hanging below her waist, her large brown eyes. Just looking at her made him giddy. And her soprano voice! "A voice that drove out bad spirits," he recalled. She was magical, and he had a feeling that they "would inevitably meet up."

It was a certainty that they would meet, these performers on the pinnacle of achievement in that close world of folk music. In 1963 her manager, Manny Greenhill, was looking for material—protest songs in particular—that would deliver Baez from her narrow rep-ertoire of ancient ballads to a broader audience. In a hotel room Greenhill played her an acetate disk of Dylan performing his songs and she said, "I was stricken by the genius of it all." Of course they would meet, and she would sing his songs, some of them better than he could; it was perhaps destined that they would become lovers, these two attractive young people, the same age, in an era when such youngsters were more likely to become lovers than not.

"I wanted people to hear him," Baez remembered. "I think we liked each other, and I really loved him." Her impressions of Dylan in her memoirs are touching. She recalls an afternoon they spent in a hotel overlooking Washington Square. "His eyes were as old as God, and he was fragile as a winter leaf. . . ." She thought of herself as a "fellow outlaw, queen to his jack, and a twin underground star." He was self-absorbed and restless with her. "His indescribably white hands moved constantly: putting a cigarette almost to his mouth, then tugging relentlessly at a tuft of hair at his neck, inadvertently dumping the cigarette ashes in dusty cavalcades down his jacket. He would stand thinking, his mouth working, his knees flexing one at a time, right, left, right, left." She loved his dry humor. She describes a characteristic expression as he started to laugh. "His lips would move from a genuine smile to a pucker. Then instantly, he would tighten them back in, until a tiny convulsion of laughter would bring them back to the smile. . . ." The flickering smile and pucker—à la early Brando—became a lifelong feature of Dylan's performing mask, so that his face sometimes looks like a ground of comedy and tragedy struggling for domination.

Because she adored him and admired his songs she wanted him to be as successful as she was. "I wanted to take care of him. . . . I mean, brush his hair and brush his teeth and get him on stage. . . . I wanted to have as many people hear him as possible." That was fine with him. They sang together at Newport in July 1963 and everybody loved it. If she wanted to invite him onstage to sing with her at the Camden County Music Fair in New Jersey a few days later he would not refuse. It pleased Joan Baez to have him sing with her at a concert in Asbury Park on August 10, and at concerts in Connecticut and Massachusetts before she introduced him as her special guest to a crowd of 15,000 at Forest Hills Stadium in New York on August 17, 1963. People had paid good money to hear Joan Baez solo. Yet in deference to the Queen of Folk Music they listened to Dylan howl the epic "Hard Rain" and the gut-wrenching "Only a Pawn in Their Game" before she joined him in the spotlight for three of his compositions, including "Blowin' in the Wind."

At the Hollywood Bowl in October some of Baez's audience politely protested Dylan's taking up fifteen minutes or so with the "long version" of the pantheistic artsong "Lay Down Your Weary Tune." Joan Baez did not care what the crowd thought, although her management may have. She had achieved her goal in advancing Dylan's career.

A year later they would perform together again, but he would mostly be inviting *her* onstage to sing duets, at Newport, in San Jose and San Francisco. He was glad to return the favor she had done him. They spent much of the summer of 1964 together at Albert Grossman's house in Woodstock. The lovers talked of marriage, both of them ambivalent about it. "Luckily," Baez recalled, "we both had enough sense to realize that it would have been a complete disaster." Perhaps they understood that the same fate that had swept them together, a stream of music, could draw them apart.

When Baez left Woodstock, Dylan invited an older woman to keep him company there, Sara Lownds, a roommate of Sally Buhler, Grossman's girlfriend. Lownds and Baez were not aware of each other's importance in Bob Dylan's life at the time, or that a romantic triangle existed.

Sometime during the winter of 1964–65 Dylan took rooms at the Chelsea Hotel in New York, where he spent time with Sara Lownds, a stunningly beautiful divorcee with a colorful past. Her father, a Jewish scrap-metal dealer, was murdered by a drunken employee enraged over losing his job. He was shot in the face while standing in a candy store. Lownds, born Shirley Marlin Noznisky in the town of Wilmington, Delaware, in 1939, married the magazine photographer Victor Lownds in New York in 1960, and in October 1961 gave birth to Maria Lownds. Divorced soon after, the bright, energetic woman worked briefly as a model, waitress, and Playboy bunny before taking a position as a secretary and office manager for Drew Associates, a film production company in the Time & Life Building.

Filmmaker Robert Drew remembered her as "extremely gracious and competent." Pennebaker knew her then. He and his partner Richard Leacock "had an operation down on Forty-third Street. She worked as the liaison between that office [Drew Associates], which was organized—with specialized people, reporters or cameramen they would hire we wouldn't have access to normally—and our end, which was half a dozen people we had taken off the streets who were just as crazy as we were, and all they wanted to do was make films. And Sara was the conduit. I really appreciated her. For a while she roomed with Sally."

Dylan's passion for the Jewish scrap-metal dealer's daughter gradually put an end to his affair with Joan Baez, the woman he called his "counterpart" in music, the one whose voice was the perfect complement to his. At first she knew nothing of Sara Lownds, although Baez suffered a growing tension with her lover as they went on tour together in February 1965. Princeton, Newark, Buffalo, Pittsburgh—by the end of the tour in late March they were sleeping in separate hotel rooms. They quarreled over politics. He criticized her activism, calling her naïve; she scolded him for his refusal to "take responsibility" for the youngsters who looked to them for guidance. He was becoming more interested in rock and roll, which left her cold. Despite their differences he found it difficult to let go of his artistic partner, nearly as difficult as breaking up with Suze Rotolo. At the end of March he joined Sara in Woodstock, but in mid-April he was there once again with Joan, who stayed with him until she had to return to work on the West Coast playing solo concerts.

Whatever else he may have felt about Baez, he could be certain of her devotion and a friendship that can only be known between equals. For the time being she was his equal in the world in which they moved. Joan Baez represented a musical tradition and a set of values that had formed him and that he was rapidly outgrowing. In New York he had smoked marijuana with the Beatles. In January he had begun recording songs with an electric guitar and a rock band, songs such as "Maggie's Farm" and "Subterranean Homesick Blues."

Johnny's in the basement
Mixing up the medicine
I'm on the pavement

Thinking about the government
The man in the trench coat
Badge out, laid off
Says he's got a bad cough
Wants to get paid off

There was no way on earth this could pass for folk music: it was up-to-the-minute, streetwise rock of the first order. The fact that it was also first-rate poetry would serve as no excuse for critics that were put off by the drumbeat.

In March of that year, around the time Pennebaker met Dylan to discuss the tour of England, the folksinger's fans were assailed by the curious sound of their hero singing rock and roll on the jukebox. "Subterranean Homesick Blues" had been released as a single. When a journalist from the *L.A. Press* questioned him about the changeup, Dylan said, "I'd rather listen to Jimmy Reed or Howlin' Wolf, man, or the Beatles, or Françoise Hardy, than I would listen to any protest song singers. . . . Sure, you can make all sorts of protest songs and put them on a Folkways record. But who hears them? The people who hear them are going to be agreeing with you anyway." The interviewer mentioned that the folk magazines and many of the folk music fans and performers were putting him down. His explanation was simple: "It's that I'm successful and they want to be successful, man. It's jealousy."

One person Dylan could be sure would not be jealous of him happened to be the Queen of the Folksingers herself, Joan Baez. She loved him and she was successful. This is probably the reason he invited her to come with him to England. On the eve of a major tour in a foreign country where he would be performing acoustic "folk music" solely—a style he had begun to disparage as irrelevant—the twenty-three-year-old poet was understandably anxious. Baez would stand by him no matter what happened. She would see him through this.

Why Baez accepted the last-minute invitation (she had to cancel concerts to accommodate him) is less clear. They were still lovers, although the affair was in limbo. She had always found it difficult to say no to him. Years later she explained that in 1964 she was supposed to do a concert tour in England and "in the middle of that Bobby's rise to fame came so fast that a few months later, we thought we'd go together and do split concerts." Evidently Grossman and Greenhill planned for the joint American tour that winter to continue in England in April, but by 1965 he was more famous than she was.

An article in a British music journal on January 9, 1965, headlined "BEATLES SAY—DYLAN SHOWS THE WAY" launched Dylanmania in the British Isles, a fever at first scarcely noticeable from across the Atlantic except by people who make their living from such phenomena. It no longer made business sense for Dylan to share the stage with Joan Baez in England, whatever he might have thought of the aesthetics.

Maybe he had led her on. Somehow she got the impression that he planned to invite her to sing with him. "I thought he would do what I had done with him, would introduce me, and it would be very nice for me because I'd never sung in England before." Later he denied misleading her: "I told her while we were in the States—that she couldn't sing with me. I told her that before we left. And she came on like a little kitten. . . . Hey, I can fit into her music, but she doesn't fit into my music, my show. It would have been dumb. It wouldn't have added to me, and it would have been misleading to the audience." As films and recordings of the English tour reveal, Dylan is correct. The performances he offered that spring were dark, hypnotic, and intensely personal, a one-man tour de force. They left no space for Joan Baez's folk romanticism and earnest politics.

"Hey sure, sure, come to Europe, you can help me out," is what she recalls him saying. "I thought that meant I would sing with him, and I think probably, originally, he planned on it and then decided against it." But his idea of her helping him had nothing to do with singing. He wanted her there for security, to reenforce his credibility as a folksinger and to help run interference with an increasingly hostile press.

What Pennebaker saw—what he calls Dylan's "abstraction"—was the unraveling of a love affair under the pressures of Dylan-mania in England. As Baez later told writer Anthony Scaduto, "I should have understood his kind of psyche and how he was going to feel. . . . When the plane landed in England, I think Bobby was torn because he was scared and he wanted me by his side." She did not realize this immediately. Baez walked ten feet behind him through a constellation of flashbulbs, not wanting "to impose on his scene." Several times he appealed to her for help before or after a press conference. "Maybe I should have, 'cause maybe he needed me then." But she didn't help because she didn't want to cut in. "Then after that he never asked again, so then I never saw him." That is, she did not see him intimately, although she showed up in the hotel room where Dylan, Grossman, and Neuwirth were entertaining the glitterati of the English folk and rock world, "that stupid revolting scene," she called it, where people blathered, and got drunk and stoned, and worshipped Bob Dylan, and threw dishes out the windows.

"Whatever had happened in Bobby's mind," Baez told Scaduto six years later, "I'd never seen him less healthy than he was in England—he was a wreck and he wouldn't ask me on the stage to sing. And I was really surprised. I was very, very hurt." Pennebaker shot a particularly ugly scene in *Dont Look Back*, in which Dylan and Neuwirth are tormenting Baez and teasing her about her looks, and she is smiling bravely through her tears. "I couldn't believe that he was just being so hurtful." The film captures the moment she kisses him on the head, walks out of the hotel room and out of his life. Sara Lownds replaced her in his bed, although no one could ever replace her onstage as a performer, his counterpart and equal. Together they were magical.

Tom Paxton and his wife, Midge, were present at a notorious party Dylan hosted at the Savoy Hotel in London—the one where

Dylan blew up because some fool had thrown a glass out the window. Paxton told me he was so appalled by the scene, "an awful, awful party . . . we made a point of staying out of the range of the camera. This was not Bob Neuwirth's finest hour, he was really behaving very badly." I asked Paxton to what extent drugs, amphetamines in particular, fueled the deviltry. "I don't know. All I know is that these people around Bob, who were definitely egging him on, were behaving extremely badly *with his imprimatur.*"

Pennebaker did not plan on making a movie about a rock star crashing and burning. He says that he went to England with his handheld camera and no preconceptions apart from an aesthetic preference for the dramas of Henrik Ibsen. If he succeeded, Penny believed, any story he told might have the power of a drama by the great Norwegian playwright. Decades later he has not lost his sense of awe over what he saw through the eye of the camera. Not just Dylan and his entourage but the English public who met them.

"It was a fatter world than Dylan expected. And not just the concerts. In a way they were nothing, bored him a bit, because he just had to stand out there and do it. And people made such a big deal out of it. It was hard for him to back away from it and say, 'Wait! I want to do something else!'"

As the tour progressed, a phenomenon unlike anything the filmmaker had ever seen or heard of was occurring in the English provinces. The American company would show up in a small city like Newcastle where there was *no evidence* that Dylan was appearing. There had been no promotion in advance, "no posters, no ads, no nothing. And there would be people, forty people sitting outside the theater, on the steps, like a Druid Council, waiting for us. It was a funny thing. I thought: Do people know something I don't know yet? I'd better be careful." The groups grew larger as the tour moved through the countryside; they became crowds. "Something was going on that never went on in my life, I guess, so I was interested just to watch. That's what I had learned to do. I'm watching with no idea what to do with it or even where it's going, but just in my head. I'm trying to figure out what is it that interests me here, *why* am I interested in this?"

The answer is simple. Dylan is always interesting in *Dont Look Back*. You cannot take your eyes off him because he consumes the energy of the scene around him.

Eric Andersen actually believes that Dylan is wired differently than the rest of us. "He's a living human being, and I think he has very much *struggled* to be human because his wiring is completely different from everybody else's. I think he was born that way. He picks things up that other people just don't see. Most people would say, 'I see. I've seen enough, that's it, and I'm going to go along with my life and get my pension' or something. They don't want to see any more. The earmark or hallmark of Bob Dylan is his curiosity, and that kind of restlessness would make anybody nervous. And he can't stop. I mean, he is a driven maniac."

Mike Seeger's wife, Alexia, a perceptive lady, felt that it was obvious, encountering Dylan in a casual social situation, that he was taking in far more information than anyone else. He is a conduit, and this sometimes makes him radiant and at other times curiously dark.

"I'll tell you what I think," says Pennebaker, as if he were puzzling over a problem of particle physics. "I've talked to Eric [Andersen] about it. What was Dylan like when I first knew him? It was like the first time you saw a black hole, you thought, what is that? And you keep thinking, I will figure it out. I will watch it and I will figure it out, and you never do."

Pennebaker recalls that the people turning out for Dylan all over England were not kids, by and large; they were intellectuals, older people, university students and graduates. "I mean, it was a very stunning group of people that turned out for him everywhere." And the words that Pennebaker kept hearing: *Well, I like his music but he is no real poet.* "And of course, that's the *land* of poets, so they are thinking of, what, who knows? But I thought right away, he *is* a poet. It's just . . . he hasn't quite learned to speak the language yet."

Darkness at the break of noon
Shadows even the silver spoon
The handmade blade, the child's balloon
Eclipses both the sun and moon
To understand you know too soon
There is no sense in trying.

"He is working on the language. And that's about as interesting a time to meet a poet as you can imagine. You just knew, when he would say things like *She's true like ice like fire*. Like fire! And I thought: Shit, that's astounding! That's really as good as you can do. I thought, he is a poet but he is not a formed one. He is not fully tuned. He is like a guitar with only three strings or something."

So the black hole, the mystery, has something to do with a poet in the state of becoming. More interesting than a "complete" poet is this poet being made, who is drawing the energy of the universe to himself in order to make his poems, and in the process creating a magnetic field that also attracts people, crowds of them, without the help of advance drummers and PR flacks.

"So I kept watching him to see what would happen. I didn't have any idea what to do with it as I shot, none. But I just couldn't stop."

And what about this blend of naïveté and hipness Pennebaker said was unique—the fact that Dylan was naïve and yet somehow always knew what was going to happen and what to do? It reminded me of Andersen's comment concerning Dylan's unerring theatrical instinct.

"Well," said the veteran filmmaker, "Dylan is like . . . I picture the hit men, the hired guns who are waiting to shoot somebody that they know is going to go through a door or his car is going to come around the corner, and they wait. What they are thinking about, what's going on in their head is unimportant because they know *exactly* why they are there. They don't have any question about it. Whereas nobody *else* knows why they are there, until it happens. Dylan had that quality."

CHAPTER 8

Wired for Sound

When Bob Dylan left for England in March 1965 he was a popular American folksinger and songwriter better known for his writing than for his performing. When he returned from London in June, with the lovely Sara Lownds on his arm, he was an international star. Like Robert Frost, T. S. Eliot, and Ezra Pound, he was able to generate a level of excitement in the island nation, adoring crowds, ecstatic reviews, and endorsements he may never have gathered in his sprawling homeland.

Fifty thousand tickets to the eight concerts in England had sold out in hours. It helped that his record company, CBS (Columbia's English affiliate), had begun to promote his records there. His four LPs were in England's Top Twenty, and *Bringing It All Back Home* (with its bold electric side 1) was the number-one album in England. Dylan, Columbia Records, and Albert Grossman all understood that this sort of success would translate into American dollars, and they were hell-bent on "bringing it all back home" to the American public. Upon Dylan's return the record company launched a national promotion campaign that featured the slogan "No One Sings Dylan Like Dylan." Who could argue? What percentage of the public knew what that meant?

What he was bringing home to America at age twenty-four was a different sound and attitude than he had left with. In England he had performed the last of his magical "all-acoustic" concerts that had endeared him to the folk audience and the young intellectuals. He had done so under duress. As Baez recalled, she had never seen him so unhealthy. On his birthday he fell ill of a stomach virus and had to be hospitalized in Paddington for a week. When Baez went to the door of his hospital room to see him, Sara Lownds turned her away. Dylan had turned away from Joan Baez, leaving what fans called "folk music" because the style had begun to seem irrelevant. He was tired of it. "I'd rather see me do rock," he declared. He had already written "I Ain't Gonna Work on Maggie's Farm No More," a personal protest against the pressures he had experienced briefly in the folk music world. And upon returning to Woodstock in June he wrote the bitter and scathing revenge lyric "Like a Rolling Stone," which he likened to a "long piece of vomit" in its mood of composition. "All about my steady hatred directed at some point that was honest. In the end it wasn't hatred. Revenge, that's a better word."

As we listened to him sing "Like a Rolling Stone" in Madison Square Garden a decade later, shouting the lyrics above the carnival piping of Garth Hudson's organ, Dylan still sounds madder than hell at us, every one of us, so full of venom that his voice loses all trace of the melody.

> *Once upon a time you dressed so fine*
> *You threw the bums a dime in your prime, didn't you?*
>
> *Now you don't seem so proud*
> *About having to be scrounging for your next meal. . . .*

Did he have someone in mind when he wrote the tirade, "seeing someone in the pain they were bound to meet up with"? The song is pure theater, theater of cruelty as Dylan had studied it in the smoke-filled bars and railroad flats of Greenwich Village. It struck a chord because most of us have experienced hatred and longed for revenge.

That summer, while "Like a Rolling Stone" was blaring from the jukeboxes, rolling to the top of the charts as Dylan's first popular hit, the singer was fulfilling a long-standing commitment to perform once more at the Newport Folk Festival. Only two years earlier at Newport, flanked by Pete Seeger and Joan Baez, he had been anointed Prince of the Folksingers. And there, the next year, surrounded by his mind guard and handlers, he had disappointed some of the audience by singing more personal compositions, "Mr. Tambourine Man" and "It Ain't Me, Babe," instead of his revered "protest" songs.

This year he would give the performance to end all performances at the folk festival. After a night of rehearsals and a nervous sound check in the late afternoon, Dylan donned a black leather jacket and strapped on a sleek solid-bodied Fender electric guitar for the main, climactic concert, Sunday night. Under a scythe of moon Pete Seeger, in a dulcet-toned introduction, dedicated the show as "a message to a newborn baby about the world we live in," a world where music hath charms to build bridges, create trust, and foster harmony.

Dylan mounted the main stage in the company of blues guitar wunderkind Mike Bloomfield, organist Al Kooper, pianist Barry Goldberg, bass player Jerome Arnold, and drummer Sam Lay. The crowd was taken by surprise, wondering if it was a joke, but they weren't given much time to wonder. The band blasted off with "Maggie's Farm," the guitar riffs sending squeals and squawks of feedback through the overloaded, faulty amplifiers. Dylan was the panther in the parish cat show. The volume was earsplitting. People began to shout and scream and boo. Oscar Brand said, "The electric guitar represented capitalism, the people who were selling out." The assault squad kept rolling. They played so loud the chairs and camp stools shook, hearing aids squealed, people covered their ears, their children's ears, as if the noise were blasphemous. Bloomfield grinned demonically, dominating the mix. When they finished "Maggie's Farm" they played "Like a Rolling Stone" and Pete Seeger had to be restrained—he threatened to cut the wires with an ax. They played one more number, "Phantom Engineer," before retreating to the shadows, discharged in a cacophony of applause, cheers, booing, and invective almost as loud as the music that had provoked it.

Many people have compared this event to the 1913 premiere of Igor Stravinsky's *Le Sacre du Printemps* at the Théâtre du Châtelet in Paris, where the audience booed and threw things and stormed the stage, outraged at the composer's dissonances and savage rhythms. Producer Joe Boyd, who was the stage manager at Newport, has written perceptively about it in his memoir, *White Bicycles*: "Anyone wishing to portray the history of the sixties as a journey from idealism to hedonism could place the hinge at around 9:30 on the night of 25 July, 1965." Boyd wrote this forty years later. His perspective was shaped by a distinguished career in the music business, as parochial as most businesses, and as prone to exaggerate its importance. The claim is grandiose and yet aptly conveys the impact of Dylan's "going electric" on his fans, a million intelligent citizens and their friends, and quite a few self-interested journalists and cultural commentators always inspired by conflict. There was not a riot among the peaceable folk at Newport the night of July 25, but there were a lot of very upset and angry folk music fans. They found themselves arguing with more open-minded spectators, younger ones mostly, who thought Dylan's new sound was just fine. The old guard felt betrayed—politically and aesthetically.

According to many who were with Dylan that night, including his close friend the blues singer Maria Muldaur, he was unrepentant but shaken by the experience. The crowd's response had exceeded his calculations. When asked to dance at a gathering afterward, he told Muldaur, "I'd dance with you, Maria, but my hands are on fire," and then went to sit alone. Like a bold child who has deliberately put his hand on the steam iron, he was blistered and astonished by the heat that made no exceptions, not even for him. Anyone who thinks

Dylan was unaware of the likely hubbub he was creating that night has only to recall Pennebaker's allusion to the professional assassin, or Andersen's comment that Dylan never made a mistake in terms of theater. He would have had to kill someone onstage in order to arouse as much excitement.

A month later Dylan formalized his stage show. He put together a rock band that included the handsome and brilliant guitarist Robbie Robertson, the equally gifted drummer and singer Levon Helm, multi-instrumentalist Al Kooper, and bass player Harvey Brooks.

At Forest Hills Stadium on August 28, 1965, he opened the show solo, with his guitar and harmonica, playing a stunning forty-five-minute set that included "She Belongs to Me," "To Ramona," "Gates of Eden," and a new composition, the eleven-minute, surrealistic tapestry "Desolation Row."

> They're selling postcards of the hanging
> They're painting the passports brown
> The beauty parlor is filled with sailors
> The circus is in town
>
> And the riot squad they're restless
> They need somewhere to go
> As Lady and I look out tonight
> From Desolation Row.

Dylan had been writing some of his greatest songs that summer, exhilarated by his new celebrity and, intoxicated by the poetry of Rimbaud, the Beat poets, François Villon—and of course, Dylan Thomas.

To understand Bob Dylan's experience of literary surrealism and its influence on the ferocious lyrics of 1965 you need look no further than an LP released by Caedmon Records in 1952: Dylan Thomas reading from his works. On one side there is the complete text of that plum-pudding paean to childhood and yuletide "A Child's Christmas in Wales," full of light and sweet laughter; on the dark side of the album are five of Thomas's poems, including "Fern Hill" and "In the White Giant's Thigh," and most importantly the fifty-four-stanza "Ballad of the Long-Legged Bait," Thomas's homage to Rimbaud, an English "Drunken Boat" full of overstuffed metaphors and tortured syntax and gorgeous vowel music.

Whales in the wake like capes and Alps
Quaked the sick sea and snouted deep.

As a holiday gift the Caedmon album made its way into every middle-class household in America in the 1950s and '60s with a pretense to culture, smuggling under its sleeve the contraband, subversive poem "The Ballad of the Long-Legged Bait," a thinly disguised allegory of a marathon sexual encounter and its consequences. Thomas's Welsh accent was gorgeous, seductive. We listened to "A Child's Christmas" until we had memorized most of the story, and wanted more. Curious about the poems beneath, we turned the black vinyl over and discovered "Fern Hill," "Do Not Go Gentle into That Good Night," and "The Ballad of the Long-Legged Bait," and memorized those, too.

The impact of that Caedmon album on the poets born in the 1940s was immense, because more than any book on the shelf it was a three-dimensional presence every December, like Nat King Cole's "Christmas Song." People who had never heard of Rimbaud, André Breton, or Federico García Lorca were suddenly hypnotized by the dislocated, mind-expanding metaphors of Dylan Thomas, challenging logic, probing the subconscious. If logic and science had failed our parents and sent us scurrying under our desks for cover then perhaps this beautiful *dérèglement des sens*, this poetry of hallucination, might be the key to salvation.

The crowd loved Bob Dylan's solo set at Forest Hills that August. But when he came back after the intermission with his rock band they were not welcome. There was booing. Catcalls and insults mixed with the applause. The new songs, including the surrealistic pageant "Tombstone Blues" and the bitter "Ballad of a Thin Man," were confrontational, as if they had been written to complement or answer the hostility.

> *Because something is happening here*
> *But you don't know what it is*
> *Do you, Mister Jones?*

So they booed him in Forest Hills and it made headlines. The *New York Post* sent Nora Ephron and Susan Edmiston to interview him in Grossman's Manhattan office. Dylan sat bouncing his knee and chain-smoking cigarettes, wearing an op-art patterned blue and red shirt, a blue blazer, and high-heeled boots with sharp toes. They asked him about his new sound, which people were calling "folk rock." And how did it feel to be booed? "I thought it was great, I really did. If I said anything else I'd be a liar."

The journalists wanted to know why he had gone from making acoustic folk music to playing with a rock quartet. Dylan explained that he was doing fine before, "it was a sure thing, but I was getting very bored with that. . . . I was thinking of quitting. Out front it was a sure thing. I knew what the audience was gonna do, how they would react." So his performing had become automatic and his mind would wander. "It's so much of a fight remaining totally there all by yourself. It takes too much. I'm not ready to cut that much out of my life."

He would never be ready for that sacrifice again. In fact, Bob Dylan gave no more than fifty-five solo concerts in his career, from Carnegie Chapter Hall in November 1961 to Royal Albert Hall, London, in May 1965. This now seems incredible but it's true. Perhaps two hundred thousand people saw those recitals live—if that many—and yet he would always be held to the standard he set in them, a level of intensity he confessed he was not willing or able to sustain.

Dylan tried to explain to the interviewers—and there were many that year—that the band provided not only musical support for new songs, but moral support in the vulnerable posture one assumes in live performing. "It's very complicated to play with electricity. . . . You're dealing with other people. Most people [musicians] don't like to work with other people, it's more difficult." Of course he meant more difficult technically, not emotionally. He told the journalists that when he started out there was no way he could maintain a band, as much as he might have preferred that. "And I like people. What I'm doing now—it's a whole other thing. . . . I know what I'm going to say, what I'm going to do. . . . The band I work with—they wouldn't be playing with me if they didn't play like I want them to." The interviewers remained puzzled, rephrasing the tiresome question: *What made you change? Your trip to England?*

"I like what I'm doing now. I would have done it before. It wasn't practical to do it before. I spend most of my time writing." At last he has come to the crux of the matter. He is first and foremost a poet, and the presentation of the songs has always taken a backseat to their creation, ever since he began composing songs in earnest. Does Nora Ephron, or Robert Shelton, or even Pete Seeger have any idea of what it is like to write "Hard Rain" or "Mr. Tambourine Man," the labor and the ecstasy of bringing such works into the world? Watch the film footage of Dylan performing "Mr. Tambourine Man" for the first time at Newport 1964, and you can see the joy in his face; he is positively incandescent. As he once told Mick Jagger: "The difference between you and me is that I might have written 'Satisfaction.' You could not have written 'Mr. Tambourine Man.'" This is not vainglory but a simple statement of fact from friend to friend. The cynic H. L. Mencken once said that if the German people had known the degree of Beethoven's pleasure in the act of composing his violin concerto they would have lynched him in a fit of envy.

"I had to get where I was going all alone," he told the women, struggling to explain that the new songs were only possible to perform with the band he had neither the time nor the resources to employ when he was starting out. "And I know it's real," he added, meaning that the feeling in the songs was as authentic as ever. "No matter what anybody says. They can boo till the end of time. I know that the music is real, more real than the boos."

So they booed him at the Hollywood Bowl on September 3, though not so furiously. He played an encore for them, "Like a Rolling Stone," and then went to a huge party where he met Marlon Brando. The band was headed for Texas for two concerts, and Al Kooper begged off for fear of his life: if they had killed John F. Kennedy in Dallas, what might the crowd at the Southern Methodist University Coliseum do to the band that had corrupted the Prince of Folk Music? Kooper had underestimated the appeal of the new sound. In Texas the audiences were more receptive than they had been in the North.

At his homecoming at Carnegie Hall on October 1 they were too hip to boo the electric Dylan. But the next night at Symphony Hall in Newark the booing started again after the acoustic set, as the band cranked up "Tombstone Blues."

The sweet pretty things are in bed now of course
The city fathers they're trying to endorse
The reincarnation of Paul Revere's horse
But the town has no need to be nervous.

That was the number that got under their skins, disturbing the peace, the one where Mama is in the factory, barefooted, and

Daddy's in the alley
He's lookin' for the fuse
I'm in the streets
With the tombstone blues

The long, drawn-out vowel of the last word rhymed with the boos in the hall, an invitation, a musical provocation. They booed him up and down the eastern seaboard, from Atlanta to Baltimore, in Princeton, Providence, Burlington, Boston, Hartford; they booed him all October in the East and then in November they booed him in the Midwest, in Minneapolis, Buffalo, Cleveland, Cincinnati. In big auditoriums people were paying good money and lining up to see the old Dylan play his acoustic set, and then to yell, stomp, and boo through the second half of the show. Robbie Robertson told biographer Howard Sounes, "It was a very interesting process to pull into a town, set up, play. People come in. They boo you. You pack up. You go on to the next town. You play. The people boo you. And then you just go on. You go all the way around the world with people just booing you every night." It wasn't always like that. Sometimes the audience was more polite.

Some of the band members were discouraged and demoralized by the experience. Levon Helm quit in November and went to work on an oil rig. To this day he marvels at Dylan's courage in the face of the crowd's constant antagonism: "By God, he didn't change his mind or direction one iota," Helm told Sounes. "Bob is a funny guy like that. He don't care, you know."

Dylan didn't care about the booing because he was having the time of his life, writing and performing many of his greatest songs—the pieces that would dominate the set list we heard in Madison Square Garden in 1974: "Just Like Tom Thumb's Blues," "Rainy Day Women #12 & 35" ("Everybody must get stoned"), "Just Like a Woman," "Like a Rolling Stone." He was in a magical zone. In August he finished recording the album *Highway 61 Revisited*, including "Tombstone Blues," "Ballad of a Thin Man," "Queen Jane Approximately," the title cut, "Just Like Tom Thumb's Blues," and "Desolation Row." Within a half year he would write most of the songs for his next album, *Blonde on Blonde*: "Visions of Johanna," "Leopard-Skin Pill-Box Hat," "Just Like a Woman," and "Sad-Eyed Lady of the Lowlands." Swept up in an inspiration like that, fueled by mob hysteria, media attention, and pharmaceuticals, the twenty-four-year-old poet was not fazed by the booing that became a predictable part of his reception.

He was not like Levon Helm or Robbie Robertson, the guys in the band; he was—for a time—an American Orpheus, son of Apollo and the muses, fireproofed for a romp through hell.

Dylan had purchased a rambling house on a woodland hill in the Catskills, a mile from Woodstock Center, on Camelot Road, in the old artist's colony of Byrdcliffe. "Hi Lo Ha" was a dark, Arts and Crafts–style mansion with eleven rooms, a spacious garage, a basketball court, and a mountain creek that fed a swimming hole.

In October Sara was in her third trimester of pregnancy. On a rainy, chilly Monday before Thanksgiving, November 22, 1965, a judge married them in a private ceremony at the county courthouse in the village of Mineola, Long Island. There was a new moon—it was a time for beginnings. No one witnessed the nuptials but the late Albert Grossman, a lawyer named Saul Pryor, and a maid of honor whose name is probably known only to the Dylans.

Bob Dylan did not want it known that he was married, and when rumors circulated, as they will, he denied them, even to friends like Jack Elliott. Five days after he said his vows, Joseph Haas of the *Chicago Daily News* was interviewing him in the Windy City. When Dylan was asked about his family he replied: "Well, I just don't have any family, I'm all alone." When Haas said that he sounded as if he was terribly separated from people, Dylan explained that it was simply a habit. "It's just the way I am. I don't know, I have an idea that it's easier to be disconnected than to be connected. I've got a huge hallelujah for all the people who're connected, that's great, but I can't do that. I've been connected so many times. Things haven't worked out right, so rather than break myself up, I just don't get connected."

There were two good reasons for the Dylans to keep the marriage quiet as long as they could—not including her advanced pregnancy, which in 1965 would raise eyebrows. One was personal: Bob Dylan was beginning to weave the cocoon that would protect his wife and children from the public scrutiny that had disrupted his private life over the past year and a half. He sensed that the intrusion might get much worse before it got better, and he was right. The less people knew about his wife and children the better it would be for all of them; look what had happened to Frank Sinatra, Jr.

The second reason was professional. For most of the twentieth century, young entertainers were perceived as more marketable if they were unattached. The wedding of a sex symbol like Frank Sinatra or Elvis Presley would send a hundred thousand female fans into mourning; upon recovering from the trauma, the bobby-soxers would go in pursuit of someone else's records, another handsome face, presumably available. Dylan had established himself not only as a sex symbol in the mold of James Dean; he had also been set up as the rebel poet, the existentialist outsider who disdains conventional politics, education, manners, and morals. Marriage, by a justice of the peace, might seriously dent Bob Dylan's increasingly bankable image. Mind you, this did not keep the man from getting married to the woman he loved, but it did keep him from talking about it.

Sara stayed home while Dylan kept touring. A shy, introspective lady, she did not relish the world of rock stars, late nights on the road, or the loud music. And even if she had enjoyed these things, the road would be no place fit for a woman in her condition. So he continued touring in the West as he had in the East, writing surrealistic songs on his private Lodestar jet and in hotel rooms. They booed him in Seattle on the first of December, and then in Berkeley and San Francisco later that week. In San Francisco, Allen Ginsberg introduced him to his lover Peter Orlovsky and fellow poets Lawrence Ferlinghetti and Michael McClure.

The Beat poets were fascinated by Dylan, an upstart poet who somehow could fill thousands of seats in the Masonic Auditorium. They posed with him, standing shoulder to shoulder, fatally cool, laughing, smoking, outside the City Lights bookstore on Columbus Avenue, where Larry Keenan took their picture. They ate at Asian restaurants, drank coffee in Tosca's Café and red wine at Mike's bar. When time came to continue the tour, Dylan and the band piled into Ginsberg's Volkswagen bus, and Orlovsky drove the poets and musicians on to San Jose, Pasadena, and Santa Monica, where the crowd booed the entertainers. On December 20, he flew back to New York.

Dylan's first child, Jesse Byron, was born on January 6, 1966. The singer had little time to bond with his new family, even if he had the inclination. He was back in Studio A on January 21 working on new songs for the LP that must follow and supersede the excellent *Highway 61 Revisited*. That day, and on the twenty-fifth and twenty-seventh he recorded half a dozen songs intended for the new album. It would take six more sessions in February and March, at Music Row Studio in Nashville, to complete the work of *Blonde on Blonde*, which was wrapped there on March 10, 1966.

Meanwhile, he was touring with the band from February 5 until May 27, twenty-one shows in America, including Hawaii, and twenty-three in Australia, Europe, and England, capitalizing on his new notoriety as a rock-and-roll singer. The half-life of a rock star, unpredictable in the face of audiences impatient for novelty, is usually short; success bears no reliable correlation with the intrinsic value of the product. Albert Grossman understood this and meant to squeeze every dollar out of Dylan's turn in the spotlight. The star himself was an eager partner in the enterprise—at least at first—so Grossman cannot be blamed for the toll that season took upon the poet's body and mind. Nevertheless, a year later, assessing the damage, he would mutter mysteriously about not writing anymore until a certain score was settled: "Not until some people come forth and make up for some of the things that have happened."

While Dylan was on that manic journey, he said it was exhilarating. But he appears to have been in the state of confusion that Clausewitz might call the "fog of war."

Dylan's antagonistic tour in 1966 was unlike any other in American musical history. Entertainers book theaters and sell tickets because the audiences love their work. In Dylan's case the difference between the perception and the reality—the folksinger whom some bought tickets to see and the folk-rock star who then showed up onstage—was so jarring it made people angry. Although he still played his acoustic set first, he did not bring his old enthusiasm to the task. He dressed in a tight Carnaby Street–style houndstooth check suit, and had long frizzy hair, took too much time tuning his guitar, and sometimes slurred the words to the songs or forgot them altogether.

Thin to the point of emaciation, he affected a fay, limp-wristed pose as he played with the band, in imitation of Mick Jagger. At first the audiences were shocked, then they were furious. As news of his renunciation of his old style preceded him the audience *showed up* angry and would call down curses even before the band's electricity was turned on. The shows became interactive, like the experimental theater of Jerzy Grotowski and Julian Beck. No matter how well the band played or how clever the new songs were, a loud contingent of the audience hated the sound because it was unlike the Dylan of the first three albums, the Dylan they thought they had paid to see.

So in addition to the normal pressures of touring—jet lag, the grinding rehearsals for a complex repertoire, the sound checks, natural performance anxiety, and the need to maintain an explosive energy level—there was the added weight of the public's hostility. The historic tour of Dylan and his band in 1966 was a little like guerrilla warfare on both sides of the footlights. This may have been exhilarating but it was hardly pleasant.

And all these demands and assaults had to be met in the heat of a treacherous historical moment: 1966 was the year the international community raised its voice against U.S. policy in Vietnam. The bombing of North Vietnam began one week before Dylan began his U.S. tour in the mid-Atlantic states, and in the major cities here and abroad there were International Days of Protest. If Bob Dylan, our de facto poet laureate of protest, had nothing to say on the subject (and he refused to comment on it), the public, especially abroad, might interpret his silence as tacit approval. They would be even more likely to assume this when his song lyrics smacked of anarchy.

Many hipsters, influenced by Timothy Leary's bestseller *The Psychedelic Reader*, were experimenting with LSD and other mind-expanding drugs. They had followed the Harvard psychologist's advice to "turn on, tune in, drop out." These youngsters, fans of the psychedelic Jimi Hendrix and the Jefferson Airplane, were not interested in political activism against the war in Vietnam, or much else. They rose above and beyond such mundane conflicts in a haze of hashish. Logic had failed America, and now young Americans were rejecting it wholesale—the logic of war, of politics, the logic of legal and religious institutions—in favor of a pure and playful hallucination, a new Dadaism. The Bob Dylan of 1966, the composer of the anarchic "Rainy Day Women #12 & 35," sang a pleasing ditty to the Dadaists.

> *Well, they'll stone you and say that it's the end.*
> *Then they'll stone you and then they'll come back again.*
> *They'll stone you when you're riding in your car.*
> *They'll stone you when you're playing your guitar.*
> *Yes, but I would not feel so all alone,*
> *Everybody must get stoned.*

The song, in the face of furious protest by parents, teachers, preachers, and pediatricians, reached number two on the *Billboard* charts in 1966.

Bob Dylan's use and abuse of drugs is documented in the works of other biographers (Clinton Heylin, Robert Shelton, Bob Spitz, and

Howard Sounes). The singer himself has referred to his drug and alcohol use in interviews and other public statements. What matters here is not so much what Dylan did with drugs as what controlled substances did to him.

There is a widespread belief that Dylan began writing his more personal and surrealistic lyrics under the influence of "mind-expanding drugs." The song "Mr. Tambourine Man," in which the singer begs the musician to "take me disappearing through the smoke rings of my mind," is presumed to have been composed in a hashish fog while Dylan sat on the floor of a room over a Woodstock café cutting and pasting kaleidoscopic collages. He has repeatedly denied writing under the influence of drugs, and as candid as he has been about his drug use there is little reason to doubt him on this issue.

The idea that writers get stoned in order to write great poetry is a canard, a romantic notion begotten of a single anecdote in the life of Coleridge and a few poems of that exceptional teenager Arthur Rimbaud. Writing poetry at the technical level of "Mr. Tambourine Man" requires both talent and an intense focus, unclouded by drugs or alcohol.

Several interviews from 1966 capture Dylan's state of mind, his manic energy at the edge of exhaustion, his anger and paranoia. It is hard to say what part drugs might have played in Dylan's mood shifts. Robert Shelton sat across from him on a midnight flight from Lincoln, Nebraska, to Denver on March 13 and recorded hours of conversation on a reel-to-reel tape recorder. The widely reprinted "eight miles high" interview with Dylan is not so much a dialogue as a hyped-up rap rhythmically similar to what was going on after hours in college dormitories from Cambridge to Berkeley.

"It takes a lot of medicine to keep up this pace," Dylan began, exhaling a blue cloud of cigarette smoke. "It's very hard, man. A concert tour like this has almost killed me. It's been like this since October. . . . It really drove me out of my mind." So why is he doing it? "Because I want everyone to know what we're doing." Yet he insists, vigorously, that "I really just don't *care*—honestly don't *care*—what people say about me. I don't care what people think about me. I don't care what people know about me."

He cares about them knowing, but he doesn't care what they think.

When Shelton asked Dylan what would make him happy, the poet gave him an answer that has remained constant, in variations, throughout the years, in many interviews. "I'm happy just to be able to come across things. I don't need to be happy. Happiness is a kind of cheap word. . . . This next year, I'm going to be a millionaire, but that means nothing. To be a millionaire means that next year you can lose it all." The one sure thing is the music: "I love what I do. I also make money off it. . . . Hey, I sing honest stuff, man, and it's consistent." He really appreciates that the money enables him to employ people. Musicians first. And then assistants like chauffeurs and bodyguards, ironically so that he can recapture the peace of mind he had before he was famous. "If I had no money, I could walk invisible. But it costs me money now to be able to walk invisible."

The composer David Amram, a pivotal figure in the New York art world who linked uptown with downtown, Leonard Bernstein and Arthur Miller with Thelonious Monk and Jack Kerouac, met Dylan in the early sixties. One night he and Dylan were strolling through Greenwich Village, and they passed a splendid town house. Dylan has always been fond of peering in folks' windows—seeing without being seen. Through the front window they spied some well-dressed middle-aged people sipping cocktails, making conversation. For a while the musicians just watched from the street, invisible to the partygoers. They looked prosperous, dignified, and to Amram, like "a bunch of rather tense people, not like the people we would be hanging out with."

Dylan said, "I don't know what kind of scene that is. But if I walk in there it's going to change." And so they knocked on the door and announced themselves. "We walked in there, and sure enough everything changed. There was dead silence. Then all of these older, very prosperous-looking people began fawning and gawking at Bob, forgetting whatever they had been doing before we walked in the door. It was like the pope had arrived. I was just blown away by it. Imagine what it must be like to deal with that all the time."

Dylan would spend the rest of his life as a public figure striving for, and craving, "invisibility." For some celebrities this is a simple matter of wanting to be left alone by fans and the press; for Bob Dylan there is the further complication of needing "to come across things" as an artist, to explore the world and human interaction without disrupting it by his presence.

Flying high with Robert Shelton on the plane toward Denver, Dylan talked candidly and volubly about everything from drugs to poetry. Did he consider himself a poet? On this subject he is always humble—or evasive. "To tell anybody I'm a poet would just be fooling people. That would put me in a class, man, with people like Carl Sandburg, T. S. Eliot, Stephen Spender, and Rupert Brooke. Hey, name them—Edna St. Vincent Millay and Robert Louis Stevenson and Edgar Allan Poe and Robert Lowell."

The only living poet he praised unconditionally was his friend Allen Ginsberg. "I know two saintly people. I know just two holy people. Allen Ginsberg is one. The other, for lack of a better term I just want to call 'this person Sara.'" Of course this is Dylan's wife, who is at home nursing the two-month-old baby. "What I mean by 'holy' is crossing all the boundaries of time and usefulness. . . ." *How is Sara holy?* "I want to keep her out of this. I don't want to call her 'a girl.' I know it's very corny, but the only thing I can think of is, more or less, 'madonna-like.'"

I want to keep her out of this. He was successful. In the words of David Amram, who knew her well, Sara was "extremely beautiful, sensitive, a lovely woman, and I always enjoyed her company. She was wonderful with all those kids, really fun to talk to and to be with." She was also an intensely spiritual, reflective woman who knew the tarot cards and the *I Ching*, and had read Dante well enough to in-form her husband that there was a special place in hell reserved for critics. Maria Muldaur called her "beautiful, elegant, and serene."

At the time when Dylan and Shelton were flying toward Denver and his three-month international tour, Sara was his lifeline, his earthbound connection with home and the future ("crossing all boundaries of time and usefulness"). Shelton perceptively commented on the volatility of the poet's emotions: "Dylan's ambivalence has confounded everyone who has ever been close to him." And Shelton knew not only Dylan, but Rotolo, Van Ronk, Baez, and Neuwirth. All would agree. "It sometimes confuses him." Shelton recalled that during that night flight in mid-March Dylan "was swinging widely." At one point he confessed: "I have a death thing, I know. I have a suicidal thing, I know. . . . A lot of people *think* that I shoot heroin. . . . I do a lot of things. Hey, I'm not going to sit here and lie to you. . . . I do a lot of things, man, which help me. . . . And I'm smart enough to know that I don't depend on them for my existence, you know. . . ."

Of course, if he was talking about drugs, the twenty-five-year-old performer was not yet smart enough to know that nobody is that smart.

In Los Angeles, early April 1966, before flying to Hawaii and then Australia to perform, Dylan attended a screening of *Dont Look Back*. Watching himself onstage in England nine months before, he had mixed feelings. First he told Pennebaker he wanted cuts because there were scenes in the film that made him uneasy. Twenty-four hours later, after viewing the film again, he told Pennebaker it was okay as it stood. But now he wanted another movie, a movie that would be "more real," one that he himself would direct with Pennebaker in the role of cinematographer.

That is how Penny found himself in England in May 1966, up close to Bob Dylan during his second tour of the British Isles. He was there to shoot footage for the documentary that would be called *Eat the Document,* a film that would never amount to much in theaters although the scenes he captured are quite dramatic and revealing.

The psychologically astute filmmaker watched in fascination as a tragedy unfolded. The difference between the Dylan he had filmed in 1965, whom the Britons had embraced and glorified, and the Dylan who returned to England in 1966 was terrifying. It wasn't the music, which was superb; it wasn't the performances, although the conflict with the audience had reached its highest pitch, with catcalls and booing so loud during the electric set that the band members could scarcely hear themselves think. The shows were uneven but mostly riveting, as Dylan's fury matched the crowd's. The terrifying thing was that the young poet was unraveling, having driven himself beyond exhaustion to a state where he was not likely to survive long with or without medication.

The effect of drugs is evident in the performances captured in the movie. At times Dylan is scarcely able to keep his eyes open during the acoustic set, nodding, slurring his words, losing track of them. At other times, in the electric set, he is manic, twitching, jumping around the stage "like a cricket," to borrow Pennebaker's phrase. "One night when I stayed up all night with him," Pennebaker recalls, "he was trying to instruct Robbie [Robertson, the lead guitarist], and Robbie wasn't really accepting it but he was going along with it. Eventually that led to their severance or something. But at the time Dylan was only thinking about the performances and he really loved being on that stage, jumping around with that band." Pennebaker saw that Dylan was taking amphetamines and other drugs, and recalls "he was scratching all the time, on his cheeks, and somebody said, 'oh, that's the amphetamine.'" In fact it was probably not speed that was causing the itching. That is a distinctive symptom of opiate abuse in its early stages, before the drug user has built up much tolerance.

The most disturbing incident Pennebaker recorded that year occurred in late May, shortly before the final Royal Albert Hall show of the world tour. It was seven o'clock in the morning. The sun had just risen over Hyde Park, and Tom Keylock, the clean-cut English bodyguard in coat and necktie, had been called to take Bob Dylan and John Lennon on a pleasure drive through the streets of London and environs while Pennebaker filmed the stars in conversation.

Keylock is in the driver's seat on the right of the limo while Pennebaker with his camera sits beside him on the left with Dylan directly behind him; Lennon sits to the right behind the driver. Bobby Neuwirth is in a jump-seat across from Lennon. Everybody is smoking cigarettes and wearing sunglasses, but Dylan keeps removing his shades to rub his eyes.

The conversation is rambling and flippant. Dylan looks out the window and declaims: "There's the mighty Thames. That's what held Hitler back, the mighty Thames. Winston Churchill said that." That is about as lucid a sentence as we get from Dylan during the eighteen minutes of film. He sips from a bottle in a bag, and teases Lennon about his crush on Mama Cass, the earth mother singer from the Mamas and the Papas. They trade jokes about the mediocre singer Barry McGuire, each insisting that the other is McGuire's friend. Lennon and Dylan are both intoxicated, but Dylan is dangerously impaired, reeling, slurring his words. He complains of nausea.

"I wanna go back home," he says, mournfully. "I wanna go back home man, see a baseball game, all-night TV. I come from a land of paradise, man." Lennon grunts in a thick English accent, "Sounds great."

"Well, I could make it sound so great that you wouldn't have the capacity to speak."

They roll on in silence, Dylan clearly suffering from vertigo.

"Hey, I'm very sick, man. . . . I'll be glad when this is over, 'cause I'm getting very sick here."

"With the tremors?" John asks.

Dylan asks Penny if he is getting sick, too. Penny leans out the window to get a shot of the wan bard from outside. Dylan begs Penny to come back in, it's too cold. He groans, overcome by nausea. "Aw! How far are we from the hotel, Tom?" The driver assures him it is only five minutes more.

"Oh God, I don't wanna get sick here." Holding his head in his hands, he mutters, "What if I vomit into the camera? I've done just about everything else into that camera, man. I might just vomit into it."

Pennebaker admits, "It'd make a nice ending wouldn't it? Cooking with Dylan, we'll call it."

This outtake from *Eat the Document* ends with Dylan removing his shades, rubbing his eyes, begging the others to get him back to the hotel before he gets sick. Forty-two years later, Pennebaker recalls what occurred after the camera was turned off, as the limousine pulled up to the Mayfair hotel.

"John [Lennon] was terrified because he thought Dylan was going to die. He was on something, and it was like he was OD'ing. John and I had to take him up the stairs of the hotel and John kept looking at me, and I could see that his instinct was to bolt because he didn't want to be around if something happened. He didn't want to get caught up in it. But he stuck with us. And John was a very good friend of Dylan's. John just loved him. And vice versa. They adored each other. And the rest of the Beatles? Paul would come in and play something and Dylan would get up and walk out of the room."

In a later interview with *Rolling Stone* Lennon said that he and Dylan had been using "junk" (heroin) that day.

———

There is another clip, a snippet caught by the filmmaker, of Dylan at the end of his rope, at the end of the line, really—not as notorious as the sequence with John Lennon in the limo, but just as sad.

Sitting on a couch across from a European booking agent, Dylan is wearing a beautiful striped shirt with a fabric like Joseph's coat of many colors. The Italian agent is proposing that Dylan extend his tour to include Italy. The performer is emaciated, pale, and twitching on the couch. He pleads with the suave promoter, who seems unable to take no for an answer. "I wanna go home," he cries, in a voice that is childlike, more terrified than petulant or rebellious. He is rocking back and forth on the couch automatically, as if moved by an engine he can't turn off. He talks wildly of people going up in airplanes, people like Buddy Holly and the Big Bopper, how the planes go up and the planes go down and they crash, and he can't do that.

"I just want to go home," he wails. "I don't wanna go to Italy, no more. I don't want to go anywhere, no more. You end up crashing in the mountains of Tennessee. Or Sicily." He is propping his eyelids open with his index fingers.

"When are you coming back?" the Italian asks.

"I don't know. I just wanna go home. You know what home is? I don't want to go to Italy."

At the end of May Sara went and got him. They flew to Spain for a few days of vacation before she took him home to Woodstock.

His demons pursued him in the shape of overwhelming business obligations and health issues. Two years earlier he had accepted a $10,000 advance from the Macmillan Company for the experimental novel he would call *Tarantula*. He had been working on it, now and again, with little confidence; then, under the pressure of a deadline, he had submitted a draft of the book. Reviewing the galley proofs that spring, he knew it was not good enough for him, no matter what the editors thought. "I knew I just couldn't let that stand," he recalled. "So I took the whole thing with me on tour. I was going to rewrite it all. Carried a typewriter around the world. Trying to meet this deadline. . . . They just backed me into a corner. A lot of invisible people." The invisible people at Macmillan had begun a highly visible promotional campaign with shopping bags and button badges that read Bob Dylan: *Tarantula*? Upon his return from Europe the editors informed him that they wanted his revisions immediately.

Tarantula was not the worst of his problems. Albert Grossman had scheduled an American concert tour of sixty-four dates that was to begin in early August with a performance in New Haven,

Connecticut. Meanwhile, Dylan was working day and night with filmmaker Howard Alk to cut and splice the hundred hours of raw footage Pennebaker had shot for *Eat the Document*; ABC planned to air the film in the fall.

He was in no shape to write a book, edit a film, or play music in New Haven. He was not well enough to negotiate a sensible compromise in fulfilling any of those obligations.

On Friday, July 29, 1966, the news came over the radio: Bob Dylan had been badly injured in a motorcycle crash. The details were vague and troubling. Rumors abounded: the singer was dead, paralyzed, horribly disfigured; he had broken his neck, his back, his nose. There were inevitable premature eulogies comparing him to Shelley, James Dean, and the late Richard Fariña, Dylan's friend, who had died in a motorcycle crash sixty days earlier.

Few people now know what really happened the morning of July 29, and none of those has agreed to be quoted on the subject. The police were not called to the scene immediately, so there is no police report. No one took Dylan to the hospital nearby in Kingston, fifteen minutes away, so there are no medical records. The picture of the doom-driven rock star bent forward on his Triumph 500 motorcycle, his curly locks blown back in the wind, looking the Grim Reaper in the eye as he takes a hairpin turn on a country road—it is an image of romantic immolation that could hardly be improved upon.

Thank heavens there was no motorcycle crash in the neighborhood that morning. There was a motorcycle, and there was a very weary, clumsy poet who wanted to ride on it. He said he had not slept in three days. The dusty, disused vehicle was in Albert Grossman's garage in Bearsville, not ready to be mounted because the tires were flat. Bob Dylan was walking the heavy motorcycle from Grossman's drive down Striebel Road toward Glasco Turnpike, where he would get the bike repaired, and Sara was following him in the car. Somehow Dylan lost his balance on the slippery road and the motorcycle fell on him. That's how he got hurt. That was the motorcycle accident.

Hearing the news in his Manhattan office, Albert Grossman exclaimed: "How could he do this to me?"

Sara drove her husband to the home of Dr. Edward Thaler in Middletown, fifty miles from Woodstock. The physician and his wife Selma made up a bed for Dylan in a guest room on the third floor of the spacious Victorian house. He stayed there on and off until mid-September, and sometimes Sara stayed with him. Thaler had his own surgery and cures. At the Thalers' he was safe from curious reporters and fans, free of agents, publicists, impatient editors, record executives, and television producers. In that sanctuary, and later at his home in Woodstock, Dylan found time to recover from the wounds, psychic and physical, he had sustained during the previous two years.

In an interview with Jann Wenner of *Rolling Stone* late in 1969, Dylan admitted that he stopped touring because "it wore me down. I was on drugs, a lot of things. A lot of things just to keep going, you know? And I don't want to live that way anymore." In that interview he indicates that the motorcycle accident was more symbolic than literal. "I still didn't sense the importance of that accident till at least a year after that. I realized it was a *real* accident." In other words, for at least a year he regarded it as unreal, or feigned for effect, an opportunity to regroup. "I mean I thought that I was just going to get up and go back to doing what I was doing before . . . but I couldn't do it anymore." He may have thought at first that the incident would buy him a year of rest and then he would go back on the road. But a few months into recovery convinced him that he needed years, not months, to reclaim his life.

Pennebaker visited Dylan a few days after the accident, to see how his friend was doing and to discuss the documentary film.

The musician was at home, wearing a soft flesh-colored surgical collar but otherwise all right. "I never quite knew what happened," says the filmmaker. Dylan was extremely irritable and Pennebaker was not sure why. "I found him very unpleasant and also not so interesting. It was like he was caught up in some struggle that he wasn't doing very well in." Pennebaker had the feeling that Dylan might be angry at him because of the way the film was going—although the film was Dylan's project and not his. "These guys, same with Norman Mailer, they don't have the patience to stick with anything. They want it to happen like a stage performance and be done, and that's it. The thing that he was pissed about was that he thought Robbie had taken out his guitar solos. And put Robbie's in instead. And this was unfair. He was having some problem with Robbie. And this was reflected in everything he said to anybody. And I thought: that's not very interesting."

Evidently there was talk of Pennebaker continuing to shoot scenes of Dylan for the film, but Dylan no longer was "interesting" to Penny as a subject. What had fascinated the great documentarian were Dylan's performances and his interaction with the public; now these things had given way to a sullen retirement and convalescence.

On August 19, Allen Ginsberg came up from Manhattan to visit, toting a bag of books, poetry mostly—Pound, Eliot, Yeats, Cummings, and "some ancient poets like Sir Thomas Wyatt, Campion, Dickinson, Rimbaud, Lorca, Apollinaire, Blake, Whitman." Upon returning to New York, Ginsberg told Robert Shelton "he didn't think Dylan was seriously hurt." He needed time to rest, read, and reflect. He had never been a fast reader. When he was younger he lacked the attention to sit for long hours with a book; then for years there had been so many distractions. Now he would build his own library in the living room of Hi Lo Ha and study the books he had not read in college.

Down the hill from the house where Dylan and Sara raised their children in the late 1960s Happy Traum still lives in an elegant contemporary wood-and-glass home he and his wife, Jane, designed. Traum has been a musician all his life, and has been married to Jane for half a century—a rarity in the entertainment world. Could Bob Dylan have enjoyed a similar stability in his family life?

"The only time I might have thought that," says Traum, "is when he was married to Sara, because it appeared to be very stable and he seemed to have completely changed his life in substantial ways. That seemed to be a solid relationship at the time." Traum speaks for quite a few people who knew Dylan in those years. He had spent a good deal of time with him in the early sixties, but "after John Kennedy was shot, I kind of lost touch." For a few years the friends had less contact because of Dylan's altered status in the music world. He moved in a different stratum, while Traum pursued his own career with the New World Singers and as a guitar teacher.

Woodstock drew them together again. The Traums settled in Woodstock in 1966, "and Dylan was living right up the hill here at the time, in Byrdcliffe, right above us. We started a friendship that lasted until he left for the West Coast." Until then they were in touch on almost a daily basis.

Jane and Happy Traum had three children. Their oldest, Merry, became good friends with the Dylans' daughter Maria, who was five years old in 1966; later Traum's son Adam was a playmate of little Jesse Dylan. "We spent a lot of time with him and his family. It was right after his motorcycle accident, so he was . . . well, you didn't see any signs of that. I never saw him struggling with injuries or anything, but I knew the doctor that took care of him. But he really settled down. He stopped smoking for a while. Stopped drinking. Stopped doing anything. He became very much a homebody. We totally enjoyed that. The kids grew up together. It was very much, you know, a family thing."

They went to Hi Lo Ha several times for holiday dinners. "In fact, the first time I ever met the guys from the Band was Thanksgiving of sixty-eight. We were up at their house here in Byrdcliffe, and Bob said 'the boys' or somebody was going to come over. And suddenly in came these guys, looked like they came from the backwoods somewhere, and it was a great night. I remember Richard [Manuel] sat down at the piano and played, and Rick [Danko] sang. It might have been the first time I ever heard 'I Shall Be Released.'"

> *They say ev'ry man needs protection,*
> *They say ev'ry man must fall.*
> *Yet I swear I see my reflection*
> *Some place so high above this wall.*
> *I see my light come shining*
> *From the west unto the east.*
> *Any day now, any day now,*
> *I shall be released.*

Good Thanksgiving fare, the hymnlike tune that Dylan had just written, and Traum is genuinely moved by the recollection of the scene. "That's a pretty great experience to hear something like that around the piano." Everyone, all ages, gathered around the piano while Richard Manuel played and Rick Danko sang "I Shall Be Released," when a few months before it had not existed. The song might never have existed if the poet had not leapt from the runaway train.

"It was an amazing transformation," Traum affirms. "Although I wasn't personally with him during the 'Like a Rolling Stone' period or the trip to England, I've seen footage of that several times, the whole tour. *Eat the Document.* We actually viewed that film with Bob up there in his living room. Kind of fun. I remember him setting up a projector." The film footage leaves little room for doubt that Dylan was manic during that period, out of control. "But when we saw him here, he was transformed into this calm, thoughtful kind of person who was interested in things, and very private. Very quiet. That was the other thing, that he was extremely protected. Not so much by bodyguards or anything, but even the townspeople were reluctant to tell anybody where he lived."

A persistent stream of people came wandering through Woodstock looking for Bob Dylan. They would trespass on his property, knock on his door. "Some creepy things happened, and he got very freaked out about his kids, as you would.

"I think he was trying to live as normal a life as possible. But the fame and adoration and everything else that went on was exacerbated by this period when he withdrew, because suddenly there was even *more* of a mystery about him than usual." So, in a sense, his strategy failed. "In a way it did," Traum agrees. "But in a more important way it really didn't. Pretty much the whole time he was still writing songs and playing music."

"There must be some way out of here," said the joker to the thief,
"There's too much confusion, I can't get no relief.
Businessmen, they drink my wine, plowmen dig my earth,
None of them along the line know what any of it is worth."

"No reason to get excited," the thief he kindly spoke,
"There are many here among us who feel that life is but a joke.
But you and I, we've been through that, and this is not our fate,
So let us not talk falsely now, the hour is getting late."

(FROM *"All Along the Watchtower,"* 1967)

In the spring and summer of 1967, Dylan joined Robbie Robertson, Garth Hudson, Richard Manuel, Rick Danko, and Levon Helm in a makeshift studio in the basement of a pink house they had rented nearby in West Saugerties. At noon every day, five or six days a week, Dylan would show up at Big Pink, make coffee for the slug-a-bed musicians, and start pounding on the typewriter, waking them up.

Between June and November, Garth Hudson recorded about 150 songs on a reel-to-reel tape recorder that ran day and night while the musicians played and raised hell. A poodle named Hamlet dozed on the floor. The poodle was one of the first creatures on earth to hear songs like "Quinn the Eskimo," "Tears of Rage," "This Wheel's on Fire," "Too Much of Nothing," and "You Ain't Goin' Nowhere."

These Dylan originals arose like vapor phantoms out of a cauldron, the stew and brew of American folk and popular music. He would arrive at Big Pink with a list of old chestnuts for the band to cover, ballads such as "Young but Daily Growing" and "Wildwood Flower"; an Everly Brothers tune like "All You Have to Do Is Dream," a soul song like "People Get Ready," Johnny Cash's "Folsom Prison Blues," the flotsam and jetsam of the American song bag, everything from "She'll Be Comin' 'Round the Mountain" and "Nine Hundred Miles" to "Spanish Is the Loving Tongue." The boys would jam with the cover tunes to get the juices flowing, and sooner or later Dylan would pull out the lyrics, some or all of the lines of a new song in progress. He would begin weaving the stanzas and choruses upon the loom of Robertson's guitar riffs, Hudson's rich organ chords, the sharp harmonies of Danko's singing voice.

The Basement Tapes, as they have come to be called, are a precious record of Dylan's creative process—his antecedents and influences, as well as the improvisational, spontaneous shaping of the lyrics in the rhythm of the moment, so what begins as a howl, mumbling, or gibberish gradually takes shape as articulate language. "He would pull these songs out of nowhere," Robertson recalled. "We didn't know if he wrote them or if he remembered them. When he sang them, you couldn't tell." Entire books have been written about the Basement Tapes, most notably Greil Marcus's historical meditation *The Old Weird America* (originally titled *Invisible Republic*), in which the author places the thirty-odd new songs Dylan recorded then in the context of the 1960s folk revival. "If they are a map, what country, what lost mine, is it they center and fix? They can begin to sound like an instinctive experiment, or a laboratory: a laboratory where, for a few months, certain bedrock strains of American cultural language were retrieved and reinvented."

This work with the band inspired and revived him. "We were playing with absolute freedom," Robertson told Marcus; "we weren't doing anything we thought anybody else would ever hear, as long as we lived." Because of that exhilarating freedom Dylan was able to write—in the privacy of his study—a sequence of lyrics whose themes were liberty and confinement, privilege and duress, license and commitment. Knowing the advantages of compartmentalization, he did not share this work with Robertson, Danko, or his other bandmates, fellows of the musical revels at Big Pink. It was secret, occult work that demanded a different mood. In Dylan's living room/library there was a short lectern on which rested an open Bible. Of all his books this was the one he turned to most often. The King James version of the Bible, its rich language and tone, would have the greatest influence on the dozen songs he was writing for his new studio album, *John Wesley Harding*.

"All Along the Watchtower," which takes a cue from the prophecy of the fall of Babylon in Isaiah 21, came to him in a burst of inspiration, during a thunderstorm in the Catskills.

CHAPTER 9

The Poet in the Garden

The big difference between seeing Bob Dylan in 1963 and seeing him in 1974 is that now you could hardly see him. You could hear the band fifty yards away but as one of twenty thousand spectators in a sports arena you had no illusion of intimacy with the singer. You had the feeling he preferred it that way.

He appeared and he disappeared without ceremony. He sang five songs with his band. After shouting the lyrics to "It Ain't Me, Babe," and delivering the spooky, withering put-downs of "Ballad of a Thin Man"—

You try so hard
But you don't understand
Just what you'll say
When you get home

Because something is happening here
But you don't know what it is
Do you, Mister Jones.

he vanished. Covering his exit, the Band sang, pointedly, the song "Stage Fright." They played on for fifteen minutes without the star but we didn't mind much because their songs were terrific; the Band had become famous in its own right, recording pieces of instant Americana such as "Up on Cripple Creek," "Rag Mama Rag," and "The Night They Drove Old Dixie Down." After they sang Dylan's "I Shall Be Released" without him, he reappeared as if the song had summoned him, released him from a self-imposed exile.

In fact, while the Band played "Stage Fright" it dawned on me that Dylan's rapid-fire delivery at the beginning of the concert resulted from nervousness, perhaps terror, as he faced the expectations of tens of thousands of fans. He rushed through "Lay Lady Lay" like a bad dream, his voice quavering and dodging the melody. Then he sang "It Ain't Me, Babe" through clenched teeth, frowning, querulous and defensive, sometimes scolding. The arrangement, particularly Hudson's looping organ lines, sounded curiously like the Beatles' "Rocky Raccoon."

One of my favorite songs, "Just Like Tom Thumb's Blues," a delicately nuanced ballad that chronicles the hero's journey through a drug-induced mindscape south of the border, was leveled by the singer's snarling and shouting of lyrics, especially at the end of lines and stanzas.

> *Now if you see Saint Annie*
> *Please tell her thanks a lot*
> *I cannot move*
> *My fingers are all in a knot*
> *I don't have the strength*
> *To get up and take another shot*
> *And my best friend the doctor*
> *Won't even say what it is I've got*

Tonight Dylan seemed impatient with the story, wanting to put the pathos behind him, like some old embarrassment that might carry him too close to the audience. Stage fright stalked him, fear of the public and anxious concern for a body of work that left him too exposed, too vulnerable, a raw nerve. So on songs like "Tom Thumb's Blues," he took refuge behind a melodramatic vocal surface, "talk-singing" and generally avoiding melody where it might lead to sentiment.

The voice that was once a clear window had become a screen.

Perhaps Happy Traum was thinking about this screen when he later said "the first three or four songs, I didn't like it, and then I realized why. I had expectations." Traum sat with Allen Ginsberg that night. I knew Allen from the poetry world, a small, factious colony in which Allen was always a friendly and accessible spirit. Nearly every time I talked to Ginsberg the conversation turned to Bob Dylan. Allen had been in love with Dylan from the moment they met back in 1963. He probably did not have the same expectations Traum had, having met Dylan after the spirit of irony banished the notes of sentimentality that touched his early work.

Like me, Traum had expected Dylan to show some vulnerability, and sensitivity toward his material. He probably had not heard Dylan play onstage in a decade. "I felt there was no emotion in the concert. It was powerful in a certain way. And there was some kind of emotion, maybe it was anger . . . which is very powerful, but maybe there was a lack of gentleness." That was the flaw: the show was fascinating—full of rage, terror, and ironic humor—but it was pitiless, lacking the pathos everyone knew was in the blood of the songs themselves. Of course, Traum concluded, if Dylan's performance at Madison Square Garden *had not* been so carefully defended against sentiment, "it really would have wiped people out, because those are the most powerful songs."

The bittersweet aroma of cannabis spiced the air.

The last three songs of the first set represented three phases of Dylan's career before and after the manic flowering of the mid-sixties: "All Along the Watchtower" (late 1967), "The Ballad of Hollis Brown" (1962), and "Knockin' on Heaven's Door" (1973).

We learned the words to "Watchtower" when the song came out in that anxiously awaited, pensive album *John Wesley Harding*, Christmas of 1967. Dylan appeared on the sepia cover, smiling, with a fringe of beard, looking no worse for wear, standing against a tree trunk flanked by two wandering Indian minstrels in robes and beads, the Bengali Bauls. In 1967 rock and roll had gone rococo and psychedelic. After the Beatles released *Sergeant Pepper's Lonely Hearts Club Band* and the Jefferson Airplane put out *Surrealistic Pillow* that year, Dylan's *John Wesley Harding* album sounded old-fashioned, almost quaint. Some fans of *Blonde on Blonde* and *Highway 61 Revisited* were so disappointed by the new record's humble production values (only a bass, a drum, and a steel guitar to support Dylan's voice, guitar, and harmonica) and the songs' archaic tone, they gave up on the singer. Like those who stopped listening to Dylan after *Bringing It All Back Home* (1965)—after he went electric—some fans of *Blonde on Blonde* would not sample Dylan's music after the motorcycle accident, no matter what he sang.

Pete Seeger once confessed that he didn't listen to records much. But when *John Wesley Harding* came out in the winter of 1967–68 he listened to it over and over. Near his house in Fishkill, New York, he had built an indoor skating rink with an outdoor sound system. He would put Dylan's album on the turntable and meditate on the lyrics as he skated round and around the rink. In 1968, Seeger was one of many who were relieved that Dylan had survived some sort of ordeal that began to look as if it were not physical. Once again he had returned from that place "where black is the color and none is the number," with a dozen songs, a song cycle really, as powerful and cohesive as any he would ever write.

Albert Grossman observed that while most lyrics proceed in a linear fashion from beginning to end, many of Dylan's songs are written in a "circular" fashion. He meant that the narrative or the rhetorical movement of the lyric ends where it begins, returning at last to its source. Perhaps such songs are more like a Möbius strip;

when one has come to the end of the verses one is on the inside rather than the outside but once more at the beginning.

In his year and a half of seclusion and convalescence, Dylan had constructed a dramatic persona fit to utter the parables, meditations, and optimistic love songs that make up *John Wesley Harding*. As restrained as it sounded in 1968—a turbulent year of antiwar protests, assassinations, and race riots—*John Wesley Harding* had infinite depths and dimensions. This was a work of deceptive ambition. From the opening title track, the legend of the western Robin Hood who "traveled with a gun in every hand" and "was never known / To make a foolish move," to the gentle, consoling "I'll Be Your Baby Tonight," which turns the lights out, Dylan wove an allegorical tapestry of the outlaw who takes up arms against the world of men and ideas, seeking redemption and freedom; at last he finds salvation in the arms of his true love.

The figures of his allegory are explicit. In "Drifter's Escape" the hero is tried for a crime he cannot understand, and is saved from the "cursed jury" when a bolt of lightning strikes the courthouse; the epistolary "Dear Landlord" is a thinly veiled plea to all agents, managers, producers, and editors not to put a price on Dylan's soul.

> *My burden is heavy,*
> *My dreams are beyond control.*

His art, like his dreams, will not answer to any authority, politics, or the needs of the marketplace. "Dear Landlord" is delicately balanced, a letter that states his case with all due respect to the proprietor, closing with the surprising promise:

> *Now, each of us has his own special gift*
> *And you know this was meant to be true,*
> *And if you don't underestimate me,*
> *I won't underestimate you.*

This is as clear a statement of hard-earned wisdom as we could ask of the man who has suffered from a business connection that demanded more of him than he estimated, while expecting he would endlessly deliver a product that was elusive and wildly variable.

Madison Square Garden was no place for the poet to render the allegorical subtleties of "Drifter's Escape" or "Dear Landlord"; it was a cavernous arena that demanded sound and fury, and more sound.

So the only selection from *John Wesley Harding* he played for us was the oracular, portentous "All Along the Watchtower." The force of the song is monolithic, a boulder running downhill that does not depend upon the precise functioning of intricate parts. The Joker tells the Thief essentially the same thing Dylan tells the Landlord: businessmen have consumed his goods without any idea of their value. The Thief explains that he and the Joker have passed through that state of ignorance. The two of them—both sides of Dylan's Gemini personality—can look toward a more serious destiny. But the hour is late.

Two riders were approaching, the wind began to howl.

The song, as performed, was one long howl from beginning to end. The melody is little more than four measures that follow three basic chords, A minor, F major, and G major, the same chords and notes over and over again for forty-eight measures. To say that the tune is monotonous is beside the point; like "Masters of War," when played forcefully—as it was in the Garden—with the machine-gun fire of Robertson's guitar and the buzzing, circus tone of Garth Hudson's organ, the effect is hypnotic. This is one of Dylan's shortest lyrics and no one ever wished it a line longer.

On this night Dylan sang "Watchtower" quickly, growling, drawing out the last word of every line, shouting some, and at the end leaving time for his lead guitarist to tear off a wild, wailing guitar solo in homage to Jimi Hendrix. The avatar of psychedelic rock had covered the song in 1968 and made it his own, dressing the simple melody in the ornate outfit and guitar embellishments suitable to the high sixties. Hendrix, himself a victim of the confusion and excess the song portends, lived just long enough to make it famous, dying in 1970 of an overdose. When Dylan started performing this piece live, in 1974, with his band, he played it in the florid manner of Jimi Hendrix, in honor of that ghost of the 1960s.

After the cheers and the whistling died down we heard the plucking of a minor melody on Robertson's lead guitar. Then he strummed forcefully, and Levon Helm started up the bouncing 2/4 rhythm on the drum kit. It might have been the opening to a down-and-dirty Billy Boy Arnold tune like "I Wish You Would" or a Bo Diddley shaker. But when Dylan started singing, the lyrics came as a surprise.

> *Hollis Brown he lived on the outside of town*
> *With his wife and five children*
> *And his cabin breakin' down.*

The performance of this 1962 composition—one of Dylan's first great songs—demonstrated that a piece that had been made for solo performance on acoustic guitar could feed the energies of a quintet. The rock arrangement of the early song was a perfect fit for the tragedy's inexorable momentum. He sang "breakin' down" instead of "falling down," the original lyric. Was this a slip of the tongue or an expressionistic variation?

> *Way out in the wilderness*
> *A cold coyote calls*
> *Your eyes fix on the shotgun*
> *That's hangin' on the wall.*

Now as he sang he followed his melody while concentrating on the story. At last he was telling the story, as he had a decade earlier, inhabiting that world of hardship and desperation where catastrophe is certain. His voice, which tonight had been a screen (a fascinating painted screen), became a window. He was in fact *inside* the story more completely than he had been in 1963, older now, a husband and the father of five children himself.

After the driving rhythm of "Hollis Brown," Dylan and the Band slowed down to pick up a new character, the town sheriff of the movie *Pat Garrett and Billy the Kid*. Dylan had spent most of the winter of 1972–73 in Durango, Mexico, acting the role of "Alias" in Sam Peckinpah's film. His performance was only tolerable but he did write some memorable music for the sound track. A year earlier he had composed "Knockin' on Heaven's Door" for a scene in which a wounded sheriff is dying while his wife watches over him:

> *Mama, take this badge off of me*
> *I can't use it anymore.*
> *It's gettin' dark, too dark for me to see*
> *I feel like I'm knockin' on heaven's door.*

The song was recorded the same month the cease-fire was declared in Vietnam, officially ending U.S. involvement in that long and demoralizing conflict. The lyric suited America's mood. Elegiac, falling from D major to A minor at the end of every verse, the song is simply two quatrains and the refrain "Knock, knock, knockin' on heaven's door," a tune easy to learn, so everyone could sing along. Released in July 1973, it became a surprise hit.

Now Dylan delivered the lyric—as he had sung "Hollis Brown"— with his heart and soul in the melody. Rick Danko and Richard Manuel added their voices in soaring harmonies on the chorus.

This was the last number before intermission. Lights came up as the musicians moved to the shadows. My sister and I stayed near our seats, speechless at first, then comparing notes on what we had heard. We agreed that tension and terror had strained Dylan's vocal chords, and made him quaver and rasp; he shouted and "oversang" in order to deliver the notes as best he could. What we were hearing was something graver than common stage fright after years of retirement.

He had good reasons to be afraid of his audience.

In 1965 Phil Ochs had said, "I don't know if Dylan can get on stage a year from now. I don't think so. I mean that the phenomenon of Dylan will be so much that it will be dangerous. . . . Dylan has become a part of so many people's psyches and there are so many screwed up people in America, and death is such a part of the American scene now . . . I think he's going to have to quit." In December of that same year an interviewer at a televised press conference confronted Dylan with Ochs's appalling prophecy; the performer shrugged it off, saying only, "Well, that's the way it goes, you know. I don't, I can't apologize certainly."

Dylan once promised us: "I'll let you be in my dreams if I can be in yours." That was in 1963. A poet who enters somebody else's dream can as easily walk into a nightmare. No one could imagine the kind of impact Bob Dylan was going to have on people's psyches for good or ill in 1963, and while he might have wished for the outcome he had unwittingly created a monster, out of his control, that was making life difficult for him and his family.

For a year or more after his motorcycle accident the world permitted Bob Dylan to live in peace. This was a grace period, a ceasefire. Neighbors in Woodstock were protective, refusing to reveal his whereabouts. His daughter Anna Leigh was born on July 11, 1967, and Dylan's parents came to Woodstock that summer to see the new baby. One of the benefits of Dylan's retirement was that he was able to resume a more regular communication and contact with his mother and father. It was no simple matter to be the parents of a man who—for whatever reason—denied he was your son.

Pennebaker recalls that after visiting Woodstock, Abe Zimmerman came to call on him in Manhattan. Introducing himself as "Mr.

Dylan's father," Abe showed up on Penny's doorstep with his hat in his hand. He spoke meekly, and referred to his wife as Mrs. Dylan. Back in May *Dont Look Back* had premiered in San Francisco, and now the film was in wider release. Abe had not seen it, he said, but some of his friends had. He was concerned that his son had used some off-color language in the documentary and asked the filmmaker if the swear words could be taken out. Gently Pennebaker explained that this was impossible, and that within the context of the movie the language was not generally regarded as offensive.

The Zimmermans' visit to Hi Lo Ha that summer came none too soon. Within the year Bob Dylan would lose his artistic father, Woody Guthrie, who succumbed at fifty-five to Huntington's chorea on October 3, 1967; then Abe Zimmerman, his natural father, died of a heart attack on June 5, 1968, at age fifty-six.

Sara was seven months pregnant and also needed to stay home with the infant, Anna. So Dylan flew alone from New York to Minnesota the next day. His brother met him at Chisholm-Hibbing Airport in the rain. They found the little house where they had grown up filled with friends and relatives, and Dylan wanted to be alone with his immediate family. At the Dougherty Funeral Home on First Avenue the day before the funeral, Bob and David endured an unconventional—and probably unexpected—"viewing" of their father's remains (open caskets are frowned upon in Jewish funeral ceremonies). At the cemetery in Duluth Bob gave in to his emotions, sobbing as the rabbi spoke the final prayers and the dirt rattled upon the coffin. There is no grief like the grief of a son or daughter caught short of time to say goodbye or make amends. There were words he wanted to say and things he wanted to do for his father. Abe had been a more loving and attentive parent than Bob had been a son, and there had not been time to even the score. Dylan was only twenty-seven years of age, and most of the past decade had passed in a firestorm of rebellion, on an epic scale.

When the new baby came on July 30, Bob and Sara named him Samuel Abram, after his late grandfather.

Dylan tells us in *Chronicles* that not long after returning from his father's funeral he got a letter from Archibald MacLeish. At the time MacLeish was the most famous and revered poet living in America. He had won three Pulitzer Prizes, most recently for a Broadway verse drama called *J.B.*, a modern-day telling of the book of Job. He had also served as librarian of Congress, and assistant secretary of state under FDR. This was the sort of poet and man of affairs of whom Beatty Zimmerman and perhaps the late Abraham would have approved. He appears, providentially, in Dylan's memoirs just at the time the poet admits that he longed to share some important things with his late father.

He had always admired Archibald MacLeish, just as he had admired Carl Sandburg and Robert Frost. When Dylan heard that the old poet wanted him to write some songs for a stage play based on *The Devil and Daniel Webster*, he decided to go and see him. He does not say he was flattered or thrilled by the prospect of collaborating with MacLeish, only that visiting him seemed like the civilized thing to do. So in the autumn of 1968, four months after his father died, he and Sara got in the car and drove to Conway, Massachusetts, to MacLeish's stone cottage in a maple grove.

He writes of MacLeish that he was a gentleman of enormous strength and "power bred of blood." With his military bearing and aura of authority, he did not look like any poet of the Left Bank or Greenwich Village. The venerable MacLeish had a good deal to say about Dylan's poetry, all of it pleasing. That the seventy-six-year-old laureate—who had known Pound, Eliot, and Frost—had listened carefully to Dylan's work and took it seriously was a compliment in itself. MacLeish appreciated the lines from "Desolation Row" in which the poet describes the two modernist poets Ezra Pound and T. S. Eliot fighting each other in a tower while calypso singers make fun of them and fishermen stand by holding flowers. He said that he understood what Dylan meant about the poets fighting (although he does not say what, exactly). MacLeish's feeling was that Pound and Eliot were too "bookish," and younger poets would have to make their peace with such commanding figures.

MacLeish said a lot of things to Dylan that he wished his father might have said, or at least heard; Abe Zimmerman, alas, had not quite understood him. MacLeish considered Dylan "a serious poet" and believed his songs would be "a touchstone for generations to come." This was a pleasure to hear, applause from a longed-for quarter of serious readers. In response to Dylan's curiosity about his place in history, MacLeish told Dylan he was an Iron Age poet (of Ovid's historical periods—Gold, Silver, Bronze, and Iron—Iron is the most advanced and corrupt) with a touch of the "metaphysical from a bygone era." He told Dylan how much he appreciated the way his songs engaged social problems. He talked about the distinction between art and propaganda, about Homer, Villon, and the technical challenges of versification.

As the conversation deepened in the twilight, MacLeish asked what Dylan had given up in order to pursue his dreams. Then he offered this advice: the real value of things cannot be measured by what you pay for them, but by what it costs you to gain them. And "if anything costs you your faith or your family then the price is too high." That is as useful a gift of wisdom as any father could pass on to his son.

This dialogue with MacLeish, and Dylan's failed collaboration with the poet on the Broadway play called *Scratch*, frame a full chapter of *Chronicles* called "New Morning." In those pages Dylan has less to say about the play than about his struggle to defend his family's privacy during the years before he went back on the road in 1974. This was not some sort of game of hide-and-seek he was playing with his fans, or a strategy for augmenting his mystique. He really wanted to be left alone to enjoy his wife, his children, and his work, and the public made this nearly impossible.

America in the high sixties was about as chaotic and fractious as it had ever been since the 1920s. The Tet offensive and the My Lai massacre raised the temperature of the antiwar movement. Four

Catholic priests and five activists in Maryland broke into the Catonsville Selective Service office, hauled classification records outside, doused them in napalm, and burned them in protest against the Vietnam War. Martin Luther King Jr.'s assassination caused riots in the cities, incalculable property damage, and forty-six deaths.

At the Democratic National Convention in 1968, National Guardsmen and twenty thousand Chicago police officers armed with nightsticks, guns, and tear gas grenades beat back a screaming mob of war protesters led by Abbie Hoffman of the Youth International Party, Tom Hayden and Rennie Davis of Students for a Democratic Society (SDS), and the Black Panthers. In 1969 American bombers attacked army bases in Cambodia as the war—to the horror of most Americans—escalated. At the end of that year, 300,000 protesters descended on Washington calling themselves the New Mobilization Committee to End the War in Vietnam. Metropolitan police blocked the protesters at the doors of the Justice Department.

Some students impatient with the peaceful ways of SDS formed a paramilitary organization called the Weathermen, or the Weather Underground. They explained that their name came from Bob Dylan's "Subterranean Homesick Blues," his verse that declared no one needed a weatherman to know which way the wind was blowing. The Weathermen favored small bombs, and so every time one blew up near an army recruiting station or a Selective Service office people thought, darkly, of Bob Dylan.

Despite the Paris peace talks, the war dragged on in Southeast Asia and the violent conflict over our policy there continued at home. U.S. troops encroached on Laotian territory, and more and more American soldiers were accused of war crimes and atrocities. On May 4, 1970, a thousand students at Kent State University in Ohio protesting the war—a few miles from where I was studying at Kenyon College—were met by gunfire from National Guardsmen. Four were killed and eight wounded.

Perhaps Kent State was the turning point. Colleges closed down all over America and students networked to plan strikes and demonstrations. Even President Richard Nixon could not ignore the murder of unarmed students by National Guardsmen. Secretary of the Interior Walter Hickel informed the president that his administration was provoking anarchy and rebellion, burning bridges to the next generation. The warning went unheeded. There would not be a cease-fire in Vietnam until January 1973, by which point the toll of Americans killed in combat had reached 45,958.

During these years of undeclared war in Southeast Asia and gnawing strife in America, Bob Dylan—in the manner of Confucius and the Quakers—was making peace. Neil Young could write the anguished "Ohio" about the four students murdered at Kent State. But Dylan was fostering order around him, as best he could, by creating order *within* himself. The most important thing to him was his family. The records he released from *John Wesley Harding* (1967) through *Planet Waves* (1973) were olive branches, oil on troubled waters, whether or not the world chose to hear them that way. What the government had done to subvert our constitutional rights was a horror—the conduct of the war, the promulgation of lies that passed for news. Dylan was making waves gently, awakening us to the possibilities of a nonviolent resistance.

During the four years after his father's death in 1968, Dylan's life was simpler and more peaceful than it would be for many years to come. To his friends and his family he was what he seemed; the albums he made in those years were as transparent, affectionate, and autobiographical as any he would ever make. In love with his wife, devoted to his children, and absorbed in his art, he stayed home.

By April 1968 the subtle collection *John Wesley Harding* had sold more than a quarter of a million copies. With the constant stream of royalties he was able to support his family very well in the house on the hill above Woodstock, without performing.

For a few special occasions he emerged from his retreat to face an audience: a tribute to Woody Guthrie at Carnegie Hall in January 1968; an hour-long set at the Isle of Wight Festival in August 1969 (for which he was paid the handsome sum of $50,000); a few songs for the benefit Concerts for Bangladesh in August 1971 at the invitation of his friend George Harrison. These performances allayed any fears the audience may have had about his accident, as did his appearance on Johnny Cash's TV show on May 1, 1969. He was in glowing good health. Having gained ten pounds, cut his hair, and grown a little fringe of beard, he looked more like a young philosophy professor than a rocker who had traveled in the valley of the shadow of death.

He made a modest album of upbeat country tunes, *Nashville Skyline*, which was released in the spring of 1969 (this included the hit single "Lay Lady Lay"). He tried on a new voice, singing more from his diaphragm than from the top of his head, and when critics marveled and wondered, he laughed and said this was what happened if you give up smoking. A year later he released a more eloquent and personal album. *New Morning* included tender songs of conjugal love such as "The Man in Me" and "If Not for You."

> *If not for you*
> *Winter would have no spring,*
> *Couldn't hear the robin sing,*
> *I just wouldn't have a clue*
> *Anyway it wouldn't ring true,*
> *If not for you.*

There were also songs that hinted that the woodland idyll might not last forever. Perfection has limitations and drawbacks, particularly for a man whose former life had been driven by ambition and the gap between the real and the ideal. Tedium and a slow clock are the price one pays for peace.

> *Time passes slowly up here in the daylight,*
> *We stare straight ahead and try so hard to stay right,*
> *Like the red rose of summer that blooms in the day,*
> *Time passes slowly and fades away.*

Dylan had found a balance between his artistic work and his personal life, and if the fulcrum had to favor one over the other, during those years he would choose life over art. He put his family first. And who could say that his work, during those years, suffered for that decision?

The houselights in Madison Square Garden dimmed and came up again, then the smoky space went dark. We took our seats. The audience started applauding and whistling again as the star reemerged from the shadows.

Bob Dylan returned to the spotlight alone, with his guitar and harmonica, riding waves of applause.

He launched into "The Times They Are A-Changin'" and the audience cheered as soon as they recognized the words.

> *Come gather round people wherever you roam*
> *And admit that the waters around you have grown*
> *And accept it that soon you'll be drenched to the bone*

Since my sister and I had first heard those lyrics eleven years earlier they had become entwined with astonishing events—freedom marches, assassinations, protests against the military draft, landing on the moon. Since 1963 his words and warning had proved prophetic. Now Dylan sang that song at a breakneck speed as if the mere mention of it would suffice to evoke a photomontage of faces and parades, his voice sometimes racing ahead of the guitar accompaniment. The harmonica playing too was hurried and roughshod. Maybe he was even more nervous, facing the audience solo; he performed this famous song as if he couldn't wait to put it behind him, with all that burden of personal and shared history. At the end of every verse he raised his voice above the melody in emphasis.

And the crowd answered him, whooping and applauding raucously, sometimes so loud you couldn't hear him. The people wanted to be heard. The song was theirs now and he was eager to hand it over to them. During this set the audience was never still; the applause ebbed as he sang, and returned to roaring as he finished a number. Before they were done crying out and clapping for "The Times They Are A-Changin'" Dylan started to sing "Don't Think Twice, It's All Right" in an even faster tempo, as if he were trying to run away from us, racing through that story of love gone wrong, strumming furiously instead of finger-picking, the subtlety of which would have been drowned in that din.

Oppressive anger, I thought, steamrolled the nuances of tone. Whatever the singer had given was never enough. "I gave her my heart but she wanted my soul." Dylan sounded as if he were singing in a barrel surrounded by wolves. He was calling out to everyone who had, intentionally or unwittingly, wasted his time.

> I ain't sayin' you treated me unkind
> You could have done better but I don't mind
> You just sort of wasted my precious time
> But don't think twice, it's all right.

Having learned the hard way just how precious his time was, he had settled in Woodstock with his family in 1966 and for a couple of years found peace there. Then strangers began showing up on the road to Byrdcliffe, on the woodland paths, intruders knocking on the door, entering the house day and night without warning.

He and Sara would come home to find strangers copulating in their bed; they would hear the footsteps of spies on the roof. Dylan figured there must be maps to his house posted all over America "for gangs of dropouts and druggies." At first he assumed random homeless people were stumbling onto his property; then it became clear that there was a stream of pilgrims who were looking for the latter-day prophet, the author of "The Times They Are A-Changin'" and "Chimes of Freedom," to come out and preach on the mountainside, to engage in Socratic dialogues with political radicals and organic farmers, to lead "the movement."

He had pistols in the house and a Winchester rifle. And while he disliked the thought of actually pointing a gun in anger, he was exasperated when the local chief of police informed him that he must not fire so much as a warning shot or he would be charged with assault.

And so in September 1969 when Sara was pregnant with their fifth child they bought a house in Manhattan at 94 MacDougal Street. Fortunately, they kept their home in Woodstock because the situation in Greenwich Village was even worse. The big city has provided asylum and relative anonymity for many celebrities of the twentieth century, from John Barrymore and Edna St. Vincent Millay to Greta Garbo and Woody Allen. But not for Bob Dylan. I can remember passing by his house on MacDougal Street in 1970 and seeing red-striped sawhorse barricades on the sidewalk and policemen on patrol.

Even here, in the sophisticated city of New York, strangers were knocking on Dylan's door at all hours. Creeps were going through his garbage looking for clues to his secret life. Demonstrators applied for permits to march up and down in front of the poet's house, shouting for him to show his face and speak, to explain his mysterious retirement, to "lead them somewhere." A pudgy man with a bullhorn lectured and pleaded with him to come out and accept his destined role, his responsibility as the spokesman of his generation.

The neighbors hated this almost as much as the Dylans did, and they could not help but blame him for the disruption of their lives. He said they began to look upon him like a sideshow freak. Soon he gave up and moved out, buying or renting houses in Long Island, Arizona, and California. At each new residence they could count on a few weeks of privacy before some scout would release their address to the local papers; then the whole tour of gawkers and parade of protesters would start all over again.

———————

For him to sing solo tonight, to stand onstage alone, must have taken great courage. For some people in the audience—Happy Traum, Allen Ginsberg, Mike Porco, and Nora Guthrie, friends who had heard Dylan in recital halls in 1963—the solo set the poet delivered in the Garden was the artistic peak of the performance. It did not come easily. The first two songs, "The Times They Are A-Changin'" and "Don't Think Twice," he had offered dutifully and without much finesse by way of warming up his vocal chords and finding his center in that colossal arena with 40,000 eyes upon him.

Ten minutes into his solo set he was ready to navigate the rapids and depths of "Gates of Eden." Written in the late summer of 1964, the lyric is one of several that mark Dylan's transition from the Brechtian speakers of the protest songs to a more personal, authorial voice influenced by Dylan Thomas, William Blake, and the French surrealists. He had been spending a good deal of time with the poet and novelist Richard Fariña in Woodstock and Carmel. In friendly competition Fariña wrote songs while Dylan wrote poems and literary sketches. His concentration on the written word reenforced a dimension in his songwriting that had first come to light in "Hard Rain" and "Lay Down Your Weary Tune," the beauty of language for its own sake, apart from any service to a concept or message.

"Gates of Eden" has a moral design as well as a religious frame of reference. But this is no allegory from *Pilgrim's Progress*, or Miltonic Adam surveying the Eden of Genesis and the surrounding territory. This is a very modern poet in the garden, assessing Eden's place in the scheme of things. His Eden is perfect and unchanging, the world outside chaotic. He begins each stanza with an elaborate flight of fantasy, improbable, illogical, sometimes cruel, the detritus of ambition and longing: a cowboy angel riding on four-legged clouds, holding a blackened candle; a savage soldier and a deaf, barefoot hunter stand on a beach watching ships bound for the Gates of Eden:

> *The motorcycle black madonna*
> *Two-wheeled gypsy queen*
> *And her silver-studded phantom cause*
> *The gray flannel dwarf to scream*
> *As he weeps to wicked birds of prey*
> *Who pick up on his bread crumb sins*
> *And there are no sins inside the Gates of Eden.*

The guitar accompaniment was spooky, underscoring the surrealism of the lyrics, sliding from G major down to F major, tonic to leading tone between stanzas.

The Eden of Dylan's song is an island of the blessed, perfect and pure, defined mostly by what it excludes. There are no kings there, no sins, and no trials. No sound comes from the Gates, although laughter may be heard within, at "promises of paradise" muttered by pretenders outside such as Aladdin and the Utopian monk. Eden is above all the domain of truth: outside the gates truth does not exist; petty discussions of what is and is not real have no place in Eden. This is the one realm in which the cowboy angel's candle can overcome the darkness.

During the applause for "Gates of Eden" I remembered the song that followed it on *Bringing It All Back Home*, "It's Alright, Ma," a meditative lyric much longer and just as concentrated as "Gates." I don't think we could have absorbed "It's Alright, Ma" right away, and perhaps that song would have been too intense for Dylan to sing it live in sequence. So the performer took a breath, tuned his guitar, and sang a very popular short song that had been a Top Forty hit in 1966.

> *Nobody feels any pain*
> *Tonight as I stand inside the rain*

Everybody knows
That baby's got new clothes . . .

We had heard Richie Havens croon this, in his golden-rich voice; we had heard Joe Cocker howl it, and Nina Simone and Roberta Flack transform "Just Like a Woman" into a dark lullaby.

She takes just like a woman, yes she does
She makes love just like a woman, yes she does
And she aches just like a woman
But she breaks just like a little girl.

When he got to the last word of the chorus he drew out the vowel and the *r* sound, making an angry and taunting growl, *girrrrll*, like a boy teasing some sissy in the school yard.

A few feminists had seized upon "Just Like a Woman" as exhibit A of Bob Dylan's misogyny, as if the character depicted in the song was not a particular woman with various attributes of maturity and vulnerability, but all women seen with a jaded eye. Now that seemed absurd—one more case of critics interpreting Dylan's lyrics to satisfy an agenda. There were thousands of critics, hundreds of agendas. None of it mattered, as the singer put all of his feelings into the bridge of the song, changing the chord from the tonic G to the mediant B. The lyric is architectural, framing an interior and exterior space. At the musical bridge the singer comes in out of the rain, dying of thirst, entering the metaphorical house of the relationship (water, water, everywhere, but not a drop to drink). His lover has put a curse on him that will haunt him forever, but far worse than the curse is the pain he suffers *within*, in the heart's home. He is doomed to abandon the place where dwelled his highest hope for sanctuary.

With a full, lush chorus on the harmonica, Dylan finished "Just Like a Woman," indulging the melody to remind us he was more than a wordsmith; he was a composer who had crafted some tunes that the customers could walk away from the show humming.

But no sooner had the applause ebbed to a drone of whispers than we could hear the engine of the guitar start up again, the drop-D tuning the poet so often used for the drumbeat of an epic. Some people began shouting encouragement before he sang the first words.

> *Darkness at the break of noon*
> *Shadows even the silver spoon*
> *The handmade blade, the child's balloon*
> *Eclipses both the sun and moon. . . .*

This was the song above all others that I had longed to hear him sing that night: the companion piece to "Gates of Eden." It was Dylan at his vitriolic best, like Juvenal cataloging the vices of the Roman Empire. The difference in Dylan's composition is the tone; with the exception of the wry title, the lyric is deadly serious. "It's Alright, Ma (I'm Only Bleeding)," weighing in at 113 lines and nearly seven hundred words, was one of Dylan's longest pieces, and as one can tell from the first quatrain scarcely a word would go to waste.

The darkness at noon is a caption metaphor for humankind's interference with nature—this is the song's overarching theme. The simplest inventions, the knife and the balloon, the useful and the playful, separate us from the rest of the animal kingdom. Our consciousness, our tool-making ability, eclipses the light of the sun and moon so that no one is spared from the darkness, not even the rich and privileged, those born with silver spoons in their mouths.

In Dylan's bonfire nothing is spared: he skewers fire-and-brimstone preachers, avaricious educators, ad agencies, old lady judges who legislate sexual morality, bankers, propagandists, and demoralized poets.

> *. . . even the president of the United States*
> *Sometimes must have*
> *To stand naked.*

On January 30, 1974, these lines got the greatest outburst of applause to be heard that night: shrill whistles, catcalls, a hullabaloo and clamor. Headlines in the *New York Times* that morning focused on the scandal in the White House. For nearly two years the police and the Senate had been investigating a break-in at the Democratic Party headquarters at the Watergate building, and evidence led to the Oval Office—a criminal conspiracy to steal secrets from the Democrats during the election campaign. "The ranking Republican in the House Judiciary Committee said yesterday that President Nixon could not use executive privilege to withhold information from the impeachment inquiry," wrote Bill Kovach. And in bolder headlines in the column right next to this was JUDGE WILL ORDER NIXON TO TESTIFY AT EX-AIDES' TRIAL. In Los Angeles a judge declared that he "would order President Nixon to testify in person at the trial of John D. Ehrlichman and two other former White House aides, now under indictment here for the 1971 break-in at the office of Daniel Ellsberg's former psychiatrist." An antiwar activist, Ellsberg leaked the top-secret *Pentagon Papers* to the press, and Nixon hoped for private information that might be used to punish him.

So now the guardians of justice were closing in on Richard Nixon from coast to coast, and Bob Dylan was singing from a bully pulpit to 20,000 potential voters that the president *must have to stand naked* (with that redneck redundancy "must have to" stressing the nakedness at the line's end), and indeed he would. When Dylan wrote "It's Alright, Ma" in 1964 Lyndon Baines Johnson had been president. Poetry, as Allen Ginsberg reminded his friends, is news that *stays* news. Dylan had cast his lines into the future—a full decade—to prophesy the impeachment of our chief of state.

Thematically the song is an epilogue to the 1962 odyssey, "A Hard Rain's A-Gonna Fall," the eyewitness report the younger poet had promised to deliver. How has mankind become removed from the natural order of the universe? How does this cause us to suffer? What can we do about it? Who among us has arrogated to himself the powers of God? What leaders and what institutions have abused their power and authority?

As Dylan answers these questions one by one, with earnest care, evoking a bleak social landscape of hypocrisy, lethal pride, avarice, and above all idolatry, he keeps reassuring mother that it's all right, everything is all right. That is the vinegar of irony he packs the poem in to keep it from going off, from sounding like a tantrum. He will endure despite the fact that the world is not what he had hoped it might be. It is, after all is said and done, "life, and life only," prob-ably no worse than life has been since the beginning of the human experience, and perhaps not so bad as it might have been. "Hard Rain" is a song of innocence. "It's Alright, Ma" is a song of experi-ence bitterly achieved.

As the singer bowed for the applause at the end of his acoustic set the Band rejoined him: lithe Levon Helm mounting the drum kit, hulking Garth Hudson noodling at the organ, Robbie Robertson checking sound levels on the guitar.

The show had been going on for two hours and we had not yet heard a song from the new album, *Planet Waves*, recorded in No-vember and released in time for this tour. The record was mainly a collection of love songs to Dylan's wife, valentines for the most part, here and there laced with a bitter verse or interrupted by a poison-pen letter. Marriage at best is a hazardous adventure. Alongside the "Wedding Song" that attests "I love you more than life itself," Dylan recorded "Going, Going, Gone," an apology for stepping out: "I been hangin' on threads / I been playin' it straight, / Now, I've just got to cut loose / Before it gets late."

In a slow, tender voice, now Dylan sang a sweet song from *Planet Waves* for his children, "Forever Young."

May your hands always be busy,
May your feet always be swift,

May you have a strong foundation
When the winds of changes shift.

They had pitched the melody in such a low key Dylan's baritone could not quite scoop the bottom notes in the fourth line, but this did leave more room for his voice to soar on the high notes of the chorus.

May your heart always be joyful,
May your song always be sung,
May you stay forever young,
Forever young, forever young. . . .

Dylan recalled that he had written the song in Tucson, Arizona, about the time he was making the gunslinger movie with Sam Peckinpah. He said that he was "thinking about one of my boys and not wanting to be too sentimental. The lines came to me, they were done in a minute," one of those moments of inspiration when the lyrics come as an unexpected gift. "I was going for something else; the song wrote itself . . . you never know what you're going to write." The performance, with a simple, understated accompaniment by the Band, was prolonged at least a minute by a long high-wire act of a guitar solo by Robbie Robertson, demonstrating the youthful exuberance the hymnlike, solemn lyrics request. Robertson was appealing, with a boyish, gap-toothed charm that contrasts with Dylan's ageless, angst-ridden looks.

So I found myself wondering if Bob Dylan had ever known the pleasures of being young, having been caught up since adolescence in an obsession that rushed him headlong into a stormy adulthood. At nineteen he had tried, and mainly succeeded in, sounding like an old man. In "Forever Young" he was praying for charity, courage, righteousness, and a strong foundation that had often eluded him since he left home—all but the courage.

Now, as a thirty-two-year-old poet, troubadour, and adventurer, he was not likely to lead the life he dreamed for his children. Dylan's destiny and self-proclaimed obligation was to go into the "deepest black forest" again and again, to the perilous place "where black is the color, where none is the number," and that odyssey was not conducive to a stable home life.

Eric Andersen claimed that "the reason Bob is inspiring to other people is because he has seen the other side—has gone to the dark and come back and reported on it. Like the old pharaohs, the priests, the medicine men. Folks would give them potions and put them out and they'd go under—almost to the point of death. If they weren't paralyzed; if they could be awakened so they could speak again they had enormous powers of insight, and prophecy."

And so it is with Dylan, but he has had a high price to pay.

He had been happy living with his family in seclusion, in Woodstock. The musician had recovered his physical and mental health and written a hundred good songs while he was free of the burden of performing them live. He was, during those years, the man he appeared to be, singing the delights and consolations of marriage, the tranquillity of living in the country, "Watching the River Flow," and expressing gratitude to God.

The problem with paradise on earth, as one might suspect, is the day-to-day sameness. There is little variety in perfection and one might find it boring—particularly an artist who thrives on the tension between the real and the ideal, the knowledge of suffering and longing, his own and other people's.

> *Outside the lights were shining*
> *On the river of tears,*
> *I watched them from the distance*
> *With music in my ears.*
>
> (FROM *"Went to See the Gypsy,"* 1970)

Two distinct musics arose from the years in the Catskills, representing two warring impulses in the artist. The hard-rocking,

Dionysian Dylan of *The Basement Tapes* stood back-to-back with the Apollonian, domestic Dylan of the commercial albums *Nashville Skyline* (1969), *New Morning* (1970), and *Planet Waves* (1974).

Andersen, Pennebaker, and others who visited Dylan in Woodstock noticed his restlessness, his recurring obsession with the possibilities of performance. At times he was like the condemned character in "House of the Rising Sun" with "one foot on the platform / And the other foot on the train," by day living the life of the quiet scholar and family man, and by night rocking out with the choirboys of hell in the frat house basement of nearby Big Pink.

The snake in the garden was the artist himself. Although Bob Dylan may have blamed the public for disrupting his family life in the 1970s, it is difficult to separate the poet from the public he had charmed. There was a mutual and irresistible attraction. As MacLeish once advised him, "things can't be measured by what they cost," but rather by what it cost a man to get them. If something costs a person his faith or his family, then it isn't worth the price. This was a lesson Bob Dylan would pay dearly to learn.

Maria Muldaur, one of the greatest white blues singers of our generation, has been friends with Dylan since 1961. Born Maria Grazia Rosa Domenica D'Amato in New York in 1943, she was singing in jug bands in the Village when Dylan blew in there from Minnesota. From the start of her career she has blended magnetic sex appeal, keen wit, and unerring instincts as a storyteller to deliver American music in her wide-ranging alto voice.

After joining the Jim Kweskin Jug Band in 1963 she fell in love with the lead guitarist and singer Geoff Muldaur, married him, and moved to Cambridge, Massachusetts, the same year. Under Albert Grossman's management the band made half a dozen successful albums in that decade, first with Vanguard, then with Warner Reprise. The group disbanded in the late sixties but Grossman continued to handle the Muldaurs as a high-profile duet. With their daughter, Jenny, they gravitated to Woodstock because Grossman was there.

Her memories of the Dylans in Woodstock go back to 1967, when Warner Bros. gave the Muldaurs money to move there, buy a house, and rehearse. "Those were the days!" she recalls. "They paid us all a salary just to hang around in the woods and rehearse songs and try out musical ideas. Woodstock, on the surface, just looked like a sleepy little town in the middle of sleepy hollow, in the Catskills. But lurking in the woods were Paul Butterfield and his whole band, Todd Rundgren and his band, John Sebastian, Happy and Artie Traum, Bob Dylan and the Band. So here was this rich, fertile soil of all these great musicians just hanging out and jamming and doing a lot of musical experimentation."

Her daughter, Jenny, was two years old when they set up housekeeping in Woodstock, and Jesse Dylan was a year younger. "Sara would bring him over so they could play. I remember meeting Sara and thinking how beautiful and elegant and serene she was. We would sit on Albert's porch and talk about our kids and what was it like living in Woodstock and so forth. When we actually moved there, there were several occasions when we got the kids together for playdates. By the time we moved I think she had had a couple [of children]. She and Bob had two or three in rapid succession.

"One time they invited Geoff and me and Jenny over for dinner, and there were several kids, just rug rats running everywhere. They had a nice, big old comfortable house." Photographs show big picture windows looking out over the wooded hills, antique Persian carpets, a concert grand piano, book-lined walls, large overstuffed chairs, and a couch. "They had a nanny, like a domestic helper, but everything was very casual. When we had dinner I noticed that the plates didn't match. Everything was not real hippyish, but it was casual and not all put-together."

Sara did some of the cooking and a nanny helped out. "I mean, there were children crawling *everywhere*. So it is understandable that she had help. Then we all sat down. The kids got along great. I remember thinking to myself how cool it was that they had every kind of dish and cup that didn't fit. It was all just cool stuff. Nobody was trying to put on airs.

"I remember this conversation we had. Dylan started talking about, 'You know I think it would be great if we all got on a train, we could take a train across the country. I could do it with the Band and you and your band and Butterfield . . .' He had this great notion. And we talked about how Bessie Smith had traveled around the country, and he said, 'Back in the old days a lot of the blues and jazz musicians traveled by train.' We thought it was a great idea. And we all chimed in with our thoughts about this train tour, and that's the kind of evening it was. Then we sat around and played a little bit of music. But by that time there were all these children to be put to bed."

Maria Muldaur always speaks of Bob Dylan with deep affection, as if he were a kind and wayward big brother. After so many years of friendship, and sharing roots in an ancient folk music and blues tradition, she has seen many sides of him. A generous spirit, she will never judge him for what he has done or failed to do. She attributes the longevity of their platonic connection to the fact that she wants nothing from him, and he seems to have wanted nothing from Maria apart from the affection and acceptance she has extended to him for so long.

She was in his life before, during, and after his marriage to Sara. She recalls Bob playing with the children Jesse, Sam, Anna; "they would be climbing all over him and he would be very tolerant of it all, he was very devoted." Also, "if they were being too rambunctious he would say, 'No, you have to put that down'; he would discipline them gently. He wasn't harsh or anything. It was all very easy and I think probably Sara's degree of grace and equanimity made it all seem mellow."

So what happened? Were there any signs of restlessness when he was in Woodstock, indications that he wanted to get back on the road?

"He was born restless," she says. "But I think he really gave it his all. 'Okay, I'm going to be a husband and father, and I'm going to do *that.*' And he really tried to do it, did it to the best of his ability considering people were peering in his window every other minute. He just wanted to do things like wash the car and walk the dog and take out the trash. There weren't lots of servants running around or anything."

In May 1969 the Dylans moved to the other side of town, to a larger house on thirty-nine acres of land on a hill overlooking the Hudson River. They hoped for more privacy there but it didn't work out, so in September they bought the house on MacDougal Street where strangers harassed them day and night. For a while the family moved from house to house. Happy Traum's brother Artie lived in Hi Lo Ha one winter after most of the furniture had been removed to the new residence. There was nothing in the dim attic but an old steamer trunk. Curious, Artie lifted the curved lid of the trunk. It was filled to the brim with letters addressed to Bob Dylan, all of them unopened.

"Meanwhile," Maria said, "he has got this raging creativity. I mean, once he had gotten a good *rest*—which he really needed because he was on a trajectory to . . . just imploding in some way—then the creativity started to bubble up and, you know? All the stuff you hear about . . . well, it was not surprising because I have seen it with everybody. I saw it in my own marriage. People go out on the road. They start fooling around, you know. Then even if they are *not* fooling around they are away so much that the connection gets kind of loosened up if you are not working on it. And we were all so young! We didn't have all the skills to keep it together. Then you add in the rock star domain and the fact that groupies are literally throwing themselves at you twenty-four hours a day. And he was no saint, you know?" Under the circumstances, Bob and Sara's separation was inevitable.

"But I do think he gave it his all and she certainly did as well. And he has remained a very devoted father and even grandfather. Even after they broke up, he has taken care of his kids very well."

When he had finished singing "Forever Young," the song for his children on *Planet Waves*, he sang a song for his wife. In an interview with John Rockwell of the *New York Times* Dylan had singled it out: "I particularly like the song 'Something There Is About You'; it completes a circle for me, about certain things running through my pattern." This was a curious choice from a ten-track album that includes seven songs about married life; five of them are clear hymns of praise, thanksgiving, adoration of his bride. There are lyrics like "You angel you / You got me under your wing" and such stanzas as

You gave me babies, one, two, three, what is more you saved my life,
Eye for eye and tooth for tooth, your love cuts like a knife,
My thoughts of you don't ever rest, they'd kill me if I lie,
I'd sacrifice the world for you and watch my senses die.

(FROM *"Wedding Song"*)

But the song he chose to sing that night in Madison Square Garden, for witnesses that included so many old friends and Sara herself, was a more complex personal statement. "Something There Is About You" concerns the mystery of love. Why does he care for this woman so much? Is it the way she moves, or the way her hair flows? Does she remind him of some romantic figure from the past, an aura or glory lost in time? He thought—so his verse goes—that he had given up the search for such things when he was a boy in Duluth.

Something there is about you that brings back a long-forgotten truth.
Suddenly I found you and the spirit in me sings
Don't have to look no further you're the soul of many things.

I could say that I'd be faithful, I could say it in one sweet easy breath
But to you that would be cruelty and to me it surely would be death.

The singer had reserved a well of tenderness that he now drew upon in the simple melody in moderate 4/4 time; he was crooning the lyrics, caressing the notes of the middle register, holding the last notes instead of shouting them. He loves her so deeply he can only tell her the truth: no matter how much he loves her he cannot promise to be faithful, even though

Something there is about you that moves with style and grace.
I was in a whirlwind, now I'm in some better place.

The whirlwind was the onslaught of fame and fortune arriving at the same time as superabundant creativity, feeding it, feeding upon it, and a storm of flashbulbs and reporters with mad and foolish questions. The whirlwind was the surrounding mind-guard phalanx and rolling theater of cruelty in Max's Kansas City and the Kettle of Fish, where idolators and groupies were skewered and consumed. It was the predatory management of Albert Grossman and a culture of greed and envy. It was *Blonde on Blonde*. The whirlwind was England in 1966, drunken parties where folks popped pills to stay awake and pills to go to sleep wherever they crashed. It was the world that cheered and booed as Bob Dylan sang "Like a Rolling Stone" and "Tombstone Blues" and "Everybody Must Get Stoned."

The "better place" was Hi Lo Ha, the house in the Catskill Mountains where he lived with his graceful wife, where they raised their children, the house on the hillside where he built his library and read and studied the Bible, Walt Whitman, William Blake, Emily Dickinson, W. B. Yeats, and T. S. Eliot. Hi Lo Ha was where he wrote the wise allegories of *John Wesley Harding* and the epithalamiums of *New Morning* and *Planet Waves*. Home was a better place to thrive and to learn, whether or not it was also a better place to create music.

When he had finished singing the song for Sara the lights went out on the stage to signal that the main show was over. The audience began their plaintive clamor for the encore that they knew was coming from the previous reviews of the show—a triple-decker encore that was pure show business. The tune started without much hesitation. The lights came up and we could hear a misleading introduction to the otherwise predictable flag-waver "Like a Rolling Stone." The crowd rose to their feet, everybody singing along.

> *How does it feel*
> *To be on your own*
> *With no direction home*
> *Like a complete unknown. . . .*

Someone recalls the flickering of several thousand cigarette lighters in the semidarkness, little torches by way of visual applause, but that must have been on some other night because all I can remember is the crowd voices drowning out Dylan and the Band until they paused to segue into the next encore. There had to be more than one encore to this colossal performance and the next one brought us full circle: Dylan sang again—in its entirety—the valedictory "Most Likely You Go Your Way (and I'll Go Mine)."

> *I'm just gonna let you pass*
> *Yes, and I'll go last.*
> *Then time will tell who fell*
> *And who's been left behind,*
> *When you go your way and I'll go mine.*

He would not leave us, his friends, his family, his public, on that bitter note. His parting words on this winter night would be the verses of the kinder song that most of America first knew him by:

> *How many roads must a man walk down*
> *Before you call him a man?*

Yes 'n' how many seas must a white dove sail
Before she sleeps in the sand?
Yes 'n' how many times must the cannonballs fly
Before they're forever banned?
The answer my friend, is blowin' in the wind,
The answer is blowin' in the wind.

It was a wizened riddle rhyme that sent us on our way brimming with questions, full of wonder. The concert in the Garden offered one certainty among many questions: Bob Dylan had left home after years of stability and had taken to the road again. The show started out in Chicago on January 3, then played to Philadelphia, Toronto, Boston, and Washington before touring the South. What we had seen and heard tonight he would perform again tomorrow on the same stage, twice, for a matinee and for an evening audience. Then he would visit Ann Arbor, Bloomington, St. Louis, Denver, Seattle, Oakland, and finally Los Angeles.

After New York he would never again sing that bittersweet song for his wife. That part of Bob Dylan's life was over.

CHAPTER 10

Midwinter: An Interlude

We got the call from Bob Dylan's office in mid-December of 1980—
the dreary week after John Lennon was shot outside the Dakota
apartments on the Upper West Side of Manhattan. Dylan was on his
way, we had heard, to visit Lennon's widow, Yoko Ono. Dylan's rep-
resentative asked if we would please come to his office downtown
early in the new year. Bob was interested, we were told, in exploring
ideas for a Broadway musical, and he wanted our feedback.

"We" were an ad hoc committee of dramatists: the musical director John Richard Lewis, playwright and lyricist Murray Horwitz,
and me. We were all in our early thirties and had worked with Joseph Papp at the Public Theater down on Lafayette Street. One of
my verse dramas, *Jenny and the Phoenix*, was then under option to
be produced there. Lewis and Horwitz had collaborated on a musical comedy review at the Public called *Hard Sell*. Horwitz was well
known as the author of *Ain't Misbehavin'*, the Broadway hit based on
the life and songs of Fats Waller. The show was in its third year of a
lively run at the Plymouth Theatre. John Lewis was the rare director
who knew how to cobble together a musical out of rock or country
numbers; he would soon distinguish himself as the director of the
hit *Big River*, based on *Huckleberry Finn* and the tunes of Roger Miller.

Sometime in the autumn of 1980, Ben Saltzman, Dylan's office manager, had visited Gail Merrifield Papp, Joe Papp's wife and the director of play development at the Public Theater, to discuss Dylan's interest in a Broadway project. Gail Papp rang for Murray Horwitz, who then recommended his collaborator Lewis, and me.

Horwitz, Lewis, and I met the morning of January 7 at Pete's Tavern, an ancient literary hub at the corner of Eighteenth Street and Irving Place. Pete's had served spirits continuously since the Civil War—the Prohibition years included. Walt Whitman, Eugene O'Neill, Edna St. Vincent Millay, and Nathanael West had been customers; O. Henry wrote "The Gift of the Magi" in a front booth. Bob Dylan had raised many a glass at the carved rosewood bar. This morning we had come for coffee and to brainstorm for the 10:30 meeting at Dylan's office nearby.

There had been a snowstorm the night before and now Manhattan lay under the white swath that seems to work a greater magic in that place where there is so much grit, and grime, and tumult to assuage. The snowplows were scraping Park Avenue. The wrought-iron gates of Gramercy Park were tipped with white.

January 1981 was the bleak midwinter of Bob Dylan's career as a performer. With characteristic passion he was singing gospel music in small theaters. Most teenagers had little interest in folk music or the dated phenomenon of "folk rock." Disco music had taken over the jukeboxes and radio airwaves in the late seventies—the shrill voices of the Bee Gees, the Jackson Five, and Donna Summer. They left room for the burnished rock sounds of Steely Dan, Fleetwood Mac, and Rod Stewart, and somewhat less for the hard-edged ballads of the young Bruce Springsteen and Elvis Costello.

In 1980 the king of popular music was the self-effacing, sentimental falsetto crooner Christopher Cross ("Sailing," "Never Be the Same," "Ride Like the Wind"), whose album *Christopher Cross* won more prizes and sold more copies than the rest of the field combined.

The decade started with an overwhelming listener's vote for music of escape, predictability, and ease. America had seen too much strife and protest, and the public did not want to be reminded of these things in its leisure hours. The brief ascendancy of folk music and cerebral rock had been a curious detour in the progress of popular entertainment. Now the public wanted the lullabies of Lionel Richie, Billy Joel, and, by an inexorable logic, the sedative, forgettable Christopher Cross—a name that erases itself.

Bob Dylan, the man who reluctantly owned the 1960s, had scarcely a place to hang his hat as the decade of the 1980s began. After the 1974 tour (the one that brought him to the Garden) his marriage began to unravel. This inspired one brilliant album called *Blood on the Tracks*. There were songs of furious disappointment in the romantic and domestic ideal: "Tangled Up in Blue" and "Idiot Wind"; tender and heartbreaking songs of parting like "You're Gonna Make Me Lonesome When You Go," "If You See Her, Say Hello," and the mesmerizing "Buckets of Rain" (Dylan's last inventive performance on acoustic guitar).

> *Life is sad*
> *Life is a bust*
> *All you can do is do what you must.*
> *You do what you must do and ya do it well.*
> *I'll do it for you, honey baby*
> *Can't you tell?*

That song and some others on the album may have been composed not for the singer's wife but for Ellen Bernstein, a twenty-four-year-old record executive he had met while he was on tour in February 1974, in San Francisco. He took up with her a few weeks after we had seen him at the Garden in New York. During the early months of Dylan's first marital separation in the summer of that year she spent weekends with Bob and his children on a farm he had purchased on the Crow River in Minnesota. There in the north country he wrote the songs for *Blood on the Tracks*.

Everything from the title to the last verse of that album seemed sublime to me, capturing emotions that until then had been inaccessible to the American voice. I thought this was the best record he had made in at least ten years, whatever it had cost him personally; and we heard through the grapevine it would cost him half his fortune, his immediate family, and maybe his sanity. In the three years from the end of the 1974 tour until the divorce from Sara was finalized in 1977, Bob Dylan passed through an odyssey almost as violent and transformative as the three years that led to his motorcycle accident in 1966.

Blood on the Tracks was released on January 17, 1975, and sold very well by word of mouth even before the rock music critics set upon it. I knew from the day I first heard the record that someone fussier than I would have to come along to find fault. Within a month *Blood on the Tracks* had moved more than half a million copies (gold record honors), more than any previous Dylan album in its first weeks. The reviews were mixed, an appropriate response to a rangy and disturbing masterpiece that critics naturally regarded as autobiographical and thereby exhibitionistic.

First Robert Christgau, writing in the *Village Voice*, noted "moments of anger that seem callow, and the prevailing theme of interrupted love recalls adolescent woes, but on the whole this is the man's most mature and assured recording." *Time* magazine dismissed the work as inconsistent. Jon Landau in *Rolling Stone* concluded that *Blood on the Tracks* contained powerful writing but was doomed because the production overall was shoddy. Paul Cowan, in the same pages, called it "the excruciating cry of a man who is tormented by his own freedom," and described Dylan's peculiar dilemma: "He seems unable to establish warm, lasting relationships, but he's too eager for love to make the cold decision to sacrifice his private life to his art, as Joyce or even Mailer can." The critic argued that this was a great album because it fully confronted that problem.

Robert Shelton, who knew Dylan personally, was having none

of that particular psychobabble and cautioned his colleagues about misinterpreting the artist's role-playing. Who would assume Shakespeare was guilt-ridden because Lady Macbeth scoured her hands? "Even if *Blood on the Tracks* was literally confessional," Shelton later wrote, Cowan's view was wrong. True enough, Dylan *had* for a time been "a cruel, self-centered loner." But that was before the motorcycle accident in 1966. Afterward "he tried to change his ways. After his move back to the Village in 1969, he was also trying to rekindle old friendships. . . . Dylan has wanted to be liked, but he tried to balance that need with trying to be true to his many embattled artistic selves."

The balancing act had been impossible. There were far more "friends" than any one man could satisfy, and so most people felt alienated. The real dilemma, I suspect, was mathematical and not personal.

For a long time Dylan had dreamed of reviving the kind of artistic community he had known in the early 1960s: Jack Elliott, Dave Van Ronk, Paul Clayton, Joan Baez, Allen Ginsberg, Bobby Neuwirth & Co. "From the summer of 1975 onward," Shelton recalled, "Dylan made an even more concentrated effort to forge a community of singers." The opportunity came only "after he had purged his feelings, and those of many others, with the brilliant catharsis of *Blood on the Tracks.*"

> *I been double-crossed now for the very last time and now I'm finally*
> *   free*
> *I kissed goodbye the howling beast on the borderline which separated*
> *   you from me.*
> *You'll never know the hurt I suffered nor the pain I rise above*
> *And I'll never know the same about you, your holiness or your kind of*
> *   love,*
> *And it makes me feel so sorry.*
>
> (FROM *"Idiot Wind"*)

That album was a catharsis as well as a declaration of independence. He was not yet free of marriage but he was no longer bound by the conventions of matrimony and the domestic arrangements that had suited the Dylans of Woodstock, 94 MacDougal Street, and now Point Dume, Malibu, near Los Angeles. There they were building a copper-domed palace, a Xanadu. The couple had managed some sort of accommodation—a middle ground between marriage and divorce—maybe not quite an open marriage, rather a casual conjugality that allowed for intimate time together and unexamined time apart.

Exhilarated, he returned to Greenwich Village in the spring of 1975 looking for signs of artistic life. The war in Vietnam had ended. Gerald Ford had pardoned Richard Nixon, declaring "the long nightmare is over." Dylan showed up at the Bottom Line on June 25, playing harmonica behind Muddy Waters and Victoria Spivey. Three nights later he attended Patti Smith's performance at the Other End, where Bob and Patti posed for photographs together. The thirty-four-year-old Dylan slept in a borrowed loft on Houston Street. One night he was driving along Thirteenth Street toward the East Village when he noticed a tall, long-haired girl walking by, carrying a violin case over her shoulder. He asked her if she knew how to fiddle. When she claimed she did, he told her to get into the car, and she got in and slammed the door.

That was the Irish Italian beauty Scarlet Rivera, who until that summer day had never seen the inside of a recording studio. Her playing was idiosyncratic and weird, with a lot of body English. Before the night was over Dylan had heard her play not only in his recording studio but also onstage with Muddy Waters. He was introducing Scarlet as a member of his new band.

From the streets and lofts of Soho, from the clubs and transient hotels of Manhattan he was gathering not only a band but a small tribe, an extended family that he would lead out of the disco wilderness of the seventies like a patriarch of old to rediscover America, a paradise lost. The company he would soon call the Rolling Thunder Revue was drawn from Dylan's past, present, and future. Rivera, picked up on a street corner on a whim, represented his future, her gypsy violin leading him through strange measures in fantasy songs like "Isis."

I married Isis on the fifth day of May,
But I could not hold on to her very long.
So I cut off my hair and I rode straight away
For the wild unknown country where I could not go wrong.

According to Ramblin' Jack Elliott, Dylan first mentioned the idea of the road show in mid-July 1975 when Jack was playing a gig at the Other End. Dylan said, "Come on, Jack, you and me'll round up a bunch of players and get on a bus and play all over, in ballparks and church halls and theaters."

"And that was it," Jack recalled. "Then we just did it."

Bobby Neuwirth was back on the scene, playing at the Other End. Somehow they had gotten over whatever bitterness had passed between them and Neuwirth once again would become Robin Goodfellow, master of revels and unofficial stage manager of a rowdy caravan. As the idea waxed in Dylan's mind he would call upon Louis Kemp—a figure from his very distant past, a childhood friend from Minnesota—to produce the Rolling Thunder Revue. They had attended Camp Herzl together in the 1950s. Louis was heir to Kemp Fisheries Incorporated of Duluth, took over the family business in 1967, and expanded it deftly and profitably in Alaska and Minnesota; he was well on the way to selling his trademark to Tyson Seafood when Dylan tapped him for Rolling Thunder.

Almost nobody could say no to Bob Dylan. Joan Baez would come along and so would Sara Dylan, the children, and even grandma Beatty Zimmerman. Sam Shepard, one of the greatest playwrights in America, agreed to join up and write dialogue for a film Dylan planned to make with Joan, Sara, Neuwirth, Ramblin' Jack, Allen Ginsberg, Roger McGuinn, and a few others. The film was about the road show and the road show was obsessed with the film. The troubadours became actors, wearing masks and hats and feathers, painting their faces. Art and life intermingled.

All of this would come to pass in October. But the music, as always, came first. New songs and melodies would create the sound track for Dylan's movie, his Revue, his life. He sat in a booth in the back of the Other End drinking red wine and listening to the young musicians. He liked Mick Ronson, the lead guitarist who played with David Bowie. He met Rob Stoner, who played bass for Ramblin' Jack. He liked drummer Howie Wyeth (Andrew Wyeth's nephew), the virtuoso guitarist Eric Clapton, and the sweet country voices of Emmylou Harris and Ronee Blakley. Then there was the nineteen-year-old David Mansfield, a one-man band who played guitar, violin, mandolin, dobro, and pedal steel. Allen Ginsberg called him "the boy with the Botticelli face."

Dylan fell in with the psychologist turned theater director (*Oh! Calcutta!*) Jacques Levy, who had collaborated with the Byrds' Roger McGuinn on song lyrics for a musical. In a loft on La Guardia Place one night they wrote the mystical song "Isis." Encouraged, they retired to a house in East Hampton, Long Island, for three weeks, and coauthored half a dozen more songs that made up the backbone of the fleshy, exotic album called *Desire*. The title says it all—or rather, the title when taken with Dylan's prose poem called "Desire (liner notes)" leaves very little to the imagination. The stream-of-consciousness "liner notes" touch upon each of the nine songs: *Romance is taking over. Tolstoy was right . . . from Lowell to Durango oh sister, when I fall into your spacey arms, can not ya feel the weight of oblivion and the songs of redemption on your backside. . . . We have relations in Mozambique. I have a brother or two and a whole lot of karma to burn. . . .*

Blood on the Tracks had been thematically focused, close to the bone, intense. The drama implied unity of time and place, locating the singer in familiar settings, addressing his beloved, sometimes in anguish, sometimes with delight. *Desire* is the id untrammeled, exploring all of time and space, the traditional and the taboo, from Brooklyn to Durango to Mozambique, from an Atlantic sea beach where he frolicked with his wife and children to a fantastic arctic landscape where pyramids were embedded in ice, a tomb where Isis has sent him. The melodies have a Middle Eastern or Moorish cast to them, and Dylan's voice sometimes quavers in the Greek or Arab style as he sings "One More Cup of Coffee" and "Oh Sister." He had learned from Om Kalthoum, the great Egyptian songstress. Allen Ginsberg thought the minor inflection was Jewish or at least Semitic.

Dylan had been studying painting with Norman Raeben in his Manhattan studio. Raeben, born in Russia in 1901, was the son of the Yiddish writer Sholem Aleichem, and what he had to offer Dylan was not merely instruction in the art of drawing and painting, but a new way of seeing the world. "I had met magicians," Dylan recalled, "but this guy is more powerful than any magician I've ever met. He looked into you and told you what you were." He told Jonathan Cott of *Rolling Stone* that Raeben had taught him "how to see. He put my mind and my hand and my eye together, in a way that allowed me to do consciously what I unconsciously felt." He also learned from Raeben a technique for writing songs that escape from the tyranny of time, as do paintings. "You've got yesterday, today, and tomorrow all in the same room, and there's very little that you can't imagine happening."

Turning from *Blood on the Tracks* to the album *Desire* is like leaving a show of Picasso's structured "blue period" and entering a gallery of riotous Delacroix epics, the world of the turban, warriors on horseback, the harem. Gypsies. Gladiators. Mobsters. We hear the indulgent protest song defending a prizefighter, Rubin "Hurricane" Carter, a black man Dylan thought had been framed on a charge of murder in the first degree. Then there is a sentimental elegy for a slain gangster, Joey Gallo—an outsider, like the artist—guilty of doing business on society's margins, outside the law and flouting the covenants of his criminal colleagues. In these songs and in the love lyrics of *Desire* Dylan's passion is breaking down the distinctions and barriers that separate black and white, criminal and legitimate commerce, sister from lover and brother from friend.

> *Oh, sister, when I come to lie in your arms*
> *You should not treat me like a stranger.*
> *Our father would not like the way that you act*
> *And you must realize the danger.*

The audience might think this a flirtation with incest; if so, it was certainly a way of getting people's attention. But that was not the point, not by a long shot. He was playing upon the vernacular—black, southern usage as well as the religious meanings of the words *sister* and *brother*. We are all, as God's children, sisters and brothers whose Father in Heaven would not look kindly upon our estrangement from one another. Having known the pleasures and agonies of Eros—the possessiveness of romantic and conjugal love—the freewheeling poet now praised a more relaxed manner of lovemaking, something with more of the generosity of friendship or familial affection, still sacred and in some measure erotic but not confining.

I have a brother or two and a whole lot of karma to burn. On the road to fame Dylan had left a lot of people behind. It was inevitable. As an artist moves forward he often travels on the boats and coattails and shoulders of other people. Bounding ahead of them, he hitches rides with others. Eventually there was a crowd that stood behind, forlorn on the shore, shading their eyes, watching Bob Dylan sail off into the sunset. Some, like Joan Baez and Bob Neuwirth, felt angry or betrayed; others simply were sad they had lost touch with a dear and captivating friend. The late Mike Bloomfield spoke movingly on this subject to Larry Sloman, who wrote a superb book about the Rolling Thunder Revue.

"There was a time when he was one of the most charming human beings I had ever met and I mean charming . . . someone who could beguile you with his personality. You just had to say, 'Man, this . . .

guy's got a bit of an angel in him,' God touched him in a certain way. And he *changed*, like that guy was gone or *it must not be gone*, any man that has that many kids, he must be relating that way to his children, but I never related to him that way again." Bloomfield's comment is highly perceptive: a man who wants to be a good father may not have much time for people other than his children.

Acquaintances, from different periods of Dylan's life, have remarked in interviews that he is a "user," that he was never above wielding his charm in the name of friendship to achieve his purpose. After this, the "friend" would find himself suddenly abandoned. Of all those who have told me off the record that Bob Dylan has used people, not one has claimed that he or she was "used." The inference is always that it was somebody else who was ill treated. The victim is never the person telling the story; the storyteller always remembers fair treatment personally, and sometimes generous treatment in his relations with Dylan. So the impression remains vague.

It is difficult to be a good friend to half a dozen people and very easy to disappoint a hundred.

In any case, by 1975 Bob Dylan felt there was a gulf of his own making between him and the community of musicians that had nourished him, and he wanted to bridge that gulf. "I have a brother or two and a whole lot of karma to burn"—bad karma presumably, or he would not have been talking about burning it. He had succeeded, wildly, while others had foundered, and some felt that his success had come at their expense. There were debts to pay, old scores to settle with Joan Baez, Bob Neuwirth, Jack Elliott, Phil Ochs, Roger McGuinn, Joni Mitchell, Allen Ginsberg, not to mention the ghosts of Paul Clayton and Richard Fariña, too many to name, far too many to fit on the Rolling Thunder Revue bus, not to mention the stage. But Dylan would include all he could, everyone who fit the bill (Ochs, a tormented drunk, alas did not). He would load up the bus with them, and the roadies and sound and light crew for *Renaldo and Clara*, until the springs groaned. And he would feed and lodge them and provide them with creature comforts and incomparable fellowship. He was back on the path he had learned in the Guthrie household, high on the "family" of people with shared values who don't need everything explained.

"What I want," he told one agent, "is to have a sort of traveling carnival that would eventually have its own tents and railroad cars. Something like Ringling Bros. does, only with musicians and their families."

By the time the carnival took to the road in late October it had another karmic purpose: raising consciousness about the black prize-fighter Hurricane Carter, serving a life term in a New Jersey prison for a murder he claimed he had not committed. In July Jacques Levy and Bob Dylan had written the protest song for Carter that was recorded for *Desire*. Now Dylan would sing "Hurricane" at every stop on the tour that started in Plymouth, Massachusetts, on Halloween and moved on to Lowell on November 2. In a cemetery outside Lowell, Dylan played guitar and Ginsberg played harmonium at Jack Kerouac's grave, improvising a song and a scene while the cameras rolled. Dylan read aloud a poem of Kerouac's from Ginsberg's copy of *Mexico City Blues*.

In Providence, Rhode Island, and Springfield, Massachusetts, Dylan sang "Hurricane" twice a day, at matinee and evening shows, backed by the swaying Scarlet Rivera on fiddle, Wyeth on drums, Rob Stoner on bass, Mick Ronson and Steven Soles on guitars, and the dark-eyed beauty Ronee Blakley singing harmony.

Here comes the story of the Hurricane,
The man the authorities came to blame
For somethin' that he never done.
Put in a prison cell, but one time he coulda been
The champion of the world.

The song has a peculiar tone that may be the fault of the late Jacques Levy: No matter how many times or with how much feeling Dylan sang the saga it never rang true. There was somehow too much effort, or self-consciousness; the singer was *trying* to sing a protest song, something he'd never done before.

The Bob Dylan who wrote "Hollis Brown," "Hattie Carroll" and "It's Alright, Ma" was not trying to write a protest song, he was just telling the truth about the state of affairs and his own feelings. Those songs simply *existed* as nature had breathed them into being; there was no exertion or artifice. But this "Hurricane" was a different kind of creature, one that seemed to have arisen out of the need to sing a song of protest—against racism, against an unjust justice system, against cruel and unusual punishment. That was all very well. But the song, as a narrative sermon, never convinced me.

Most people did not know at the time that Levy and Dylan had gotten the facts wrong: Rubin Carter was not a great boxer; his guilt or innocence was hotly disputed, although the trial was a travesty of the jury system; he certainly was not boxer enough to have been champion of the world. None of that mattered much then or now as far as the song goes, but the song did not go very far or very deep, notwithstanding its righteous rage and a vivid narrative sequence.

Sometimes the show would open with Bobby Neuwirth singing a country song like "Good Love Is Hard to Find," then Jack Elliott in his ten-gallon hat would ramble on and sing a few songs, notably Carter Family favorites and the Kingston Trio song "South Coast." The tall Texan T-Bone Burnett, guitarist, songwriter, born-again Christian, took his turn in the spotlight, singing the blues, then Roger McGuinn, Mick Ronson, and Ronee Blakley.

Allen Ginsberg, dressed in a baggy brown suit and a necktie, read a poem. Then he would step down into the audience to watch Dylan perform solo, singing the poignant love song for his wife "Sara."

> *I can still hear the sounds of those Methodist bells*
> *I had taken the cure and had just gotten through,*
> *Stayin' up for days in the Chelsea Hotel,*
> *Writin' "Sad-Eyed Lady of the Lowlands" for you.*

Sara, Sara,
Wherever we travel we're never apart.
Sara, oh Sara,
Beautiful lady, so dear to my heart.

Ginsberg, smiling, turned to the journalist Larry Sloman and said: "He revealed his heart. For Dylan to reveal his heart completely is for me a great historical event. . . . It gives other people permission to reveal their hearts." Dylan then sang "Just Like a Woman." Ginsberg declared: "It's brilliant to go from that complete announcement of his totally open heart to some ancient open heart song—completely transformed for them now. Everybody has thought of Dylan endlessly for ten years and now he's . . . putting out the definitive statements. . . . All the fantasies people had about his children and his wife, he's out there doing them." Ginsberg pointed in wonder. "He's right out there now, giving. He's completely in his body, completely in the song, completely at one with the universe."

Sara was in the audience, listening, whenever she decided to come along. The shows went on for five, six hours. She was still the main woman in his life if not the only woman, and she was a part of the movie fantasy of Dylan's world, *Renaldo and Clara*, playing scenes with Joan Baez and actresses Ruth Tyrangiel and Helena Kallianiotes.

He stuck a feather in the hatband of his dove gray gaucho hat. He had a number of masks he wore: a Nixon face, a Hubert Humphrey, a scary clear mask, masks of comedy and tragedy. He wore a pale dueling shirt unbuttoned to the sternum and a demonic medallion on a chain. He wore a black vest with satin trim, and boot-cut jeans onstage, strumming his Martin guitar. Sometimes he swirled a Tibetan scarf around his neck. His curly hair was nearly shoulder-length. In heavy mascara and white pancake makeup on the broad planes of his cheeks and jaw he looked almost pretty, an androgynous Pierrot gunslinger, a Parisian street mime.

He sang cheek to cheek with Joan Baez: "The Times They Are

A-Changin'," "Oh Sister," "I Shall Be Released," and she was grateful. They looked deeply into each other's eyes. Sometimes he kissed
her on the lips, ready or not. The crowd loved seeing the King and
Queen of Folk Music together once more. They sang together and
they sang contesting, seeing who could hold a note longer or arrive
first at the end of a chorus. She dressed as his twin so from an angle
you might think she was Bob Dylan, or that he was Baez.

Ginsberg asked Dylan if he was getting any pleasure out of the
tour.

"Pleasure? I never seek pleasure. There was a time years ago
when I sought a lot of pleasure because I'd had a lot of pain." What
was the cause of the pain? Was it the breakup with Suze Rotolo? Or
the ache of conscience during the Cold War, horror of the bomb,
the Vietnam War, the assassinations? Was it the anguish of being
misunderstood by his friends and his audience?

"But I found there was a subtle relationship between pleasure and
pain," he went on. "I mean, they were on the same plane. So now I
do what I have to do without looking for pleasure from it."

The masquelike, commedia dell'arte style of the Rolling Thunder
Revue owed something to the informal stage directions of Jacques
Levy, and the Dylan/Neuwirth predilection for obfuscation and
mummery. Masks suited Dylan, a master of the dramatic lyric who
cultivated mystery. It might be true, as Ginsberg said, that Dylan
was revealing his heart completely. But at the time he could manage
this only while wearing a mask or playing a role and appearing—
outside the sacred boundaries of his home—in a social or theatrical
environment where the scenery and actors shape-shifted so cease-
lessly that the hero could never be precisely identified.

The commune maintained a hierarchy: poets, performers, film
crew, and roadies. Dylan and his nearest and dearest of the moment
rode in a private coach, a green and white camper; all others piled
on to the boisterous, jouncing tour bus, forty or fifty comrades,

the number varied as the company took on more performers or let some go. "Joni Mitchell flies in from the coast and tunes up in the bathroom," Sam Shepard observed. "Dylan is a magnet. He pulls not only crowds but superstars. Who wouldn't play with Dylan if he asked them?"

Jammed on the bus they looked like a collision of gypsies with Buffalo Bill's Wild West and the cast of *La Bohème*, with their head scarves and bandannas, their ten-gallon hats and black berets, buckskin fringes, black leather, beads and gold chains, their Navajo ponchos, embroidered scarves and vests. The uniform was only below the belt: a consensus of blue jeans and pointed cowboy boots.

The musicians stormed the stage of the Palace Theater, Waterbury, Connecticut; Veterans Memorial Coliseum, New Haven. Young Bruce Springsteen sat in the audience, wide-eyed, with Patti Smith and Albert Grossman. Smith had turned down an invitation to join the troupe because Dylan would not let her bring her band. Grossman and Dylan had drifted apart in the late sixties as the singer struggled to regain control of his performing schedule and his song catalog (in which Grossman would hold a substantial interest until his death in 1986). Now the shrewd manager was amused to see this ragtag, itinerant road show, the promiscuous squandering of resources and talent, with its naïve goal of "playing for the people," without notice or hype, without regard for budgets or profit.

At first the publicists announced to *Variety* that Rolling Thunder intended to play small halls and theaters. But five dates into the run, the Providence Civic Center seated 12,500. What happened to the utopian plan to play small venues? The idea had collapsed under the weight of expenses: a company of seventy to feed and house and in special cases to pay a per diem, and the simultaneous filming of *Renaldo and Clara*, whose daily cost amounted to tens of thousands of dollars. Dylan insisted that he himself was drawing no salary, and every dollar that did not go to subsidizing the Rolling Thunder Revue was being plowed into the movie. In the face of these costs it would be madness to play a "small hall" in Quebec for the pleasure of five hundred fans if—on two weeks' notice—you might book the Quebec Coliseum for the delight of ten thousand. When the press got wind of the change in venues they cried foul and wanted to know what had become of the musicians' ideals and where the money was going. In fact, hardly anyone was making money, least of all the musicians.

On Thanksgiving Day, November 27, producer Barry Imhoff set the table for eighty at a snowbound Holiday Inn in Bangor, Maine. Roast turkeys, mashed potatoes, bread stuffing, and cranberry sauce were heaped high. Sara Dylan was there for the week acting in *Renaldo and Clara*; Dylan's mother, Beatty Zimmerman, was on hand to help with the children: Jesse, nine, Anna, eight, Sam, seven, and five-year-old Jakob. They took great delight in the colored balloons floating above the table, and in the food fight that broke out toward dessert time when the food began to run out. Turkey bones, dinner mints, and cashews flew across the room.

They were on the border, about to cross into Canada. Quebec Coliseum, Quebec City, November 29; Maple Leaf Gardens, Toronto, December 1 and 2; Montreal Forum, December 4. Their final destination: Madison Square Garden on December 8 for a show billed as "The Night of the Hurricane," a benefit for the boxer still in a prison in Clinton, New Jersey.

That show in the Garden was more than four hours long. Dylan himself sang twenty-one songs. Muhammad Ali, dressed in a black leisure suit, delivered a passionate speech on behalf of Rubin Carter and spoke to poor Carter via a live telephone hookup. Sometime during the intermission Dylan took a call from Carter, who excitedly explained that he had a new trial date, and he would be released from prison in two weeks. A band member recalled Dylan's elation. Embracing Stoner, he cried, "We really accomplished something. This is what it's all about!" As he tuned up for the second act Dylan planned to announce the news from the stage.

Fortunately, someone double-checked with New Jersey governor Brendan Byrne's office before Dylan addressed the crowd. There was no trial date. He was shaken by the misinformation, and at least temporarily disillusioned. The troupe had been led to believe the Rolling Thunder Revue would go on for years, maybe forever, but now cracks in the foundation were showing. He lit a cigarette. Nothing was permanent for sure and nothing was quite what it appeared to be.

At the end of the night, at the postconcert party at the Felt Forum, the band members were surprised to find a bonus, an extra week's salary in their pay envelopes. Some were pleased while others were suspicious. There were no stated plans as far as anyone knew for the future of the Rolling Thunder Revue. The bonus might in fact be a pink slip in disguise.

Dylan had not given up on Hurricane Carter's cause or the Rolling Thunder Revue. "We're regrouping," he told a reporter in mid-December 1975, "then we'll be out there again."

"Making music, making movies, making love, it's all in my blood," he confided to Larry Sloman. "Look, I'm just outgrowing, er, settling my old accounts but the restoration of honor is still in my blood." He referred to Hurricane Carter's honor as well as his own. Like Blake's fool ("if the fool would persist in his folly he would become wise") Bob Dylan wisely or foolishly continued to push for the vindication of the jailed boxer. Dylan would not admit the possibility that the man whose song he had been singing, day in and day out for tens of thousands of people, protesting his cruel sentence, might actually be guilty. Perhaps if he sang it enough times, the song itself, like an avenging angel, would unlock Rubin's cell. For a man who—as Eric Andersen said—"never made a mistake in terms of theater," this may have been the exception that proves the rule. (Carter was retried a *second* time and convicted. He was then released in the 1980s upon a writ of habeas corpus and prosecutors decided not to try him a third time.)

On January 22, 1976, Dylan called the band together to rehearse in a Los Angeles studio in preparation for a second "Night of the Hurricane" to raise more money for Carter's legal defense. For reasons now lost to history Dylan and his producers decided to debut the 1976 Rolling Thunder Revue in the 70,000-seat Houston Astrodome, a stadium three times the size of Madison Square Garden, with atrocious acoustics.

Why Texas? The masks and pranks of Rolling Thunder made sense, more or less, in the antique culture of the Northeast—think of Hawthorne's "May-Pole of Merry Mount" or Peter Schumann's Bread and Puppet Theater—and might have hoped for a warm welcome in Los Angeles or fanciful San Francisco. But Houston, on the banks of the Buffalo bayou? Yearly host of the biggest livestock and rodeo show on earth? Booking the Astrodome on a few days' notice? True, Dylan's star at the moment was ascendant. *Desire* was released on January 16 and quickly rose to the top of the charts in England and America—his bestselling album to date. He was on the cover of *People* magazine in November and the cover of *Rolling Stone* on January 15; a month earlier he appeared on PBS-TV in a musical tribute to his producer John Hammond. But even granted all this personal publicity, it was an act of enormous courage or hubris—hinting of delusions of grandeur—to book that colossal sports stadium in Texas, to raise legal funds for a black man convicted of murder one.

"Night of the Hurricane II" was not successful by any standard—financial, artistic, or moral. Even the addition of Stevie Wonder and Stephen Stills to the star-studded lineup could not sell enough tickets to fill three quarters of the Astrodome. Egos clashed, out of control. Everyone played too long. Howie Wyeth recalled, "Everybody did too much. There were too many stars there. . . . All these guys brought their own bands. They weren't doing it the way we'd been doing it. . . . We lost the whole togetherness thing." That *togetherness thing* was the inspiration that had brought the Rolling Thunder Revue into being, from a chat in the Other End with Jack Elliott to a jam session at Studio Instrument Rentals on West Twenty-fifth

Street in late October. The idea was that a community of poets and musicians would travel together and play for the people, putting their egos aside for the glory of art. Now Jack Elliott had been let go and Joan Baez was nowhere to be seen. What was left of the Rolling Thunder Revue was lost in the incomprehensible spaces of the Houston Astrodome, forlorn mimes, scattered voices that could hardly hear their own echoes in the gloom.

With nearly a half-million dollars in overhead the show did not lose money but after the bills were paid there was not a windfall for Hurricane Carter's relief fund. Accounts vary from $10,000 to $50,000. If the take was on the high side that was certainly nothing to apologize for—although, given the scale of the event, it was nothing to brag about. At a hundred dollars an hour in 1976 you could get a lot of lawyering done for $25,000. On March 17, Rubin Carter was granted his retrial by the New Jersey Supreme Court and released on bail. But Bob Dylan, in the vast and impersonal distances of the Houston Astrodome, had sung his song "Hurricane" for the last time.

He also sang "Sara" that night—for the last time in public. Insofar as the song was autobiographical (and he had presented the piece as such since recording it in July 1975 while Sara watched), he could no longer perform it without distress. The marriage was not over when the Rolling Thunder Revue resumed their tour in April 1976, but the Dylans spent little time together that year and their time was deeply troubled.

Joan Baez rejoined the troupe when they reconvened in Clearwater, Florida, to rehearse for the second leg of the Revue. She was essential. Baez had cut her hair short and Dylan was so angry he wouldn't rehearse with her for days. "Bob had a thing about wanting me to grow my hair long, the way it was in the beginning." But he had graver concerns than Joan's hair.

For most of the rehearsal period Dylan was in a black mood and ignoring almost everyone, leaving the band to rehearse on their own or under Rob Stoner's direction. Dylan had gone down to Florida in high spirits, encouraged by the number of dates that had fallen into place for the Gulf Coast circuit, not to mention a TV special that was planned for the Bellevue Biltmore Hotel in Clearwater. But his euphoria did not last much longer than a couple of lively jam sessions in the "Pool Studio" of the Biltmore.

On the evening of April 10, he was having dinner with Scarlet Rivera, David Mansfield, and others when he received the news that folksinger Phil Ochs had hanged himself in the New York apartment he shared with his sister.

By all accounts Dylan took it hard. Ochs badly wanted to be part of Dylan's Revue, and he may have held out hope until the last. The composer of "There but for Fortune" had attended the end-of-tour party at the Felt Forum before Christmas and made his desires known. Bob Dylan—with the best intentions—would not have coldly rejected Phil Ochs in that situation, face-to-face. When Jack Elliott asked why he had been let go, Dylan evaded the issue, saying he had nothing to do with who stayed on the tour. He would have been no more direct with Phil Ochs, who—in his alcoholic haze— might have construed his old friend's ambiguity as encouragement.

Anyway, Phil Ochs had taken his life, and while Dylan was not responsible for it, he was vulnerable to the grief and anger that the folksinger's suicide evoked. *I have a brother or two and a whole lot of karma to burn.* Ochs was like the annoying little brother who loves and hates you and won't leave you alone. And so you torment him. Sometimes Dylan was not kind to Ochs, although he suffered his company. And in fact, during the mid-sixties when Dylan and Neuwirth were directing the Greenwich Village Theater of Cruelty, Dylan was cruel to poor Ochs in memorable and picturesque ways.

No one could deny that Ochs loved Bob Dylan notwithstanding the demon of envy. The sentiment was clear to everyone who had attended Mike Porco's sixty-first birthday party at Gerde's Folk City back in October. When the tipsy Ochs took his turn on the stage, he played an achingly beautiful rendition of "Lay Down Your Weary Tune," looking at Dylan as the composer listened in the back row.

Ochs joined the growing community of the dead that included Paul Clayton, Geno Foreman, Edie Sedgwick, Richard Fariña, and Brian Jones—all of whom would continue to haunt Bob Dylan because they couldn't get enough of him in life. For days he kept to himself. According to some accounts he drank whiskey. When at last he returned to the rehearsal room on the night of April 15, with Rob Stoner, Howie Wyeth, and Scarlet Rivera, he wanted to sing "Knockin' on Heaven's Door," and Paul Clayton's classic "Gotta Travel On." If he could not bring himself to sing a song by Phil Ochs, so recently departed, then a song by another suicide must fill the bill.

When the show premiered at the Civic Center in Lakeland, Florida, on April 18, "Gotta Travel On"—which insiders knew as a surrogate elegy for Phil Ochs—had a prominent place on the bill, as the last ensemble encore.

The Thunder rolled through Florida in late April: Lakeland, St. Petersburg, Tampa, Orlando, Gainesville, Tallahassee, and Pensacola, playing huge civic centers and college stadiums, looking out at a lot of empty seats. Like the fiasco of the Houston Astrodome, the booking of the Gulf Coast tour seemed illogical and ill-fated. A review of the first show in Lakeland described the audience as "unimpressed and bored with the entire evening." There were more notices like that. Recordings and film footage indicate that the repertory and performances were powerful, but the crowd chemistry was wrong.

The headliner had a positive memory of Texas because in 1965 the audiences in Austin and Dallas had not booed him. This did not mean that a decade later they would welcome him with open arms. Ticket sales were so poor in Austin that one of the two shows had to be canceled. Shows were also canceled in Houston, Dallas, and Lake Charles, Louisiana; in other cities they had to downsize the event to smaller venues so as not to leave so many seats vacant. In Houston the producer added Willie Nelson to the bill, but even with the drawing power of that country-western star several thousand tickets went unsold in the 11,000-seat Hofheinz Pavilion.

Bob Dylan rarely allowed any audience, great or small, hostile or adoring, to compromise his music. With characteristic courage and grim determination he went about his business in April and May 1976, and his business that year was to achieve a level of performance art that transcended the exuberant spectacles of the 1975 tour.

The Rolling Thunder Revue as it had debuted in Plymouth in the autumn of '75 was spontaneous, magical, and often playful. Sometimes Dylan sang in a small, little-boy voice, with a tremor. He was charmingly vulnerable when he sang his love songs. The filming of *Renaldo and Clara*—the masks, makeup, and tomfoolery—helped to deflate those real-life intrigues that were going on backstage, the main drama being the winding down of Dylan's marriage. There were also a number of sideshows that featured Dylan's efforts to burn karma or pay debts of gratitude to old friends. Any of these themes might find their way to the stage: everybody knew that back when Dylan was singing "Sara" he was addressing his "mystical wife," the mother of his children, begging her never to leave him. When he sang "It Ain't Me, Babe," the words could have been for Joan Baez. When he sang "Oh Sister" one might imagine he was thinking of a budding relationship, platonic or erotic, one that somehow challenged the conventions of courtship. But all the masks and makeup, and the role playing off and onstage, took the edge off the real passions beneath the skin of the songs.

In 1976 Dylan stripped off the masks. There was no decorative face painting, no movie cameras or role playing. Joan Baez stopped dressing up like his twin. Dylan's wife was a rare and awkward guest. The keenest description of Sara in those days comes from Baez: "Her skin was white and translucent, and her eyes were huge and black. Everything about her face looked frail: the rings under her eyes, the tiny dents in her forehead that would come and go when her mood changed, her hair thin and fluffy like black angel hair, her pouting lips and perfect nose, her high arched eyebrows. Sara was cold in winter; she didn't seem to have enough energy."

Dylan spent time with a woman who taught him the art of tight-rope walking (on a real rope stretched between poles, not the figurative line he had been walking between marriage and freedom). Another, a pretty herbalist, catered to body and spirit, inasmuch as herbs and potions can restore the powers of a musician who gives them up, nightly, for the pleasures of a capricious audience. Meanwhile, the ghost of Phil Ochs hovered above the stage, a memento mori, reminding everyone of the transience of this world and reminding Dylan, in particular, of his karmic responsibilities.

He grew a fringe of beard. He got rid of his feathered gaucho hat and covered his long curls in a white cloth, knotted behind and held to the brow by a string of beads, Arab style. Soon the other band members followed suit, tying their hair back with rags and colored scarves until they looked like a company of Algerian desert soldiers (wearing blue jeans and cowboy boots) instead of a covey of French mimes. Dylan got very serious. He performed more than twenty songs a night, half of them solo. His voice, at age thirty-five, had good range, a variety of placements, and nuance of tone; the voice had reached a peak of strength from which—undermined by tobacco and fatal vocal dynamics—it could only decline as he entered his forties.

Although the set list varied, on a typical night he would sing "Mr. Tambourine Man" then "Tangled Up in Blue" solo, for starters. Neuwirth would join him on "Vincent van Gogh." Then, backed by the band, he belted out "Maggie's Farm," "One Too Many Mornings," "Mozambique," and "Isis." After the intermission Dylan and Baez came on to perform the archival "Railroad Bill," Woody Guthrie's "Deportees," "Blowin' in the Wind," and "Wild Mountain Thyme." The band would step up behind them for an upbeat, rock version of "I Pity the Poor Immigrant." Then they sang another dozen tunes from a list that included "Shelter from the Storm," "I Threw It All Away," "You're a Big Girl Now," "Oh Sister," "Lay Lady Lay," and "Idiot Wind."

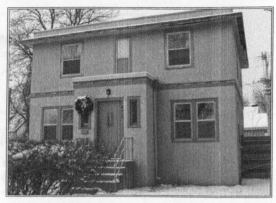

Dylan's childhood home,
Hibbing, Minnesota
(*Courtesy of the author*)

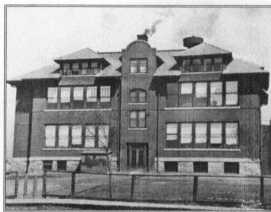

Alice Elementary School,
Hibbing (*Courtesy of the author*)

Dylan's elementary-
school class picture,
Dylan seated, center
(*Courtesy of the author*)

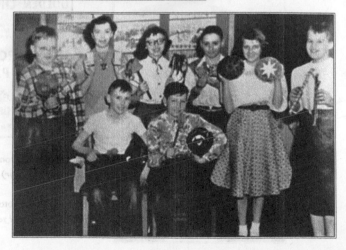

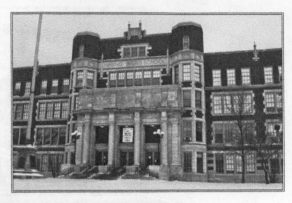

Hibbing High School
(*Courtesy of the author*)

Hibbing High
School auditorium
(*Courtesy of the author*)

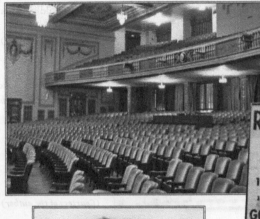

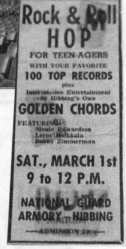

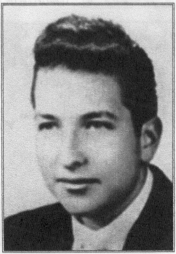

Dylan's first band, concert ticket
(*Courtesy of the author*)

Senior yearbook photo
(*Hibbing High School yearbook*)

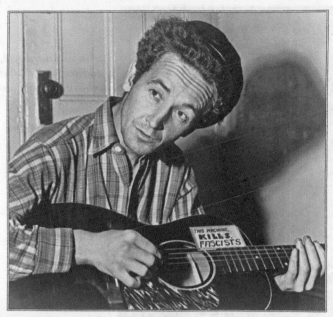

Woody Guthrie, March 1943 (*Library of Congress, Prints & Photographs Division, NYWT&S Collection*)

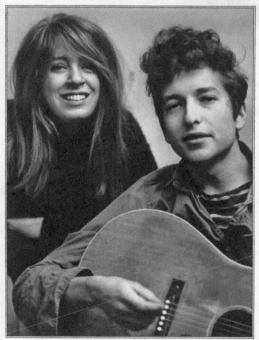

With Suze Rotolo in New York, 1963 (*Getty/ Michael Ochs Archives*)

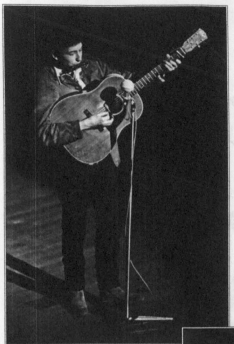

Dylan at Carnegie Hall, 1963
(*Southern Folklife Collection,
University of North Carolina*)

Dylan at St. Lawrence
University, 1963 (*St. Lawrence
University yearbook*)

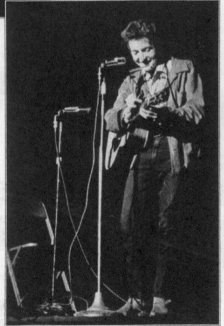

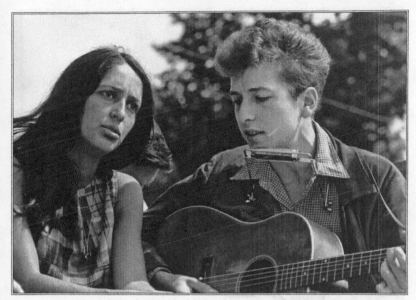

With Joan Baez at March on Washington, 1963 (*Still Picture Records Section, Special Media Archives Services Division [NVWCS-S], National Archives, ARC Identifier 5420210*)

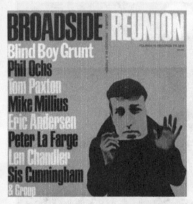

Album cover, 1972, Dylan as "Blind Boy Grunt" (*Courtesy of Smithsonian Institution, Center for Folklife and Cultural Heritage*)

Dylan, circa 1964 (original pen-and-ink drawing by Milton Glaser) (*Courtesy of Dale Bellisfield*)

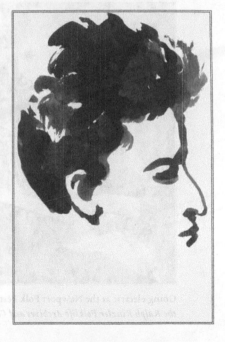

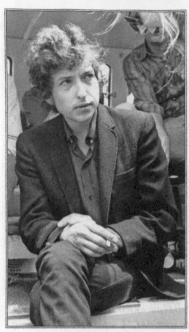

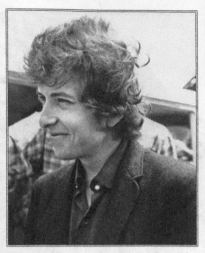

Dylan at Newport, 1965
(*Diana Jo Davies, courtesy of the Ralph
Rinzler Folklife Archives and Collections,
Smithsonian Institution*)

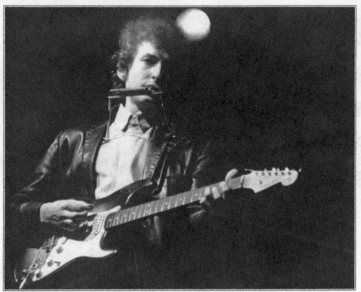

Going electric at the Newport Folk Festival, 1965 (*Diana Jo Davies, courtesy of
the Ralph Rinzler Folklife Archives and Collections, Smithsonian Institution*)

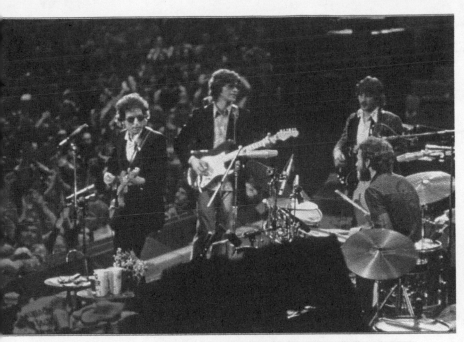

Dylan with the Band, 1974
(© Tom Zimberoff)

Sara Dylan, March 1975,
San Francisco
(© Michael Zagaris)

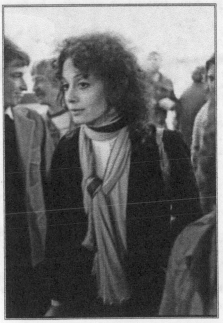

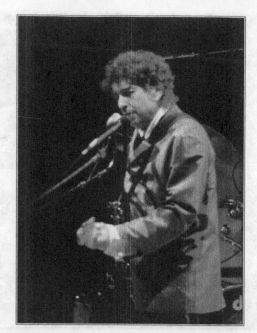

Dylan in performance, 1997 (© *Colin Moore*)

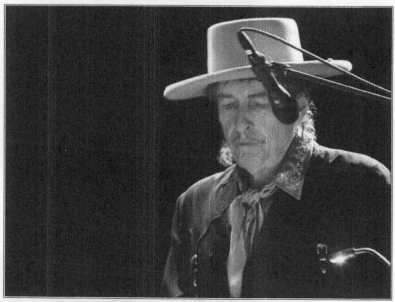

Dylan in concert, Aberdeen, 2009 (© *Bud Fulginiti*)

The scope and quality of those shows went largely unnoticed at the time. Now most of them are lost, in the afterlife of live performances: the dance dramas of Nijinsky and Martha Graham, the interactive psychodramas of Lenny Bruce, Lord Buckley, Spalding Gray, and Lily Tomlin. In Madison Square Garden, 1974, Dylan had sounded belligerent and defensive, mostly keeping his distance from us. In 1975, throughout Rolling Thunder Revue 1, he had been not only approachable but endearing, chatting with the audience and his bandmates, sharing his music and the moments of performance. In 1976 he was still connecting, but now he was aggressive, colossal, and furious. When he sang "A Hard Rain's A-Gonna Fall" in a dirgelike tempo, the band members sang along on the chorus. But he was far removed from them. Neuwirth, Kinky Friedman, Rob Stoner—they're all grinning like this is just one more good-time sing-along while Dylan's face is tragic, he is trumpeting his prophecy like Isaiah before the fall of Jerusalem. Only Baez in her gypsy-red turban, the profound eyes of Joan Baez, reflect the mystery of the lyric. Dylan looks like the one man on the stage who really knows what the words mean.

The change in the set list reflected the change in his mood. Shelving most of the songs on *Desire*, notably the tendentious "Hurricane" and the nostalgic "Sara," he replaced these with wrenching love songs, the lyrics of remorse and longing from *Blood on the Tracks*, that incomparable record of a broken marriage. Even older songs were recast so that they began to sound like outtakes from that album. In fact, the second leg of the Rolling Thunder Revue was virtually the live enactment of *Blood on the Tracks*, the spectacle of love gone wrong, broken promises, dreams shattered. Dylan was heartsick and he was angry—you could hear this in the slashing intro notes of "Maggie's Farm," a Chuck Berry riff that came to Dylan by way of the Rolling Stones' Keith Richards.

I got a head full of ideas
That are driving me insane.

It's a shame the way she makes me scrub the floor.
I ain't gonna work on Maggie's farm no more.

In 1965 Maggie's farm had been the close, precious world of folk music. Now in 1976 the trap was the structure of traditional marriage. He was pouring out his vitriol in Sara's direction, whether or not she was in the audience—he seemed even angrier when she was present—and upbraiding himself as a party to the hypocrisies of the marriage contract.

The delivery of the love songs, old and new, for Sara and others, was endlessly inventive, intense, and authentic. When he sang "I Threw It All Away" he sounded like he was sobbing. "Lay Lady Lay" he had transformed from a lilting country tune, a courtly seduction, into a knockdown doo-wop pickup number out of the fifties with cynical new lyrics: "Forget this dance / Let's go upstairs! / Let's take a chance / Who really cares?"

His singing on the melancholy love song "One Too Many Mornings" (1964) was precise, wide-ranging, and full of harmonic surprises. The original three-chord ballad had been enriched by a chord progression that now moved the melody through a major chord to a minor and back to the tonic in the first four measures. Dylan's voice deftly picked out notes from the major chords to the minor, anticipating the mournful pealing of the pedal steel guitar, singing harmonies over and under the melody before the tagline. And he was making up verses on the spot, addressing a lover and a moral situation that was more real than art can ever be:

I've no right to be here
If you've no right to stay
Until we're both one too many mornings
And a thousand miles away.

The centerpiece of the new set list, the rock on which the whole psychodrama rested, was the caustic, hypnotic "Idiot Wind," the

Divorcees' National Anthem. This had replaced "Sara," the tender plea for mercy and understanding, pushed it out of the way for the time being and then forever. He sang the song very slowly. He sang it with rancor, engraving every syllable in stone, his eyes murderous, and he sang it for a very long time (ten minutes).

Idiot wind, blowing through the dust upon our shelves,
We're idiots, babe,
It's a wonder we can even feed ourselves.

Sara heard him perform this on a rainy afternoon in May at Colorado State University, Fort Collins, on the eve of his thirty-fifth birthday. She flew in from Southern California with Dylan's mother, Beatty, and the children and surprised him. He had plans that did not include them. As much as he loved all of them he was not fond of such surprises, even on his birthday, and so he brought a renewed vehemence to his performance on Saturday afternoon. Joan Baez, who by now looked upon Sara with affection, stumbled upon a scene that night she said reminded her of something out of a silent melodrama: through the open door of a dressing room, in garish light, she saw "Sara in her deerskins and oils, perched on a straight-backed chair. Her husband was on one knee in front of her, bare-headed and apparently distraught. . . . Bob in whiteface and Charlie Chaplin eyeliner, Sara all ice and coal and bits of rouge."

She was running out of ways to forgive him, and the posture of the suppliant was unendurable. Soon they were separated and in March 1977 Sara filed for divorce. The decree was finalized in June, but the dispute over the children's custody dragged on, in and out of court, for the rest of that year, pouring brine on the wound.

Back on the Malibu coast of California the summer after the tour, Dylan spoke to reporter Neil Hickey of *TV Guide*. He told Hickey that his temperament was influenced by his astrological sun sign,

Gemini. "It forces me to extremes. . . . I go from one side to the other without staying in either place very long. I'm happy, sad, up, down, in, out, up in the sky and down in the depths of the earth." After apologizing to the reporter for being inarticulate, he went on to talk for an hour about himself, the media, music, and religion— eloquently, and with generosity toward the stranger.

Of all the myths about Bob Dylan there is none more laughable than the idea he doesn't give interviews. He has given hundreds of interviews on four continents, most of them polite, many of them gracious, and at least a dozen of them witty, profound, and revealing. It is, once again, a matter of perception. For every interview he grants he turns down forty, and he gets more attention for being audacious and enigmatic than for being serious. So the reporter begins by congratulating himself on his rare catch, unaware that the complete interviews with Bob Dylan would make a fascinating book the size of *Anna Karenina*.

"The press has always misrepresented me. They refuse to accept what I am and what I do. They always sensationalize and blow things up. . . . It makes me feel better to write one song than talk to a thousand journalists." That stands to reason. Nevertheless, he goes on talking, about the shallowness of TV news, about Rimbaud, Melville, Conrad, Joyce, and Allen Ginsberg, about the mystery of anti-Semitism. He even talks about God.

"There's a mystic in all of us," Dylan reflects. "Some of us are shown more than others. Or maybe we're all shown the same things, but some make more use of it."

Hickey asked him how he imagined God.

"I can see God in a daisy. I can see God at night in the wind and rain. I see creation just about everywhere. The highest form of song is prayer. King David's, Solomon's, the wailing of a coyote, the rumble of the earth. It must be wonderful to be God. There is so much going on out there that you can't get to it all. It would take longer than forever."

His principles, he confesses, are so removed from the norm that he finds most people's values baffling. "Greed and lust I can understand, but I can't understand the values of definition and confinement." He means marriage, and the pigeonholing of music; he means race and denominations of religion—everything that needs space to breathe. "Definition destroys. Besides, there's nothing definite in this world." This is the romantic, anarchic cry of the creative spirit that must be free; Dylan, the Gemini, had been driven once again to an extreme. In the next breath he might as sincerely insist upon strict definitions that harness a song's energy, the chain of command in a fighting force, or the life-giving matrix of the nuclear family.

In closing, the reporter asks if Dylan has any messages to the world.

"I've been thinking about that. I'd like to extend my gratitude to my mother. I'd like to say hello to her if she's reading this."

Sara and the children—and an old-fashioned marriage—had rescued him in 1966. They guarded him for the eight years he needed to convalesce and compose the music and lyrics for nine albums. These included, among others, *John Wesley Harding*, *The Basement Tapes*, *New Morning*, *Planet Waves*, *Blood on the Tracks*, and *Desire*—nearly a hundred of the best songs he would ever produce.

After the Rolling Thunder Revue rolled into oblivion, after Dylan's thirty-fifth birthday party, there would be no more touring for nearly two years, and no new songs or records until spring of 1978. Dylan was adrift, tangled in miles of celluloid in a Warner Bros. back lot screening room. He was editing his movie *Renaldo and Clara*. He sat in the darkness for much of that year looking at film footage of himself and his wife; of Joan Baez, Jack Elliott, Allen Ginsberg; and others, trying to cut eighty hours of film down to a size fit for distribution. Given the movie's autobiographical imagery, the viewing must have been excruciating when it was not numbing, a painful immersion in the tragedy of his marriage—an act of penance.

Losing his beloved wife and the unity of the family would cause a shock to his system as great as the trauma that had led him to retreat to the Catskills a decade earlier. What would rescue him now? Another woman? The wisdom of Ginsberg? The power of music? Perhaps he was counting on the success of his movie.

Renaldo and Clara opened in Los Angeles and New York in late January and was a dismal failure with the critics and at the box office. The movie was a financial disaster for Dylan, who had paid for it with his own money. This must have hurt. Now the question—as important a question as who, or what, would save him during this ordeal—is this: what, if anything, did he need rescuing from? There is a simple answer and a complex one. The simple answer is "the everyday vices" (the three D's) that ambush rock stars, the excesses of Drink, Drugs, and Debauchery that undermine health and productivity. Dylan admits to having succumbed, in part, to "the everyday vices" in another interview, conducted in November 1977 with Ron Rosenbaum. In that conversation he also explains the hazards of performing really well: "You do lose your identity, you become totally subservient to the music you're doing in your very being. . . . It's dangerous, because its effect is that you believe that you can transcend and cope with anything. That it is the real life, that you've struck at the heart of life itself and you are on top of your dream. And there's no down.

"It's the appearance of the Devil. . . . The Devil is everything false, the Devil will go as deep as you let the Devil go. You can leave yourself open to that."

Bob Dylan had left himself open to that. He went back on the road in 1978 to replenish his bank accounts, with a new backup band that featured three comely black vocalists, Helena Springs, Jo Ann Harris, and Carolyn Dennis. He wore white jumpsuits and heavy eyeliner. His new production owed more to Las Vegas and Neil Diamond than to Rolling Thunder. The eight-month, 115-show tour debuted in Japan in late February. He played in Australia and New

Zealand before returning to Los Angeles in mid-April to record the songs for a new album, *Street Legal.*

> *China doll, alcohol, duality, mortality.*
> *Mercury rules you and destiny fools you*
> *Like the plague, with a dangerous wink*
> *And there's no time to think.*

(FROM "No Time to Think")

The first week in June they played seven dates at the Universal Amphitheatre in Los Angeles in preparation for the European journey that hopscotched through Great Britain, Holland, Germany, France, and Sweden. The tour ended in triumph before an audience of 200,000 at the Blackbushe Aerodrome in Surrey, England, July 15. *Renaldo and Clara* and the divorce had cost him tens of millions, and he meant to recoup his fortune. After a two-month break the band reconvened for a sixty-five-date North American tour, coast to coast, a tour that took its toll on Dylan's psyche as well as his vocal chords.

> *You've murdered your vanity, buried your sanity*
> *For pleasure you must now resist.*
> *Lovers obey you but they cannot sway you*
> *They're not even sure you exist.*

(FROM "No Time to Think")

In Portland, Maine, he gave a warm introduction to the band members, especially to "my current girlfriend, Carolyn Dennis." Two days later he introduced her as his ex-girlfriend. In Springfield, Massachusetts, on September 16, he acknowledged "on the left my fiancée Carolyn Dennis; and in the middle my current girlfriend, Helena Springs"; in Greensboro, North Carolina, in December he called for bows from "my ex-girlfriend Jo Ann Harris, my new girlfriend Helena Springs, and my fiancée Carolyn Dennis." Of course this was all in fun, but it underscored the fact that he had come a long way from the domestic security of Hi Lo Ha and the temperance of his life in the late sixties. He was counting on red wine or brandy to ease the transition from one ecstatic performance to the next.

By November he was burned out, physically ill. In San Diego on Friday night, November 17, 1978, near the end of the show, Dylan was running on empty. A year later in the same theater he told his audience: "Someone out in the crowd, they knew I wasn't feeling too well. I think they could see that. And they threw a silver cross on the stage. . . . I put it in my pocket. I brought it with me to the next town. I was feeling even worse than I'd felt when I was in San Diego. I said, well, I need something tonight. I didn't know what it was. I was used to all kinds of things. And I looked in my pocket and I had this cross."

He took to wearing a cross around his neck onstage for the rest of the 1978 tour, and he changed the lyrics in "Tangled Up in Blue" so that the woman he meets in the topless bar is not reading "an Italian poet / From the thirteenth century" but verses from the Gospel of Matthew instead.

In January 1979 Bob Dylan accepted the Lord Jesus Christ into his life as his personal savior. He met with the pastors of the Vineyard Fellowship in West Los Angeles and "prayed that day and received the Lord." He began attending Bible study classes at the School of Discipleship, studying the life of Jesus four days a week for the rest of the winter.

This is the point in time and in the progress of Bob Dylan's career where I lost him. Or rather he lost me, and most of his fan base. It was not his religion that put me off, but the fact that a religion had taken over not only his inner life but his songs and his performances. I had thought that, like Henry James, Dylan had a mind so fine that no idea could violate it. I was wrong. For the next two years he wrote and performed nothing but religious music, fire-and-brimstone gospel tunes of the most fundamental, doctrinaire, and judgmental ilk. There were gems among the coals, such as "Every Grain of Sand" and "Gotta Serve Somebody." Some of it was fine musically, but most of the twenty-seven songs on *Slow Train Coming* (1979), *Saved* (1980), and *Shot of Love* (1981) are downright preachy. And Dylan was also preaching in front of the curtain, thus:

You know you're living in end times—I don't think there's anybody here who doesn't feel that in their heart. . . . Men shall become lovers of their own selves. Blasphemous, heavy, and high-minded. . . . I'm telling you now Jesus is coming back, and He is! And there is no other way of salvation. . . . Jesus is coming back to set up his Kingdom in Jerusalem for a thousand years.

(Albuquerque, December 5, 1979)

It's called the Truth, the Light and the Way. There's only one. There can't be but one. Satan will tell you there's all kinds of ways, but there's only one Way. And which kind of way do you think that is? Alright. Remember earlier the story you heard about Jesus? Well, Jesus is called 'The Solid Rock Before the Foundation of the World.' I know there's some that think it sounds incredible. I know it does. But you watch when you do need some help—when you've exhausted everything else, when you've had all the women you can possibly use, when you've drunk all you can drink. You can try Jesus. He'll still be there.

(Albany, New York, April 27, 1980)

I did not want to be preached to by Bob Dylan or anybody else in 1979, and I was not so diehard a Dylan fan that I would keep listening to his records no matter what. I had begun to lose interest in his new work after *Desire*, and by the time I got the call from Saltzman about a Bob Dylan stage play I was not as thrilled as I would have been four years earlier. Even the prospect of meeting the man was not very appealing, given his reputation for surly behavior and his current avocation as an evangelist.

Ben Saltzman, a kindly gentleman in his shirtsleeves, put us at our ease as soon as we entered his office. Murray Horwitz later recalled him as a soft-spoken, middle-aged fellow with thinning hair who talked like someone in the garment business downtown. His wife, Naomi, an efficient, attractive lady in her forties, moved in and out of the office with papers and notes. She answered a phone in the next room.

We sat on a couch and armchairs in a room dominated by Ben's desk on one side and a wall of shelves on the other with books and albums. There were all of Dylan's records, bootlegs and foreign pressings included, and every book that mentioned Bob Dylan or his music—already a sizable library thirty years ago. On the wall behind the desk was Milton Glaser's iconic silhouette portrait of Dylan with psychedelic hair (the poster hung on dormitory walls all over America in the sixties) and several framed shiny gold and platinum discs.

Saltzman put his palms up in a gesture that took in the room. He nodded in the direction of Naomi, who had just passed by. He said, "We are Bob's *yiddishekop*," a term difficult to translate. It means literally "Jewish head." What the manager was trying to tell us, in this context, is that he and his wife took care of the practical and worldly matters in Dylan's life so that the artist could concentrate on his music. For a long time Albert Grossman had done that, but Grossman had taken advantage of his position as personal manager, particularly as it pertained to Dylan's income from publishing and recording his songs. In addition to the 20 percent he got from booking Dylan, Grossman—by dint of an outlandish contract—collected 25 percent of Dylan's royalty income. That year, 1981, Grossman and Dylan would begin a lawsuit over unpaid royalties that would drag on for nearly seven years.

Naomi Saltzman had been the secretary and bookkeeper of Grossman's management company, but she preferred working for Bob Dylan. Husband Ben soon joined her in the New York office.

No doubt by using that Yiddish term, Ben was also referring, obliquely, and for the benefit of an audience that was entirely Jewish, to Dylan's surprising conversion to Christianity—as if to say, we are the keepers of an ancient flame, the guardians of Robert Zimmerman as well as Bob Dylan.

One of us asked if Dylan would be coming to the meeting. Saltzman said no, unfortunately Bob would not be present today. He shrugged and smiled, perhaps anticipating that someone might ask where Dylan was. Nobody asked and I had a feeling no one could have answered.

"You know," said Saltzman reflectively, casting a glance toward the door, "if he walked in here right now and sat down, he wouldn't say a thing. He would just look at you." The manager stared at me hard as he spoke. "And you would wonder, 'What have I done? What could I have done?' And that's how it would be. So, gentlemen?'" He was inviting us to pitch him ideas.

Those dramaturgical ideas of thirty years ago have mostly escaped my memory. Murray and John talked about the musical structure of *Ain't Misbehavin'* in which the various themes of Fats Waller's life are developed through the performance of his songs by a small cast of gifted singers and dancers. Saltzman listened carefully, nodding. Then he said he thought that what Bob wanted was a play with solid narrative structure, a beginning, a middle, and an end. He turned to me.

I thought of Bertolt Brecht and *The Threepenny Opera*, the epic theater that had made such an impression on young Bob Dylan. I described a play in which a young man with a guitar comes from a small town in the West to find his name and his fortune in New York City during the Cold War. He meets extraordinary characters, poets, comedians, and folk musicians in the coffeehouses of Greenwich Village. Although he is not the most talented musician on the scene he learns fast; most important, he has a powerful vision and a dream. He is a poet, and he wants to write songs that will express the passions, fears, and ideals of folks his age. His writing at first is imitative and tentative.

Then the young hero falls in love. He meets a New York girl who sees the greatness in him; soon he is writing not only sublime love songs but songs of protest like "Blowin' in the Wind" and "Hard Rain." Against the backdrop of the 1960s—projections of Freedom Riders, mushroom clouds, JFK and Martin Luther King Jr. speeches—we see the young bard composing his poems and singing his songs. Soon he has a devoted audience, and he's happy for a while. But then his beloved leaves him, breaks his heart, and the honey of the love songs turns to gall.

He becomes a rock-and-roll star. Fame and the pressures of facing larger and larger audiences make him frantic and then cynical ("Positively 4th Street"). The songs become surrealistic and furious ("Gates of Eden"), reflecting his trauma as well as all of America's in the mid-sixties. Marriage to a good woman and the experience of fatherhood rescue him from a collision course; he sings of those joys and fascinations for a while ("Wedding Song," "If Not for You," "Forever Young"). Then the marriage fails and the performer once again returns to the withering, dangerous life of the rock star. At last he turns to Jesus for salvation—

Saltzman held up his hand, like a cop stopping traffic.

"I get the picture," he said. "Very interesting. I don't know about the part after the marriage. Or just how much of the drama should be based on Bob's personal experience. We can talk more about that. The main idea here"—the manager paused for emphasis—"the main idea is to create a permanent showcase for all those songs that Bob Dylan will never sing again."

None of us knew what to say.

By that he meant most of Dylan's extraordinary work preceding 1979, all of the songs before his conversion. I hoped that this was some kind of a misunderstanding. I hoped that it was a passing notion, perhaps prompted by the tragedy of his friend John Lennon's assassination. Dylan had been known to change his mind and even to alter what he thought about his mind.

In this case, fortunately, he did change his mind. By the spring of 1981, during his European tour, he was mixing secular and religious songs in the set list. Gradually he would phase the gospel tunes out of the rotation until only a few remained. He would preserve his greatest work by continuing to interpret it as no one else ever would. Perhaps this is why we never heard from Dylan's office ever again.

PART III

Tanglewood, 1997

ORCHESTRA BOB DYLAN
LOCATION ANI DIFRANCO/BR5-49
PATRON# 365387 GROUNDS OPEN AT 4:00 P.M.
3 J 9 PRESENTED BY BSO/DON LAW CO.
SEC. ROW SEAT
NO REFUNDS OR EXCHANGES
97T804 02
TANGLEWOOD - SHED
9706171051
PRICE $28.50 MON AUGUST 4, 1997 6:00 PM

❊ CHAPTER 11 ❊

Young Blood

The Tanglewood Music Center near Lenox, Massachusetts, in the Berkshire Mountains, features a fan-shaped outdoor "shed" that covers a large stage and 5,000 seats, with a lawn for additional concertgoers stretching outside. The Boston Symphony Orchestra has been giving summer concerts on the site since the 1930s. In 1940, conductor Serge Koussevitzky started a summer school for young musicians there, and it's still thriving.

My wife and I had enjoyed several classical music recitals at Tanglewood while vacationing in the village of Tyringham, ten miles south. But we did not think of attending any rock concerts until Bob Dylan put the Berkshires on his schedule in 1997. Knowing of my long-standing interest in Dylan, she secretly purchased two tickets as near the stage as she could get for his concert under the shed for August 4, as a surprise birthday present. She wanted me to go with my son Benjamin.

A promising drummer and guitarist, Ben knew Bob Dylan mostly by name, as a legend rather than a flesh-and-blood performer. My son was born in February 1983, about a year after my meeting in New York to discuss the Dylan musical. As a teenager, his tastes ran more to Nirvana, Jane's Addiction, Metallica, and Pearl Jam than to any artist of the 1960s.

Now it dawns upon me, with some sadness, that there was no Bob Dylan in my son's life, as there had been in mine. Dylan had been a giant in my world, a poet and something of a prophet, someone you could trust to tell the truth of his perceptions. He saw deeply into history and the human heart. The poet was a reliable moral quantity—incorruptible, in this sense. But there was no one like Bob Dylan in the Reagan-Bush era, and recently the man himself had become a shadowy presence, heard and seen in glimpses beyond a barrier of his own making.

He was not idle and he was hardly forgotten. He showed up for benefits like the Live Aid concert for Africa's famine relief fund in 1985, and Farm Aid for American farmers soon after. He toured with Tom Petty in 1986 and with the Grateful Dead in 1987. On a lark he joined his friends George Harrison, Roy Orbison, Jeff Lynne, and Tom Petty in a band they called the Traveling Wilburys, which enjoyed some success with studio albums they released in 1988 and 1990. In 1988 he was inducted into the Rock and Roll Hall of Fame, and at the ceremony his colleague Bruce Springsteen said: "Bob freed your mind the way Elvis freed your body."

But Bob was not taking care of his mind or his body, and by the late 1980s alcohol appeared to be affecting his performances. In January 1986 the singer Carolyn Dennis gave birth to Dylan's third daughter, Desiree Gabrielle Dennis-Dylan; Dylan and Dennis were wed in June 1986 but the secret marriage provided only short-lived stability in a life that work and love had rendered chaotic. Six years later the marriage ended as quietly as it had begun—to the larger world as if it had never happened.

On February 20, 1991, a friend and I tuned in to a telecast of the thirty-third Grammy Awards ceremony at Radio City Music Hall in New York. We had heard that Dylan would be getting a lifetime achievement award and singing a song. Jack Nicholson introduced the disheveled singer, who was dressed in a rumpled dark jacket and wearing a gray, short-brimmed fedora. He reminded me of the tipsy tramp the comic Red Skelton had made popular back in the days when people still thought drunks were funny. Guitarist César Díaz, who played behind Dylan that night, said he was ill, and maybe he was. Singing "Masters of War" he jammed the words so impetuously I could hardly make them out. I was glad when the racket was over and hoped Dylan would go and lie down. But no, Nicholson had to present him with a trophy. Dylan stared at it for a long time, squinting, as if it were an artifact he could not quite see or comprehend, before mumbling this acceptance speech:

> Well . . . my daddy, he didn't leave me much. You know, he was a very simple man. But what he did tell me was this: he did say, "Son?" he said . . . [pause] He said so many things, you know [laughter]. "You know it's possible to become so defiled in this world that your own father and mother will abandon you, and if that happens, God will always believe in your ability to mend your own ways." Thank you.

My companion, who was visiting me from Holland and knew his way in and out of a gin bottle, turned to me and said, in his Dutch accent, "Dan, I think your friend Bob Dylan is three sheets in the wind."

I turned off the television set and went to bed with a heavy heart. For the next five years I paid very little attention to Bob Dylan.

In fact what got my attention at last was not any new music but the surprising weight of our mortality. Allen Ginsberg, whom I saw quite a bit of in the 1980s and '90s, died of liver cancer on April 5, 1997. And on May 25, the day after he turned fifty-six, Bob Dylan was admitted to St. John's Hospital in Santa Monica for chest pains and shortness of breath. He was diagnosed with pericarditis, an inflammation of the conical membrane around the heart, caused in his case by the fungal infection histoplasmosis. He had probably inhaled the spores while riding his motorbike on the roads near Memphis.

We read in the newspapers a few days later that Dylan was gravely ill with a "potentially fatal" condition. Released from the hospital in early June he gave this statement to the press: "I'm just glad to be feeling better. I really thought I'd be seeing Elvis soon." That very moment I told my wife we ought to go and hear Bob Dylan, for better or worse, before he caught up with Elvis and John Lennon.

In order to prep my son for the concert I decided to play him some Dylan albums. I would not play anything from the antediluvian sixties or seventies; I would try out some music that would be more likely to sound like what we were going to hear in August at Tanglewood.

Dylan had not released a major studio album in the 1990s (although one had just been recorded). The 1980s had not been a prolific decade for him, either—by his own standards—but even in that difficult period he managed to make two very good albums six years apart: *Infidels* in 1983 and *Oh Mercy* in 1989. So those were the records I dusted off for a spin on our turntable.

Infidels is a transitional work, a departure from the pearly gates of the gospel world where so many of us had left the singer. All eight of the songs show traces of Dylan's born-again experience, but the best of them transcend the gospel genre, exploring abstract metaphysical questions ("I and I") or addressing timely geopolitical and even economic problems ("Neighborhood Bully" and "Union Sundown").

A curious interview—one of only two Dylan granted that year—took place on July 5 at the Empire Hotel in New York. The reporter was Martin Keller of the *Minneapolis City Pages*; the short dialogue, printed under the title "Religion Today Bondage Tomorrow," provides some insights into the poet's state of mind as he was selecting and mixing the songs that would add up to *Infidels*. Keller asks only three questions, but they elicit intriguing answers.

Keller opens with the New Age icebreaker: "Do you believe in reincarnation?" Dylan says that he does, there are no new souls on

Earth, in his opinion. "Caesar, Alexander, Nebuchadnezzar, Baal, Nimrod. They've all been here time and time again. Spirit talks to flesh—flesh talks to spirit." The problem, as he sees it, is that you cannot know who is addressing whom, body or spirit. Then, abruptly, Dylan declares that he is not seeking the truth, and he never was. "I was born knowing the truth. Everybody is. Trouble is they get it knocked out of them before they can walk." He denounces the intoxication of the "drugs of illusion." Humankind seems to be deaf to the sounds that can offer salvation, "while pursuing . . . a strange mirage. Seeking freedom where freedom isn't . . ."

Keller wonders aloud if the forthcoming record, *Infidels*, will address those issues that fans expect Dylan to tackle: freedom and oppression, true faith versus idolatry, the "drugs of illusion," and the deadening effects of consumerism and mass communication.

"I hope so," Dylan answers. "But no one's gonna buy anything or talk about anything that they don't understand. My work is understood in the blood of the heart." People get confused, he says, when they try to talk about his work. "The most they can do is try to categorize it. They call it folk-rock or white rhythm and blues or country-punk or religious message music. And it means nothing." What seems to matter most to people now, in Dylan's opinion, is the consumer culture—the marketplace has co-opted popular music. "When you go into a department store to buy an umbrella, your mind is attacked by a fictitious sound—The B–52's, The Pretenders or somebody—and you kind of end up drifting in and out while the cash registers ring. I don't remember that being the purpose of music." Dylan's career—at least during the twentieth century—may be seen as a crusade against the violation of music's true purpose.

"The purpose of music is to elevate the spirit and inspire. Not to help push some product down your throat. To those who care now where Bob Dylan is at, they should listen to 'Shot of Love' off the *Shot of Love* album."

Not many people in 1983 *did* care where Bob Dylan was at. Nevertheless, taking him at his word, before listening to *Infidels* let's have a look at this title song from that widely ignored album of 1981. It's a tight, percussive reggae rocker, with the great drummer Jim Keltner keeping time. Fred Tackett and Steve Ripley cover the guitar parts, and the wailing, hooting quartet of Clydie King, Regina McCrary, Carolyn Dennis, and Madelyn Quebec does the backup vocals. "Shot of Love" delivers a bitter sermon with the punch of a .45-caliber handgun.

> *Don't need a shot of heroin to kill my disease*
> *Don't need a shot of turpentine, only bring me to my knees,*
> *Don't need a shot of codeine to help me to repent,*
> *Don't need a shot of whiskey, help me be president.*

What the singer needs, he announces in the refrain, is a shot of love. And it is not erotic love, as he insists over the course of six stanzas of righteous renunciation.

> *Doctor, can you hear me? I need some Medicaid.*
> *I've seen the kingdoms of the world and it's makin' me afraid.*
> *What I got ain't painful, it's just bound to kill me dead*
> *Like the man that followed Jesus when they put a price on his head.*

"It's my most perfect song," he informed Keller. At that moment in his life Dylan probably believed what he was saying, as extravagant as it sounds. A reliable feature of his consciousness is his immersion in the present moment, whether he is singing for an audience or sitting for an interview. This was something his friend the Buddhist Allen Ginsberg greatly admired about Dylan. Many people talk about the importance of being in the moment but few actually practice it.

On that day in July 1983 Dylan was not thinking about the protest songs of 1962, the love songs of 1964, or the surrealistic collages he had hammered together in the mid-sixties. "Shot of Love" represented the best of him at that point in time. "It defines where I am at spiritually, musically, romantically and whatever else. It shows where my sympathies lie. No need to wonder if I'm this or that, I'm not hiding anything. It's all there in that one song."

Bearing this in mind, I sat my son Benjamin next to the stereo and played for him—the next generation—the album *Infidels*, from 1983.

The first track, and probably the best known, is "Jokerman." The singer addresses a character central to his iconography, the Joker, the trickster who creates illusion and is himself a victim of his own trickery. In this song, he casts bread on the waters, walks on clouds, manipulates crowds, and twists dreams. This joker might be Christ, he might be Bob Dylan, or he might be the remote God of the Old Testament who sees the world's madness and injustice but seems to be unmoved by our needs.

> *It's a shadowy world, skies are slippery gray,*
> *A woman just gave birth to a prince today and dressed him in scarlet.*
> *He'll put the priest in his pocket, put the blade to the heat,*
> *Take the motherless children off the street*
> *And place them at the feet of a harlot.*
> *Oh Jokerman, you know what he wants,*
> *Oh Jokerman, you don't show any response.*

At the age of fifteen my son was no literary critic, so I don't suppose that the image of the Jokerman dancing in the moonlight meant much more to him than did the colorful Joker card in the Bicycle card deck or the villain in *Batman*. Nevertheless, Ben was fascinated by Dylan's nasal, incisive singing, especially the long, drawn-out syllable of the chorus, "Ohhhh, ohh, oh [two full measures] Jokerman!" And then, of course, the graceful duet of Mick Taylor and Mark Knopfler on guitars. This was solid, surefire rock and roll, Alan Clark droning on the organ, Sly Dunbar keeping an easy beat on the drums.

Ben was bouncing his knee and nodding his head, amused by the fanciful lyrics riding on the back of a conventional rock tune: a new-born baby with a serpent in each fist; the Jokerman shedding skins like a snake, and dozing in fields under the stars while a dog licks his face; then a jumble of images—a water cannon, tear gas, nightsticks, padlocks, and a Molotov cocktail. What did it all come to? Maybe it sounded like nonsense but it was glorious, soaring nonsense. One might say that the song was deconstructing the myth of the hero: the joker is a figure for all men and gods, embodying good and evil, darkness and light. It was my son's turn to see what he could make of Dylan's verses.

"My work is understood in the blood of the heart," Dylan had told Keller, and he meant that the emotional appreciation of the songs ought to precede a mental understanding of them. This is more obvious with songs than with purely literary works, because the melody and phrasing deliver the meaning over and under the text of the lyrics. "Jokerman," like many of Dylan's best songs, is monomorphic. In other words the piece has similar structure and meaning in all of its parts, so that if you arrive late, leave early, or nod in the middle, you may still get the gist.

"Jokerman" reminded Ben of the Beatles. The teeming imagery really is reminiscent of the kaleidoscopic lyrics of the Beatles' late period, "Strawberry Fields," "Penny Lane," "The Fool on the Hill," even "Lucy in the Sky with Diamonds." As strange as it seems, when I was growing up there were a dozen poets writing such profuse song lyrics. Now perhaps there was only one, or two if the Canadian poet Leonard Cohen had emerged from the monastery and taken up his pencil.

My son really liked "Neighborhood Bully," a number driven by the backbeat of Sly Dunbar's snare and high-hat, the grinding of Robbie Shakespeare's bass, the spare duet of Knopfler and Taylor's guitars, Taylor importing the attitude he had learned from onetime bandmate Keith Richards of the Rolling Stones. For years people said that Dylan's music was not meant for dancers, but this was no longer true. The tempo and riff smacked of the Stones' "Honky Tonk Women," although the subject was far removed.

> *The neighborhood bully been driven out of every land,*
> *He's wandered the earth an exiled man,*
> *Seen his family scattered, his people hounded and torn,*
> *He's always on trial for just being born.*
> *He's the neighborhood bully.*

I did not mention that the "bully" in the song was widely believed to be the state of Israel in the early 1980s after the embattled Jews had bombed an Iraqi nuclear reactor and invaded Lebanon. There were rumors that when Dylan's evangelical fervor began to cool he had studied with Hasidic Jews of the Chabad movement. His song was not so much a defense of specific policies of Prime Minister Menachem Begin as an expression of pride in a nation that had survived against the worst oppression.

> *Every empire that's enslaved him is gone,*
> *Egypt and Rome, even the great Babylon.*
> *He's made a garden of paradise in the desert sand. . . .*

My son's favorite song on the album was "Union Sundown," with guitarist Taylor carving out Muddy Waters riffs from the traditional "Rollin' and Tumblin'," and hammering them into the text of Dylan's wicked satire.

> *Well, the dog collar's from India*
> *And the flower pot's from Pakistan.*
> *All the furniture, it says "Made in Brazil"*
> *Where a woman, she slaved for sure*
> *Bringin' home thirty cents a day to a family of twelve,*
> *You know, that's a lot of money to her.*

The lyrics were so heavy-handed there was no mistaking the message that greed had the U.S. economy in a fatal squeeze: on one side the rapacity of capitalist companies, and on the other the hoggishness of the unions that opposed them.

The more romantic, slow dance numbers on *Infidels*—"Sweetheart Like You" and "Don't Fall Apart on Me Tonight"—made less of an impression. The exception, to my surprise, was the mysterious, mystical "I and I" with its haunting minor melody.

> *Been so long since a strange woman has slept in my bed.*
> *Look how sweet she sleeps, how free must be her dreams.*
> *In another lifetime she must have owned the world, or been faithfully*
>   *wed*
> *To some righteous king who wrote psalms beside moonlit streams.*
>
> *I and I*
> *In creation where one's nature neither honors or forgives.*
> *I and I*
> *One says to the other, no man sees my face and lives.*

The narrative stanzas tell a simple tale. A man has gone to bed with a "strange woman"—at least he is watching her sleep in his bed. He leaves her side to go out for a walk, to have his thoughts to himself and avoid conversation with the woman should she awaken. His thoughts are philosophical: the race goes not to the swift but to the worthy who know the truth; the world might end tonight but that would be all right; and finally the singer confesses—like the proverbial shoemaker—that he has made shoes for everyone else but goes barefoot himself.

What intrigued my son, who has a knack for riddles, is the chorus (the second quatrain quoted above). Dylan sings the quatrain five times, weaving it in and out of the little story like a child's riddle rhyme. Ben asked me what the song meant, and I returned the question to him.

"I guess he's talking about the two eyes in your head, eye and eye, or maybe two people are looking at each other eye to eye," Ben offered.

That had not occurred to me. I thought of the Bible verses where God speaks to Moses: "Thou canst not see my face: for there shall no man see me, and live." Then I pointed out the title of the song on the album jacket, "I and I," so that Ben could appreciate the pun on "eye and eye" (the phrase actually turns up in the third stanza). I suggested that maybe one self is talking to another self—two parts of a single person, maybe two people, or perhaps even a god might be conversing with a man.

He asked me where they were, and I told him they were "in creation." God's creation? "Probably not. It is a very particular creation, maybe the creation of the singer, maybe the world of those two people, the man and the woman in the room, because in that creation nature neither honors nor forgives. We know that in God's creation nature can both honor and forgive."

"It's a very lonely song," my son concluded. "Let's listen to it again."

No portrait of Bob Dylan in the 1980s would do him justice if it left out the cameo story of Larry Kegan.

Kegan was one of several teenagers with whom Robert Zimmerman bonded at the Jewish summer camp Herzl in 1954. The boys began performing their favorite rock and blues songs for the other campers, using the piano in the common lodge. Kegan, who grew up in St. Paul, had a good singing voice. As soon as Bob got his driver's license he would drive to visit his friend Larry in the Twin Cities, where they would go to parties together and play and sing for anyone who would listen.

In 1958, Larry Kegan made a bad dive in shallow water off the Florida seashore that left him paralyzed from the waist down. Young Bob regularly visited his injured friend in the hospital; he would wheel Larry into the sun parlor on a gurney. There they would sing songs until Larry got tired and then Bob would roll him back into his hospital room and tuck him in.

Although Kegan would never walk again, he found the courage to finish college and earn a master's degree in communications. While Bob Dylan was making his fortune in the 1960s, Kegan took on the management of a citrus farm in Florida, and later a resort for disabled veterans in Mexico. He also contributed to an evaluation of the attitudes toward sexuality in disabled persons, a study that became the basis of a required course at the University of Minnesota's medical school.

Meanwhile, he continued to make music. He formed a rock band named, ironically, the Mere Mortals (in contrast to the übermensch Dylan). And Bob Dylan never lost sight of him. Whenever Kegan was willing and able he joined the Dylan entourage on the road. And so he traveled with the Rolling Thunder Revue in 1975 and the gospel shows of the 1970s and '80s. A director named Billy Golfus, who later made a film about disabled persons featuring Kegan, recalled how Larry and his Mere Mortals bandmates "would load up Larry's handicapped equipped van and catch up with the tour and hang out as long as they could. Sometimes they'd stay for weeks as Bob's personal guests. Bob put the word out to the crew that these were his friends and they were to be treated right and 'make sure they don't get in the way or arrested.'" According to the same source, Larry's vehicle would caravan behind Dylan's bus, and some nights the old friends would talk on the citizens band radio until Larry drifted off to sleep.

Like Dylan's other close friends, Larry Kegan did not speak to the press or any other strangers about such favors, what Wordsworth has called "that best portion of a good man's life, / His little, nameless, unremembered acts / Of kindness and of love." In such a spirit Dylan called Kegan to the stage of the Holiday Star Theater in Merrillville, Indiana, on October 19, 1981. Instead of singing the scheduled encore "Knockin' on Heaven's Door" the star yielded his spot to Larry Kegan. Rolling onstage in his wheelchair he sang Chuck Berry's "No Money Down," while Dylan made squawking sounds on a borrowed saxophone. Two nights later and a thousand miles away, in Boston, Kegan was invited to play mouth harp on "When You Gonna Wake Up" late in the concert, and then stayed on to reprise his solo "No Money Down" as the encore that brought down the curtain.

As David Braun, Dylan's attorney in those years, related, "Catch him in the right mood, he was very warm and friendly. I can remember a kid on our block wanted his signature, and he takes a piece of my foolscap paper. He asked, 'What's the kid's name?' I said, 'Herbie.' He draws a picture of himself and he says, 'To Herbie, I could never have made it without you, Bob.'" And then there was the story Happy Traum told about a surprise visit Dylan paid him at his home in Woodstock around the same time. Dylan, Clydie King, and Jesse Dylan showed up in a big SUV. "He just knocked on the door and came in, and spent several hours playing records. He asked me what I was listening to, and I played him some songs that he ended up putting on some records [Paul Brady's "Arthur McBride," and "The Lakes of Pontchartrain"]. And I called John Herald [of the Greenbrier Boys] and my brother Artie. We hung out and played records and reminisced. He was asking about people that he had known here and whether they were still around and what's the town like, and all that. . . ."

Traum also recalled an incident that may have occurred during the same visit, when Dylan showed his natural generosity with children. "It was a funny story. My son Adam had been going to boarding school down in Poughkeepsie. That weekend he came home with a friend, this painfully shy Korean boy. Adam was playing the guitar at the time, he must have been fifteen. They were up in Adam's room. The kid played bass, and so they were up there jamming. Bob was here, sitting around, and then he said, 'Oh, what's the music upstairs?' I told him it was Adam and a friend of his. And you have to understand, this boy was *so* shy. Adam is very personable and outgoing, and for him Bob wasn't such a big deal. He'd known him since he was a kid, 'Jesse's dad,' see? But this Korean was so shy he couldn't even look at us.

"So the boys are upstairs jamming in Adam's bedroom. Then Bob goes up there, and he picks up a guitar and starts jamming with them. And this kid . . . I think he thought the heavens had just opened up. He was speechless the rest of the time. Bob played a few songs with them and then came downstairs. It was sweet. A very nice visit. And totally by chance that we were home."

A lawyer who once represented Dylan, humorously describing himself as an amateur psychiatrist (a useful sideline for an entertainment lawyer), has a long-standing theory about the notoriously guarded poet: "I think—and it's true—if you can get to Bob, you can almost get anything you want out of him, so he shuts himself off. Do you follow me? I think it's part of his defense mechanism. He will only talk through Jeff [Rosen] now about business. I think that is Bob's idea. And those two or three friends he has [Louis Kemp, for one], he knows they don't want anything from him. Everyone is picking on him now, they want something. And along with the natural paranoia of stars, for Bob there is the fear that if they get to him, they'll get what they want. He doesn't know how to say no."

Oh Mercy (1989), which I had always considered a superior effort to *Infidels*, proved to be a harder sell to the next generation—at least to the delegate in my household.

Ben could not sit still for the length of the first track, "Political World." He kept begging for a chord change: it never came. He found this monotonous and I could not really argue with him because musically he was correct.

He didn't like the next cut, either, the lugubrious "Where Teardrops Fall," with the scrub board scratching and the Hawaiian lap steel sobbing in the shadows; he said the singer sounded like he had a terrible cold. Dylan kept dropping his voice an octave at the end of every chorus drearily. But then, happily, the tough bass notes of Tony Hall's lead guitar cracked the ice for Daryl Johnson's four-on-the-floor drumbeat and Daniel Lanois's ringing dobro. The band was rocking at last, on the song "Everything Is Broken."

> *Broken lines, broken strings, broken threads, broken springs,*
> *Broken idols, broken heads, people sleeping in broken beds*
> *Ain't no use jiving, ain't no use joking,*
> *Everything is broken.*

The verse is sad and very funny at the same time, the rhymes piling up like potsherds and crippled furniture at the town dump. That song, alas, trailed off all too quickly. The next track is the magnificent gospel number "Ring Them Bells," and I made Ben sit there and listen, because I knew if he gave it a chance he would appreciate the words.

> *Ring them bells, ye heathen from the city that dreams*
> *Ring them bells from the sanctuaries cross the valley and streams*
>
> *Ring them from the fortress for the lilies that bloom*
> *Oh the lines are long, and the fighting is strong*
> *And they're breaking down the distance between right and wrong.*

The rest of the album held little interest for my son. He declared the program was dreary and plodding and dull, with the exception of the spooky downbeat "What Was It You Wanted," in which the singer plays hide-and-seek with some friend or lover. It is a bit like an Abbott and Costello routine scripted by John Lennon.

> *What was it you wanted*
> *I ain't keepin' score*
> *Are you the same person*
> *That was here before?*

Is it something important?
Maybe not
What was it you wanted?
Tell me again I forgot.

Both of us found this clever. The song was clearly—to me at least—based on a real dialogue, maddeningly insistent and repetitive, that had been going on between Bob Dylan and his public, and between Dylan and countless friends, relatives, and strangers, for about thirty-five years. Things like this are funny only when they are happening to somebody else.

Dylan had given the world a great deal by the time he was in his forties, but the demands the world made upon him were endless. In a good-natured radio interview he granted Bert Kleinman and Artie Mogull in November 1984, Kleinman mentioned the great expectations the public sustained for Dylan's next album, his next song, his next performance.

Kleinman asked: "Have you been able to get beyond that, to stop worrying about what people expect from you?"

"Who expects what?" Dylan replied. "I mean, anybody that expects anything from me is just a borderline case. I've already given them enough, you know; what do they want from me? You can't keep on depending on one person to give you everything."

In his memoir, *Chronicles*, Dylan speaks candidly of the 1980s as the nadir, and also the turning point, of his career. By the time he was touring with Tom Petty in 1986, he confesses, the live performances no longer captured the spirit of his songs. There was no intimacy in them, and no focus. The ten years from 1977 to 1987 had rendered him "whitewashed and wasted out professionally." Minutes before showtime it would occur to Dylan that he wasn't keeping his word with himself, and he couldn't even recall what the word was.

He says in that book that he had shot himself in the foot too many times. People will pay to see a legend, but only once. If a performer does not deliver on his promise then he is wasting his own time and everyone else's. He speaks movingly of there being "a missing person inside of myself," and how desperately he needed to find him. He felt "done for, an empty burned out wreck." The songs he had written—the vast majority of them—had become strange to him; he could no longer understand their origins or their meaning, and so he could not make the emotional connections he needed to perform them. He was ready to pack it in, to retire.

The road back, or rather the road forward, to vital performance had a lot of twists and turns, as Dylan humbly recalls. One night in early June 1987, he was rehearsing with Jerry Garcia and the Grateful Dead in their Front Street studio in San Rafael, north of San Francisco. After an hour of playing the core set of tunes he was used to performing with Tom Petty, the Dead wanted to go deeper into the master's catalog. They wanted to play some of the older, neglected works, things like "Chimes of Freedom," "Tangled Up in Blue," and "Simple Twist of Fate." Dylan got really jittery, doubting that he could connect with the old songs well enough to sing them with conviction.

He excused himself, saying that he had left something in his hotel room, and walked out, into Front Street, in the rain. It is a two-block dead-end street of concrete warehouses overhung with power lines. Dylan didn't intend to go back as he turned the corner. Passing a bar near the harbor, he heard a jazz ensemble. He went inside, ordered a gin and tonic, and stood four feet from the little stage where the piano, bass, and drum kit were set up against a brick wall. The old vocalist was singing ballads like "Gloomy Sunday" and "Time on My Hands," his voice casual, relaxed, convincing, reminding Dylan of the 1940s pop star Billy Eckstine. The man had natural power. In an instant of illumination Dylan understood the source of the singer's energy.

The scene, as he describes it, has a cinematic flavor. It is similar to the melodramatic encounter Joni Mitchell describes in "Real Good for Free"—the moment when the star, having lost her muse in the welter of fame and commerce, finds it again in the sound of a nameless street musician, a horn player inspired by nothing more than the plain emotion in his song. This is a stock scene, a cliché almost, but it might well have happened. Dylan does not tell us exactly what he learned from the singer in the dive in San Rafael, only that the man "sang with natural power," and that his *voice* was not the source of it. The power source came from the blood of the song or from the singer's ground of being or from the Holy Spirit—or maybe some combination of the three. He never tells us.

What he does tell us is that he returned to the Grateful Dead's Front Street studio that rainy night and found his voice, following the example he had just studied in the bar. At first the process was painfully difficult. Drawing upon a number of stratagems, old and new, Dylan discovered that he could perform his old songs effectively by bypassing his brain, somehow releasing the song from the tyranny of the lyrics. This was a revelation. He was able to get through his June and July performances with the Grateful Dead with ease, singing old and new material, whatever Garcia and the band wanted to play. It was all the same to Dylan.

This does not mean that he was out of the woods yet. In September 1987 he flew to Egypt en route to Israel, where he was to begin a European tour with Tom Petty and the Heartbreakers. Dylan traveled to the land of the pyramids with his sons Jesse, now twenty-one, and Samuel, nineteen. It was important that his children get a sense of how he spent his working days. He was singing diligently, a variety of sets (nearly fifty different songs on the first three shows), but he was still planning to hang up the guitar and call it quits when this tour was over in the autumn. His fan base had dwindled; he had the impression that in Europe people were showing up mostly to see Petty. The performances had become monotonous rituals—no longer draining, he recalls (although the recordings indicate vocal fatigue), but they were tedious to him because he felt no connection to the audience.

For twenty shows, from Tel Aviv to Milan, Italy, on October 4, Dylan was on automatic pilot. Gazing out over the heads of audiences in Switzerland, Germany, Holland, Finland, and Sweden, his eyes were fixed on retirement, the prospect of taking his ease with his friends and family on a yacht cruising the Bahamas, or in one of a half-dozen homes he had purchased in America and Europe. He had had his fill of this charade, performing for a public that scarcely knew him, and that he no longer cared to know. Word came that the advance sales in Paris had been so poor there would be only one show. He didn't much care.

And then one night the world-weariness caught up with him.

On Monday, October 5, the company found themselves in a jewel-like Renaissance town on Lake Maggiore in the Swiss Alps. The town of Locarno was known for its gardens of camellias, oleanders, and magnolias that bloom on lakeside promenades and the terraces that step down to the arcaded Piazza Grande, the main square. On a crag overlooking Piazza Grande stands the sanctuary of Madonna del Sasso, where brother Bartolomeo d'Ivrea had his vision of the Blessed Virgin five hundred years ago.

Under a full moon in Locarno Bob Dylan was about to sing for a crowd of thousands gathered in the Piazza Grande. The wind was blowing hard over the lake. He suddenly felt like he was falling. There is a moment when a swimmer is crossing a bay or channel and knows he is midway—as far to go forward as turn back—the perfect spot to drown in the deepest water. Then it is not fatigue that is the enemy, but panic. Actors have nightmares in which they walk onstage, open their mouths to speak their lines, and no sound comes out. This is the most extreme form of stage fright and professional players develop methods to overcome it. Dylan was on the verge of a panic attack and none of his compensatory techniques was working.

He later described the experience to a reporter. Struggling to gain his composure, Dylan had an auditory hallucination. "It's almost like I heard it as a voice. It wasn't like it was even me thinking it. *I'm determined to stand, whether God will deliver me or not.* And all of a sudden everything just exploded *every* which way." He started singing like he had never sùng before. "And I noticed that all the people out there—I was used to them looking at the girl singers, they were good-looking girls, you know? And like I say, I had them up there so I wouldn't feel so bad. But when that happened, nobody was looking at the girls anymore." They were riveted on Bob Dylan, the lead singer.

"After that is when I sort of knew: I've got to go out and play these songs. That's just what I must do."

When the tour concluded with four triumphant shows in London in October, Dylan decided to postpone his decision to retire. "I had a revelation about a bunch of things," he told Robert Hilburn of the *Los Angeles Times.* "This gift was given back to me and I knew it. . . . The essence was back." He sat down with his tour manager, Elliot Roberts, at the St. James Club in London, and told him he wanted to play two hundred show dates in 1988. He wanted to cultivate a new audience; the folks who had grown up on his records could no longer accept him as a new artist. That audience was "past its prime and its reflexes were shot." He had burned them too many times and their anger had not yet died down. He wanted young blood, a "crowd who didn't know what yesterday was."

Roberts, having witnessed Dylan's highs and lows in 1987, was cautious, if not skeptical. He suggested the performer take a couple of years off. They finally reached a compromise: Dylan would take a six-month break from touring and Roberts would see what kind of a tour he could book for the spring of 1988. It was a good thing they came up with this plan, because some time before Christmas Bob Dylan's hand was badly injured (in an accident that remains mysterious) and it would be months before he could perform again.

One of the most baffling distortions in Dylan's *Chronicles* is his account of the period from late 1987, when he injured his hand, until March 1989, the weeks in New Orleans when he was making *Oh*

Mercy with producer Daniel Lanois. For some reason he conflates the years 1988 and 1989 so that in effect 1988 ceases to exist in memory. It's like a blackout. His vivid account moves directly from his convalescence in Los Angeles in early 1988—during which he wrote songs for the new album—to the Victorian rooming house on New Orleans's Soniat Street where Lanois had set up a temporary recording studio in 1989. (A close reading turns up a reference to an "autumn" meeting with Lanois in New Orleans that could only be autumn of 1988. There are no other references to the events of that year.) Thus he bypasses the recording of the slipshod album *Down in the Groove* (May 1988) and more importantly a grueling American tour of sixty cities in the United States and Canada, seventy-one shows between June and October 1988 that took a toll on Dylan's vocal cords.

His self-portrait during these years of artistic turmoil includes some affectionate memories of Carolyn Dennis, the thirty-four-year-old singer who became his second wife. Dennis was known to read John le Carré novels for diversion and liked to go on long rides on the back of Dylan's Harley Police Special, over the damp back roads of the bayou. During the dark days of winter, when he feared he would never play the guitar again, he was grateful for Carolyn's presence. He describes her as a companion with desires similar to his, a woman open to his singular energy. She accompanied him to New Orleans, where the family lived—daughter Desiree was three—in a big old house on Audubon Place during the weeks he was recording *Oh Mercy*.

Sitting down to dinner at a little inn near the port of Morgan City, he looked to her to order from the exotic Cajun menu, admiring her self-reliance: Dennis, he recalls, was one of those rare spirits who never looks to someone else for the key to their happiness, not to him, nor to anyone else. "She's always had her own built-in happiness." He trusted her implicitly.

It is curious that the writer of *Chronicles* blots out that year of his life, because 1988 may have been the year most crucial to his development as a performer. The revelation in the jazz club in San Rafael had given him courage; the epiphany under the full moon at Locarno in 1987 gave him resolve. But not until June 1988 would he truly put himself "in the service of the public," to use his own phrase. No more Dylanettes, no more girl backup singers or string sections, not even a keyboard at first. Dylan played no harmonica that year. The band consisted of G. E. Smith, the lanky, hollow-cheeked rocker with the blond ponytail familiar to TV audiences as the lead guitarist on *Saturday Night Live*; Kenny Aaronson, skinnier than Smith, plucking a funky bass; and the versatile Christopher (Toph) Parker on drums. That was it, at the beginning, a lean, hard-driving quartet that interpreted songs from every period of Bob Dylan's career.

An intense, sixty-five-minute performance that began with "Subterranean Homesick Blues" (the first live version ever) and ended with "Maggie's Farm" at the Concord Pavilion in Concord, California, on June 7, 1988, was the world premiere of what would come to be known as the Never Ending Tour. The show grew, from a dozen songs to as many as twenty, and so did ticket sales as Dylan crisscrossed the nation and Europe, reaching out to his new audience.

> *It's all the same tour—the Never Ending Tour—it works out better for me that way. You can pick and choose better when you're just out there all the time, and your show is already set up. You know, you just don't have to start it up and end it. It's better just to keep it out there with breaks . . . extended breaks.*

After a break in the autumn and winter he did ninety-nine shows in Europe and America in 1989.

His performances were erratic, spontaneous, and unpredictable. They depended on Dylan's state of mind, and the chemistry between himself and his bandmates, himself and the audience. Never has any improvisational singer, mime, or dancer remained more firmly fixed in the moment of performing than the principal player of the Never

Ending Tour. People heard he was great and they heard he was terrible. He was both, often on the same night. There were rumors of inebriation and bad temper and cross words; there were, on most nights, brilliant renditions of songs familiar and little known. But there were the tunes that got rushed or mumbled. Some nights he would perform with an anorak hood over his head.

More and more people showed up to see him because they were curious about what he might do. He could be relied upon to be authentic in the moment they were watching him. Fans began to follow the Dylan tour for days and nights on end, like the "Deadheads" who followed Jerry Garcia. "There are a lot of people that come to our shows lots of times," Dylan observed, commenting on the variable set list, "so just for them, it's a good idea to do different things. It's not like they come and see me once."

About four hundred shows later, in 1992, Dylan told the journalist Robert Hilburn that there was little glamour in life on the road. "There are a lot of times that it's no different from going to work in the morning. Still, you're either a player or you're not a player. It didn't really occur to me until we did those shows with the Grateful Dead [in 1987]. If you just go out every three years or so, like I was doing for a while, that's when you lose touch. If you are going to be a performer, you've got to give it your all."

By giving his all, 100 nights a year, Dylan had found his new audience, people from their teens to their sixties. And in the process he found himself. He told Jon Pareles of the *New York Times* in 1997 that, unlike some musicians who dislike touring, for him it was as natural as breathing. "I do it because I'm driven to do it, and I either hate it or love it. I'm mortified to be on the stage, but then again, it's the only place where I'm happy. . . . You can't be who you want to be in daily life. I don't care who you are, you're going to be disappointed in daily life. But the cure-all for all that is to get on the stage, and that's why performers do it." The man who, thirty-five years before, had bypassed the boundaries of daily life by reinventing himself as Bob Dylan had finally accepted his fate and duty as a "player." For two hours out of twenty-four he could experience the perfection of a world where he had maximum control, a zone in which magic could, and did, occur.

And so, nine years and 879 performances after the show debuted in California, my teenage son and I headed toward the 880th episode of the Never Ending Tour.

CHAPTER 12

Finding the Beat

We drove up to Lenox in the late afternoon. The grounds of Tanglewood opened at four for the six o'clock show, so we had plenty of time to get sandwiches and find our seats, two folding chairs in the fifth row to the left side of the stage.

My wife, purchasing "the best seats in the house," had set us up within twenty feet of the biggest stack of full-range megawatt loudspeaker cabinets I had ever seen up close—far too close. Fortunately, I had a wad of napkins in my pocket. I could roll the napkins to make earplugs.

Dylan had tapped the twenty-seven-year-old singer/songwriter Ani DiFranco to open for him at Tanglewood, so it didn't take long to test the sound system. Sexy, hyperactive, young Ani, a Jewish Italian bisexual punk rocker from Buffalo, had enormous dark eyes full of mischief and a demonic grin full of teeth. She chuckled, or cackled in counterpoint to the long, staccato introduction to her song, strumming with admirable percussive force.

And Ani had one hell of a percussionist in Andy Stochansky. Between the two of them, Ani and Andy created a polyrhythmic beat as stirring as an African or Baja marimba band. Ani, the original "righteous babe," was known then mostly for her social politics, anarchistic, libertarian. She was a rabble-rouser, we could tell immediately, and the first thing she did that night—after blasting our eardrums with sixteen measures of polyrhythmic guitar strumming and rhythmic laughter—was rouse the rabble.

The song she opened with, I believe, was the rocker "In or Out." It was one of those ghetto-blasting numbers that nobody wants to sit still for; you just have to get up and move to it. And at Ani's bidding the audience, several thousand of us, got up off our folding chairs—and some got up *on* the folding chairs—bouncing and bumping to the African cadence. People danced out of their seats and into the aisles and Ani was shouting encouragement. She hadn't even started singing yet. Then came the cops, the fire marshals, and ushers, their arms raised, calling for order.

I wondered what Bob Dylan thought of this hullabaloo, if he was backstage or in his trailer watching this folk rocker—who owed so much of her style to him—warming up his audience to the boiling point before she had even finished one song. He had never done that sort of a thing to a crowd. Or had he?

Soon the aisles were cleared, Ani finished her song, and there was a roar of approval. She tuned up and started in again. People danced in their allotted places as the charismatic singer completed a stunning set of about ten songs, exquisitely written and precisely rendered. She offered a brief encore, and then bowed out although the crowd begged for more. As the warm-up act, DiFranco played by the rules.

The stage lights dimmed, houselights came up while the road crew came onstage in their black T-shirts to roll away DiFranco's equipment. Then they set up the drum kit, pedal steel, and guitar stands for the Eleventh Never Ending Tour Band.

The crew took their time, and around nine o'clock Dylan and the band took their places onstage. As he came on the audience shouted greetings, cheered, and applauded. David Kemper gave a terse drumroll; Larry Campbell played a few guitar notes. Then a booming circus ringmaster voice came over the PA system:

"Good evening, ladies and gentlemen! Will you *please* welcome Columbia recording artist *Bob Dylan*!"

He was wearing a scarlet lamé frock coat and a dark blue "string" bow tie, and strumming a low-slung Stratocaster. My first impression was that he looked not quite old at fifty-six but something beyond middle-aged, and vaguely androgynous. I don't mean effeminate but rather soft around the edges. His lined face had broadened and he was no longer slender. There was a little gray in his mop of tousled hair and he looked deadly serious, like a sea captain about to weigh anchor on a shaky vessel in lowering weather. The man had been deathly ill—this was only the second performance he had given since he left the hospital in June.

The cheering that greeted him that night was the sound of relief and gratitude for an artist who once again had come from the dark place—the other side—to share his words and music.

Dylan stood just to the right of center stage, in front of the round-faced, beaming drummer, David Kemper. Far right, Bucky Baxter was seated at the pedal steel guitar, sporting a black fedora, shades, and a Vandyke beard. Next to Kemper stood the dark-skinned, mustachioed Tony Garnier on the string bass; to the far left was Larry Campbell, the lead guitarist. Campbell had long, dark, straight hair that hung down to his shoulders, and he was so handsome, or beautiful, that he might be mistaken for a girl. He moved around more than the other sidemen, depending on the song and the instrument he was playing, sometimes guitar, sometimes mandolin, drawing close to Dylan as they riffed between stanzas, backing away when the star returned to the microphone.

They opened with a moderate-paced boogie. It was so loud that at first I couldn't make out the words. But the rhythm was solid, hard-edged, like Chuck Berry or Lynyrd Skynyrd. I stuffed more paper in my ears and tried to get Ben to try some. I was surprised by Dylan's voice (once again!); what a rusty rasp there was at first as he sang the phrase "it gets so hard" in the middle range, but when he reached up for the high notes on the tagline the sound was clear as a cavalry bugle.

But where are you tonight, sweet Marie?

So that was the song, the richly poetic, hyperspatial gem from *Blonde on Blonde* (1966), written then in a blaze of manic creativity, "Absolutely Sweet Marie."

No rock-and-roll song is honor bound to make sense. Many, such as "Tutti Fruiti" and "Hound Dog," make a virtue of nonsense. The pleasure of certain Dylan songs from his "surrealistic" period is that they play off sense against absurdity in a lyric sequence that adds up to uncommon sense. In "Absolutely Sweet Marie," the question "Where are you?" comes from a man trapped in many situations that make it impossible for him to meet his sweet Marie. Frustrating predicaments keep him and his beloved apart: a railroad gate (hers) that he cannot get over, a traffic jam, illness. There are prisons and jails and locks he cannot open although she promises deliverance. This is a classic anxiety dream where rescue or the object of desire retreats just as one seems to be reaching it. The song has a famous line, "to live outside the law you must be honest," and I hoped that my son would recognize it over all the din. I wished I might translate the lyrics for Benjamin, but there was no talking to him; he would have to understand the songs "in the blood of the heart," just like everybody else. I waited for Dylan to sing the renowned words, just as the narrator of the song waits for sweet Marie, and Dylan held us in suspense by *not* singing the lines where they belong, in the middle, but waiting for the last chorus.

> *Well, six white horses that you did promise*
> *Were fin'lly delivered down to the penitentiary*
> *But to live outside the law, you must be honest*

I know you always say that you agree
But where are you tonight, sweet Marie?

The six white horses are a figure from American folk music, songs like Blind Lemon Jefferson's "See That My Grave Is Kept Clean," the glorious horses that draw the hearse to the cemetery, another form of deliverance.

So what is the metaphoric calculus here? Sweet Marie, the beloved, promises the white horses of deliverance to the trapped narrator, *but*—and it is an immense and thorny qualifier—"to live outside the law, you must be honest," and maybe he isn't, or wasn't. In the penitentiary of this life we are all stuck if we are not honest enough to envision a greater and more compelling reality, or form of penitence. The singer has not quite achieved that clarity of vision, and so he cannot find his beloved, for all the promises she has made to free him. In the end it appears she is as lost as he is.

And now I stand here lookin' at your yellow railroad
In the ruins of your balcony. . . .

One last guitar riff, a crash of cymbals, and then the cheering and hooting sounded, calling forth the waves of applause.

Bucky Baxter plucked some mournful minor notes on the pedal steel guitar, Kemper started a slow drumbeat, and Dylan sang, pleadingly, "Señor? Señor?" I noticed a meaningful progression from the playful metaphysics of "Absolutely Sweet Marie" to the religious drama of "Señor (Tales of Yankee Power)" that graced the neglected 1978 album *Street Legal*. In both songs the singer is lost or trapped, struggling to contact an important woman. I did not expect the show would have a narrative logic but here it was unmistakable.

Who knew what the master of the Never Ending Tour did in his trailer all afternoon? He must select thirteen or fourteen songs out of an inventory of seven hundred and arrange them in some order that would be taped to an amplifier or a music stand under the title "set list." One must, of course, begin with an up-tempo number to get the crowd's attention and give the band and the singer movement enough to loosen up, to make mistakes; the opener cannot be too subtle or slow. Then one must create a balanced mix of old and new, borrowed and blue, selections from a range of years and tempos. Then Bob Dylan must memorize the songs, at least some of them, the ones he has not performed in a while.

Part of the magic of the Never Ending Tour shows is that Dylan performs unexpected songs, so you can watch him revive and update the work in a spontaneous creative act. And sometimes during the hours of preparation he will shape a program thematically, as he had clearly done for Madison Square Garden in 1974. If so, the program itself becomes a dramatic work of art. At the start of the show in Tanglewood I glimpsed such a shape.

The character "Señor" in the song of that title is the confidant or companion the singer addresses as they travel together. We are overhearing a conversation between the singer, who is in danger, and Señor, a guide, or guardian angel. This time the words were not only loud but clear, and my son could hear all of them.

Señor, señor, can you tell me where we're headin'?
Lincoln County Road or Armageddon?

Lincoln County Road alludes to the range war in 1878 between the ranchers and the merchants in New Mexico. Armageddon, the site of the last battle between good and evil before Judgment Day, can only be known from the Revelation of St. John the Divine; it has become a symbol for any catastrophic clash of arms. This road the men are traveling could lead to a regional skirmish or the most crucial challenge for the human spirit, the war to end all wars.

Where is his lady love, his comfort and salvation, his sweet Marie, now that he needs her? He asks his guardian where she is hiding.

And when they arrive there, will there be any solace? The singer moans:

> *There's a wicked wind still blowin' on the upper deck,*
> *There's an iron cross still hangin down from around her neck.*

As the journey continues our hero sees dreadful signs and he can hardly stand the suspense. Just where are they going and who can he talk to when he gets there? Dylan's rearrangement of the lyrics in this performance sharpened the story's logic. He warns of how hardhearted the host will be where they are headed, then asks for a moment to gather his strength; at last he says he is ready.

The lyric signals a time shift. The sinuous strains of the pedal steel guitar, twisting and turning, lead the singer to reflect on the moment *after* the catastrophe, the arrival, the confrontation.

> *Well the last thing I remembered before I stripped and kneeled*
> *Was that trainload of fools bogged down in a magnetic field.*

A gypsy with a twinkling ring tells him this is no longer a dream—it is reality: holocaust images of people stripped naked, brutalized, "bogged down in a magnetic field" of the material world, false idols, greed, corrupt governments, racism. Who, or what, can possibly save them?

> *Señor, señor, let's overturn these tables,*
> *Let's disconnect these cables. . . .*

Their destination, like the cities of Sodom and Gomorrah that Abraham tried to save from God's wrath is so bewildering and terrible that the singer must take it upon himself (as at the end of "Hard Rain") to do the work of salvation. He calls upon his companion (*Señor* is one of the titles Spanish-speaking peoples give to the Savior) to join him in overturning the tables—just as Christ overturned the tables of the moneychangers in the temple—and cut the whole reeking barge loose from its moorings.

"Señor" was one of the last songs Dylan wrote before his conversion to Christianity, and was as good an acknowledgment of that chapter of his story as any of his gospel songs would have been. When he had sung the last lines, and Kemper's drumroll signaled the ending, Dylan humbly acknowledged the warm ovation:

"Thanks, everybody."

At this point, hearing the assertive backbeat of David Kemper's drums as the band kicked up the hard-rocking "Tough Mama," I might have given up on the thematic thread that connected the first and second numbers. He had chosen this one for the quicker tempo, following the stately "Señor."

In my opinion "Tough Mama" is one of Dylan's best rock-and-roll songs, if rock and roll is to be judged by the gold standard of Chuck Berry, Buddy Holly, Otis Redding, and Elvis—the sheer clarity and precision of the beat and the blue notes that change from major to minor, the *danceability* of the sound. In the 1930s dancers wanted a band that could "swing," that dished out that six-count, bouncy rhythm a couple could jitterbug to, or Lindy hop, or double shag. In the 1960s the dancers preferred a moderate rhythm that "rocked." The standard was Chuck Berry's "Carol" or "Little Queenie," both reinvented by the Rolling Stones; Elvis's "All Shook Up"; Junior Walker's "Shotgun"; Martha and the Vandellas "Dancin' in the Street"; Tina Turner wailing "Fool in Love"; practically anything by James Brown.

Bob Dylan made funny self-deprecating comments about his own songs being undanceable and this was mostly true. The tempo of "Subterranean Homesick Blues" was too fast, "Like a Rolling Stone" lacked a firm backbeat, and "Rainy Day Women" was in 6/8 march time; the Dylan songs that made it as far as the jukebox would clear the dance floor—all the more remarkable that people sat back and played them anyway. But "Tough Mama," composed for *Planet Waves* (1974) under the influence of the hard-rocking Robbie Robertson and Levon Helm, broke new ground for Dylan. It was the shuffle drumbeat that did the trick, a syncopated backbeat that the lead guitar could grind against with growling boogie progressions.

As Dylan ducked into "Tough Mama" he looked possessed, transported by the rhythm, beyond language—and the song's language is a force to be reckoned with. He was drawing from the original lyric about love and freedom like a palette, transposing words and phrases, rearranging stanzas or deleting them as the spirit moved him, throwing anything at the canvas that would stick. "Tough Mama," to continue the theme of the evening, might well be the Madonna/redeemer of "Sweet Marie" as well as the woman with the iron cross in "Señor." He calls her "Sweet Goddess" and "Silver Angel."

But now he has caught up with her. At last he and his angel are together, and now what does he want from her? He wants her to move over and make room, to cut him some slack. Now the time has come for him to enter the world again, become a stranger, "to carve another notch," which happens to be exactly what the real Bob Dylan did when he took to the road again in 1974.

Working back and forth through his text, he snatched or slashed lyrics until he got to the final stanza. This he sang word for word, in its entirety.

> *I'm crestfallen.*
> *The world of illusion is at my door,*
> *I ain't a-haulin' any of my lambs to the marketplace anymore.*
> *The prison walls are crumblin', there is no end in sight*
> *I've gained some recognition but I've lost my appetite.*
> *Dark beauty*
> *Meet me at the border late tonight.*

Drumrolls, crashing cymbals, and Kemper rang down the curtain on a number that made the most of his rock-and-roll skills, a number he has stamped with his own peculiar artistry.

Of all the great drummers who have traveled with Dylan, including the immortal Levon Helm, the excellent Howie Wyeth, Christopher Parker, and George Receli, David Kemper is my favorite.

A round-faced, animated fellow with thinning hair and a cherubic smile, Kemper, my age and seven years Dylan's junior, replaced drummer Winston Watson in the band in 1996 and played with them until 2001. He played 569 concerts. He is small, compact, and gentle. In some ways Kemper is an unlikely-looking rock-and-roll drummer, an intellectual who reads Borges and Kafka, a studio painter whose pictures of cats and domestic scenes fetch good prices in galleries here and abroad. The drummer for the Jerry Garcia Band from 1983 to 1993, after that he divided his time between painting and session work before going on the road with the Never Ending Tour.

Kemper lives with his wife and daughter in a spacious, bright house in West Hollywood. There are lots of his lighthearted cat paintings on the walls.

He has two different stories about how he met Bob Dylan.

"We bumped into each other way back in 1973, literally." Dylan and his band were busy at Village Recorder studio in Los Angeles, Studio B, early in November, recording *Planet Waves*. Kemper was working on another album in the same building. He was on a break, sick with the flu, and standing in the hall dazed, his back to the door. "And I was complaining to my girlfriend, 'Oh baby, you know, God, I got the flu,' and then all of a sudden the doors burst open and this guy bammed into me. I said 'sorry' and he said, 'That's okay.' That's Bob Dylan and there goes the Band. Holy-moly." Like a runaway train, about to record "Forever Young" and "Tough Mama." And Kemper mused: "Am I in the right place at the right time?" Los Angeles, November 1973, a drummer colliding with Bob Dylan? Well, he was *almost* in the right place at the right time.

Then in 1980 Kemper was playing sessions and club dates with T-Bone Burnett, who had sung his own songs and played guitar behind Dylan on the Rolling Thunder Revue. In a house in Malibu on short notice Kemper played drums for an album session that yielded Burnett's *Truth Decay*. "And then we would work around town in nightclubs and we played some Chinese place in Santa Monica, I believe. Bob was in the audience. After the show there was a knock on the door. I opened it, and there was this hand and it said, 'David, I'm Bob.'" Kemper looked up from the handshake. "And I thought, Jesus. Blue eyes. He has got really blue eyes. Because to me it was—it was iconic. I never really had thought I would meet the guy. It was just out of my league, you know?" And then Dylan introduced his beautiful companion, the singer Clydie King.

Kemper had worked with the backup singer before, so the two greeted each other cordially. Kemper was the only one of the company who was not born-again; this was at the height of Dylan's gospel phase. T-Bone had exercised some influence, reading aloud to Dylan from the Bible, Leviticus 20:6: "And the soul that turneth after such as have familiar spirits, and other wizards, to go a whoring after them, I will even set my face against that soul, and will cut him off from among his people." Dylan seems to have taken this to heart, reading it as a comment on his own dealings with astrologers and fortune-tellers, as he found himself separated from his wife and children in 1979. That was the year he converted.

Not until 1996, several years after David Kemper's decade with the Jerry Garcia Band, would the forty-eight-year-old drummer be invited to join the Never Ending Tour, following the resignation of Winston Watson. For more than four years the band had consisted of Watson, Baxter, Garnier, and the guitarist John "J.J." Jackson. Fans were hoping for a change and so was Dylan. The ensemble had settled into predictable routines; there were rumors that authorities such as Van Morrison had fingered Watson as the cause of the stasis. Watson was a methodical, enthusiastic young percussionist who used two metronomes and overplayed the triangle. He looked up from the drum kit, grinning more broadly and more often than is seemly for a drummer. Dylan would—paternally, kindly—nod for him to get his head down. Be that as it may, if one is to rebuild a band from the ground up, there is no better place to begin than with the percussion.

Nineteen ninety-six had been a relatively uneventful year in a slack decade of Dylan's career. All winter and spring rumors were flying that a new album was in the making, one called "Coupe de Ville"; in the summer the hearsay continued, though the name changed to "Stormy Season." It had been so long since he had released an album of significant original work (*Under the Red Sky*, 1990, was negligible), his fans were ready to conjure one out of the silence. His live performances were fair, though there were thirty fewer of them—86 shows compared to 116 the year before.

In January he had been nominated for three Grammys: Best Male Rock Vocal for "Knockin' on Heaven's Door," which he had performed on the MTV *Unplugged* special; Best Contemporary Folk Album for *MTV Unplugged*; and Best Rock Song for "Dignity," a piece Dylan had written in one day after hearing of Pistol Pete Maravich's death on January 5, 1988. Pistol Pete was one of the greatest basketball players ever to dribble a ball and the most graceful. He died of a heart attack at the age of forty-one. "He could have played blind," said Bob Dylan. Of his own songs "Dignity" became one of Dylan's favorites. He must have been reading T. S. Eliot.

Someone showed me a picture and I just laughed
Dignity never been photographed
I went into the red, went into the black
Into the valley of dry bone dreams

So many roads, so much at stake
So many dead ends, I'm at the edge of the lake

Sometimes I wonder what it's gonna take
To find dignity.

He recorded this during the *Oh Mercy* sessions in 1989, but then did not release the track until the *Greatest Hits Volume III* came out three years later.

When Ellen DeGeneres announced the awards at the Shrine Auditorium in Los Angeles the night of February 28, 1996, Dylan's name was not among the winners. But he was pleased to see that his friend Tom Petty had won the laurel for the Best Male Rock Performance, Ramblin' Jack Elliott had won Best Folk Album for his *South Coast*; John Lee Hooker had pulled down Best Traditional Blues Album for *Chill Out*. The committee was on the right track, and Dylan's turn would come soon.

He took his band on the road April 13, the week after Easter Sunday. They started in the mid-Atantic states, then rolled through New England, the Midwest, and Canada before closing in Burgettstown, Pennsylvania, on May 18. After a month off they began a twenty-eight-show European tour in Aarhus, Denmark. Dylan's friend Van Morrison joined him at the Molde Jazz Festival in Norway a week before the summer tour ended on July 27 at the Lollipop Festival in Stockholm. During that week Van Morrison, a veteran bandleader, engaged Dylan in a heart-to-heart talk about touring bands. The best of them have a natural life expectancy, not too long or too short, and this band in particular—Dylan, Watson, Garnier, Baxter, and Jackson—might be losing its traction.

Chemistry was a mysterious thing in a band and burnout was inevitable. Dylan might not be setting the world afire in the 1990s but he owed it to himself and his audience—which he had rebuilt by a heroic effort—to make the most of his opportunities on the road as well as in the studio.

So after two shows at the House of Blues, a wigwam set up in the Olympic Village in Atlanta on August 3 and 4, Winston Watson, feeling the heat, crestfallen, submitted his resignation to the road manager, Jeff Kramer. He said he was homesick. After certain disparaging comments Van Morrison had made within his hearing in Molde the month previous, Watson could not muster the confidence to continue. Dylan had said nothing discouraging or unkind, but somehow the connection between the singer and his drummer had faded, and now it was time for Watson to move on.

Meanwhile, David Kemper had been in touch with the executors of Jerry Garcia's estate. Garcia had died about a year earlier of a heart attack at age fifty-three, and the estate had formed a record company. They planned to issue some rare concert recordings of Garcia's band from tapes that had been made from the console in the middle of the audience. John Cutler, who had been Garcia's sound man, was mastering a new tape from a Cleveland concert, and he sent it to Kemper, wanting the drummer's opinion.

"I don't know why," Kemper recalls, "but John Cutler sent Dylan a copy of it. Bob and Jerry were very close, and I know Bob liked the way Jerry interpreted his music." When Garcia died Dylan had released this statement to the press: "There's no way to measure his greatness or magnitude as a person or as a player. . . . He was that great, much more than a superb musician with an uncanny ear and dexterity. He is the very spirit personified of whatever is Muddy River Country at its core and screams up into the spheres. He really had no equal." Dylan went on to say Garcia was like a big brother who had taught him more than he realized. Although Dylan did not make a custom of attending funerals, when Garcia was laid out at St. Stephen's Church in San Francisco on August 10, 1995, Bob Dylan was there.

The most important thing Jerry Garcia had taught him in the summer of 1987 was how a troubadour, by *staying* on the road, making a life of performing, could bond with his audience: If you give, you'll receive. The Never Ending Tour came to resemble nothing on earth as much as it did the Grateful Dead's road show. So now when Dylan listened to the tape Cutler had sent him he was struck once again by the authenticity of Garcia's sound, and at the center of it a heartbeat. He picked up the telephone and called John Cutler.

"Who is on drums?" Dylan asked the sound man. "Is that Kemper on drums?" Cutler confirmed that it was. "Do you know how to reach him?" Cutler gave Dylan the phone number, before calling Kemper to say, "I think you are going to be getting a phone call." A year after Garcia's death and three years after David Kemper had last cracked the snare for him, Bob Dylan was looking for a live wire that would link him to the Grateful Dead and the Jerry Garcia Band.

He knew Kemper's sound and he knew something of his character from bumping into him here and there, in T-Bone Burnett's company, and from the late eighties when the drummer was with Garcia. Dylan would sometimes show up an hour before showtime, and he and Jerry, and the hirsute roadie Steve Parish, promoter Bill Graham, and David Kemper would sit around in the dressing room telling stories and joking. They would gang up on Graham, a natural stooge.

"What's in an egg cream, Bill?" Parish inquired.

"Well, it's got . . ."

"Come on, Bill! What's in an egg cream?"

Bill Graham was a German Jew raised by foster parents in New York, a would-be actor from New York City who—of all of them—should have known the ingredients of the Brooklyn soda fountain beverage, the egg cream.

"Well, it's got . . . egg?"

That is when Kemper learned "there is no cream and there is no egg in an egg cream," and doubled up with laughter on the couch listening to Dylan and the others teasing Bill Graham. "In fact," he recalls, "I thought Steve Parish was the funniest man I had ever met until I met Bob. I think Bob could be a comedian. Bob is very, very funny and the humor is real dry and it just sneaks in. There are no obvious bombs he has been practicing all day. He's not that kind of a jokester."

Among the earmarks of intelligence a sense of humor is one of the most delightful. Wanting a bandmate with a connection to Garcia, Dylan also wanted a man of subtle intelligence, and he had found this in Kemper.

The day he got the call from Dylan's office he had just picked up his daughter from school. "The phone was ringing, and it's Jeff Kramer, one of Bob's managers. And he said, 'Bob would like you to join the band. Would you be interested?' Of course I would. 'He would like you to join for a period of years—not just for a tour or a month. How would you feel about it?' And I said, 'I'm good for the rest of my life except for January. But, what are you going to use for material? No, just kidding. January. For two days I have an art show and a gallery has already printed up posters and mounted some pieces and I really need to be there.' And Kramer said, 'That's not a problem. Okay, I'll get right back to you.'"

Then Kemper hurried to the closest music store, Virgin Records, and bought the Dylan albums he did not already own. "I sat on my bed and learned two hundred songs in four days."

Meanwhile, he and the manager hammered out the details. "I may never know, really, *how* I did. At that point I wasn't too concerned. The first offer was a decent offer. And I said, 'Okay, I will accept this if we can renegotiate once you see how I change the band.' And Kramer said that sounded fair enough.

"Bob was very generous. He treated me with respect. He would support me when others would say, 'Kemper, I think you are not playing the right part,' or 'Are you slowing down, are you speeding up?' Bob would say, 'No, no, no, *David* is fine. In fact, are *you* in tune?' He would do these kinds of things, and he really ushered me into the job in a very gentle, supportive way. 'Don't worry about it, be confident, you are here because I want you to be here.' That kind of thing, which is wonderful for a drummer or any artist.'"

Accounts and reviews of the summer 1996 Never Ending Tour by Dylan enthusiasts like Andrew Muir and Michael Gray, as well as critics like Andy Gill of the London *Independent*, concurred that the show was in a decline before Kemper arrived. Kemper refuses to take any credit for the change, yet the facts speak for themselves.

Michael Gray, one of the most knowledgeable and dedicated music critics and "Dylanologists" in Great Britain, saw Dylan with Watson in Liverpool on June 26 and 27 that year. He could not resist comparing the shows to the ones he had seen thirty years before. "The band is one tenth as good as The Band [with Robertson, Helm, Hudson, Danko, and Manuel]; Bob Dylan isn't one tenth as energetic or innovative or communicative or accurate or acute; only the ragged rapture that greets him is greater than it was."

Gray suspected that Dylan, fifty-five, and approaching the eight hundredth date of the Never Ending Tour, had become a victim of his own success. "Ironically, now that Dylan has got so much less to say, and cares even less how he says it, he's knee deep in Lifetime Achievement Awards and disproportionate adoration. This time half the audience comes to both shows, and the Bobcats who descended from all corners of the land occupy all the front rows; the usual eighteen faces peering up at Bob's. . . . They spend the whole show on their feet, whooping at every number . . . regardless of how well or badly Dylan sings it." Andy Gill's newspaper review of the Hyde Park show on June 29 was dismissive, accusing Dylan of "subverting his own material, rendering some of the most well known of rock anthems virtually unrecognizable, both to the audience and, at times, to his own musicians."

Kemper's first show with Dylan was in San Luis Obispo, California, on October 17. There were four days of rehearsals in Los Angeles the week before, six hours a day. "So in the first rehearsal," he recalls, "the first break we take, I'm really not sure how to deal with this man. I just kept thinking, *He is this icon.* I can't deal with an icon, you know? It's too scary."

Dylan's lawyer David Braun, who spent a good deal of time with Dylan in social situations and in private, was fascinated by this effect he had on people. "For some reason, grown men, established artists in their own right, feel uneasy in Dylan's company. And I mean *everyone* famous that you can think of. I never figured it out. It's his look. He has an appearance that is awesome. If he's in a room, people know where he is, they approach him. They shift their weight from foot to foot, because he never says, sit down, let's talk. Doesn't do that. And they don't know quite what to do. And yet when he is alone—with me at least—he is fun to be with. We used to have long conversations about life. I have missed many a dinner because of him."

And so David Kemper decided he would have to try to deal with Dylan as if he were no different from anyone else—a difficult thing to do with the man you are working for. "I'm just going to deal with him exactly how I do with you. Hey, man! Where did you get those shoes? And I said, 'Bob, how do you remember the words?' And he says, 'Oh man, they are just stuck in here,' pointing to his head."

Dylan asked Kemper, "How do you play so—with the groove—so unrelentingly . . . you know, so unchanging?" And the drummer explained that he had worked for a long time to be able to do that. Dylan's question about the regularity of Kemper's tempo was a special compliment coming from a musician who possessed, from the early years when he was playing solo, the most precise sense of tempo. Dylan would start a song like "Boots of Spanish Leather" at 102 beats per minute and finish the last verse at 102 and you could set your metronome by it. This was one of his greatest natural gifts.

"Tempos are a very funny thing," said Kemper. "One beat more or less can make the difference from the most soulful groove you have ever heard and, 'Why is this uncomfortable?' There is a strict association with how fast you play *this* song in this version or style, and the emotional impact." I thought of the Rolling Stones' immortal recording of "Honky Tonk Women" and the sorry efforts of garage bands to cover it, often by playing too fast. I thought of "Tough

Mama" shaking the tent poles at the Tanglewood music shed, and how it had *rocked*. The problem with Dylan's band in the mid-nineties is that it didn't rock, at least not consistently.

Dylan does not actually call for a number of beats per minute. "No. He was all about feel and what he felt at that moment, and he would start the song." The drummer would watch the back of the leader's head, the movement of his shoulders. The sign was visual and telepathic. "He would play the song. And one night it would be a shuffle beat. And the next night it would be a straight eighth-note feel. He purposely wanted it to be that way. And me, I wanted to hear 'Lay Lady Lay' played the way it was on the record because I thought the recordings of the songs were the ultimate."

Sometime that October, having gained the new drummer's confidence, Dylan drew him aside for a chat after a rehearsal. He had brought Kemper aboard not simply for his technical chops but as a veteran of Garcia's band and a player who knew the galaxy of rock and roll. Casting about for an apt figure of speech, the bandleader said something to the effect that he wanted this band to make the Rolling Stones "roll over a bit" so we might come up, so to speak, into their space.

His tongue was probably in his cheek, the phrase was not literal but hyperbolic, yet he wanted to know what Kemper thought of the idea. "I looked around," he recalls, "and I said, 'We can't get there from here.'" This was the most honest and innocent response to the question, implying no criticism of anybody, himself or the boss included. Kemper has the highest regard for his colleagues, including the drummer he replaced, Winston Watson. No one was to blame for the fact the band did not cook like the Rolling Stones, or the Black Crowes, or B.B. King. They weren't really expected to. The truth was that if Dylan wanted more funk, and punch, and dance moves to this show, the organic chemistry had to change. From the top down or the bottom up, one way or the other, there must be a metabolic shift. He had taken a small step in changing drummers, and perhaps one more step in confiding the direction he wanted the band to pursue. The giant step would be his own, over the next three months, the composition and recording of eleven songs that would add up to *Time Out of Mind*, rock for the ages.

Up until now my son had heard nothing familiar, and I began to wonder if the Tanglewood program would include any of the Dylan chestnuts, songs we had sung at bedtime or on long automobile journeys. Now, four songs into the set, the drummer framed a moderate, upbeat, 4/4 tempo; Baxter twanged the simple chord progression on the pedal steel, G major, A minor, C major, and back to G. In eight measures we were home again as Dylan sang:

> *Clouds so swift*
> *Rain won't lift*
> *Gate won't close*
> *Railing's froze.*
> *Get your mind off wintertime,*
> *You ain't goin' nowhere.*

There was nobody in this audience who had not heard this ditty: on his mother's lap, on her boyfriend's knee, or around a campfire, although they may not have named the author. "You Ain't Goin' Nowhere" is one of those American tunes like "She'll Be Comin' 'Round the Mountain" or "Old Dan Tucker" (it sounds a *lot* like "Old Dan Tucker") that is so elemental and homespun you might think that no one could have made it up, no one person. The song could only have been picked up or recollected by some minstrel who heard or overheard it as a child from an ancient woman beating clothes out on a rock at the river's edge:

> *Oowee, we're gonna fly*
> *Down in the easy chair!*

This was a song that came with a place to sing it, down in the easy chair, on a cold winter day, waiting for the bride to come. On the chorus Baxter and Campbell joined Dylan in singing the delights of flying over the winter landscape in the warm comfort of the winged easy chair. And the crowd joined in singing.

I thought of how much the world had changed since I first heard "You Ain't Goin' Nowhere" in 1968. I was a junior in college. Bob Dylan had been missing in action for almost two years and nobody I knew had any idea what had become of him. I had a friend named Fletcher DuBois, a superb folksinger (who would later make records) who was so small you could pick him up like a doll. Some fraternity brothers would do that in greeting him in the lounge, and they would not put him down until he promised to sing them a song.

Fletcher had an antique Washburn guitar that was also very small, an amber-hued parlor guitar he played with delicacy and a sure rhythm, and he usually had new songs for us—at least they were songs we had not heard. From Fletcher I first learned "I'll Keep It with Mine," a very obscure Dylan song for anyone to be playing in the 1960s because Dylan had not released a recording of it.

> You will search, babe
> At any cost
> But how long, babe
> Can ya search for what's not lost

As of 1969 you could only hear this piece on recordings by Judy Collins, Nico, and the Fairport Convention. Fletcher played it in 1967 about as well as anyone ever has, belting out that glorious, wide-voweled, soaring chorus:

> But if I can save you any time
> Come on, give it to me
> I'll keep it with mine.

My friend learned the tune, and sang the song for us when none of us had ever heard it before, and we were grateful.

Then, in the autumn of 1968, at the end of an impromptu recital in the student lounge, in front of the stone fireplace, with wintertime looming, Fletcher introduced a new song, a world premiere. It was "You Ain't Goin' Nowhere." And for that audience of undergraduates at a men's college on a lonely hill in Ohio, with a harsh winter coming on, the song spoke to us; it became an anthem that promised to carry us through until spring. We would make up verses to it, as the form invites one to do.

Oil the locks
Boil the socks
Roll me a beer
Keep the runway clear
By quarter to two I'm getting out of here
You ain't goin' nowhere.

Dylan himself never tired of making up new lyrics to "You Ain't Goin' Nowhere" as if he himself had first heard the song from the old lady on the riverbank and could not resist tinkering with it.

Now the point of this story is this: Fletcher DuBois, a nineteen-year-old folksinger in the village of Gambier, Ohio, twenty years before the Internet, in a time when boys lined up at the phone booth to make long-distance calls with spare change, somehow had learned a Bob Dylan song less than a year after it was written in secrecy. None of us thought to ask him how he did this. So it remains a mysterious testament to the telepathic power of a certain kind of poem or folk song like "Boots of Spanish Leather" or an obscene drinking song like "Waltz Me Around Again, Willie." Once it has been sung, even in a close space like the makeshift recording studio at "Big Pink" in West Saugerties, the thing cannot be contained. It spreads like gossip or a volatile element that instantly disperses itself into the atmosphere.

From the country-twang languor of the easy chair, the band leapt up to the double-time rhythm of "Silvio," a rock tune too fast for dancing. But the song had a winning chord sequence, tonic to leading tone to subdominant, like the three-chord underpinning to "Louie Louie," the Kingsmen's classic; it made a great opportunity for the lead guitarist Larry Campbell and the bandleader Dylan to whip up bracing guitar duets between choruses. Bucky Baxter added wailing high notes on the pedal steel to make it a wicked trio.

Stake my future on a hell of a past
Looks like tomorrow is coming on fast
Ain't complaining 'bout what I got
Seen better days but who has not?

Silvio, silver and gold
Won't buy back the beat of a heart grown cold
Silvio, I gotta go—
Find out something only dead men know

Dylan's voice had opened up completely. He was eliding the penultimate syllables of lines, like "what I . . . got" sounding open vowels like "days" with full vibrato, and hitting the notes, high and low, right in the center.

"Silvio" had been rescued from the shipwreck of an album called *Down in the Groove* (1988), which Dylan made during his association with the Grateful Dead in the late 1980s. Jerry Garcia actually sang backup on the original recording, made in Los Angeles in April 1987; so did the Dead's Bob Weir and Brent Mydland. Dylan had been playing "Silvio" regularly in concerts since Garcia's death in 1995, for its main force and the racy guitar riffs, and as a tribute to the man who had so profoundly influenced his performance style.

As "Silvio" wound down Kemper backed off the snare, suspending the backbeat and playing nimbly on the cymbals, letting the guitars finish. He rolled the drums and Dylan cut the song off.

He called out to us, "Thank you, everybody."

Kemper called his first show with Dylan "a real trial by fire. San Luis Obispo. Cal Poly Auditorium. The monitor mix at sound check was fine. During the show that fineness all disappeared." That is, the clarity of the amplification and the balance of the instrument volumes and voice levels somehow got warped. This was not uncommon but nonetheless annoying, and the musicians would have to adjust onstage as best they could if the engineer failed to correct the balance from the sound board. For a new drummer, trying to keep a dozen new rules in his head, adjusting his volume was one more challenge to a player already overwhelmed with them. The set list included fifteen songs: it started with "To Be Alone with You" and "If Not for You," and included "Jokerman," "Silvio," "My Back Pages," "Masters of War," "It's All Over Now, Baby Blue," "Maggie's Farm," among others. The last encore was "Rainy Day Women #12 & 35."

"Bob gave a great and inspired performance. He leaned over his amps and put his hand up and gave me a high-five." Two months had passed since the band's poor showing in Atlanta, and Dylan was relieved to hear the difference.

Kemper read to me from his diary: "Eight hour bus ride to Las Vegas for the day off. October 19, 1996, Jean, Nevada. Star of the Desert Arena. Jill and Barry attend, friends of mine. I think this was the most amazing night of my life. The sound onstage was primo." The set list included nine songs the band had not played at the previous concert, including "Crash on the Levee (Down in the Flood)," "Señor," "Simple Twist of Fate," "Mr. Tambourine Man," and "Everything Is Broken." The last always got a rise out of the audience.

"At one point about five hundred people spontaneously rushed the stage. Then they just started screaming." Dylan's band was not the Rolling Stones but they were getting the kind of physical response a rock-and-roll band gets sometimes when they're really cooking. A couple of times during the first half Dylan held up his hand to salute Kemper. "On our break, he just said to me: 'That was scary. We were never able to do this before.' And then I said to him, 'I'm glad my friends were here to witness it.'"

By that point Kemper felt that he was going to be useful. He had seen Dylan on a television show, probably MTV *Unplugged* late in 1994, when he performed a lackluster "With God on Our Side," hiding his eyes behind sunglasses, and he looked like he didn't really care. Of course neither the new drummer nor any other player could make Dylan care or not care, and maybe the TV performance was unusual. Nevertheless, there are useful hints and influences that a mindful bandleader may hear from his sidemen, if they come at the right time.

At an early rehearsal Kemper noticed a departure from the custom he had learned from a decade of playing with Garcia. At the end of the song the drummer fires off a drumroll, and the guitar slices the final note off. It is customary for the bandleader to "cut the songs off," just as it is his prerogative to count off at the beginning. The drummer noticed that somebody else in the band was cutting the songs off, and he thought this was strange. He asked Dylan about it. From that day forward Dylan cut the songs off in the way the leader usually does. To an outsider this may seem like a small thing, but such gestures can significantly alter the mood of a band.

"And he never told me, 'Hey, back off, smart-ass.'" Dylan's bandmates knew how to make suggestions, to have input verbally or musically, and the boss was confident enough in his authority to pay attention.

❋ CHAPTER 13 ❋

Telling the Story

Understanding Bob Dylan's life and work since the 1990s depends
mostly upon knowledge of his conduct on the road and in the studio with other musicians. This is in part because the mature man
in his sixth decade succeeded in his struggle to keep his private life
secluded, and largely because he has organized his affairs around his
intense touring, writing, and recording schedule. What is left of his
"private life" is either mysterious or self-evident, depending on your
prejudices. With a wry smile he has told interviewers that he has no
private life; while that is an exaggeration it is truer for this famous
man than it is for most of us.

Dylan has six children, a beloved brother, David, nieces, neph-
ews, and many grandchildren, all of whom adore him. He is by all
accounts a devoted father, brother, grandfather, uncle, and nephew.
He collects houses in America and Europe, and is as likely to be
found in some castle in Scotland as in his hilltop home in Malibu
overlooking the ocean. He collects antique cars and there are quite a
few vehicles from the 1950s rusting away on his property behind the
green slat fence in Point Dume. There is also a paddock, visible from
his windows, where he keeps some very fine Thoroughbred horses.

Like any other prolific artist, he spends a *lot* of time alone. No extrovert could accomplish what he has. He may spend most of his hours alone, so if you do the math—hours per day, days per year—you get the picture.

He attends some weddings, Yom Kippur services and Bar Mitzvahs, a few funerals—schedule permitting—and holiday dinners from Thanksgiving till New Year's, mostly with his children. When he is not composing, watching television, or reading books he often passes the time drawing and painting.

In the 1980s he took up boxing, hiring the professional opponent (and amateur comedian) Bruce "the Mouse" Strauss as his trainer and sparring partner. Strauss is a fine-looking fellow for a Jew who has been knocked out a hundred times, and his wit is as nimble as his footwork. Dylan owns a coffee shop in Santa Monica, and behind it a gym where boxers train and spar. There is a regulation boxing ring surrounded by seats, where club fights are held on Saturday nights, and you must buy a ticket for admission.

Dylan has never lacked female companionship when he has desired it, so one may assume that he has it when he likes. I think it is also significant that—as one of the most famous men in the world, a world in which celebrity gossip is a pastime for many, and daily bread for journalists—Dylan has an admirable record for avoiding scandal and generally keeping his name out of the tabloids.

Historian Daniel Boorstin once noted a shift in American values that had replaced the classic hero with the celebrity. "The hero was distinguished by his achievement; the celebrity by his image. . . . The hero created himself; the celebrity is created by the media." He added, darkly: "The very agency which first makes the celebrity in the long run inevitably destroys him. He will be destroyed, as he was made, by publicity." The tragedy is familiar, from the lives of hero/celebrities like F. Scott Fitzgerald and Janis Joplin to Kurt Cobain and Tiger Woods. That Bob Dylan, more famous than any of them, has for forty years managed to avoid immolation by the media tells us more about his character than a team of investigative journalists could.

One might say that he has been too busy to make mischief, but that would fly in the face of what we know about busy celebrities. As he spends most of the year on the road performing with his band, it is in that context we ought to look for him.

Does he travel alone?

David Kemper says: "He has his own bus that he and his family travel in, if any of the children are with him. We don't all travel together." The band and the road crew, including the caterers, have separate buses. The crew is always the first to arrive at a location, usually by 4 A.M. They sleep until eight, get up and make coffee, and the cooks make breakfast for the crew. Then they set up the stage and heavy equipment. They take showers in the locker room or whatever facilities are available in the stadium, civic center, or theater. Then they get the finer gear prepared, the amplifiers and microphones and instruments. By midday the stage is ready and the musicians show up for the "sound check." A sound check is not just a testing of the sound system. It is a rehearsal of an hour or two. Sometimes the band rehearses songs on the evening set list; sometimes they play a grab bag of tunes the band wants to play. Kemper says this is one of the only bands he has ever been with that did a sound check before every performance.

Was Dylan usually there?

"No, Bob was usually not there. But he would come frequently. He might have an idea about changing a song or a tempo. 'Let's try something different with this.' Tweaking." Dylan had plenty to do without attending the sound check. On any given night he might be singing four or five songs he had not performed the night previous, or in a month's time, or for ten years. The singer did not go onstage without reviewing and in some cases relearning the lyrics from songbooks. This cannot be done at the last minute, no matter how spontaneous he wished to sound. A song to be played on Friday night might be studied Monday or Tuesday and played at a sound check on Thursday.

From Albuquerque they drove to Dallas and then to Austin.

Kemper's wife, Norma, and his little daughter, Chloe, joined him in Austin. When Kemper introduced the family to his boss at the hotel, Dylan took time to get to know them. "He played with Chloe. He has kids. He knows how to get down on their level. He knows you have to get down on their level literally." And so fifty-five-year-old Bob Dylan got down on his knees, smiled, cocked his head, and looked out of the corners of his blue eyes at shy Chloe.

"He was very gracious in putting in the few minutes that you know meant so much to my family." It was the beginning of a long voyage, five years with this legendary captain, and so Dylan had to send Mrs. Kemper some reassuring signals that he had been a family man himself.

Kemper had written in his diary, on October 23, 1996: "It's great to be with Chloe and Norma. It's also too hard to leave them. If I didn't have to support us I wouldn't be doing this band thing." Twelve years later he looks at it differently. "Well," he says, wistfully, "I said that then. But I would give anything to be back in that band. I miss it. And I miss Bob."

Dylan introduced the new band member to his children as they came to join him on tour, now and then: Jakob the musician, twenty-eight; Jesse, a promising filmmaker in his early thirties; and Anna, a year younger than Jesse, a studio painter who had gone back to college. One day Dylan approached Kemper for advice. He said he had a teenage daughter who was learning to play the drums. This was Desiree Gabrielle, his youngest, who needed a set of drums, so her father asked Kemper where he might look for them.

Kemper offered to give Desiree the drums he had used when he played with Jerry Garcia. After Garcia's death in 1995, "it was just too painful" for Kemper to be reminded of the decade he had traveled with the great bandleader, so the drums gathered dust.

Dylan gratefully accepted the offer.

A couple of months later, March 28, 1997, the band was rehearsing in New York. Dylan came up to Kemper during a break and told him how much his daughter was enjoying the drum kit. Then

Dylan said that he would like to do something nice in return, and the drummer replied that would not be necessary. But the boss was insistent. "You meet me at noon in the lobby tomorrow."

So at noon Kemper was waiting. Dylan and his bodyguard stepped out of the elevator and led him across Park Avenue at the stoplight. The best Italian clothing designer of the day, Giorgio Armani, had a boutique at Sixty-sixth Street and Madison Avenue. The bodyguard opened the glass door to Armani's for the two musicians to enter.

Dylan told Kemper to pick out a suit he liked. So he looked at the racks of elegant handmade garments and finally picked out "this beautiful silk and black linen suit." Dylan watched his drummer try on the coat and turn in front of the three-way mirror. "That looks good," said the boss, nodding approval. "It's great to have a special suit for a special occasion."

Kemper says the suit is so beautiful he has nearly worn it out. He recalls that Dylan tried on three suits that day, and had a great deal of fun while he was at it. At noon on any day of the week Bob Dylan was likely to draw a crowd in Armani's, so the management and the bodyguard had their hands full. Dylan was enjoying the free time, and he knew how to make the most of it.

The salesman held the suit coat up for his famous customer; he put his right arm in the sleeve and then the salesman held up the other sleeve. And then Dylan would turn *away* from the befuddled clerk. "And the guy would walk around and he could never get the other arm in. Bob wouldn't let him. He would twist as the guy would walk around. And then he would say, 'I'll take it!' And come to the next suit."

The first time he did this it seemed awkward. The second time, people started laughing. "The guy would walk around. 'I'll take this one, too.'" It was clever physical humor, Marx Brothers–style slapstick. "And the third suit, you get the right arm in, walk around—*I'll take that, too, okay. Wrap them up.*"

Dylan's show at Tanglewood in the summer of 1997 was typically structured: the opening five songs were "electric" with drums; next came a set of songs with "acoustic" arrangements, where the guitarists used hollow-bodied instruments and the drum was optional.

So after Dylan cut off the last note of "Silvio," Kemper put aside his drumsticks and walked offstage. He would not be needed for a few minutes. Dylan strapped on his Martin guitar and started flat-picking a G-major chord in easy 4/4 time.

I am a roving gambler
Gambled all around.
Wherever I meet with a deck of cards
I lay my money down.

Larry Campbell fell in behind Dylan with his mandolin, and Baxter on a second guitar. The song has but one chord change, G to C in the fourth line. And when they came to the chorus—repeating the ballad's last line—Campbell and Baxter chimed in with rough harmonies. Campbell, with his long hair and matinee-idol profile, looked like the riverboat gambler in the song.

Lay my money dowwwn . . .
Lay my money down.

Campbell recalls that the acoustic part of the program was always his favorite: "Great tunes, all of them. 'Roving Gambler' was always a lot of fun because I just love those old folk tunes, those traditional tunes. Being able to do those with Bob within a rock-and-roll setting, you know, that was very cool to me." Campbell admired the range of styles Dylan encompassed in rehearsals, and how long-forgotten songs would appear on the set list. Dylan was fascinated by the "close harmony" country singers of the 1940s and

'50s, brother duos like the Louvin Brothers, and Johnnie & Jack, who somehow managed to integrate Latin and black rhythms into the country idiom. Dylan and Campbell played Johnnie & Jack's gospel tune "The World Can't Stand Long" and later "Searching for a Soldier's Grave." They sang "Roving Gambler," uproariously, savoring the refrain.

> *I gambled up in Washington,*
> *Gambled over in Spain.*
> *I'm on my way to Frisco town*
> *To knock down my last game. . . .*
>
> *Knock down my last gaaaame . . .*
> *Knock down my last game.*

"Bob just grabbed from that old country lexicon, and he would make those tunes into something else. Tony [Garnier] and Bob would write up the set list before the show every night. There were songs we would do almost every night, like 'Tangled Up in Blue' or 'Watchtower.' They became regulars; so did 'Silvio.' But nothing was determined in advance. It's not like the set lists were compiled before the tour started. It was always done before the show every night."

Larry Campbell joined the Never Ending Tour only five months before we saw him at Tanglewood. Born in 1955 in New York City, he was well established as a versatile session player by the early 1980s. A close friend of Happy Traum, Campbell played on Traum's album *Bright Morning Stars* in 1980; he worked with Kinky Friedman, Rob Stoner, Shawn Colvin, and Edie Brickell before getting the call from Jeff Kramer, Dylan's manager in Beverly Hills.

Campbell had never met Dylan before, but he had known Tony Garnier for twenty years. Garnier played bass fiddle for the band Asleep at the Wheel before quitting in 1978 and moving to Manhattan, where he became part of G. E. Smith's combo on *Saturday Night*

Live. Campbell recalls the vibrant scene in New York that year, the renaissance in country music that centered on the Lone Star Café. "There was the whole urban cowboy fad thing just starting to kick in, which was, on the fashion and pop music side, a sorry state of affairs. But the upside—the upshot of that—was that there were a lot of great country music bars in New York at the time. And if you were into the real thing then this was a great opportunity to be playing that kind of stuff. The Lone Star Café opened around then." The great slide guitarist Cindy Cashdollar remembers playing there with Levon Helm and Rick Danko when she was in her twenties. She first met Dylan at the Lone Star.

The Café was the watering hole for all the best American roots musicians, including Garnier and Campbell, Helm, Danko, and Richard Manuel of the Band. Through that network Garnier got the job with Dylan in 1989. "Then in 1997, when Bob was looking for a new guitar player," Campbell relates, "well, Tony had recommended me before that."

John Stigler Jackson, who had been a solid lead guitarist for Dylan's band since 1992, left the Never Ending Tour at the end of February 1997, after their tour of Japan. Many fans were sorry to see him go, but Dylan and Garnier looked ahead. "Bob knew what I had done with other musicians," Campbell recalled, "but it was through Tony, really, that I first started playing with Bob."

When Kramer first telephoned Campbell to invite him to a rehearsal, the guitarist balked. "At first I didn't want it. I refused because I didn't want to be on the road anymore." He had just returned from a tour with k. d. lang—a good experience, but now he was getting a lot of calls from New York studios to do session work and he wanted to concentrate on that. So when Kramer called about joining Dylan's band, Campbell thought, "No, I don't want to do it."

"But then I got off the phone, and I said to myself: Wait a minute. This is Bob Dylan. This is somebody I've wanted to play with since I started playing guitar and here is the opportunity." So he called the manager back and said he was, in fact, interested.

The rehearsal was in Manhattan at the end of March. As Campbell remembers, it didn't seem like an audition so much as a jam session. Dylan talked to him, about friends in common, about the various instruments Campbell played, and old songs. "Mostly that rehearsal was just playing. Technically it wasn't an audition. It was just to see, to feel it out. Did everybody feel good playing together." Mostly they played old rock-and-roll tunes and country songs; they played one or two of Dylan's.

David Kemper remembers that particular rehearsal, and a quality Dylan was seeking in the new guitarist. "I learned a long time ago that finding a rhythm guitar player is the hardest thing in this town—just an electric guitar player that has taken the time to understand what the role of a rhythm player is, and then mastered it." By this, he does not mean a guitarist who only strums chords. The position Larry Campbell was called to fill was lead guitarist, but a lead guitarist plays "lead"—melodies, riffs, and breaks—only part of the time. During most of the song he will be keeping the beat, and the accuracy of this can make or break the rock-and-roll ensemble. "Keith Richards is a fantastic rhythm player. And Larry Campbell is a fantastic rhythm player. Just beautiful. And this expansive thing he brings into rhythm is not just strumming. It's a combination of licks and lines and melodies as he plays rhythm.

"And when we got Larry," Kemper recalls, "I was thrilled. First, I mean, the man himself. Part of being in a band is how you get along. And like everybody else, I fell in love with Larry right away. He was so good." But the audition, as he recalls it, was rocky. "His audition was terrible. He was nervous and fumbling. And later he told me, 'I had a terrible audition.' But I knew right away this was the guy."

Dylan saw the same qualities, and when the band hit the road in April, Campbell was one of them. Hiring a new guitar player was the second major personnel decision in six months and now Dylan had a band that rocked, one of the finest touring ensembles he would ever lead. "Three days of rehearsal," Campbell remembers, "and not much playing of *his* music, either, and then we started the tour.

Mostly songs I had never played before, and some I had never heard before. I had to just go out there and play them."

Five months and twenty-six shows after Campbell joined the band, Benjamin and I were watching him heat up the acoustic set under the shed at Tanglewood. After the last chorus of "Roving Gambler" David Kemper returned to the drum kit. Baxter started up a repeating figure on the electric mandolin, D major to D suspended fourth and back again, four measures, a jangling, modal folk sound. Then Campbell entered with a soft boogie progression, ABC walking boogie guitar against the drone of the mandolin—totally surprising and right for the introduction of "Tangled Up in Blue."

> *Early one morning the sun was shinin'*
> *He was layin' in bed*
> *Wondrin' if she'd changed at all*
> *If her hair was still red.*

A tangled tale for the audience at Tanglewood; they cheered the poet as they recognized his famous lines. Probably the best-known song from Dylan's album of love gained and lost, *Blood on the Tracks*, "Tangled Up in Blue" is one of his most memorable compositions of the 1970s. It had become a nightly fixture in his acoustic set, an old story to be told again for youngsters who had not been born when it was conceived.

"Tangled Up in Blue" is the tale of a fatal attraction, a courtship that may or may not have been consummated, and the singer's obsession with the woman who remains just beyond his reach. What has fascinated generations of listeners is the curious progress of the narrative and the shifting perspective.

The love story is compelling in itself, but so is the manner of storytelling and points of view, fashionably postmodern. The song begins in medias res, with the narrator remembering his beloved and her parents' prophecy that the marriage was doomed; the first stanza and the last one frame a roving tale of romance that unfolds in the five stanzas intervening.

The narrative follows the organic process of memory rather than the comfortable chronology of fiction. So those middle stanzas are a jumble, out of sequence. When he met her she was married, he tells us in the second stanza. He stole her away, they rode off into the West, then parted soon after that by mutual agreement. But she let him know that they were fated to meet again, on the streets of an unnamed city. In stanza three he is working as a cook in a lumber camp, but he still cannot forget her. In the fourth stanza he recognizes her as she waits on him in a bar. In stanza five they are alone in her kitchen, reading Italian poetry that thrills him. In the penultimate stanza six he recalls living with a group of people, one of whom is his beloved, on Montague Street in an atmosphere reminiscent of Greenwich Village in 1962—music in the clubs, talk of revolution in the air. But then:

> *He started into dealing with slaves*
> *And something inside of him died.*
> *She had to sell everything she owned*
> *And froze up inside.*

Who are these people? Up until now he has been speaking in the first person—*I* did this and that. Now his shift to the third person either suggests that *he* and *she* is a strange couple, or that they are actually the original lovers somehow transformed. His dealing with slaves (corrupt commerce) and her selling all she owned has put the narrator at such a distance from himself and his beloved that he can no longer even speak of *them* as *we*. The bottom fell out, he recalls, and he "became withdrawn." Only in the final stanza, returning to where he began, does he vow to get her back, somehow. After all—he confesses in the final lines—the lovers always *felt* the same about each other, they just happened to see things from different points of view.

That night at Tanglewood, Dylan simplified the melody as well as the narrative. I noticed after the first seven or eight verses he abandoned the melody and rapped out phrases on two notes, the mediant F major, and D major, the keynote. The keynote he used infrequently, usually on the penultimate word in a stanza. The effect, after the first two stanzas, was monotonous, particularly as he imposed on the same two notes during his long guitar solos between stanzas. This was the only time during the first forty-five minutes of the concert that I thought Dylan was nodding or that the band had lost its direction. I could tell that my son, who has a good ear, was wondering if Dylan's guitar was stuck or if he had lost some of his strings.

Dylan simplified the narrative by telling the whole tale in the third person, and by leaving out stanzas four and five, the meeting in the seedy bar and the kitchen scene where she reads him the Italian poetry. The abridgment worked, as those stanzas do not really advance the story; and by using the third person throughout, the singer doesn't present the audience with that jarring shift in the Montague Street section: the man who deals in slaves and the woman who sells all she owns are clearly the central lovers in the romance.

As I listened to this new version of the well-known song I wondered: how much did he work out in advance, and how much was spontaneous? You would have to attend quite a few concerts and hear "Tangled Up in Blue" several times in order to answer that question. Dozens of "Bobcats," as they were called, were following Dylan from town to town for the pleasure of making such discoveries. They were waiting for "All Along the Watchtower."

When I was a kid learning blues guitar from records and itinerant pickers like Linn Barnes and Robbie Basho who held forth on Dupont Circle in Washington, D.C., and by the Duck Pond in College

Park, there were half a dozen set pieces you had to master in order to be in the game.

Most of these songs were in the keys of E and A, but there were some novelty pieces in the brighter key of C major that were fun to play, notably "Yes, Yes, Yes" (or "Yass, yass, yass" to rhyme with the body part featured in the song) and "Cocaine Blues." The first one, my mother was quick to tell me, was a well-known bawdy song when she was in college during the Second World War, and not to be sung in mixed company.

> *Mama bought a chicken,*
> *Thought it was a duck,*
> *Put it on the table with its hind legs up.*
> *Along come sister with a spoon and a glass,*
> *Spoonin' up the gravy from its*
> *Yes, yes, yes!*

"Cocaine Blues" as played by Reverend Gary Davis and Dave Van Ronk was a guitar tour de force, a talkin' blues with melody only in the refrain, "Cocaine, run all around my brain," and an endless fund of X-rated lyrics that poke fun at both sex and drug addiction.

> *Woke up this morning*
> *Put on my clothes*
> *Looked in the mirror*
> *And I had no nose:*
> *Cocaine, run all around my brain.*

Nobody I knew used cocaine in the sixties so the song we learned was a lighthearted joke without a victim.

> *Cocaine's for horses*
> *Not for men.*

They say it'll kill me
But they don't say when.
Cocaine, run all around my brain.

Come here, baby, come here quick
This old cocaine 'bout to make me sick
Cocaine, run all around my brain.

When Bob Dylan sang the "Cocaine Blues" at Tanglewood with a country-western twang, slowing the song down to a crawl, there was nothing lighthearted about it. Squeezed dry of humor the piece became a cry of anguish, the agony of a strung-out junkie. Instead of talking the verses he sang them, one note per line, changing only with the chord change and sometimes not even then. Where the stress usually goes on the second syllable of the word *cocaine*, Dylan came down hard and long on the first syllable.

Coh-caine . . . run all around my brain

And when he sang the chorus, "Come here, baby, come here quick / This old cocaine 'bout to make me sick," there was real terror and craving in his voice, an awful pathos in that plea. I had never heard the verse that way before, and although I'd known it for most of my life I was hearing it for the first time not as entertainment but as an authentic cry for help.

When the final chord of "Cocaine Blues" closed out the acoustic set, a stagehand leapt up to help with the equipment change. Dylan handed him the hollow-bodied Martin he had been playing and strapped on a Stratocaster electric. Kemper signaled a tempo by clicking the drumsticks together and the band plunged into a hard rocker, "Seeing the Real You at Last," from *Empire Burlesque* (1985).

Well didn't I risk my neck for you,
Didn't I take chances?

Didn't I rise above it all for you,
The most unfortunate circumstances?

The singer is taking a last, hard look at his lover in the final hour of their affair, but what he has to say is mostly about himself: weary and irritable, he's got troubles, and he's glad things are nearly over between them.

Well I don't mind a reasonable amount of trouble
Trouble always comes to pass
But all I care about now
Is that I'm seeing the real you at last.

The metrics of the stanza are irregular and Dylan's phrasing—getting the words to fit the measure—was stunning. The musical structure is rudimentary AABA boogie in the key of E—a good showcase for Larry Campbell's guitar skills.

For most of this song Dylan was singing just two notes, the subdominant A, and then a higher note, an octave above the keynote of E. He would sing most of a stanza on the low note, lifting his voice only on the last near rhyme, as above, "pass" and "last." Critics call this Dylan's "upsinging," and in this case there was just enough variation—the singer sometimes returning to the melody—to avoid tedium. The method suited his theme. Dylan was using his voice not as a melodic vessel but as a rhythm instrument like Kemper's snare and the strokes of Campbell's guitar. He was chopping wood with it.

Campbell theorizes that Dylan's literary gifts are so consuming that they have constricted the musical range of the compositions. There is a limit to the amount of complexity a song can bear. "There were songs that evoked so many different things in so many people, deep, emotional sources that other songwriters have never touched. 'Boots of Spanish Leather,' a song like that. There is an emotional spectrum that can conjure up the hidden valleys and crevices in your psyche that you rarely visit.

"That's the strength he has that no one else I have ever worked with has. And I don't know if it was intentional, if he set out saying I'm going to hit people on an emotional level that nobody else ever has. But that's really his strength. The musical part of it? Well, I think if he had directed his attention and creativity toward musicianship he would be another Charlie Parker or a Miles Davis—a completely innovative musician—but he didn't. His musical thing is: he has made crude, visceral music skills, fundamental skills, into something artistic and accessible. If he was more of a master of the musical side of it, I don't believe the work would be as accessible as he has made it."

Bowing, absorbing the rounds of applause like sunlight, Bob Dylan looked very happy, like a man who is keeping a good secret. "Thank you, everybody!" His introduction of the band members was swift but cordial: "On the guitar tonight—give him a big hand, Larry Campbell! On drums tonight, David Kemper. On bass guitar, Tony Garnier. And Bucky Baxter is playing the steel guitar!"

The introduction of his sidemen signaled that the main show was nearly over. They had played nine songs, more than an hour. Surely he would sing "All Along the Watchtower," a song he had played without fail as a lucky charm for seven years and about seven hundred performances in his regular set; then he would sing three or four encores.

But Dylan is a man of secrets and surprises. The tenth and last piece of the regular set was not "Watchtower" but the classic "This Wheel's on Fire," the meditation on memories and promises Dylan wrote with the bassist Rick Danko in the Catskills in 1967.

> *If your mem'ry serves you well,*
> *We were goin' to meet again and wait,*
> *So I'm goin' to unpack all my things*
> *And sit before it gets too late.*

A slow rock-and-roll song that moves from a minor to major key, the melody was heavy with the ululating of Baxter's pedal steel guitar leading the verses. Danko's fancy-wrought tune augmented Dylan's apocalyptic lyrics—Danko, a kind man marked for death, a cocaine addict whose heart would give out before he was sixty. Baxter and Campbell sang rough harmonies on the chorus.

> *This wheel's on fire*
> *Rolling down the road,*
> *Best notify my next of kin*
> *This wheel shall explode.*

As the show approached the finale Dylan used more and more of his voice, sang more notes. Now he was using his whole vocal range, eight notes from keynote to an octave above. That was pretty much all that a lifetime of singing had left him. He sang Danko's melody soulfully and forcefully—not quite beautifully—and the effort it took seemed to diminish his attention to his own lyrics.

"This Wheel's on Fire" is not a long composition, only three stanzas, but he left out the second, the one that identifies the auditor as a woman whose memory might serve her well. He had planned to tie her lace in a knot and hide it in her bag—hocus pocus, a trifle. Instead the singer had hidden the whole stanza, no great loss, and repeated the first stanza after the third, as one does in singing a round, bringing us back again to the beginning where the song was about *us*, Bob Dylan and his audience, bound in an "Eternal Circle."

> *If your memory serves you well*
> *We will meet again someday. . . .*

CHAPTER 14

The Good Secret

Dylan had an album of new songs. That was the good secret, and it could not be kept for long. As we were listening to the concert, advance tapes of *Time Out of Mind* were traveling to editors, critics, disc jockeys, and journalists from coast to coast.

He had begun writing lyrics sometime in 1996—probably earlier—and in December of that year he read them aloud to his friend Daniel Lanois, the French Canadian musician who had produced *Oh Mercy* in 1989. "The words were hard, were deep, were desperate, were strong," Lanois later recalled, and he invited Dylan to come to Oxnard, California, a port city an hour north of Los Angeles, to an old theater he was renting where he had set up recording equipment.

The architecture in the neighborhood had a Spanish colonial flavor, and Lanois called the playhouse the "teatro." "That's where we made the demos for *Time Out of Mind*, and out of that demo session came some lovely things, including that version of 'Can't Wait' which I feel has a lot of thunder in it. . . . Bob on my lovely turn-of-the-century Steinway, which has a roaring bass in it; me on my goldtop 1956 Les Paul [guitar] through a Vox, and Pretty Tony [Mangurian] on the drums." Mangurian played a sexy groove, a hip-hop beat, and Dylan came in with a gospel-style delivery, belting out the lyrics in syncopated intervals over the block chords on the piano. The sound engineer, Mark Howard, recalled, "the hair on my arms went up, it was stunning. Luckily, I was recording, and I caught it. . . . We were thinking, Wow. If it's going to be anything like this, this record is going to be unbelievable. And that's how it all started."

The process started very simply, with the idea of a trio, Dylan, Lanois (an excellent acoustic guitarist), and a drummer. In this old, echoing theater they would create loops of sound based on Mississippi Charlie Patton's 78s from the 1930s and 1950s blues records, building up tracks from those.

In mid-December the musicians were prepared to make the record in Oxnard. Howard recalled: "We were getting amazing sounds in this old theater, had all the gear set up, this really incredible atmosphere with sixteen-millimeter projectors and mirror balls, and Bob says, 'You know—I can't work this close to home. I got my family there, I can't work there. I wanna do it in Miami.' The *furthest* point away, right?"

So Lanois and Howard packed up the equipment, the vintage guitars, tube microphones and amplifiers, and the tape loops from the 1930s and 1950s, loaded them on a truck with a couple of motorcycles, and drove from California to Florida to set up at the Criteria studio in North Miami.

From the enchanting Oxnard "teatro"—where Lanois had found the aura so magical for recording the demos—to the Criteria Recording Studios at N.E. 149th Street, Miami, the distance was cosmic. It came to symbolize an aesthetic rift between Dylan and Lanois that was both a benefit and a torment. That the move resulted in a masterpiece, few would deny. That it made for high drama, harsh words, and icy silences in the studio is a matter of opinion, memories, and impressions of a dozen musicians, engineers, and producers who witnessed the creation of *Time Out of Mind*, a casebook study of how collaborative artists make works of art out of chaos.

Dylan's choice of the concrete, cinder-block quarters of Criteria Studios sent a stern message to Lanois and his engineer. "Criteria is a big, huge, soundstage room, completely white, no vibe . . . it just didn't sound good at all," Howard recalls. Suddenly he went from a space where the acoustics were perfect and he could get any effect he wanted, to having to struggle to get any kind of sound quality at all. And in a few days there would be more than a dozen musicians playing in that barren room at once.

How *Time Out of Mind* evolved from the humble, romantic vision of Daniel Lanois's teatro to the multilayered, "chunky" echo chamber some called "Atlantic Studios South," where James Brown made his records, and the Allman Brothers Band made theirs, and Eric Clapton recorded "Layla," is a drama with a large cast of characters and many crises.

When the rehearsals began on Monday, January 13, the company included Dylan's road band—David Kemper, Bucky Baxter, Tony Garnier—the drummer/pianist Tony Mangurian, and drummer Jim Keltner. The first few days Dylan strummed the guitar, scribbled lyrics, and didn't sing a note.

He was haunted by the spirit of Buddy Holly, the boy genius of rock and roll, born in Lubbock, Texas, five years before Dylan. He had made eye contact with Holly as he performed at the Duluth Armory on January 31, 1959, days before Holly perished in a plane crash at age twenty-two. Now in the car on the way to the studio Dylan heard Holly's "Rave On" playing on the radio. Walking down the hall, he heard Buddy Holly records, and as he entered the studio somebody was playing a cassette of "That'll Be the Day."

"And this would happen day after day after day," Dylan remembered. "Phrases of Buddy Holly songs would just come out of nowhere. It was spooky . . . it stayed in our minds. . . . Buddy Holly's spirit must have been someplace hastening this record in a kind of way."

Maybe Dylan was wondering what Holly might have written if he had lived to be old. "I get very meditative sometimes," he told one reporter, "and this one phrase was going through my head: *Work while the day lasts, because the night of death cometh when no man can work. I* don't recall where I heard it. I like preaching, I hear a lot of preaching, and I probably just heard it somewhere. Maybe it's in the psalms, it beats me. But it wouldn't let me go." The verse is from the Gospel of John 9:4: "I must work the works of him who sent me while it is day; the night cometh, when no man can work."

Jim Keltner recalled: "On *Time Out of Mind*, Bob called me and a lot of other guys specifically. I remember one evening, maybe the first night, he asked me, 'What do you think about Jim Dickinson for this?' And I said, 'Aw that's a great call.'" Dickinson was a veteran rock-and-roll keyboard player who had played with the Rolling Stones, Ry Cooder, Carl Perkins, and Furry Lewis. He could channel Buddy Holly, if need be. Dylan had immense admiration for him and trusted his judgment. "Next day," Keltner continued, "Jim Dickinson was there. So Bob was thinking about the sound. He put the call out for [guitarist] Duke Robillard, [organist] Augie Meyers, all those guys." These were distinguished Nashville session men, so one might have known where he was headed. Dylan's approach was not to tell people what to play, but rather to surround himself with musicians likely to play what he wanted.

They recorded in what was known as the "big room" of the studio. Dylan sat in a corner facing the drummer while the rest of the musicians formed a semicircle around the drums.

For the engineer the acoustics were a burden, but this soon began to pale in the face of the challenges the composer presented to his sidemen. As Dylan is figuring out a song, he tries out stanzas in different keys in order to discover which one best suits his voice and the tone of the piece. "So he's just been doing it in D," Howard recalls, "and now he's going to do it in E, and for the musicians, suddenly you have to change the whole map of chords, and a lot of people just can't do that straight off. But Dylan expects you to just know it. He knows every chord, and he's really great at that kind of stuff." Some of the musicians could not follow him.

They would lay down a track. Then Howard, Lanois, and Dylan

would go back to the control booth and listen to the tape. "It was all over the place—people hitting the wrong note," Howard recalled. "It just sounded so chunky, it was just awful. So Dan [Lanois] said to the musicians, 'If you're not going to make the changes—if you can't figure it out, just don't play—that's the law. Just don't make the mistake, because we're only going to get a couple of chances, and you never know if this is going to be the take.'" Dylan hated to repeat himself, and had great faith in the first and second takes in the recording process.

"Anybody who has worked in the studio knows this," the late Jim Dickinson explained. "That first cut is magic. And if you don't get it in the second or third cut, then you are talking about seven or eight. It is going to go downhill before it comes back up. And after everybody has learned the song, of course, it turns into something else—which obviously doesn't interest Bob Dylan at all."

"You had a room full of musicians," Keltner added, "some of whom Daniel wanted to be there and some of whom Bob wanted to be there. So there was this curious dynamic." The musicians all got along very well, but there was an obvious tension between Dylan and Lanois.

Dickinson believed that Dylan had unfinished business with Lanois, a conflict that had never been resolved over the making of *Oh Mercy*. "I don't think Bob was happy with *Oh Mercy*. I think he felt controlled. I think he thinks it was contrived, and it sounds to me like it is."

There was a violent incident Dylan mentions coolly in *Chronicles*—fifteen years after it happened—when he and the swarthy producer of *Oh Mercy* locked horns over the tone of the song "Political World." Dylan wanted an upbeat ballad; Lanois wanted a backdoor funk sound. Dickinson tells of Lanois "bashing the dobro, smashing it in front of Dylan's face" when words could no longer serve to make his point. And so, eight years later they are in Miami recording *Time Out of Mind*, and Dylan is asking for a certain key, Dickinson recalls, and Lanois is quibbling, and so Dylan picks up the dobro by the neck and starts waving it around menacingly, "and I don't think anybody in the room but me and Mark Howard knew the story."

Of all the players in that celebrated session, the late Jim Dickinson was the most gifted raconteur. Dickinson remembered that when Dylan's assistants picked him up at the Miami airport on Thursday, a bodyguard read him a protocol regarding the space around Bob Dylan. "Don't look at him or talk to him, don't stand in his way, etc.," rules he thought were odd, particularly since he knew Dylan socially and wouldn't dream of disturbing him.

Then, the first night Dylan saw the heavyset greybeard smoking a joint in the Criteria parking lot, he walked up to Dickinson wide-eyed and said, in mock astonishment, "Hey, didn't you used to play with Sleepy John Estes?" Estes was an honest-to-God legend, a narcoleptic blues guitarist and singer who had been famous in the 1930s and then was rediscovered during the folk revival of the early 1960s. He had been dead for twenty years, but Dickinson really *had* played with Sleepy John, so Dylan's comment was a wry form of flattery, teasing the pianist about his age while acknowledging that he was—by association—a legend himself.

"So what was I supposed to do? Walk away from him?"

And from that moment on Dylan and Dickinson conversed freely. The pianist believed that one reason he was invited to Miami was to facilitate communication, because it had become so badly strained between the producer and the singer. Dickinson explained how "there are two times in the recording process where the producer has subtle but real control of the moment: on the 'talkback' right before you actually start playing—when the producer says, 'Are you ready?' or 'Let's do it!' Whatever. Lanois never seized that moment. He never talked to Dylan prior to the recording." The other moment comes after the team has heard the first playback. "In the control room, it's protocol. That's when the producer asks, 'What do you think?' Or, 'Should we do it again?' And again, Lanois never spoke."

Dylan and Lanois wouldn't speak to each other for days on end, as Mark Howard recalls, so the engineer was relaying messages back and forth. Dylan and Howard would be sitting at the console and Dylan would ask, "What's on this track?" And Howard would say, "That's your guitar." Dylan would tell him to turn it up. Then he would ask, "And what's on that track?" When the engineer told him it was Lanois's guitar Dylan asked him to cut it. At one point, Howard recalls, "Dan would walk in and say 'Wow, this is sounding great!' And Bob would turn to me, with Dan standing right there, and he'd say, 'Did you hear something?' He was kind of playing, but it was intense."

According to Dickinson, they were about three songs into the session. The company—including two Jims—was listening to the first playback of the third song. "And again the silence. Then Dylan turns around to us and he says, 'What do you think, Jim?' Well, Jim *Keltner* answered him instantly. And after Keltner said whatever he had to say, Dylan turned to me and said, 'No, I meant him,' and pointed to me. So I told Dylan what I thought, which you are not supposed to do." That is, sidemen are not customarily involved in the process of critiquing a playback. Dickinson cannot recall exactly what song it was, but "I told him whatever I would have said had I been the producer. And it got to where this was happening a lot."

Late that night the old pianist went up to Lanois's hotel room to make amends. "It was so jive that we were all staying in different hotels, and they would round us up in a bus. It was really over the top. Anyway, I went over to Dan's room, and I said, 'Look, man, I know I shouldn't be saying this stuff, but really, it's *Bob Dylan*, and he asked me . . .'"

Lanois replied that apologies were unnecessary. "No, no," he insisted, twirling his curly black hair, "that's obviously why he's got us all here [five drummers, four guitarists, two keyboard players, etc.], don't worry about it." And then Lanois made a joke of it, rolling his eyes, putting the back of his hand to his forehead. "Oh darling," he moaned, "Bob talks to *you*, he doesn't talk to *me*. He thinks I'm a whippersnapper." Lanois is a decade younger than Dylan.

And Dickinson said, "Well maybe. I don't know." He was fascinated by the way Dylan remained in control of all those musicians, so many egos and personalities rattling around him in a situation that always seemed on the verge of pandemonium. "I had watched a bit of the *Shot of Love* sessions with Keltner so I had an idea of what was coming. You have got to be ready at any second. That session was like an hour and a half of sheer chaos and then five minutes of beautiful clarity. And it was at least twelve musicians on the floor." Dylan, Lanois, Dickinson, Garnier, Baxter, organist Augie Meyers, guitarists Duke Robillard and Robert Britt, slide guitarist Cindy Cashdollar. Then there was the drum corps. Dylan appreciates percussion. "There were three *full* drum kits!" After Kemper went home, Jim Keltner, Brian Blade, Tony Mangurian, and Winston Watson platooned on the drums. "It is twelve musicians playing, and that is like—orchestral. And with no chart. Wouldn't let you make a chart. One of the other Nashville guys and I were both surreptitiously making charts; Dylan saw us doing it and didn't stop us, though I was told he might."

Eric Andersen had observed, long before this, Dylan's tendency to create "these controlled chaos situations, where nobody really shines. Everybody is sort of off-balance, and you would record one or two takes; you might learn all of the chords or you might not. Then, bam, it is all done. So nobody really gets a lead, nobody gets a run. And the reason is: he comes out on top. So, it may stem from insecurity. To be famous *and* insecure? It's a strange combination."

"There was a lot of heart in that room," Dickinson fondly recalled, "people of a certain age . . . a lot of mortality there." There was Jim Keltner of Tulsa, who had played with John Lennon, B.B. King, and Eric Clapton, and had been contributing to Dylan albums for twenty-five years. Dickinson called him "a god of music" and now he was "playing his heart out" because he was so devoted to this music. Organist Augie Meyers from Texas, a polio survivor, had taught himself to play while being roped to his grandmother's upright piano for balance, trying to walk again. He had filled out the sound of Doug Sahm's quintet for thirty years. Dylan called him "the shining example of a musician." Blues guitarist Duke Robillard had followed Jimmie Vaughan in the Fabulous Thunderbirds. Young Cindy Cashdollar had "rewritten the book" on the pedal steel guitar. A striking blond in her late thirties, she was the only woman on the floor.

She remembers her first impression, "walking into that studio—it was garagelike but not in a spatial sense. Lots of squareness and concrete. It didn't feel warm to me. My first thought was, This is kind of a cold space, but, well, this is cool, there has been all of this great music that came out of here, and this studio has been chosen." The music and the players would provide what warmth was needed. "As everybody started setting up for the sessions, it made sense, as yet another reason to record there."

Cashdollar was so strongly affected by the song lyrics—hearing them for the first time—it was a challenge to focus on her playing. "Oh, it's hard because you are hearing this beautiful song; I am listening emotionally, but I'm also listening for where the lyrics might go and what I can do for the lyrics as well. You cannot detach. You have to open up to everything that is going on.

"All the songs were coming from such a personal place. So you are listening with your heart, and trying to feel what to play—to do both things at once but not to think. And Daniel Lanois didn't want people to really *play*, you know?" He asked the musicians to avoid ornamentation; what he wanted was texture and atmosphere.

She remembers a passage in the song "Not Dark Yet" in which Dylan's voice and her guitar blended, spontaneously, perfectly, and how "that just happened." On that track she could distinguish her own sound in the mix, but for the most part, "the contribution seemed to be coming from *everybody* in the moment those recordings were happening because it was more about texture than lead lines. Now, listening to the CD, I think *this is everyone.*

"Can you imagine all those people playing at once? Two of everything, like Noah's ark. Two drums, *two* pedal steels! And everyone listening to what everyone else is playing? Trying to figure out, 'Is he playing low? Should I play high? Should I go above the vocal or below it?'" When she heard the finished CD nine months later, it sounded exactly like it did when they were recording. "Like that room. Just like being in my little corner there, sitting in my chair. It's like reliving the moment all over again. Sonically, that record is amazing."

And what made it possible? The producer? The engineers?

"Bob Dylan. I was struck by his graciousness throughout the whole process. He was extremely generous, wanting feedback from others when it came time to listen to the playback. He was genuinely interested in what the musicians felt and thought, at times; that really struck me because some artists aren't like that."

Dylan himself later confessed that the session was fraught with difficulties. He told Mikal Gilmore of *Rolling Stone*: "It got off the tracks more than a few times, and people got frustrated. I know I did. I know Lanois did." The musicians they had assembled were top-notch, and "they had the right soulful kind of attitude for these songs. But we just couldn't . . . I felt extremely frustrated, because I couldn't get any of the up-tempo songs that I wanted. . . . It was tricky trying to steer that ship." According to Jim Dickinson, there was no conflict in the studio apart from the tension between Dylan and the producer.

Cashdollar, like Dickinson, Meyers, and others, was surprised at the ease with which Dylan transposed, moving from key to key on the acoustic guitar without a capo—and not for the reason vocalists usually change key. Many singers stick to certain keys to suit their range; Dylan sometimes settled on a key just because of the way it made the song sound, to get a particular color or tone quality.

Above all she was awed by Dylan's concentration minute by minute, his attention to the sounds and people's emotions in the studio space: it created a force field in the room all around him. "He didn't miss a trick. With all of those musicians playing at once, and him singing, he would hear a guitar line, pick it out, and say to the guy, 'Can you play that in a higher register?' At one point he came over to me and said: 'That was some Don Helms steel licks you were playing there!' I was amazed that with all those people he was hearing [including two pedal steel guitars] he picked up things like that." Don Helms was Hank Williams's honky-tonk steel guitar player in the 1940s. "It's no secret that Dylan knows so much about music history he can reference specific players and styles." He would go over to Duke Robillard and cite a certain guitar player, B.B. King, John Lee Hooker, or Roy Buchanan, if he wanted a change in tone or syncopation.

"He was so aware of what was happening at all times, I felt comfortable in his presence from the first meeting. With some artists you're just there as a worker bee, you play your part, and that's that. But Dylan was very involved with us in the whole process, personally and professionally, I felt. That was my take on it." This was also Jim Keltner's take on it. He was going through a personal crisis in the New Year. "Bob was actually talking me through it . . . there was so much going on during that recording session."

Dickinson heard Dylan say he had been working on some of the *Time Out of Mind* material since the early 1990s. "He was touring but he didn't have a strong touring show, and he said he reached a point where he thought there were so many Bob Dylan songs that there was enough—it was getting confusing to everyone. So he told his manager Jeff Kramer that he was writing songs but he wasn't going to record them." That is when he recorded the two albums of traditional folk songs, *Good as I Been to You* (1992) and *World Gone Wrong* (1993) with the guitarist /fiddler David Bromberg in his Malibu garage. "It was real frustrating for the management, you know, to hear that." But then Dylan began to notice younger and younger people in his audience. "And he figured that a new audience deserved new material."

In the studio Dickinson was impressed when he noticed that Dylan's lyrics were all handwritten on notebook paper, as if he had written the songs in study hall. He had been working on these things for maybe five or six years, and now he was *still* working on them as they were recording. His guitar tech had three steamer chests full of paraphernalia, instruments, strings, tools, charms, harmonicas, and one trunk with a flat top Dylan used for a writing desk.

He wrote left-handed, his elbow crooked out, with a pencil, because he was erasing words and lines and rewriting them. It really touched his friend to watch this because he had seen so many rock stars stroll into the studio with their hair slicked back and the typed and printed script that an assistant had just Xeroxed for them. This was more personal. "I think that for him, it is all about the songs."

An album is only as good as its best songs—with some notable exceptions, "theme" albums like *Sergeant Pepper*, *Blue*, and *Blood on the Tracks*, where the collection becomes greater than the sum of its parts. Many fans believe *Time Out of Mind* is just such an album, a dramatic song cycle about aging, love, and loss, where the lyrics of one ballad of angst bleed into the lyrics of the next, build to a climax in the seventh track, and slowly decompress in an ironic denouement.

At the beginning of the cycle, in the song "Love Sick," we find the singer "walking through streets that are dead," and thinking of his beloved, sick of love but hopelessly in its grip. In the next, "Dirt Road Blues," it appears to be the same character walking down a road, then pacing the floor, hoping his love will return to him, walking "until his eyes begin to bleed," but still looking for the bright side of love. In the third song, "Standing in the Doorway," the lover is walking through a summer night, mourning the woman who has left him crying, "in the dark land of the sun," and so on.

For every fan who embraces the whole song cycle there is another who skips over the more sentimental, redundant tracks ("Til I Fell in Love with You," "Make You Feel My Love") to get to the best ones. At least three songs on *Time Out of Mind* justify all the plaudits and laurels that have been heaped upon the album since it was released in the summer of 1997: "Tryin' to Get to Heaven," "Not Dark Yet," and "Cold Irons Bound." And there was another song as good as any of these, as fine as anything he had written in thirty-five years of versifying, a piece called "Mississippi" that never made the final cut.

As Jim Dickinson said, for Dylan "it is all about the songs," and perhaps more narrowly about the *poetry* of the songs; the choices this inspires him to make in the studio are mysterious, peremptory, and sometimes exasperating to producers and businesspeople. In making *Infidels* he left out "Blind Willie McTell" and "Foot of Pride," maybe the best songs the sessions yielded. When his friend Larry Sloman expressed astonishment and dismay about this decision, Dylan replied to the effect that it was only an album; "he had made dozens" of them and one more or less didn't matter much.

So what did matter? The poetry mattered, and the dramatic presentation.

It seems bizarre that "Mississippi" would be too good to suit the album in production and would have to lie in mothballs for four years before Dylan would try it on again (for "*Love and Theft*"). But what else are we to think? The song explores all of the themes and questions that animate the other pieces on the record—restlessness, loneliness, loss, regret, and the desperate feeling of being trapped. The speaker is the same world-weary traveler nearing the end of life's journey. But in the moderate tempo of "Mississippi" he offers us something slightly different: an apology. It is a classic apologia (defense of one's life) that is not an admission of guilt but rather an explanation of one's actions and feelings. The refrain, "Only one thing I did wrong, stayed in Mississippi a day too long," is quoted from an African American spiritual called "Rosie," and Rosie appears as the second character in the drama of Dylan's song.

"My songs," Dylan told Jon Pareles of the *New York Times* that year, "what makes them different is that there's a foundation to them. That's why they're still around." He is a creature of the folk music tradition. "They're standing on a strong foundation, and subliminally that's what people are hearing." The theme of "Mississippi" is timeless, and so Dylan built it upon a timeless old song.

The apology is the refrain and the refrain is the apology he must return to again and again—the same as in the old spiritual. He's really done nothing wrong except linger in one place when the only righteous conduct is to keep moving forward. Yet he has other things to account for, to explain, certain regrets and sadnesses: "Got nothing for you, I had nothing before / Don't even have anything for myself anymore. . . ."

Autumn is upon him. He is walking through falling leaves, feeling like an invisible stranger, filled with remorse.

So many things that we never will undo
I know you're sorry, I'm sorry too.

When Dylan sings these simple lines over the strumming of the major chord, there is such tenderness in his voice you know he means it with his whole heart, as if this is the one and only chance he will ever have to make amends. But the poem does not end there. The sentiment is far more complex and expansive.

Well my ship's been split to splinters and it's sinking fast
I'm drowning in the poison, got no future got no past
But my heart is not weary, it's light and it's free
I've got nothing but affection for them who sailed with me.

Darkness, in "Mississippi," is the turbulent background against which the singer reveals time and again the splendor of hope and the radiance of love; in the last quatrains he asks for her hand and her vow, promising that now, in this climactic moment, things are going to get *really* interesting . . .

The lyrics of quite a few Dylan songs can stand alone on the printed page (like Robert Burns songs) without the support of melody or instrumentation. They are not necessarily his best songs, they are just verses so concentrated and clear they can bear the weight of a "New Critical" reading by graduate students in an English seminar. Such songs rack rival lyricists with envy. Two such pieces were presented to the musicians at the *Time Out of Mind* sessions in 1997: "Not Dark Yet," which is often compared to Keats's "Ode to a Nightingale" without much offense taken on either side; and "Mississippi," which is like a late poem by Yeats, perhaps one of the "Crazy Jane" poems or a lost section of "Vacillation." Both of these songs created havoc in the Criteria studio as Dylan, Lanois, and businessmen wrangled over how they should be sung and produced. One of the two, "Mississippi," became a casualty of that conflict as Dylan and Lanois played off against each other and grew irreconcilably entrenched in their opinions. The album, as a whole, suffered for the quarrel, while the songs of course did not, being incorruptible.

As *Time Out of Mind* has come down to us the greatest song, by acclamation, is "Not Dark Yet," a melancholy, brooding artsong so different in texture from the blues ballads and torch songs dominating the album that the piece just barely fits the niche prepared for it. The title itself, which becomes the refrain, signals a loftier diction level. After hearing the tune once I found myself calling it "Ain't Dark Yet" because on this plainly vernacular recording Dylan had made a very literary choice in avoiding the substandard "ain't," as if to say, "Sit down and listen closely, friends, to the poetry; this is not music for dancing."

The melody for the six-line stanza is stately and simple, the root chord alternating with the subdominant (three tones higher) for two verses, a third line that boldly moves up to the dominant (four tones higher); then the structure is repeated in the last three lines, making a perfect circle of melody.

In the opening lines the singer says he is watching the shadows fall in a place where he has been resting for the entire day. He can't sleep for the heat and the sense that time is running out.

Feel like my soul has turned into steel
I've still got the scars that the sun didn't heal.

The meditation, like so many of the songs on *Time Out of Mind*, explores the limits of human space and freedom, of confinement and movement. He ends the first stanza with the complaint that he doesn't have room and freedom enough to actually *be* anywhere at all, and night is coming on fast.

The two middle stanzas mention a woman who has written him off. He says this shouldn't concern him, and yet it does. While he no longer looks to other people for fulfillment, his loss is still a terrible burden he must bear on his own. Finally:

I was born here and I'll die here against my will
I know it looks like I'm moving, but I'm standing still
Every nerve in my body is so vacant and numb
I can't even remember what it was I came here to get away from
Don't even hear a murmur of a prayer
It's not dark yet, but it's getting there.

The old pianist believed that Dylan despised the whole process of studio recording as the business had evolved in the late twentieth century. The sound studio had become a machine for elevating mediocrity and erasing authenticity. As Jim Dickinson had said, for Dylan making a record "was all about the songs," the creation and performing of them in the moment, hot-blooded. "He wants the first interpretation he can get of the song." In this, Dylan reminded him of Keith Richards, Mick Jagger, and Charlie Watts, who also were obsessed with "the moment of creation" rather than the packaged product, mixed, remixed, overdubbed, sliced, and diced. Once you had tried a particular song with such a musician three times, "he was past it."

When it came to the recording of "Mississippi" there arose a squabble over a guitar line Dylan wanted to develop that Lanois ignored; then they made a version Dickinson described as "swampy" that Lanois loved but Dylan rejected as being too obvious. "And the two of them really locked horns over that version and so it never made it onto the album." But even Dickinson never completely understood why "Mississippi" was cut.

In a sense, "Mississippi" really *was* "too good" for this particular collection. By the time Bob Dylan got to the Criteria studios in Miami he had made up his mind about one thing—that is, the dramatic persona of *Time Out of Mind*. The voice is distinctive, consistent, and unrelenting: the voice of an old man, bitter, weary, sometimes angry, impatient, and more than a little querulous. There are flashes of hope, as in "Tryin' to Get to Heaven" and "Highlands," but it is ironic hope against hope or against impossible odds. "Mississippi" would have been a ray of sunshine in the gloom, so bright that it might well have upset the photometric balance of the composition. As we can tell from hearing the lovely outtake (not released until 2008), that is exactly what would have happened.

It is fascinating to see how deliberately Dylan shaped and maintained that voice in the studio, despite formidable opposition. The voice was very low-pitched, harsh, sometimes growling, at other times moaning. We had heard premonitions of this "old man voice" in earlier albums (including his debut) and stage performances, but never so resolutely fretful and solemn. Only by listening to outtakes, especially of the Oxnard sessions two weeks earlier, do you realize that the voice he uses is a conscious choice, a *role*. At fifty-five years of age Dylan was still capable of sounding like a vigorous man in his forties, easily singing notes higher than any he allows himself on *Time Out of Mind*. And this, above all, was the bone of contention between Dylan on one hand and Lanois and the "management" on the other. Columbia Records wanted a new Dylan album that would sell units; indeed they had high hopes for a track that might catch on with radio disc jockeys as a single.

"Dylan had started the sessions at Oxnard," Dickinson recalled. "It was just a trio, the way Lanois wanted to do it, obviously." Then some Columbia executives heard "Not Dark Yet" and got excited, smelling the money. "The management had heard over the phone a version from Oxnard with Dylan singing in a higher register, and this quick and spare guitar stuff that Lanois was playing, and it had stuck in somebody's head."

So in late January, during the final days of the session, when the "suits" had not yet heard what they were longing to hear, they began throwing their weight around. "I mean," Dickinson recalled, with dismay, "they actually talked to Bob Dylan about getting on the radio—which I found really hard to sit in the same room and listen to. They had designated that 'Not Dark Yet' would be the emphasis song. We were supposed to come back in with a smaller, trimmed-down rhythm section, just seven of us, and recut it, right? Because they had heard this earlier version and they were trying to get Dylan to push it up to this higher register."

On Monday night, January 27, everyone gathered for the last session: Dylan, Lanois, Baxter, Robillard, Britt, Cashdollar, Garnier, Meyers, Dickinson, Keltner, and Blade. They always started after sundown because Dylan wanted slow tempos throughout the album, uncommonly slow, and it is naturally easier for a real player to maintain such a tempo when the biological clock is set for nighttime. The song on the docket was "Not Dark Yet" and Lanois had set up the studio simply, with a minimum of microphones, booms, wiring, derricks, and other paraphernalia. Dylan was facing a semi-circle of chairs where the musicians could come and go. He was looking somewhat the worse for wear, and the tension between him and Lanois was mounting.

"We do the song and they keep changing keys," Dickinson recalled. "Daniel said, 'Bob, will you try it in another key?' Nobody will say *this thing about putting his voice up*, right?" What the management really wanted was for Dylan to sing the song in a higher, brighter register. "So we did it in three or four different keys. One of the amazing things I found out about him on this session was just how good a guitarist he is, how fluidly he could change keys without using a capo. He was an old folk guy—I figured he used a capo. Not at all. He could play a song in E flat, just on folk guitar, never used a capo."

Daniel Lanois and the others in the booth still were not hearing what they wanted to hear. Dylan obviously could sing the song well in half a dozen keys without hitting higher notes. "We changed keys and changed keys. . . . And finally Dylan was just obviously pissed off."

"Well," Dylan called out. "We did it in E flat. And we did it in B flat. And you know what? If you ain't got it *now*, you ain't *getting* it."

And so Lanois and Mark Howard called Tony Garnier into the sound booth for a conference while Bob Dylan lit a cigarette. Of Dylan's band members, Garnier is first mate. Born in St. Paul, Minnesota, in 1955, he is the grandson of the bandleader who taught Louis Armstrong his scales at the New Orleans Colored Waif's Home for Boys; now Garnier has been traveling with Dylan for twenty years. Lanois and the others explained to Tony Garnier what they wanted. "He came out real sheepishly, and he says to Dylan, 'Do you remember when you were doing it before [back in Oxnard], you were singing it in a higher register? That's what they want,' he says, glancing back at Lanois. 'Do you think we could do it that way?'"

And at that point, Bob Dylan lost his cool.

"Tony," he asked his bass player. "How many times you heard me sing?"

And Tony shrugged and said he didn't know.

"Well? You heard me sing a thousand times?"

"Yeah."

"You heard me sing two thousand times?"

"Yeah, I guess so."

"You *ever* heard me sing it the same way twice?"

There was dead silence in the room. Nobody stirred. Tony Garnier confirmed that he had never heard Dylan sing it the same way twice.

And then, just loud enough for everyone to hear him, Dylan said: "You know, if I had taken some people's advice, I might have had more of a career."

That was the last word and the end of the sessions for *Time Out of Mind*. After that experience Dylan would do his own producing, a practice that is frowned upon in this business, rather like a playwright producing his own play. In all fairness to Daniel Lanois, whose efforts on *Time Out of Mind* earned him a Grammy for Album of the Year, Jim Keltner summed up the dynamic that was going on between the singer and the willful producer. "What I saw was that Bob was really bouncing off Daniel. That was the main value Daniel brought to the production. He really allowed Bob to know what it was he wanted—and what he *didn't* want. And I think the reason the recording ended up really beautiful was exactly because of this dynamic. . . . In the end Bob got what he wanted but . . . it was a very intense process. That's all I can really say."

Two weeks later the band flew to Tokyo to begin an eleven-date tour of eight cities: Tokyo, Kurashiki, Fukuoka, Nagoya, Osaka, Sendai, Akita, and Sapporo. They played old songs: "Crash on the Levee," "Masters of War," "All Along the Watchtower," "Silvio"; for a change Dylan sang Elizabeth Cotten's "Oh Baby It Ain't No Lie" during the acoustic set. They played no songs from the new album because it was a secret, still in development, and didn't even have a name as yet.

After taking a break in the month of March they took to the road again with the new guitarist Larry Campbell. He remembers that year most vividly, as being both exciting and surrealistic from the beginning. After three days of rehearsal in New York, they flew to Newfoundland on Sunday, March 30, 1997. They played two shows in St. John's, Newfoundland, on March 30 and April 1. Then they were supposed to board a ferry south to Nova Scotia out of Port aux Basques on April 2, and perform in Halifax at the Metro Center the next evening. But the ferry they were scheduled to sail on was canceled due to choppy seas; meanwhile, their equipment had gone on an earlier ferry that got stranded mid-sea in an ice pack.

So there they were waiting in a hotel in St. John's, far from the next gig, their gear loaded on a ferry with five hundred passengers stuck in ice somewhere out at sea off the coast of Nova Scotia. Local news was covering the crisis. Newsmen swarmed the hotel trying to interview the musicians, and according to Kemper one journalist "even interviewed Bob's dog, the mastiff Felix." The bus driver, Tom Masters, stood between Felix and the cameras. A coast guard icebreaker was on the way to rescue the passengers and the Never Ending Tour's equipment, but it would not be in time to make the schedule in Halifax.

The shows for April 3 and 4 would have to be rescheduled. The road manager had to rent equipment and drive the band three hours around the Gulf of St. Lawrence to get to Moncton, New Brunswick, to resume the tour there at the Coliseum on April 5; then on from Moncton to Halifax to do the rescheduled show on April 6. This meant that the band would have to play seven shows in a row without a break while traveling frantically and adjusting to unfamiliar sound equipment. When the crowd sees a band onstage they have no idea what madness they may have endured to get there.

On April 5, Allen Ginsberg, who had been fighting liver cancer, passed away in his apartment in the East Village. That night, from the stage of the Moncton Coliseum in New Brunswick, Dylan acknowledged his old friend, his brother in the art of poetry, dedicating the song "Desolation Row" to Ginsberg.

And the riot squad they're restless
They need somewhere to go
As Lady and I look out tonight
From Desolation Row.

"That was one of his favorite songs, the poet Allen Ginsberg. That's for him," Dylan told the people when the song was over.

One month and twenty-one performances later Dylan was tired. His voice was little more than a dry shell, a whisper. Yet his publicist announced he would continue touring in June, in Europe, on a double bill with his friend Van Morrison.

In Memphis, Tennessee, before performing at the Beale Street Music Festival in Tom Lee Park, overlooking the river, Dylan was resting in his hotel room with the windows open.

It was a dark, windy day early in May, with the smell of rain in the air. From his bed he watched the trees moving in the wind, through the sliding glass door. He saw a little cloud drift into the room through the door. It was like a gray hand groping and grasping, that kept its shape between the window and the bed, threatening, scary. So Dylan got up to close the door and the cloud fled before him except for a wisp that was cut off when the glass door slid shut upon it, "like the tail of an animal had been severed, like a snake." It made him so anxious he had to get out of the room, he told Kemper, "and so I got on my motorbike and I just started riding into the wind." He did not know that the wind off the Mississippi—the wind off Beef Island and the Loosahatchie Bar and drainage canal that runs north of Memphis—bears a rare but deadly effluvia.

Ten days later he was back home in Malibu, sequencing the tracks from *Time Out of Mind* and taking a breather before the scheduled June tour. But his breathing was labored, more and more, and he felt a weight on his chest. On Saturday, May 24, he would be fifty-six. His daughter Maria Himmelman held a family party for him at her home in Santa Monica with her siblings and the grandchildren. Grandfather was smiling and grateful but Maria heard him coughing and could see he was in pain. Like other men loath to relinquish control he avoided physicians. Maria insisted he call a doctor, and the next day Dylan was admitted to St. John's Hospital in Santa Monica for observation.

The young specialists could not figure out what was wrong with him; this was not the sort of ailment they encountered in California. It took a very old doctor, who came at last with a black bag like the venerable sawbones from the middle of the twentieth century, to ask the right questions and make sense of what had happened to the musician. The physician had seen histoplasmosis only a couple of times in his life. Rarely did the disease inflame a man's heart. Without proper treatment with antifungal drugs the singer would not have made it to Tanglewood in the summer. Bob Dylan would have followed his late friend Allen Ginsberg into the hereafter.

After the closing guitar solos on "This Wheel's on Fire," the slackening of the tempo, the drumroll and ringing cymbals, there came a full minute of applause, curtain calls, and bowing—Dylan bowing right and left. Benjamin asked me if the performance was over.

The show at Tanglewood was all over but the encores. Bob Dylan had not yet sung "All Along the Watchtower," and the Bobcats were shocked. Dylan-watcher Andrew Muir later quipped: "this rip in the space-time continuum became a tear that threatened existence throughout the galaxy."

The encores of the Never Ending Tour are a ritual of farewell, dedicated to the audience and mostly predictable: three songs, in 1997, the first of which is "Like a Rolling Stone" and the last of which is "Rainy Day Women"; at the end the houselights go up as everyone sings *Everybody must get stoned*, and people head for their automobiles.

Dylan sang his signature hit "Like a Rolling Stone" as he had in the Garden in 1974 but now he sang with more feeling and conviction, *yearning* to know "How does it feel / To be on your own / A complete unknown / Like a rolling stone?" as if one of us could tell him, because many years had passed since he had known such a life. The fact that he could bring to this song he sings nightly—a thousand and one nights—so much urgency and excitement was impressive. His voice was rough-edged but very strong, sustaining the notes, reaching and sliding, using a full vibrato at the line endings.

We were grateful and let him know it with our burning palms and hoarse cheering, a full minute ovation while he disappeared and appeared again with an acoustic guitar, strumming a major chord, commanding silence. This time he had brought the audience a surprise, an old tune he rarely performed nowadays, "My Back Pages." He had written the song when he was twenty-three. Kemper tapped the tempo with his sticks, Baxter played an introduction on the pedal steel, and the old troubadour revisited his thirty-three-year-old critique of the young firebrand who had written "Hard Rain."

> In a soldier's stance, I aimed my hand
> At the mongrel dogs who teach
> Fearing not that I'd become my enemy
> In the instant that I preach
> My pathway led by confusion boats
> Mutiny from stern to bow.
> Ah, but I was so much older then,
> I'm younger than that now.

Prophecy begins at home: the prophet foresees his own future, and then in the fullness of time he foretells the future of the world. Such a wealth of imagination allows time travel, once in a great while.

The renowned paradox, "I was so much older then, I'm younger than that now," meant more to me than ever. The singer at Tanglewood was invoking an old self, the Bob Dylan of the early 1960s, of Lisner Auditorium, the civil rights movement, the protests against the war and the atom bomb and the ban on travel to Cuba, causes that had made the most of his voice and then tried to consume him.

The man who was standing before us now near midnight, singing with all the energy he had left in him after hours of performing, after most of a lifetime of creating and delivering songs, was a new man, young in the best sense, no older than this moment. He had a good secret.

Our ears would be ringing for a long time.

PART IV

Aberdeen, 2009

JAM PRESENTS
THE BOB DYLAN SHOW
GATES OPEN AT 5:00PM
RIPKEN STADIUM
ABERDEEN IRONBIRDS
FRI JUL 24, 2009 5:30PM
RAIN OR SHINE
GAX4   GA5   14   67.50

✻ CHAPTER 15 ✻

Deaths and Entrances

Rick Danko, who wrote the enchanting melody for "This Wheel's on Fire," died in his sleep at his Woodstock home on December 10, 1999, his heart muscle burned out from cocaine, age fifty-six—a gentle soul who could not survive the millennium. Dylan had last seen him in August 1997, two weeks after Tanglewood. He invited Danko onstage in Wallingford, Connecticut, during the Never Ending Tour's show there, to join in singing "This Wheel's on Fire" as well as its apocalyptic counterpart, "All Along the Watchtower."

In January 2000, Dylan's mother, Beatty Rutman (she had remarried in the 1970s), fell ill. She had been spending the holidays at her winter residence in Scottsdale, Arizona. Beatty was flown to St. Paul, Minnesota, to consult her regular physician, and her sons David and Bob joined her there. Emergency surgery confirmed that she had cancer and there was little that could be done. She died in the hospital on January 25, and was buried the next day next to Abe Zimmerman in the Jewish cemetery in Duluth.

In her eighty years Beatty had seen astonishing things. She had lived to witness her son's triumphs in 1997 after the release of *Time Out of Mind* in that pivotal year. The whole world seemed to embrace him. She watched on television as he and his band performed for

Pope John Paul II at the World Eucharistic Congress in Bologna, Italy. In a black tuxedo Dylan stood strumming his guitar under an immense canopy while the pope sat on a throne to the right of the stage five steps above. "The Pope's idea is to get closer to young people through pop music, which unfortunately for many years has been viewed with suspicion and indifference by the church," said Monsignor Domenico Sigalini, a spokesman for the congress. "We don't want to create a Catholic rock 'n' roll, but we do want to encourage a rock 'n' roll which expresses our values." Three hundred thousand people crowded into the Piazza to hear Bob Dylan sing "Blowin' in the Wind" and "Forever Young." The pope leaned forward resting his forehead on his hand as if he were dozing but he was deep in thought, listening to the music.

Dylan put down his guitar and ascended the dais, bowed like a knight before the pope, and kissed his ring. It seemed like the thing to do. Later he did not recall this. The pope said, "You say the answer is blowing in the wind, my friend . . . but it is not the wind that blows things away. It is the wind that is the breath and life of the Holy Spirit, the voice that calls and says, 'Come!'"

The next day the Italian newspapers ran a photo of the pope and the poet together with the caption: "Who is using whom?" One thing was certain: in 1997 Dylan joined the short list of the most famous people in the world, the likes of Queen Elizabeth, the pope, the Dalai Lama, and Muhammad Ali. The telecast of the concert in Bologna was aired in more than seventy nations. Beatty Rutman's son Bob had greater name recognition abroad than any living American with the exception of Ali, Michael Jackson, President Clinton, Madonna, and a few movie stars.

In October he received the Dorothy and Lillian Gish Prize for achievement in the arts, a richly endowed cash award given annually to an artist "who has made an outstanding contribution to the beauty of the world and to mankind's enjoyment and understanding of life." Photographer Richard Avedon, who presented him with the prize at the grand Lotus Club in midtown Manhattan, also took the picture of Dylan that appeared that month on the cover of *Newsweek* magazine.

In December Beatty and her sister Ethel Crystal joined him in Washington, D.C., where he was to receive a medal at the Kennedy Center. The other honorees were Charlton Heston and Lauren Bacall. Bob was wearing a tuxedo and sneakers. Bacall, impeccably dressed, straightened the singer's tie and brushed at his shoulders. Beatty sat next to Bob in a box seat above the stage. Just before his time came to be honored he had to answer a call of nature, and when President Clinton turned to praise him his seat was empty. After making the TV crew very nervous for a minute he returned to his seat. Beatty heard Clinton declare that Dylan had probably had more impact on his generation than any other artist. His face had just appeared on the cover of *Time*, which named him as one of the hundred most influential artists and performers of the century.

In that same year Beatty's handsome grandson Jakob, twenty-seven, leading a rock band called the Wallflowers, had a runaway hit with his second album, *Bringing Down the Horse*. The record sold more copies than his father's, and in June of that year Beatty saw Jakob's portrait on the cover of *Rolling Stone*. His father said, "I'm proud of his accomplishments. He's still young, and he's come a long way in a short time. I worried about him when he started out. I just didn't want to see him get roughed up. This business can throw you into deep water."

On November 14, father and son shared a bill at the San Jose Arena. And when time came for the Grammy nominations in January 1998, Beatty's son's album was named in three categories: Best Album of the Year, Best Contemporary Folk Album, and Best Contemporary Rock Vocal Performance (for "Cold Irons Bound"), while her grandson was also competing for best rock vocal, and had also been nominated for Best Rock Performance by a Group with a Vocal. The night of the Grammy Awards, at Radio City Music Hall on February 25, Beatty watched as both of her boys won awards— Jakob for the category in which he was not competing with his father; Bob Dylan in all three categories. Bob played a song and made a gracious acceptance speech. She had always been proud of her son, but for twenty years or more much of the world had not shared her belief in his gifts. All of a sudden, everyone was proclaiming what she had known all along.

Before she became ill in January 2000, Beatty learned that Bob was to be awarded the prestigious Polar Music Prize in Stockholm— along with violinist Isaac Stern. Perhaps she might have gone to see him receive the laurel from the king of Sweden. There were rumors that Bob would win the Swedish Nobel Prize for Literature—a professor in Virginia had nominated him. Anything seemed possible for Bob Dylan. But she would not live to make that journey to Sweden, for any present or future honors. And nothing, really, could make her more proud of him than she was.

After she died that winter he began writing his autobiography. It was time. Writing about his past, in prose, was intense and lonely work. In mourning for his mother, Dylan put his performing on hold until March 10, when the spring tour began with two shows at the Sun Theatre in Anaheim, California. Then he was happy to be onstage again with his bandmates in front of a live audience. He played little guitar, leaving it up to Larry Campbell and Charlie Sexton, so he could concentrate on his singing.

He sang songs he hadn't performed in years: "Tell Me That It Isn't True" from 1969 and "We Better Talk This Over" from 1978. The band toured the western states Idaho, Washington, Montana, Wyoming, the Dakotas, Nebraska, Kansas, and Colorado, twenty-three shows in large arenas. Then Dylan flew home and returned to his writing desk.

On May 6 the tour resumed in Zurich, Switzerland, at the Hallenstadion, where Dylan sang a regular set of a dozen songs and then *six* encores: "Love Sick," "Like a Rolling Stone," "Don't Think Twice," "Not Fade Away," "Blowin' in the Wind," and "Rainy Day Women." Fans tossed flowers on the stage and he picked one up and carried it off after taking his last bow.

In Scandinavia and Germany they played to half-empty houses, mostly. But Dresden on May 24 was special. The 6,000-seat Freilicht-bühne Junge Garde, an amphitheater, was packed with fans from far and wide who had come to celebrate Dylan's fifty-ninth birthday. His manager and other friends had made the journey. The weather was perfect. In the cool twilight the audience could see the stage and the performers could see the fans. Bedsheets unrolled as banners above the heads of the crowd, with the words "Happy Birthday, Bob" painted in black letters.

He came onstage wearing just a gray western shirt, breeches, and boots, no coat or tie, holding his acoustic guitar. And as he played the first chords of "Roving Gambler" a few fans began singing "Happy Birthday." He ignored the serenaders and the band drowned them out, but as the show continued, it became clear that Dylan would offer this audience something special on his birthday. He performed "Song to Woody," the first song of any importance he had ever composed; he sang "Mama You Been on My Mind" in a tender voice, and no doubt she really was. Between numbers, as the applause rolled toward the stage, there was a lot of discussion between the singer and his bass player about what would come next. Dylan decided to dispense with the cue sheet and play whatever he wanted. He sang "To Ramona" as Larry Campbell strummed a mellow mandolin:

Ramona, come closer
Shut softly your watery eyes
The pangs of your sadness
Shall pass as your senses will rise

And there's no use in tryin'
T' deal with the dyin'
Though I cannot explain that in lines.

When he sang "Country Pie," a couple near the stage found room to waltz, and Dylan smiled at them. He sang "Just Like Tom

Thumb's Blues" and "Drifter's Escape." As he came on for the encores the crowd was singing "Happy Birthday" in a German accent, and Tony Garnier wanted to join in. He pleaded with Dylan to give in, and though the birthday boy kept shaking his head no the crowd would not take no for an answer. Garnier played the melody on the bass and David Kemper made a flourish on the drums. Dylan was visibly moved; he bowed and murmured his thanks. Instead of singing "Love Sick" ("I'm sick of love"), which was slated to come next, he cued up "Ballad of a Thin Man."

> *Because something is happening here*
> *But you don't know what it is*
> *Do you, Mister Jones?*

Women threw roses. A man tried to leap onstage with a gift-wrapped package of wine, but a security guard stopped him.

Dylan sang a lot of encores. Spying a banner that read "Happy Birthday Bob—Forever Young," he sang that song instead of "Rainy Day Women." After he had finished the last encore, "Blowin' in the Wind," and bowed out for what looked like the final exit, he returned to the microphone and—bowing once more—called out: "Thank you! I will remember this birthday for a while."

They went down to Italy for the last week of the tour: Modena, Milan, Florence, Ancona, and Cagliari (on the island of Sardinia). The audiences there in the spring were large and enthusiastic. In his late fifties Bob Dylan—more famous and adored than ever—employed a team of bodyguards to ensure his privacy and personal safety. John Lennon, lacking such security, had been murdered by a fan; George Harrison had been stabbed in his home; Dylan was stalked repeatedly. David Kemper recalled how one night after a performance in London, when leaving the theater in a car with Dylan, several youngsters jumped on the hood and roof of the automobile, and Kemper was frightened. Dylan sensed it. He leaned over to him and, patting his hand, said reassuringly, "David, it's only love. It's only love."

On the last night of the tour they played on the wharf of the ancient port city of Cagliari, the southwestern tip of Sardinia in the Mediterranean. The stage faced the seven hills of the city, the Castello with its thirteenth-century white limestone towers, St. Pancras and the Elephant Tower, the white Cagliari Cathedral, and the Art Nouveau swirls of City Hall. On one side of the stage two NATO warships were docked. Sailors and their dates were watching from the upper decks, overlooking the crowd of 9,000 on the wharves as Dylan played under the starry sky. He mostly sang songs from the sixties: "Just Like a Woman," "Masters of War," and "Like a Rolling Stone." He sang "Mama You Been on My Mind," again with feeling. That night he maintained a joyful rapport with the audience, Italians in their teens and twenties, standing up close to the stage and in the long bleachers where the VIPs had reserved seats. He was pleased to hear everybody singing along, and took many bows after the last encore.

When the show was over he did a surprising thing. The stage at the Molo Ichnusa backs up to the harbor, so there is no back road the performers can use to leave the area. They must pass through the broad pavilion where the audience had been, from the docks to the main road to the town. While the greater part of the crowd moved through the midway on their way up to Cagliari, several hundred fans pressed toward the stage and around it where floodlights illuminated the backstage area. They hoped to glimpse Bob Dylan as he made his way toward the town center.

Some police cars and vans were idling in a guarded lot. A silver Mercedes in the midst of the cavalcade began pulling away, going slow, making a path through the crowd. At first nobody was sure if Dylan had left or not. Then they could see him walking toward a van and trying to climb in, having difficulty because people were blocking the door. At last he climbed in and shut the door, but when the van made no headway, Dylan got out.

He started walking toward the lights of the city, through the crowd that was making way for the Mercedes slowly moving ahead. His bodyguard was guiding him toward the silver car where Tony Garnier was seated in back, distressed over the confusion, this hazardous breech in security. Now the crowd was making a lane in front of the Mercedes, and Dylan's bodyguards were begging him to get into the car; overhead a floodlight illuminated the scene at the wharf where Dylan was walking into the open lane and people were pressing toward him, waving their arms, jumping, bobbing their heads, stepping in front of him with programs, newspapers, maps, train tickets, anything he might scribble his name upon. And at first the security crew and bodyguards were frantic. But somehow, in a few minutes, the furor died down. "Bob was very calm, and he alone— just his presence signing autographs—managed to stop all the pushing," one fan recalled. After a while he stopped signing his name. He pulled a camera out of his pocket, held it above his head, and started taking photos of the crowd with a flash. When he had finished taking pictures, he turned toward the group of people standing thirty feet behind him, held at bay by guards, and signed autographs for another ten minutes. At last he announced that it was time to go, walked back to a minivan, and climbed inside.

"But on his way out he appeared at the window," a fan recalled, "sending kisses with his hand to the people. *Grazie mille*, Mr. Dylan."

A year later, at a press conference in Rome, the bandleader bristled when a reporter called attention to the surprising longevity of the Never Ending Tour.

"It annoys me when I hear people talking about the Never Ending Tour. Obviously everything must finish. That which ties everyone together and makes everyone equal is our mortality. Everything must come to an end."

Someone asked Dylan if he thought about death often.

"I wouldn't say often, but it certainly happens when people who are close to me die." He admitted that his mother's death had affected his recent songs, not yet released. The journalist asked—obtusely—if Dylan considered his own mortality. The poet replied, "I can see myself in other people. That's the way you can think about it. I don't think about it any more than everybody else. As soon as you enter this world you are old enough to leave it."

Friends and colleagues had been leaving this world at an alarming rate. Victor Maymudes died in January 2001, four months before Dylan's sixtieth birthday, and in the months to come he could hardly keep up with the obituaries. John Lee Hooker passed away in June, Mimi Fariña (Joan Baez's sister) in July, Larry Kegan in September—the day of the attack on the World Trade Center—and George Harrison in November. Every time a musician expired anywhere in the world the phone would ring for Bob Dylan to make a statement, a tribute, as he had for Jerry Garcia in 1995 and Carl Perkins in 1998. You would think a guitar player couldn't decently leave this world without Dylan's blessing. Of Harrison, he said, "George was a giant, a great, great soul, with all of the humanity, all of the wit and humor, all the wisdom, the spirituality, the common sense of a man and compassion for people. The world is a profoundly emptier place without him."

The year 2001 had begun auspiciously. On January 21, Dylan attended the fifty-eighth Golden Globe ceremony at the Hilton in Beverly Hills, where Phil Collins and Monica Bellucci presented him with the award for Best Original Song. He had written the tune "Things Have Changed" in 1999 for Curtis Hanson's film *Wonder Boys,* and it was released as a single in 2000.

People are crazy and times are strange
I'm locked in tight, I'm out of range
I used to care, but things have changed.

Dressed in his tuxedo, his tie slightly askew, he made his way from his seat to the stage, shouldering through the glamorous, bejeweled celebrities, and you could see how small he was. He looked handsome, trim, and youthful, his curly hair brown on top and graying around the ears, sporting a pencil mustache.

"Wow, this is . . . umm . . . something, really . . . Thanks Curtis, thanks Hollywood, thanks to my band, the record company and everybody in my family and . . . that's about it." (Laughter and applause.)

> *This place ain't doing me any good*
> *I'm in the wrong town, I should be in Hollywood*
> *Just for a second there I thought I saw something move*
>
> *Only a fool in here would think he's got anything to prove. . . .*

He happened to be home on a long break between tours, having played his 109th date of 2000 in Towson, Maryland, on November 19. He was free until the winter tour started on February 25 in Japan. Showing up for the Golden Globe event was good manners and savvy public relations; Dylan was a strong candidate for an Oscar in 2001, but the Hollywood community is sensitive to slights and attitudes.

The week of the Oscars, he and his band were in Australia. They booked a television studio, Channel Seven in Sydney, so that viewers all over the world could watch Dylan perform "Things Have Changed" live and—if he won—see him give his acceptance speech via satellite hookup.

On Saturday, March 24, the band members—minus Dylan—went to the studio to set up their gear for the lighting and sound. The Australian TV director had arranged everything to his liking, marking Dylan's spot with an X on one side of the room, and the drums on the other, and the sidemen's places carefully situated; the camera would swoop around them from above. As they played the song through they could tell that the director was proud of his artistic vision that would be beamed from his local studio into hundreds of millions of homes the world over. This sound check went okay but something about the setup made Kemper and Campbell uneasy.

The next day, Sunday the twenty-fifth, Oscar night in Los Angeles, Dylan and his sidemen showed up at Channel Seven studios a couple of hours early to prepare for the broadcast. Pleased to see the famous singer all dressed up for the occasion, the director said, "Okay! Let's get to work! We need to make a safety . . ." Someone in the band asked what that was for. "Well, just in case we are in the middle of the show and we lose a satellite feed, we'll shift to the safety and no one will know." Dylan stood where he was told, the band members took their places, and they performed "Things Have Changed" as the cameras rose and circled around them in the heat of the key light.

Dylan insisted on viewing the "safety" video. So they showed it to him.

"Whoa, whoa, whoa!" he said. "I don't like this at *all.*"

"Well, Mr. Dylan," said the director. "Everything is *set* the way it is, with the lighting and cameras. The crew has spent days getting everything right."

"But I don't like it."

"Mr. Dylan, I'm sorry. Come on now—"

"I want to be closer to the drums . . . over *here,*" said Bob Dylan, and to the director's horror, the singer picked up his standing microphone and carried it from the X spot on the soundstage and put it down with a thump about three strides to his right.

The director was fit to be tied. Now the key light would have to be repositioned, and the safety was useless. What was he to do if he couldn't get the band to remake the safety? The clock and the bandleader were against him.

It was time for lunch; after that the band would return for the live broadcast. Dylan, having no appetite just then for food, stood in the studio with David Kemper, thinking. All of the lights were off now except for a single work light in the ceiling. Against the wall was a wide, flat plasma screen and on it Dylan could see himself moving.

"Look at how the screen works, Bob. Stand by your microphone and look at that!" It looked like a Vermeer painting.

"This is what I want," said Dylan. "Just the camera on me and that light. That's how I want to do it."

He knew that if he looked directly into the monitor he would get the natural effect he wanted and the director's contrivance would have to be abandoned. The fact that the light was a work light and not a key light didn't matter to him.

As one band member theorized, the Australian director appeared to have one more trick up his sleeve. He had sent the band out to lunch for forty-five minutes even though showtime came in forty. Musicians being musicians, if he did not call them early they would not all arrive in time, and then his beautiful backup video would have to air instead of a crude live performance.

But these were no ordinary musicians, and the drummer, for one, was suspicious. "Unless I'm an idiot, they were trying to catch us off guard so they would have to use their safety that had the fancy production values." When the director called for "places" on a few minutes' notice they were all ready: Dylan, Baxter, Garnier, Kemper, and Campbell. Where Dylan was standing now the key light was wrong and no light suited him better than the plain work light he desired. As they announced his name and his nominated song in Hollywood a close-up of Bob Dylan's face appeared on a screen fifty feet high, and the glitterati laughed. In the audience, Randy Newman—another nominee—was watching, and so was Sting, once again finding themselves upstaged by a master of imagery, a musician who was always larger than life. Did anyone doubt he would win the Academy Award for Best Song?

At first he appeared to be mugging, turning his head this way and that, profile, full face, craning his neck like a bumpkin at an inaugural ball; in fact he was checking the monitor to make sure he was looking the audience straight in the eye. He looked natural, with his bushy eyebrows, his pencil mustache; he looked real, just as he had wanted it all along, without any cinematic trickery, and his eyes were piercing.

A few minutes later, when Jennifer Lopez announced that Dylan had won the Oscar for "Things Have Changed," he appeared again on the colossal screen, in his tuxedo, with a flowing black ribbon for a tie, his bandmates standing behind him, grinning. He was grateful and his humility was touching.

Oh good God, this is amazing. I've got to thank Curtis Hanson for encouraging me to do this song and everybody at Paramount, Sherry Lansing and Jonathan Dolgen. But especially Curtis, who just kept at it. . . . . Everybody at Columbia Records, my record company, who supports me through all these years. . . . I want to say hello to all of my family and friends out there watching. And I want to thank the members of the Academy who were bold enough to give me this award for this song—which obviously—a song that doesn't pussyfoot around or turn a blind eye to human nature. And God bless you all with peace, tranquility, and goodwill. Thanks.

Dylan had recorded "Things Have Changed" in the Clinton Recording Studios, New York City, in the first week of April 1999, before flying to Lisbon to begin a twenty-one-show European tour. The recording was done with no preparation and on short notice. Engineer Chris Shaw, who had never worked with Dylan before, remembers getting the call three days before the date, and wondering "Why me?" Shaw had worked for Booker T. & the MG's, and Jeff Buckley, as well as Public Enemy, but he didn't think of himself as an obvious choice to be working with the singer-composer who had made *Oh Mercy* and *Time Out of Mind*.

Shaw told journalist Damien Love that he met Dylan and his touring band at the studio on a spring afternoon. There was no producer in the room. The engineer arranged the microphones and set the levels. Dylan said, "Here's the song," and they played it. The first take had a heavy New Orleans vibe, a shuffle rhythm, and the band was pleased. But Dylan thought that this version might be "too overpowering" and suggested they try it over.

After the second take he asked Shaw to play it back while they all listened. The song was fine except for one of the guitar lines, so Charlie Sexton fixed that, then they decided that the tune wanted more rhythmic continuity, so the drummer put a shaker on it. "The very last thing Bob did was raise the shaker up like ten decibels, making it ridiculously loud, and that was the mix he wanted to go with," Shaw recalls. Shaw thought this was just a rough mix that would be turned over to Lanois or some other producer who would refine the end product, and he was surprised to learn that this rough mix was final.

That evening Dylan turned to his band members and said, "You know, I don't need a producer. I think I can produce the next record." So when the spring tour ended with a double-header at the Beale Street Music Festival in Memphis on May 6, 2001, Bob Dylan, his touring band, and Chris Shaw returned to the studio in New York to record an entire new album—with no producer. During the winter of 2000–2001 Dylan had been writing songs, quietly, gleefully, a sequence of tunes with a different tone from the dirges and torch songs that dominated *Time Out of Mind*.

"On '*Love and Theft*,' Bob really wanted to get the live sound of the band he had at that time," Shaw recalls, judging that this band— Larry Campbell, Charlie Sexton, David Kemper, and Tony Garnier—was the best Dylan has ever had. Augie Meyers came to play organ, and his brother Clay played the bongos. Dylan was unpredictable. First he told the engineer he meant to play guitar throughout the session. He had a vision of himself facing a corner of the room and singing into it like Robert Johnson as painted on the cover of an iconic album cover in the 1960s. So Shaw and his assistant spent hours the day before Dylan arrived arranging the studio equipment so that he could do that.

On Tuesday, May 8, Shaw got the band settled and set the sound levels. They were jamming when Dylan walked into the studio, unpacked his guitar, sat down in his chair, and started singing into the corner. Within ten minutes he had gotten whatever satisfaction he hoped to get from that vision of himself, cornered. It was not going to be that kind of a record. He stood up, put aside the guitar, ambled over to the piano, sat down, and started playing. Shaw had a microphone at the piano just in case Dylan might find inspiration there, and this was a good thing, because Dylan stayed in his seat at the piano for the rest of the session, except when they were recording "High Water" and "Po' Boy."

Shaw had heard the war stories about the conflict between Dylan and his producers in the studio. Now there was no problem. "The thing about Bob is that he just knows exactly what he wants. . . . The people who have said that Bob is difficult are people who were trying to put what *they* want on the record—not what Bob wants.

"For him it's all about getting the track to fit the words, and not the other way around." In twenty years of studio recording Shaw had never seen an artist approach a session the way Dylan did. Nearly every day he would go into the studio with a new song, and a "prototype," that is, some classic song that had a quality or mood he wanted for his own. "I'm kinda hearing like this old Billie Holiday song," he would say. So the band would start with the old song, and when they had gotten the feel of it the bandleader would say, "Okay, and this is how *my* song goes."

There are twelve tracks on the album, and they recorded one per day. "It's always interesting, always unbelievably exciting, and it's a lot of hard work," Shaw affirms. The first day they kicked off with the upbeat "Summer Days," a swing tune.

Summer days, summer nights are gone
Summer days and summer nights are gone
I know a place where there's still somethin' going on

The prototype was the boogie-woogie tune "Rebecca" by pianist Pete Johnson and singer Big Joe Turner, a rambunctious rockabilly number full of high spirits and humor that set the tone for the sessions to come.

I'm driving in the flats in a Cadillac car
The girls all say, "You're a worn out star"
My pockets are loaded, and I'm spending every dime
How can you say you love someone else, you know it's me all the time.

The second day, Wednesday, May 9, Dylan mystified his bandmates by inviting them to play Johnnie & Jack's "Uncle John's Bongos" from the 1950s. This was the prototype, the feeling he wanted for the deliberately grotesque Mardi Gras parade rocker "Tweedle Dee & Tweedle Dum."

Well the rain beat'n down on the window pane
I got love for you, and it's all in vain
Brains in the pot, they're beginning to boil
They're drippin' with garlic and olive oil
Tweedle Dee is on his hands and his knees
Sayin' "Throw me something, Mister, please."

It was southern fried gothic, Lewis Carroll lost in the funhouse of a Harry Crews or Flannery O'Connor novel, daring you to make sense of the allegory.

And so it went: on the third day, "Honest with Me." There was no prototype for that tune, and the band had difficulty in finding the right tempo.

When I left my home, the sky split open wide
I never wanted to go back there, I'd rather have died. . . .

On day four they created "Lonesome Day Blues," low-down, deep, and dirty. The prototype was Son House's "My Dog Can't Bark." Day five, May 12, Dylan brought in a tune in the manner of Bing Crosby, "Bye and Bye," upbeat for brushes and bass drum, thump, thump, four to the bar . . .

The singer on *Time Out of Mind* had been dour, bitter, and deadly serious, an old man cornered, looking into the mouth of a graveyard. The groove he cut on that masterful album was deep but narrow. "I got so frustrated in the studio that I didn't really dimensionalize the songs," he later admitted. "I feel there was a sameness to the rhythms. . . . I think that's why people say *Time Out of Mind* is sort of dark and foreboding: because we locked into that one dimension of the sound."

The character Dylan brought to the *"Love and Theft"* sessions is a magpie collector of old songs, jokes, and stories, a minstrel show interlocutor, the sort of gaffer Yeats says may come "proud, open-eyed and laughing to the tomb." He returned to the studio with a sense of fun and the broadest palette of styles he had assembled since the brainstorming Basement Tapes in the 1960s: western swing, rockabilly, and slow blues ballads in the style of Bing Crosby and Dean Martin. He was sorting through the prop and costume annex, the broad attic of American roots music. That was perhaps the biggest surprise: for the first time Dylan was writing pop tunes similar to the ones his *mother* loved and danced to—not folk, rock, or rhythm and blues but the foxtrot ballads of Johnny Mercer, Frank Loesser, Hoagy Carmichael, love songs with tonic verses and a key change in the bridge.

"Floater" takes its tune from Guy Lombardo's 1930s classic "Snuggled on Your Shoulder." Dylan's gentle "Moonlight" echoes a chorus from the 1925 "The Prisoner's Song" that was a parlor favorite from Vernon Dalhart's original recording of it, down to versions by Bill Monroe and the Carter Family. If the singer of *Time Out of Mind* had been isolated, walking a narrow road out of the world of the living, the persona of *"Love and Theft"* seems to have come out the other side, high above the strife and chaos, taking it all in, and gathering as much of the music of humanity as his heart will hold. An old man who has earned his second childhood, he delights in nursery rhymes, knock-knock jokes, and low humor. And there is no producer or schoolmarm in the room to put an end to the clowning.

> *Po' boy in the hotel called the Palace of Gloom*
> *Called down to room service, says "send up a room"*

Shaw recalls how much fun everyone had making *"Love and Theft."* "Bob was just having a blast producing himself, and he had one of his best bands ever with him. . . . There were ten of us in the control room, and we were all whooping and hollering the entire time . . ." A welcome guest at the studio was the television director Larry Charles, who was collaborating with Dylan on a new screenplay. "A lot of lines that didn't wind up in [the film] *Masked and Anonymous* wound up in *"Love and Theft"* and vice versa."

This was just the right atmosphere for the sublime "Mississippi," with its tender sentiments and magnanimity. On Sunday, May 20, everyone took the day off, and on Monday Dylan came into the studio with a multitrack tape from the Miami sessions back in 1997. Dylan's girlfriend had been listening to this tape, which included the outtakes from *Time Out of Mind*. After hearing "Mississippi," she said, "Bob, this song has gotten left behind." He listened to it, and admitted, "Yeah, that's a great song." The other musicians and the engineer all agreed that not only was it a great song but the performance at Criteria had been very fine. There was only one problem: Daniel Lanois's guitar was essential to the mix. Tony Garnier pointed this out and Dylan said, "If we use this it means Daniel has to be involved. So let's cut our own version." And so they did.

"Love and Theft," with its broad canvas, its openhearted inclusiveness, turned out to be the perfect home for "Mississippi," which

Dylan knew instinctively would have been out of place in the existential wasteland of *Time Out of Mind*.

My heart is not weary, it's light and it's free
I've got nothing but affection for them who sailed with me.

During the last week and a half in May, Chris Shaw and Bob Dylan worked on mixing *"Love and Theft."* The composer was demanding and impatient. Absorbed in the studio, he scarcely acknowledged his sixtieth birthday on Thursday, May 24. Larry Campbell remembers giving the boss a cigar as a token of the milestone, but there was no other celebration that he can recall. In one day, Shaw remembers, they mixed four of the songs, working for six hours straight. "It's very nerve wracking when you're working with Bob," Shaw told Damien Love, "especially as a mixer . . . because you don't get much time. . . . He really hates being in the studio, I think, on that part of the process. So you have to be on your toes."

One of the main problems in recording Dylan is that he refuses to use headphones. In rerecording or dubbing flawed lines, the standard practice is for a singer to repeat those lines while listening to the first recording through headphones. Dylan wouldn't go along. He wanted everything to be live. So they would have to get the whole band back in the studio, or as many as they could muster, to revise a single verse. The advantage of this was that you could hear, simultaneously, the sound of the original recording and the rerecording, what the engineers call "bleed" or "spill" on the tracks. The sound was large and thick, "kind of swampy," according to the engineer, but Dylan really liked it.

By June, when the band was ready to launch the European tour in Norway, the album was ready for artwork and packaging. The public relations staff at Columbia and Sony decided to break the news in Europe so it would be world news when it hit America. So while

Dylan was between gigs in Pescara and Anzio, Italy, on July 23, they invited reporters from all over Europe to attend a press conference in the magnificent baroque Hotel de la Ville near the Spanish Steps in Rome. Hours before the conference began, the thirteen journalists from twelve countries gathered in a gilded parlor with marble tables, Persian carpets, and chintz-covered sofas. They sipped white wine and nibbled prosciutto sandwiches while listening to "Mississippi," "Tweedle Dee & Tweedle Dum," "Po' Boy," and the rest of "*Love and Theft*" piped in on the stereo system.

Fifteen minutes after the appointed hour Bob Dylan strolled into the parlor wearing a cowboy hat, a two-tone western shirt of black and gray, and matching trousers with patch pockets. His pointed cowboy boots made him stand an inch taller, but he still looked small to the reporters. He was very thin, almost frail-looking. He quickly took his seat on a couch against the wall and looked out at the semicircle of journalists over a thicket of microphones and tape recorders. He crossed and uncrossed his legs. He took off his white hat. There is a startling dissonance in meeting a man whose old photographs are iconic. Dylan had aged in interesting ways. He had most of his hair, the trademark, tousled curls touching his wrinkled forehead; his face was deeply lined, especially the lines etched from the nose to the edges of his downturned mouth, accentuated by the angle of the pencil mustache above his upper lip. The winnowing of the years had uncovered contrasts and contradictions deep in the bone, weird asymmetries. It was a wise, owlish face radiating humor and ironies. One noted "pale blue eyes, frighteningly large and attentive, like the windows of a great mind that works unceasingly." He welcomed the company courteously, yet he looked anxious and puzzled.

A reporter mentioned that there had been many books written about Bob Dylan. Had he read them?

He smiled. "I stopped reading them after the Shelton biography. It's difficult to read about yourself because in your own mind things never happen in that way. It all seems like fiction."

Then the reporter asked if he had ever been tempted to write about himself, and Dylan readily replied, "Yeah. To tell the truth, I'm doing it. I think that what I'm writing has been trying to find its way out for some time now." He wanted to make the point that this book was not merely an exercise in nostalgia for his own gratification, but an effort to discover some kind of pattern in random events.

His old songs prompted his memory. "I'm studying the songs, but I look at them in a way I've never thought of before." So much of life one lives without trying to connect the dots. "Many things [in life] go from one point to another without any [apparent] reason. Why did they happen? Various bad things lead to something good. Could they have happened if something else hadn't happened? And if they seemed so bad at the time why did they bring long term benefits?" Although the project was enormous, Dylan indicated that he was writing the book in his spare time. "My impressions come from a great number of songs, and I'm trying to see things from many points of view." Studying Dylan's schedule over the previous two years one might wonder what time the songwriter had to spare for the "enormous project" of chronicling his eventful life.

In Rome he had nothing to say about his personal life, restricting his remarks mainly to two topics: his pride in self-producing "*Love and Theft*," and the insidious effect of the mass media on poetry and the public. The themes are closely entwined. Asked if he has been influenced by poets, and if he keeps an eye out for new poetic voices, he said that he does, but he doesn't have much faith that there are any, because this period of history is inhospitable to poets. "The media is very invasive. What could you possibly write that you haven't seen every day in the newspapers or on television?"

Still, a journalist insisted, there are *emotions* that must be expressed.

"Yeah, but the media control people's emotions. When there were people around like William Blake, Shelley or Byron, there probably wasn't any form of media. Just gazettes. You could feel free to put down whatever you had in your mind."

Someone else asked Dylan if he believed television and the media had killed poetry.

"Oh, absolutely. Because literature is written for the public. There's nobody anymore like Kafka who just sits down and writes something without wanting somebody to read it." These days, he argued, the mass media have preempted the precious paths of communication that once belonged to poets and their readers. We see things on television that are more horrifying, sad, or hilarious than we are likely to see in real life. "The news shows people things that they couldn't even dream about, and even ideas that people thought they could repress. . . . So what can a writer do when every idea is already exposed in the media before he can even grasp it and develop it?"

Because the media control sources of information, according to Dylan, "We live in a world of fantasy where Disney has won. . . . It's all fantasy." Characteristically, just as he was giving up the case as hopeless he insisted on the need to challenge the status quo. "If a writer has something to say he should say it at all costs. The world is real. Fantasy has become the real world—whether we realize it or not." His favorite rhetorical device—in interviews—is the paradox, and his speech, on this summer afternoon in Rome, was a maze of paradoxes, in which perplexed European journalists struggled to keep him in view without getting lost themselves.

His personal efforts to bring people to their senses—to bring us back into relation with "the real world" rather than the world of Disney—have been focused upon the recording process. He is dogmatic on this subject. Until *"Love and Theft,"* he declared, none of his recordings ever sounded the way he hoped they would. "When you work with a producer . . . he can take you in this direction or that direction if you're not particularly determined—as soon as you're not sure if a song should be in a certain way. Most of my records turned out to be compromises because of insistent producers. Often the producer or the engineers are prisoners of the legend. They don't think about how my things should *really* sound." Fans who hear him in concert often complain that the songs don't sound the way they do on the record. Of course they don't, he agrees, because they weren't recorded properly to begin with.

And so Dylan took the next bold step, dispensing with the producer altogether. "If you have your own vision, there's really not much a producer can contribute. I don't know much about sound quality, but the arrangements are exactly like I wanted them this time." He praised his engineer Chris Shaw, who simply understands the distinctive quality of Dylan's voice. "My special vocal range subverts the classical recording systems: both the low and high register disappears. On my last record [*Time Out of Mind*] they tried all kinds of effects and overdubs to make my voice sound like it does in real life. But I really think the right way is the most simple way . . . an analogic recording, realistic. . . . On this record we had a young guy who knew exactly what to do."

Time Out of Mind was a hard act to follow as far as most people were concerned, but not for the composer-producer of *"Love and Theft"* (who now had two noms de plume, Bob Dylan, the singer, and Jack Frost, the producer) still harboring some misgivings about the previous album. "There's a real drive to it [*Time Out of Mind*], but it isn't even close to the way I had it envisioned. I mean, I'm satisfied with what we did. But there were things I had to throw out because this assortment of people just couldn't lock in on riffs and rhythms all together. I could've [made it work] if I'd had the willpower. I just didn't at that time, and so you got to steer it where the event itself wants to go. I feel there was a sameness to the rhythms. It was more like that swampy, voodoo thing that Lanois is so good at."

For *"Love and Theft"* Dylan threw open the doors and windows so that all the rhythms of America could attend the party. When the CD was ready, while they were touring Italy in late July, Dylan gave copies to all of the band members. One recalls Dylan's comment as he handed him his disc. "Here," he said. "Here is *our* record. You are never going to hear a *tighter* motherfucker." Soon the audience would be divided over which album was the greater achievement—the "unsurpassable" *Time Out of Mind* or its surprising successor "*Love and Theft*." It is pretty clear which album Dylan preferred.

Soon after returning from a late summer tour in America, Dylan granted an interview to Edna Gundersen of *USA Today*. They met in a seaside hotel not far from Dylan's coffee shop in Santa Monica. He told her that the new album was more autobiographical than his others, "the way I really feel about things. . . . It's me using everything I know to be true." He recapitulated the arguments he had made in Rome. "To me, music either expresses ideas of liberty, or it's made under the oppression of a dictatorship." This was an idea he was exploring allegorically in the screenplay he was writing with Larry Charles. "The only stuff I've heard that has that feeling is traditional Anglo-American music. That's all I know. That's all I've ever known. I was fortunate to come up at a time when the last of it existed. It doesn't exist anymore." Of course that feeling of liberty does exist—in "*Love and Theft*" if nowhere else.

Gundersen pointed to the lines in the song "Lonesome Day Blues."

I'm forty miles from the mill, I'm dropping it into overdrive
Set my dial on the radio I wish my mother was still alive

And she asked if he was thinking about his mother's passing. All he would say is that "even to talk about my mother just breaks me up."

CHAPTER 16

Facing the Lion

"*Love and Theft*" was officially released on the darkest day of the dawning century, September 11, 2001, the day of the suicide attacks by Al Qaeda on the World Trade Center in New York and the Pentagon in Washington, D.C.

New books and records that month had more than the usual difficulty getting attention. But critics had received "*Love and Theft*" months before, and the runaway success of *Time Out of Mind* four years earlier had so piqued the public's interest in the "mature" Dylan that the press was bound to give him a hearing.

On 9/11 Greg Kot set the tone for the discussion, in the *Chicago Tribune*: "This is a tour of American music—jump blues, slow blues, rockabilly, Tin Pan Alley ballads, country swing—that evokes the sprawl, fatalism and subversive humor of Dylan's sacred text, Harry Smith's *Anthology of American Folk Music*." Kot, referring to the song "High Water (for Charley Patton)," said that the whole album was "a kind of homage . . . a sweeping portrait of the South's racial history, with the unsung blues singer as a symbol of the region's cultural richness and ingrained social cruelties." In short, Kot called the record "one of the finest roots-rock albums ever made."

Robert Christgau of the *Village Voice* gave it an A+, suggesting that if *Time Out of Mind* was Dylan's death album, "this is his immortality album." The music critic Paul Williams, who had been writing about Dylan and his work with incomparable sensitivity since 1966, when he reviewed *Blonde on Blonde* for his magazine *Crawdaddy*, was overjoyed: "Each song, I find myself lingering in the car or wherever it's playing so I can hear it to the end. . . . I like the wholeness, the connectedness of the album . . . the way it becomes a single experience, single narrative, in some mysterious and pleasing way." Williams noticed the recurring themes: especially the nautical perspective, in "Floater," where the narrator is on a boat fishing for bullheads; "Honest with Me," where he sings "I came ashore in the dead of the night"; "Mississippi," with its magnificent stanza beginning "My ship's been split to splinters"; and then "Throw your panties overboard" from "High Water." Most of the songs on *"Love and Theft"* feature a boat or a river moving through the lyrics—water, the universal symbol for life and renewal.

On September 25, two weeks after the terrorist attacks, Dylan met with Mikal Gilmore of *Rolling Stone* at a Santa Monica hotel. They sat at a small table near the balcony of the hotel suite, feeling the salt breeze off the Pacific through the open doors. Dylan was wearing a white western shirt and black trousers with arrows embroidered on the pocket seams, and black boots. Airplanes were taking off from the municipal airport, ascending over the blue sea, and he would pause from time to time in conversation to gaze at a plane and its vapor trail.

The point of the interview was to discuss Dylan's music, particularly the new album. He did so dutifully, thoughtfully, while leaving the impression that there were more important things on his mind.

"You're talking to a person that feels like he's walking around in the ruins of Pompeii all the time. It's always been that way. . . . I deal with all the old stereotypes. The language and the identity I use is the one I know only so well." His records, he told Gilmore, are an expression of "the entire panorama" of America, past and present, "a rising tide that lifts all ships," including the vessel of his own inspiration. The reference to the ruins of Pompeii fourteen days after 9/11 was revealing. Trying to sum up the content of *"Love and Theft"* in a few words, Dylan drummed his fingers on the table and gazed at the sea. "The whole album deals with power. If life teaches us anything, it's that there's nothing that men and women won't do to get power. The album deals with power, wealth, knowledge and salvation." No doubt about it: "Mississippi" is all about self-knowledge and salvation; "Summer Days" touches upon power and salvation; "High Water" is about power, from beginning to end; "Po' Boy" is a parable about wealth; "Tweedle Dee & Tweedle Dum" tackles all four of Dylan's professed themes. "If it's a great album—which I hope it is," he added, "it's a great album because it deals with great themes."

Dylan gives a lot of himself in his interviews. One senses, reviewing this conversation, that he was weighing his words not just for himself but for his children and grandchildren. It was a dark and perilous time in our history, and Dylan's poetry was as consequential then in refining the American character as it had been in the 1960s.

When the journalist called attention to the humor on the new album, Dylan was quick to qualify it: yes, there is humor but it is dark humor, which would never poke fun "at the principles that would guide a person's life. . . . Basically the songs deal with what many of my songs deal with . . . business, politics and war, and maybe love interest on the side."

I'm going to spare the defeated, I'm going to speak to the crowd
I'm going to teach peace to the conquered, I'm going to tame the proud
(FROM *"Lonesome Day Blues")*

Toward the end of the conversation Gilmore mentioned that some music fans had turned to *"Love and Theft"* after September 11 because there is something in the songs "that matches the spirit of dread and uncertainty of our present conditions." And finally, he asked Dylan if he had anything to say about the events of that terrible day.

Thirty years earlier Bob Dylan might have avoided the straight answer. But in 2001 he faced the solemn question with the dignity and wisdom appropriate to an éminence grise. First he quoted verses from a surprising source, the "Gentlemen-Rankers" by the poet of the British Empire Rudyard Kipling.

We have done with Hope and Honour, we are lost to Love and Truth
We are dropping down the ladder rung by rung,
And the measure of our torment is the measure of our youth
God help us, for we knew the worst too young!

Above all he was concerned for the children. "If anything, my mind would go to young people at a time like this." The author of "Forever Young," who prayed in that lyric for his children always to prize Hope, Honour, Love, and Truth, now feared for the youngsters whose worldview had been blighted by the terrorism of Al Qaeda.

"Art imposes order on life," he said, "but how much more art will there be? We don't really know. There's a secret sanctity of nature. How much more of that will there be?"

And did he see any hope in the situation?

First apologizing that he is neither "an educator or an explainer," he then quoted—without citing the source—lines from John Stuart Mill's treatise *On Liberty* (1859): "But it is time now for great men to come forward. With small men, no great thing can be accomplished at the moment." It is Mill's argument against the tyranny of the majority in a democratic society—a point of view consistent with Dylan's iconoclasm and faith in the rugged individual.

He went on to cite Sun Tzu (sixth century B.C.), the Chinese general and military theorist who wrote *The Art of War*, prefacing the quote with the admonitory aside that "whoever's in charge" of our nation will surely have read Sun Tzu: "If you know the enemy and know yourself, you need not fear the result of a hundred battles. If you know yourself and not your enemy, for every victory gained you will suffer a defeat." How could America think of waging war with the Taliban, Iraq, or in Afghanistan without a thorough understanding of those countries and their cultures? And how dependent is such an understanding upon Americans understanding themselves as a people?

"Things will have to change. And one of those things that will have to change: *People will have to change their internal world.*"

On October 19, in the midst of his autumn tour, Dylan addressed the audience in the Staples Center in Los Angeles. Madonna had performed on the same stage two weeks earlier. "She told you to think globally," Dylan commented. "I've got some advice to give you. Rethink it." He was not advocating "globalism" or isolationism; he was urging introspection.

It is this crucial work, the changing of one's interior world, that Bob Dylan was best suited to pursue, as a poet and performer, from the time he was a teenager. His songs were a graphic record of his development, and they had a rare power to influence people who listened to them. In his sixty-second year he was curious to find out if he could do, in other media, what he had done with songs.

In February 2002 he won a Grammy for Best Contemporary Folk Album for "*Love and Theft*." At the Staples Center on February 27, Dylan and his band performed "Cry a While." Bonnie Raitt loved the number, said it was "perhaps the funkiest performance by a white guy" she had ever seen. "He's at the top of his game," she decided. U2 won Record of the Year for "Walk On," which Daniel Lanois had produced. Dylan was always glad to see his friend Bono, who performed "Walk On" early in the evening. And he was charmed by twenty-one-year-old rhythm and blues prodigy Alicia Keys ("There's *nothing* about that girl that I don't like . . .") who won five Grammys that night, including Song of the Year for "Fallin'" and Best New Artist.

A lot of old friends were there: T-Bone Burnett, Eric Clapton, Emmylou Harris, Ralph Stanley. The year 2001 had been very good for American roots music, with the success of the Coen brothers' film *O Brother, Where Art Thou?* and its sound track performed by Alison Krauss & Union Station, John Hartford, Norman Blake, Ralph Stanley, and others, which won Album of the Year.

The next week Dylan was in T-Bone Burnett's studio in Los Angeles making a record with the great gospel singer Mavis Staples. He had known Mavis for forty years, since she had discovered his song "Blowin' in the Wind" and performed it with the renowned Staple Singers. As a child he had listened to her on the radio, singing "Yonder comes little David with his rock and his sling. I don't want to meet him, he's a dangerous man," and it had made his hair stand on end. Her admiration for young Dylan was mutual. "We just wondered how with him being a little white boy, how he could feel all those things we felt, you know? All this pain and the hurt, you know. How could he write these songs?"

Forty years later, the two legends found themselves back in the studio to record one of Dylan's gospel tunes for a forthcoming album to be titled *Gotta Serve Somebody: The Gospel Songs of Bob Dylan.* Upon the urging of executive producer Jeffrey Gaskill, Columbia would release the album of covers by Aaron Neville, Shirley Caesar, the Chicago Mass Choir, and other gospel groups in March 2003. Meanwhile, they asked Dylan if he would contribute to the project by revisiting one of his own religious compositions. His choice: "Gonna Change My Way of Thinking," a theme in keeping with his agenda that year. Larry Campbell played at the session, and he recalls how wonderful the chemistry was between Mavis and Bob. "Mavis, you know that's a sweetheart right there—Mavis and her sister Yvonne—great to be around. Light up the whole room, you know? Just to hear her sing, the vibe, the personality? It is just wonderful."

Dylan had asked Campbell to select some songs from the Carter

Family box set because he was thinking about making a record of Carter Family tunes. "So I grabbed a couple of tunes on a disc, and on one of them was the song 'Keep on the Firing Line' we ended up recording. I don't know that it's ever been released. But on the Carter Family disc there is this routine from a radio show they did with Jimmie Rodgers [in Louisville, 1931]. There's a knock on the door and somebody yells, 'Hey, Maybelle, look who's coming down the drive! Well. If it isn't Jimmie Rodgers.' He yodels. And they shout, 'Well, come on in, Jimmie!' There is this whole dialogue. So Bob kept making me play that record over and over again.

"The next thing you know we were doing this tune with Mavis, 'Gonna Change My Way of Thinking,' and he says, 'All right now, we will play through this first verse. Then I want you to stop everything, and there will be a knock on the door, and I'm gonna say 'Hey, it's Mavis Staples!'"

So Dylan re-created the skit between yodeling Jimmie Rodgers and the Carters, but with a millennial twist: in 2002 it is white Bob Dylan and black Mavis Staples he is inviting into his home to eat chicken and sing a duet—a kind of interracial mingling that even legends would not have been allowed in Louisville a half century before.

BOB: Why look, someone's coming up the road, boys.

(Knock, knock, knock)

MAVIS: Hey, hey! Hey there, Bobby!

BOB: Hey, it's Mavis Staples!

MAVIS: Hey, fellows! What's up? Aw, it's good to see all of you. My goodness, Bobby, you got a nice place here!

BOB: Well, welcome to California, Mavis!

MAVIS: Thank ya much! Whoa, you got a nice view!

BOB: Yeah, it is. You can sit on this porch, and look straight into Hawaii.

They agree to "knock off a few chickens and fry 'em up." He tells her he has the blues from laying up in bed with insomnia, "reading *Snoozeweek*"—the same kind of cornball humor that leavens "*Love and Theft.*" She says reading *Snoozeweek* is no way to cure the blues: what they need to do is some singing. And so they do.

> *Gonna sit at the welcome table*
> *I'm as hungry as a horse*
> *I'm gonna revitalize my thinkin'*
> *I'm gonna let the law take its course*

Dylan took the opportunity to rewrite most of the stanzas of this grim song, not to much advantage, but more in keeping with the breezy mood of the occasion.

Mavis was fascinated to see her old friend scribbling new verses in the studio. He would write a line and show it to her, write a few more and ask her what she thought. "Bobby, you write so little," she said, struggling to read the words. "He said he couldn't help it. When a person writes like that," Staples remarked, "they're humble." When she told him that, he said he'd never heard such a thing before.

Larry Campbell has other fond memories of those years, 2002–2004, when Dylan took time off from songwriting and recording but seemed more determined than ever to change his interior world and show others how it can be done. While Death stalked the singers of his generation Dylan worked as if his days were numbered. At sixty-one his energy was prodigious. He performed more than a hundred shows a year in Europe and America, wrote, coproduced, and acted in a new movie, *Masked and Anonymous*, and finished most of his three-hundred-page memoir, *Chronicles*.

The spring tour concluded in London at the Docklands Arena on May 12, 2002. The band had about five weeks off before regrouping in a Los Angeles studio to rehearse for the movie. "I read the script before we went out there. I didn't understand it," Campbell admits. "It was either too far above my head or ... I don't know."

You might think that by now Dylan would have learned his lesson about the film business, having been burned so badly before. But every day makes a new promise in an artist's life, and he had a vision for this film that was radically different from the one that had failed audiences in the 1970s.

Renaldo and Clara explored the theme of identity, Dylan's in particular, and how an individual's self-perception—as artist, lover, and friend—is affected by the community. Dylan cast the movie from his own circle, his friends, his wife, lovers, and fellow artists such as Joan Baez, Allen Ginsberg, and Jack Elliott, mostly amateur actors. Lacking firm direction, the film descended into narcissism. The new script, the one that Larry Campbell professed not to have understood, was in fact almost primitive in its dramatic structure. *Masked and Anonymous* is a morality play; the very pseudonym Dylan chose for himself as coauthor of the story, Enrique Morales (Ruler of Morals), shows his intent.

Throughout the movie we see a conspiracy or confluence of dark forces: a dictator and his ruthless police threatening to take over a nation; invasive, self-serving journalists undermining privacy, misleading the public; music industry executives interested only in profits. A cartoon villain, the "dictator in waiting," gets his kicks by maiming jazz singers and banjo players. The nation is vulnerable because its citizens have lost touch with their unique values, their roots in Anglo-American and black culture, a melting-pot experience that formerly maintained the virtues of the past. Ironically, the continuing homogenization of American culture has dehumanized it, creating this opportunity for the dictator.

What can save this country (an allegorical America) and the innocent men, women, and children who are not already lost to the forces of evil? A concert. A "benefit concert" for the good people will raise money and morale to fight the forces of darkness. This is the plot that the music promoter (John Goodman) Uncle Sweetheart and a TV producer, Nina Veronica (Jessica Lange), hatch. Unable to enlist the help of a big-name act, they decide on a legendary folk rock artist named Jack Fate (Bob Dylan). Fate, past his prime, has been languishing in prison, probably for offenses against the postrevolutionary government. They spring him from prison, get him a guitar, a cowboy outfit, and a comically large ten-gallon hat; he assembles the band (Dylan's own road band) and they begin playing despite the efforts of villains like the journalist Tom Friend (Jeff Bridges) to disrupt the concert.

"So we went out to make the movie," Campbell recalls. "And it was a great experience because you are hanging out with John Goodman and Jeff Bridges, Jessica Lange, Ed Harris, Val Kilmer, Mickey Rourke, and Penelope Cruz, incredible actors who are all great people to be around, too." If this movie failed it would not be for any lack of talent. All these stars waived their usual fees for the privilege of working with Dylan in an independent film. The problem was that the dialogue he had written was abstract and meandering, and strayed far from the action, creating false expectations. Lines like "Sometimes it's not enough to know the meaning of things; sometimes we have to know what things don't mean as well" are interesting, but moviegoers have little patience with dialogue that does not advance the story, and there was far too much of it.

"The director, Larry Charles, was a great guy, too, but I still didn't understand what was going on in the movie," Campbell recalls. What he admired, from his special vantage point, was the way the music was rendered. All of the musicians wore lavalier microphones. "Normally you see a band playing onscreen, and it's playing vacuum tracks, but this was really done, it is live. And mixed really well, I thought."

The director later said that he "wanted to make a Bob Dylan movie that was like a Bob Dylan song. One with a lot of layers, that had a lot of surrealism and was ambiguous and hard to figure out, like a puzzle." No doubt Dylan wanted the same—a perfect recipe for disaster in a stage play or a movie. It is curious that Dylan's idea of a great director is the François Truffaut of *Shoot the Piano Player*, a stickler for clarity and subtle nuances in character development.

Much of the hour and forty-five minutes of *Masked and Anonymous* captures Dylan in live performance, and the music is excellent. If Campbell or anyone else were to watch the movie with the sound turned off I think it would be clear what the movie is about. It is a picture of the world as Dylan sees it, slightly exaggerated: America in grave trouble, beset by idolaters, false prophets, rapacious businessmen, and media leeches. If there is any hope it lies in our ability to understand ourselves, to clearly view what is in us and change that quintessence for the better.

The hero of the allegory, Jack Fate, endeavors to change his way of thinking, and the world around him, through the power of authentic art. As an aspiring filmmaker, Bob Dylan reached beyond himself to make a movie that would do the same. His reach exceeded his grasp. *Masked and Anonymous* premiered at the Sundance Film Festival in Colorado on January 22, 2003. Film critic Roger Ebert observed that when Dylan entered the room he received a standing ovation, and that during the film people continued to stand, in order to leave. "And the auditorium was half-empty when the closing credits played to thoughtful silence." Ebert called the film "a vanity production beyond vanity," and the *New York Times* described it as "an unholy, incoherent mess." John Waters loved it, as he had loved all of Bob Dylan's movies. Widely panned, the movie never found much of an audience, even among Dylan's fans.

He did not waste much time that year or the next brooding over the fate of *Masked and Anonymous*. Instead he threw his energy into a project that required no collaborators, no heavy equipment or deep-pocket financiers—nothing more than a typewriter, pencil and paper, and a little peace and quiet: his autobiography.

He traveled the world with his typewriter, pounding out sentences in capital letters for convenience and the better to read them without eyeglasses. Most of the work was done at home in month-long stretches between tours. But Larry Campbell remembers "he was constantly working on it, updating it. A couple of times he gave me a draft of what he was writing."

Dylan wanted feedback from Campbell about certain chapters. "Bob and I had been talking about the New Lost City Ramblers a lot, and he gave me a rough draft of something he was writing about them. I was fascinated. Part of it was about when he had first seen Mike Seeger perform." Seeger was a member of the Ramblers, and a prodigiously gifted interpreter of old-time American music. Campbell was eleven when he first saw the Ramblers on television. "I was *mesmerized*. I had just started playing guitar, and here were these guys . . . and they weren't Doc Watson or Gary Davis. They didn't come from that region in the South. I could tell that. But they were still the real thing. I didn't know the concept at that time, but there was this *edge* to what they were doing that was fascinating." In writing *Chronicles* Dylan was trying to capture the excitement of the young 1960s "vernacular" folksingers, and now he wanted to know if a musician fifteen years younger could feel that energy in reading his pages.

"I felt honored, you know? I had a lot to say, but it was all about how intriguing it was . . . because he was talking about an era that has fascinated me my whole life. To hear Bob in the book describing people like Dave Van Ronk and Mike Seeger and these coffee-houses, and people's apartments, and listening to new records—I was hungry for details about that era. When he would show me these pages I would just read them and comment to him how it affected me."

The cancellation of a tour of Japan gave Dylan a few extra weeks in March to work on *Chronicles* before beginning the spring tour in Dallas on April 18. Personnel changes provided new challenges and opportunities for the Never Ending Tour, which had played its

1,500th concert in New Zealand without David Kemper or Charlie Sexton. George Receli, who had accompanied Mavis Staples and Dylan in the studio a year earlier, had taken over the percussion, and Bill Burnette played eleven dates of the "down under" tour before giving up his spot to the formidable guitarist Freddy Koella. As Koella was getting settled during the first shows in Texas, Dylan gave him plenty of room, playing piano and harmonica almost exclusively, letting the new guitarist do the picking, with Larry Campbell to guide him. There were moments of frustration onstage as the equipment for the steel guitar faltered, or Koella missed a chord change.

By April 23, the second night at the Verizon Wireless Theater in Houston, the band was beginning to come together. An audience of three thousand heard Dylan sing sixteen songs, from "Tweedle Dee & Tweedle Dum" and "Tonight I'll Be Staying Here with You," to "It Ain't Me, Babe," "Positively 4th Street," and "Summer Days," a hundred minutes of music. He dedicated the fourth number, "Blind Willie McTell," to the memory of Sam Houston.

> See the arrow on the door post
> Saying "This land is condemned
> All the way from New Orleans to Jerusalem."
> I traveled through East Texas where many martyrs fell
> And I know no one can sing the blues
> Like Blind Willie McTell.

A spectator, Jason Nodler, reported to a Dylan online forum that every song he played "was transformed by his effort, his engagement . . . he was there for every single moment tonight, loving it, caring, tasting each syllable, managing each moment from the band." During a Koella guitar solo, Dylan walked around the stage as if he were looking for something. He wasn't missing his harmonica or his guitar; he knew where they were. "It was like he had energy he didn't recognize and was looking for somewhere to let it loose in a different way than on a guitar or a harp or a piano. A righteous restlessness." Then he returned to the piano to finish the song. As the lights dimmed, a stagehand came to remove Dylan's guitar and he waved him away, telling him to leave the instrument there behind the piano.

A more knowledgeable source, with backstage access (writing under the initials of RJ in Houston), reported that Dylan's stroll around the platform was to "check the levels on Fred Koella's guitar. The boy had his hands full and had never noticed he was a little loud, and Bob danced over and cued the sound board to adjust."

An old-timer in the crowd said he had seen so many Dylan shows he could recall them only by decades. A youngster who had never seen one said he was beside himself with excitement. "As for me," said RJ of Houston, "some of the best moments in life are watching someone do the thing that makes them happy and being very good at making you happy you came for a look." RJ had been looking since 1974, and declared that he had always been pleased "with the message and the delivery. Now I think I am happy with the man himself. Just show up, Bob. We will be there."

The band found its groove, and Dylan was in good spirits in spite of the fact that ticket sales were not very good. By the last week of the tour, on May 14 in Asheville, North Carolina, they played to 75 percent empty seats in the Civic Center; the last show, in Little Rock, Arkansas, on the eighteenth, had to be downsized from the Alltel Arena to the 2,400-capacity Nite Life Rocks club.

Larry Campbell says Dylan never expressed the slightest concern about sales, or whether the house was half full or standing-room-only or half empty, and he showed no preference for one venue over another—Casper, Wyoming; Nampa, Idaho; or Harvard University. That didn't interest him. The maestro had his temperament—nights of anxiety, nights of exuberance, "but as far as venues go, it didn't matter where we were playing; we could be in a beautiful setting where the sound was great and everything was going well but the vibe onstage was miserable." Everything depended on Dylan's mood. That was "always the main catalyst. Moody? They need to invent a new word for it," he reflects, chuckling, but it was never in response to the crowd.

"As far as we were concerned, it was just go ahead and do it, the same thing again, just keep going and going. . . ." Le Roy Hoikkala, the drummer in Dylan's high school band, remembered an afternoon in Hibbing a half century earlier, soon after the death of James Dean. They were in the Zimmerman house reading a magazine article about the late actor, his consuming ambition and devotion to his art. Bob had looked up from the page with tears in his eyes and said to his friend, "You just keep doing your best, you always keep going and do your best, and never *ever* give up."

After the last show of the spring tour, May 18, 2003, in Little Rock, Dylan had almost two months to give his attention to *Chronicles* before beginning the long summer tour in Winter Park, Colorado. Unaccustomed to the sedentary routine of the prose stylist, he confided to David Gates of *Newsweek*: "Lest we forget, while you're writing, you're not living. What do they call it? Splendid isolation? I don't find it that splendid."

He returned to the stage in Colorado eager for interaction, recharged, ready to revive his waning audience, sporting a dark blue western suit with white trim on the coat pockets, a cowboy hat, and sunglasses. He took off his hat for the cheering crowd and stood at the keyboard, bareheaded, launching into "Stuck Inside of Mobile." Gazing out at the crowd on the ski slope he sang "Highway 61" and "High Water." He sang "Honest with Me" and when he got to the line "I'm stark naked and I don't care," a girl stripped to the waist and tossed her bra onto the stage; it landed in front of his piano.

Some songs got off to a shaky start, as Koella was still uncertain about his entrances and changes. Dylan looked frustrated at the band's mistakes. Holding his harmonica in his right hand he struck the keyboard with his left, trying to get Koella's attention. A fan noted "he sometimes slammed the keyboard with the palm of his hand . . . trying to get everyone's attention. He had mine but not always Freddy's it seemed."

Dylan looked back at the crowd and then grew animated: "Lots of points, sneers, smiles, and brow raising from behind the shades . . . lots of antics. He gave a few double points, double thumbs up." He shadowboxed, tugged at his curls, "and kept showing us the palms of his hands like they were puppets. He'd move around behind the keyboard and rock back on his heels." He crossed and crisscrossed the stage during songs and between them, faked stumbling, and then flinched like he was getting electric shocks. He spoke into Tony Garnier's ear and the bassist laughed. During the next number Dylan went behind the drum kit to have a word with the guitar technician. The tech handed him a glass of blue Gatorade and he drank it down.

"He didn't walk anywhere, he danced," another spectator noted. "After the encore he placed his cowboy hat on his head, fluffed the sides of his hair, picked up his jacket and came back out in front of the piano to gaze at the audience and enjoy the screams and applause one last time before leaving."

The next evening, under a full moon in Casper, Wyoming, Dylan was all business. There was no mugging, shadowboxing, finger-pointing, or other shenanigans, just focused, intense singing and piano playing. The new guitarist played resolutely, and missed no cues. "The guys were smiling quite a bit," a fan reported, "but Bob just had this look of concentration on his face as he stared at the keys or looked right through people as he stared into the audience." Dylan liked this show more than the last, but he was not satisfied. Perfection was not in the cards, but excellence lay somewhere between the histrionic confusion of Winter Park and the button-down recital at Casper—played to a half-empty house.

That night they caravanned two hundred miles west, high into the Teton range, to the resort town of Jackson. Monday they had the day off. On Tuesday, July 15, Dylan left his trailer in the afternoon wearing a retro two-tone bowling shirt, jeans, and his cowboy boots and hat to meet his bandmates onstage for the 4:30 sound check. The amphitheater at Snow King is beautiful: the stage looks up at the ski run and the mountains. There are some seats near the stage but most of the audience sits on the slope of the ski run beyond a beer garden at the foot of the hill.

A few early birds who had shown up to watch the sound check were thrilled with their good luck in finding Dylan on the scene. The band tuned up their instruments, set the sound levels, and began to rehearse. Dylan did not play or sing. He stood in front of the other musicians, one by one, and led them as they played. He looked like a scrawny conductor in a cowboy hat. *Tony, Larry, George, this is the tempo,* here is where you come in. He spent by far the most time leading Freddy Koella, waving his arms expressively, accenting the beat. In a field behind the stage a Little League team was playing baseball, and from time to time between songs Dylan would stop to watch the boys play or he would look up at the mountain and the sky. In the early 1980s he had attended every one of his son Jakob's Little League games, and kept all of Jakob's home run balls.

After an hour and a half of work, Dylan sent the band away and sat alone on an amplifier to the left of the stage, in contemplation, gazing at the green hillside where several thousand fans would be waiting for the performance under the stars. He would sing "Maggie's Farm" and "Don't Think Twice." He would sing "Tweedle Dee & Tweedle Dum," and "It's All Over Now, Baby Blue," and then "Things Have Changed." Roger Daltrey and Pete Townshend of the Who were passing through Jackson and they would be visiting backstage. It was going to be a good night. He would tell a joke or two.

"Larry bought a pig lately," Dylan announced, during the introductions. "I asked him where he was going to keep it. He said, 'Under the bed.' I said, 'What about the smell?' He said, 'I'm sure the pig won't mind.'" Presenting George Receli, he said George was "the best drummer on this stage."

The band was beginning to hit their marks. Tonight nobody would be disappointed.

Five weeks and thirty shows later they played their last gig of the summer at the Oakes Garden Theatre, Niagara Falls, Ontario. Against the backdrop of the multicolored, floodlit waterfall Dylan sang "Forever Young," soulfully, his voice a cappella on the chorus. He had hardly touched the guitar all summer and maybe it was because of the arthritis in his hands. During the encores, "Like a Rolling Stone" and "All Along the Watchtower," fireworks boomed, blossomed, and glittered in the sky above the iridescent waterfall.

Late summer and early autumn provided essential time for reflection and concentration on his memoirs. Through the manuscript pages the living and the dead walked side by side. In a few months the book would have to go to his publisher, David Rosenthal at Simon & Schuster. In conversation with David Gates about the process of writing *Chronicles*, Dylan alluded to the New Testament passage Acts 2:17–18: "And it shall come to pass in the last days, saith God, I will pour out of my spirit upon all flesh: and your sons and your daughters shall prophesy, and your young men shall see visions, and your old men shall dream dreams." When he was young, he told Gates, "I could see visions. The me now can dream dreams. . . . What you see in *Chronicles* is a dream. It's already happened."

For many people in their sixties the past seems dreamlike, as the future dwindles and ghosts proliferate, vying for attention. Songwriter Warren Zevon, whom Dylan admired, died of an aggressive cancer in his lungs and liver on September 7. He was fifty-six. Hearing of that fatal illness a year earlier, Dylan had kept playing several of Zevon's songs in rotation.

Five days after Zevon's death, Johnny Cash passed away in a Nashville hospital from complications of diabetes. Dylan's big brother in the art, Cash was the singer who—over the years—came to represent a unity of legend and humble humanity. When Zimmerman was a boy listening to the radio in 1955, Cash was already a colossus, the man in black singing "I Walk the Line." Just seven years later Cash wrote Bob Dylan a fan letter congratulating him on making a great record in the spirit of Jimmie Rodgers and Vernon Dalhart. He defended Dylan against hostile executives at Columbia when the label tried to drop him. Cash supported Dylan in 1969 when he went "country" with *Nashville Skyline*, and later during his controversial gospel period. A true friend from the day they met backstage at the Gaslight in 1963, Cash had stood by Dylan through all of his changes, artistic and personal.

Now when the press called upon him for a tribute Dylan answered not with a few sentences but with a four-hundred-word essay that appeared in *Rolling Stone* in October 2003.

Johnny was and is the North Star; you could guide your ship by him— the greatest of the greats then and now. . . . 'I Walk the Line' had a monumental presence and a certain type of majesty that was humbling. Even a simple line like 'I find it very very easy to be true' can take your measure. We can remember that and see how far we fall short of it. . . . Truly he is what the land and country is all about, the heart and soul of it personified. . . . If we want to know what it means to be mortal, we need look no further than the Man in Black.

Dylan had not seen Cash in a long time, "but in some kind of way," he mused, "he was with me more than people I see every day." Dylan was spending hours of each day tapping a typewriter, writing about people he had not seen or talked with in years: people like Izzy Young, who once owned the Folklore Center in Greenwich Village, where Dylan had met Dave Van Ronk—Izzy, who had put up the cash to produce Dylan's concert at Carnegie Chapter Hall in 1961. Others such as Mike Seeger, a roots musician so steeped in the American vernacular, a singer and player so exquisite in his style that Dylan was compelled to find his own rather than compete with him. Writing about old friends brings them to life again if they have passed away and brings them close to you if they are living. Izzy and Mike were still in this world. They were just far away, doing their work—Mike in the mountains of Virginia, Izzy in Stockholm, Sweden.

He would go and see them at the first opportunity.

The autumn tour commenced in Helsinki, Finland, on October 9. Jet-lagged, they played to a half-full house at the Hartwall Areena. Dylan tried to play guitar on "Things Have Changed" and "Highway 61 Revisited," but put it down in the middle of "Summer Days" in pain, or frustration, returning to the keyboard. Halfway into the show he got the giggles. It was one of those nights when a sense of humor was the only defense against exhaustion.

The next morning they flew over the Baltic Sea to Stockholm. Izzy Young was eagerly awaiting Dylan's arrival. He had been living in Sweden, where he operated the Folkore Centrum, for thirty-one years, and had not seen his protégé in all that time. "People would ask me, 'How come you haven't seen him in thirty years, Izzy?'

"Well, he doesn't call me, I don't call him. It's equal."

Eventually a mutual friend, after making many phone calls to both parties, arranged for a reunion between Izzy and Bob after the concert at the Globe Arena in Stockholm on October 11. Izzy received good seats up front and a backstage pass. He was delighted to see Dylan onstage in such good form—not at all the way he had appeared in his youth, solo, with no accompaniment but guitar and harmonica—still fit, energetic, powerful.

The star strolled onstage in a black suit with silver piping, hatless: he went straight to the keyboard and struck up "To Be Alone with You." He played eighteen songs that night, more than a hundred minutes, was in good humor, and moved easily from piano to guitar and back again. He sang "Boots of Spanish Leather," which Izzy had heard and praised forty years earlier; he sang "Every Grain of Sand," a lovely spiritual from Dylan's gospel period.

I hear the ancient footsteps like the motion of the sea
Sometimes I turn, there's someone there, other times it's only me
I am hanging in the balance of the reality of man
Like every sparrow falling, like every grain of sand.

The folklorist took pride in the seeds he had planted so long ago in his native land. When the show was over and Dylan had taken his bows, seventy-five-year-old Israel Goodman Young made his way backstage through the throng, passed through several security checks, and finally stood in a small receiving area where he waited for Dylan to recognize him.

"It was just like the old days," Izzy recalled. "He says to me: 'Izzy, it's great to see you! I wrote a chapter about you in my new book!'"

"I said, 'You're full of shit! You told me that in 1962.'"

"So he laughed, and I laughed, and now he's got the last laugh, because it's in the book. But I didn't know that at the time."

So they talked for a while. "First I embraced him, and all of the security guards went nuts. But then at one point he was telling me things and he said to me: 'I don't know why I'm doing this [a hundred shows a year], I should be taking care of my fourteen grandchildren.' And I said, 'Yeah, I think you should stop altogether. You should just take a time-out.'"

Aware that his time with his old friend would not be long, Young was unsure exactly what to say or do in the situation. "So I went to him, and I took his head in my hands, and cradled him like he was my baby. And he was smiling and laughing and happy. And the guards thought I was strangling him . . ."

The musician confided that his life on the road had become something of a grind—*boring* was the word he used.

"Boring?" Young replied, astonished. He had been living in the little shop he owned in Stockholm. "God! I only have the store, I don't even have an apartment. Maybe I can come and visit you," he offered, knowing Dylan had several residences around the world. "Maybe I can visit your *estate* . . ."

Dylan was amused by the idea. "My estate?" he said. "What are you, crazy? Well, yeah . . ."

Izzy reminded Dylan that the point of work had always been the pleasure he took in it. "I was in it for the fun. And I'm still having fun—"

"But are you really living on the street?"

Young admitted that he was—practically—living on the street, and that God was protecting him. A devout Jew, he believes that the prayers of a certain Lubavitcher rabbi are protecting both Dylan and himself.

They passed the time pleasantly backstage. And when the time came to say goodbye, Izzy recalled, "It really felt great. I felt like thirty-one years was nothing.

"So then a week later his manager Jeff Rosen calls up. And he said, 'Izzy, you know Bob Dylan had a great time with you! He's really happy. He wants your exact address.'

"So. He sent me three thousand bucks. God! He should be happy also in Berlin and Yokahama, he should be happy everywhere! I really want to see him again and say, 'Stop this shit, just give up everything, take a time-out, so you can read the papers again, meet people again, and write songs the way you used to.'"

————

Mike Seeger, seventy years old, was living in a rambling, wood-frame nineteenth-century farmhouse in the Shenandoah Valley when he and his wife, Alexia, heard from Dylan's office.

He was still collecting songs, recording, and performing. In fact he had just released one of his finest solo albums, *True Vine*, on the Smithsonian Folkways label. He called the genre old-time music, songs like "Coo Coo Bird," "Breaking Up Ice in the Allegheny," "Freight Train," "Don't Let Your Deal Go Down," and "Sail Away Ladies," all done with Mike's patented blend of tenderness and savage energy. His voice cut through time like a well-honed sickle. He was stunningly handsome, with a muffler wrapped around his neck, an English duke in exile dressed like a gentleman farmer.

The Seegers had been amused, if not astonished, to see Dylan appear in a television ad for Victoria's Secret in April, strolling through a Venetian palazzo with a half-dressed lingerie model, singing his song "Love Sick." This too had been the fulfillment of a youthful prophecy. At a San Francisco press conference in 1965 somebody asked him, "If you were going to sell out to a commercial interest, which one would you choose?" Without missing a beat he replied, "Ladies' garments."

No doubt he had been paid well to fly to Venice by private jet in January 2004. Ticket sales had not been all that good in 2003, and more than two years had passed since "*Love and Theft*." The movie *Masked and Anonymous* had been a dead loss. There were the Izzy Youngs on the street to consider, and one's children and grandchildren setting out in a harsh world and fickle economy. And who knew whether or not the author of "What Good Am I?" intended to build a hospital with his hard-earned money? At sixty-three he was probably worth several hundred million dollars. Building a hospital would have been less surprising, somehow, than his appearing in the Victoria's Secret commercial after a lifetime of denouncing the co-option of music by politics and advertising. There was a time for all things, forty years of condemning Madison Avenue and a few years of taking advantage of it. Dylan was nothing if not unpredictable and Mike Seeger knew better than to try to judge or second-guess him.

Now the Never Ending Tour with Willie Nelson was coming Mike's way, and Dylan surprised him pleasantly by getting in touch.

Dylan had enjoyed playing with Willie Nelson since the Farm Aid concert in 1985, and more recently on May 5, 2004, in the Wiltern Theater in Los Angeles, where they sang Hank Williams's "You Win Again." After Dylan's European tour ended in July of that year he and his management decided that ticket sales might benefit from a double billing of Willie Nelson and Bob Dylan in the dog days of summer. Instead of risking the costly, high-stakes coliseums and amphitheaters, the duo would try their luck in minor-league baseball parks, venues with a ready-made atmosphere of casual camaraderie and Americana. There the grandstands would fill up quickly and any number of fans could stand or sit or sprawl on blankets on the diamond as the band played under a flagpole in center field.

"We aim to touch all the bases and get home safely," Dylan said in his press release. The tour officially started on August 6 at the birthplace of America's pastime, Doubleday Field in Cooperstown, New York.

The closest he would come to Seeger's home near Lexington, Virginia, was Richmond on August 15. So Dylan invited Mike and his wife to come to the 6:30 show at the Diamond, and dine with him and the band members at their late-afternoon lunch backstage, just after the sound check.

Everything was arranged in advance, with Dylan's management providing the tickets and backstage passes. Mike and Alexia drove over the Blue Ridge Mountains and along the James River a hundred and forty miles to Richmond, to the baseball park.

The last time Seeger had seen Dylan was May 19, 1993, in a Los Angeles recording studio called Grandma's Warehouse, on Glendale Boulevard near Echo Park. Mike was producing the third of his Annual Farewell Reunion albums for Rounder Records, and he wanted Dylan to sing "Hollis Brown," his favorite of the early songs. Dylan was willing, if Seeger could come to Los Angeles, but getting clearance from Dylan's record company, Sony, was difficult. "The infrastructure," Seeger recollected, "is labyrinthine. It took more than a year." Mike offered to do the recording right there at Dylan's house in Malibu, but when he mentioned this to Dylan's agent the agent was appalled and told him to go and find a studio.

Through a friend of Seeger's son they found Grandma's Warehouse, a whitewashed former garage across the lake from Aimee Semple McPherson's Angelus Temple, "a nondescript place. He made it clear he didn't want anybody else there." So Dylan showed up at the appointed hour, carrying his guitar case. "He brought his favorite guitar, the one he uses in hotel rooms." The idea was for Dylan to sing, and for Mike to accompany him on his guitar. But Seeger wanted to use the five-string banjo instead.

"We did it in one take. I asked would he give us a cover, because I always like to have one. He laughed and said, 'Sure. Was there a problem with that one?' And the next take was *totally* different, emotionally different. The first one had all this wild passion, and that's the one we used. The other one, well, it didn't have any of that in it." Alexia Seeger commented that Dylan doesn't like to do anything twice, in terms of takes, and Mike added, "I think that's the story of his life."

The Seegers showed their passes at the gate to the Diamond baseball park, passed through security, and were escorted to an area that had been set up for artists' hospitality. "They travel with fifty or sixty people," Mike remembered. "This was the area where the food was, and we sat down at a picnic bench." They sat there for a few minutes, waiting. Then Larry Campbell came out to say hello, and Stuart Kimball, the guitarist who had replaced Freddy Koella in June, and some other band members. Mike was pleased to discover that the young musicians all knew his work. "I didn't know the extent to which they knew about traditional music. It turned out they were *collectors* [i.e., musicians who foraged for forgotten tunes and recordings].

"So then, without any warning, this guy with a baseball cap and a wig on, a blond wig, comes up behind me, and taps me on the shoulder and peers around and says, 'Hey! Howdy! Hello!' And I didn't know who that was. Dylan has a way of being theatrical, no matter what time." Alexia added, "He had just come from his trailer through the public area, accompanied by a rather large man. And he was definitely in disguise; otherwise he might have been trampled."

Tom Paxton recalled once attending a banquet just after Dylan was inducted into the Songwriters Hall of Fame. Paxton had sung

"Blowin' in the Wind" (scrambling the stanzas, to his embarrassment) and presented the citation. "We were at the next table. I was sitting with Harold Leventhal and his wife, and Bob was at the next table. About thirty photographers suddenly showed up at his table and stood there clicking, clicking, clicking. And I thought, at what point have they got their picture? And I remember turning to Harold and I said: 'Fame, isn't it wonderful? Isn't it *wonderful*?' The poor bastard, just being fried with flashbulbs over there. I mean, that can't be what someone has in mind when they think, God, I would like to be famous."

Dylan took off his cap and his blond wig and sat down at the picnic table with the Seegers. "He was *really* glad to see Mike," Larry Campbell remembered. "That's what it felt like to me. He would avoid people most of the time; people would come to see him, and they would sit there and wait, and if he had a minute to say hi he would say hi. If not he wouldn't say anything at all. But there is something real and deep in Mike Seeger that's not common, you know." Bob and Mike and Alexia sat for a long time in the afternoon talking about music and old friends. "It was just about the time that *Chronicles* was coming out. He said, 'They've been talking about me for years and now I'm going to throw it all back at them.' He was quite humorous and wonderful to talk with."

"And remember he was talking about some system of threes?" Alexia added. "I don't know if it was rhythmic, or harmonic? Some musical idea."

Seeger explained: "There was a great black guitarist who was also a great fiddle player of the twentieth century, Lonnie Johnson. He was one of the classic players but ended up playing lounge music in the sixties when Bob struck up a friendship with him. This guy told him about a philosophy of music based on a system of threes. I couldn't understand it. He talks about it some in *Chronicles*." Alexia added that this "was an idea he was playing with onstage, as he played off other musicians."

"Another thing," he continued. "He talked about why he performed. He had some wonderful images about that. *'Facing the lion,'* was one of the images. 'I wanna see if I can still do it.' He has a demanding schedule. I mean, he's sixty-eight!" It must be very hard on someone's voice to sing so much. "Especially if you're singing that way, having a very loud band. Their whole idea is not to leave any decibel unturned. That's what rock and roll is all about, having constant music, no up-and-down dynamic, constant sound. It's got to be terrible for your voice, feeling you have to sing above that. Now I think his voice has deteriorated some, it certainly sounds like it; I don't think it's an affectation—I think he's trying to adapt to it."

As the old friends conversed in the lengthening shadows, Mike Seeger mused upon the phenomenal range of forces that moved Bob Dylan: how as an artist he has always liked to be at the "meeting of vernacular music in the broadest sense of the term, and literary tradition and ideas." And how, as a man, he is at once passionate and removed. "It is the poet in him: it's almost like he's . . . not amused, but whimsical. There's almost, like, a distance in him; he looks back at himself as an observer, toward his ability to write, and what he's done, and so forth. He was tickled by certain things he'd written about me. And he was looking over at Larry Campbell, with that same expression of delight. Pleased or amused? It's intriguing."

Then the time came to say goodbye, time for Bob Dylan to go to work. One of the last things he said to Mike Seeger was "Well, I hope you can hear the words." It was very important to him. "I couldn't," said Mike, chuckling.

"If life is movement," Alexia concluded, "Bob Dylan was in motion constantly. He is more animated than anyone I have ever been around—in perpetual motion. It was fascinating just to be in his presence."

Dylan had managed to convey that vibrant presence in the book he was writing, and the reviewers who received advance copies of *Chronicles: Volume One* during the summer were pleasantly surprised.

Publishers Weekly, the weather vane of the publishing world, gave it a starred review. "After a career of principled coyness, Dylan takes pains to outline the growth of his artistic conscience in this superb memoir. . . . This book will stand as a record of a young man's self-education, as contagious in its frank excitement as the letters of John Keats and as sincere in its ramble as Jack Kerouac's *On the Road*." Like other memorable autobiographies from St. Augustine's to Ben Franklin's, Dylan's book is a bildungsroman, a novel of education, a book in which the poet explains, again and again, how he was able to change his internal world. *Chronicles* made the bestseller lists soon after publication in October 2004 and stayed there for five months.

On December 5, Ed Bradley interviewed Dylan on CBS's newsmagazine *60 Minutes*. This was the first network interview Dylan had given in America in almost twenty years. He sat in a high-backed chair, dressed in a black coat and gray shirt, head cocked to the side, a smile flickering at the corners of his mouth as he parried Bradley's questions about his role as spokesman of his generation. The face he had prepared for Bradley was impassive, tight-lipped. He looked a bit like the strong and silent heroes of 1950s westerns, and his accent sounded more like Johnny Cash or Wyatt Earp than the Dylan of *Dont Look Back* or the relaxed Westwood radio interview of 1984.

"I never wanted to be a prophet or savior. Elvis maybe. I could easily see myself becoming him. But prophet? No." As Bradley insisted that the world saw him in that role, the singer pushed back, in earnest. "If you examine the *songs*, I don't believe you're going to find anything in there that says I'm a spokesman for anybody or *anything* really."

Of course, one could make a compelling argument from two songs alone: "Hard Rain" and "It's Alright, Ma."

When the broadcast journalist asked him why he was so opposed to the media that he deliberately misled reporters, Dylan explained: "I realized at the time that the press, the media, they're not the judge—God's the judge. The only person you have to think about lying twice to is either yourself or to God. The press isn't either of them. And I just figured they're irrelevant."

There was so much humor beneath the surface of Dylan's dead-pan responses you could see that Ed Bradley, a seasoned interviewer, was struggling to control his laughter. He had been amused by a line Dylan had written suggesting that the unsettling thing about fame is that nobody really believes you are who you are. So he asked him exactly what he meant by that.

"People, they'll say, 'Are you who I *think* you are?' And you'll say, 'I don't know.' Then, they'll say, 'You're him.' And you'll say, 'Okay, you know, that—yes . . .' And then the next thing, they'll say is 'Well, *no*,' you know? 'Like are you *really* him? You're not him!' And, you know, that can go on and on."

After Bradley read him a list of recent honors and laurels, Dylan softly acknowledged that it was all very well, "this week . . . but who's to say how long that's gonna last?"

Finally the interviewer asked Dylan what kept him out there, on the road performing, after so many years. "It goes back to that destiny thing," he replied. "I mean, I made a bargain with it, you know, a long time ago. And I'm holding up my end." What kind of bargain? Bradley inquired. "To get where I am now," Dylan said. And with whom had he made this pact? "With the chief commander," Dylan concluded, laughing. "On this earth?" Bradley asked, laughing along with him.

"On this earth and in the world we can't see."

The writing and publication of *Chronicles* substantially changed Bob Dylan's dialogue with the American public, because it was far more revealing than it seemed at first glance. Many readers complained that the book was oddly focused, that Dylan had passed over the very subjects and decades that most interested them—most of the 1960s and '70s, the years with the Band, the making of *Blonde on Blonde* and *Blood on the Tracks*. He had largely avoided talking about his marriages and family life, his friendships with John Lennon,

George Harrison, Mick Jagger, Allen Ginsberg, Van Morrison, and other luminaries of the literary and music worlds. Some had hoped for a comprehensive, linear celebrity autobiography, a tell-all that would answer their questions about Dylan's loves, quarrels, and disappointments, his religious life, how many houses he owned and how much time he spent in each of them.

An autobiography, unless it is Casanova's twelve-volume *Memoirs* or the *Diaries of Samuel Pepys*, is a small and leaky vessel. The best modern examples, such as Sartre's *The Words* and Nabokov's *Speak, Memory*, are strictly selected, like Dylan's, and highly concentrated. What the writer chooses to recall is not the most important thing— in Dylan's case it is the year he arrived in New York; the years after his father's death, when he made *New Morning* and struggled to protect his family's privacy; and 1989, the year he recorded *Oh Mercy*. What counts is the manner in which he tells the story, how he relates to his human subjects, and the self-representation of the narrator. In Dylan's book the self-portrait that emerged must have been a wonder to everyone but his closest friends, more eye-opening than a laundry list of sexual conquests, more enlightening than a stack of tax returns.

The narrator of *Chronicles* is witty, nostalgic, and humble. The humility is impressive, because he is in no doubt about his talents. While respecting his accomplishments, he can be very hard on himself when it comes to analyzing his failures. It is not surprising that the poet who wrote *Blood on the Tracks* and *Time Out of Mind* is a capable prose draftsman, depicting characters as different as Izzy Young, Mike Seeger, and Archibald MacLeish with such color and insight that they fairly rise from the pages in three dimensions. Nor was it unexpected that the author of "With God on Our Side," "Only a Pawn in Their Game," and *John Wesley Harding* would be well-read in history, philosophy, and literature.

What did come as a surprise was the generosity of spirit with which he approached the subjects in his life, people and places, rich and poor, famous and obscure, everyone from musicians of the sixties to former wives and lovers, from Hibbing, Minnesota, to Greenwich Village to New Orleans—Mike Porco, Suze Rotolo, Dave Van Ronk, Joan Baez, Tom Paxton, Bono. There is enormous affection and gratitude expressed on every page of *Chronicles*, and not much irony except when he is talking about the press, the music industry, intrusive fans, and the government. Not many readers anticipated that the author of the bitter verses in "Positively 4th Street" and "Ballad of a Thin Man" could be so tenderhearted.

Somewhere in the bayou country below New Orleans he spent hours in conversation with the proprietor of a soul food restaurant, a dark-skinned Asian American he calls Sun Pie. When Sun Pie asked him if he was a praying man, and what he prayed for, Dylan replied: "I pray that I can be a kinder person." In writing *Chronicles* he had answered his own prayer.

This was the Bob Dylan we would get to know in the twenty-first century, a wise grandfather, kindly, humorous, a veteran of the Cold War with a fierce loyalty to the best of tradition and solicitous hope for our children.

CHAPTER 17

Aberdeen: July 24, 2009

On the delta of land where the Susquehanna River flows south into the Chesapeake Bay lies the town of Aberdeen, Maryland, population 15,000. It is known chiefly for the Aberdeen Proving Ground, a site for the design and testing of ordnance matériel, tanks, chemical weapons, and High Mobility Vehicles. The APG was installed just after the United States entered World War I, the first cannon was fired there on January 2, 1918, and the natives have endured the sound of warfare for ninety years, many of them becoming "deaf" to it through habituation.

Aberdeen was as close to my home in Baltimore as Bob Dylan would perform in the summer of 2009, and I wanted to see him once more.

I wondered if he would take time to look for the house where the late Frank Zappa spent his formative years. The brilliant composer and musician, father of the Mothers of Invention, grew up near Aberdeen, where his father worked at the chemical warfare facility. Frank recalled that the arsenal stored mustard gas, and so the family kept enough gas masks on hand in case of an accident. Young Zappa was fascinated by his father's work with chemicals, germs, and germ warfare; between that and the background noise, the firing of guns and cannons, Aberdeen had a profound effect on Zappa's cerebral rock and roll.

In his spare time Dylan liked to visit the childhood homes and haunts of rock stars. On November 2, 2008, he was in Winnipeg, Manitoba, to perform at MTS Centre and took an hour in the afternoon to visit the duplex on Grosvenor Avenue where Neil Young spent his adolescent years. Such surprise appearances always cause excitement in the neighborhood, and when Dylan's cab showed up, the owner of the house, John Kiernan, was stunned. "These guys were standing at the front of the house about to get back into their taxi. I noticed he was wearing these expensive-looking leather pants tucked inside these world-class boots. Then I studied his face and tried to keep cool." The singer was unshaven and wore a knit cap pulled down close to his bushy eyebrows. Kiernan offered to show Dylan and his companions the house. The host observed that Dylan "was very articulate and introspective." He asked thoughtful questions about how the place had changed since Young lived there. When Kiernan showed him the singer's old bedroom, Dylan inquired, "Would Neil have looked out this window when he played his guitar?" Dylan spent about a half hour in the house, thanked the owner, and went on his way.

A year later, visiting Liverpool on a tour of England, Dylan had his road manager telephone John Lennon's childhood home and arrange to get him a ticket on one of the guided tours. Dylan took the number 16 bus with the other tourists. He spent a lot of time in Lennon's former bedroom, where Lennon wrote some of the Beatles' earliest hits. According to a spokesman for the National Trust, which maintains the house, "He spent ages going through photo albums and was thrilled at all the memorabilia."

Incredibly, no one recognized him.

Dylan would like to have seen Bruce Springsteen's childhood home in New Jersey, where he had just performed, but he wasn't sure where it was. Maybe he would look for Zappa's home in Aberdeen.

Frank Zappa was six months older than he, and despite their differences in style they admired each other. Zappa was so impressed when he first heard "Like a Rolling Stone" on the radio in 1965, it made him want to give up music. "If this wins and it does what it's supposed to do, I don't need to do anything else." Of course Zappa went on to do a great deal else, making groundbreaking records that fused rock and roll, jazz, and classical music, directing films and traveling the world as a cultural ambassador. Dylan thought enough of Zappa to seek his advice in 1982, when he was transitioning out of his gospel period and writing the songs that appear on *Infidels*. He showed up at Zappa's gate in Los Angeles on a cool day in December, unannounced. At first Zappa didn't recognize him on the security video monitor. "I get a lot of weird calls here. . . . I sent someone down to check, to make sure it wasn't Charles Manson. . . ."

Dylan played him eleven new songs, and Zappa thought they were good. "He seemed like a nice guy," he recalled. Dylan asked the notorious composer if he would consider producing his next album. "Didn't look like it would be too hard to work with him," Zappa thought. He asked if there were any Jesus songs on the list and Dylan assured him there were none. "When I took him upstairs to give him a sandwich, my dog barked at him." Zappa explained that the dog didn't like Christians; Dylan was not amused.

In recent years Aberdeen has become known as the cradle of a baseball dynasty. The great shortstop Cal Ripken, Jr. (the Iron Man) and his brother Billy, the second baseman, born here, anchored the Baltimore Orioles while their father coached third base. Ripken Stadium, home of the Aberdeen IronBirds, provides an open-air venue for bands like Def Leppard, Counting Crows, and Steppenwolf. In 2004, when Bob Dylan and Willie Nelson began their summer tour of ballparks, Zappa's hometown was the second stop on the circuit, two nights before Dylan dined with Mike Seeger in Richmond. I missed the concert in 2004, which received good notices; Dylan had given a heroic performance in the face of torrential rains, singing thirteen songs, including "A Hard Rain's A-Gonna Fall" and a duet with Willie on "Milk Cow Blues."

So when I heard that the Never Ending Tour would be returning to Ripken Stadium in July 2009 I paid my eighty dollars to Ticketmaster online. The price of a ticket to a Bob Dylan concert (general admission) had increased exponentially since we paid four dollars for our orchestra tickets in 1963; so had the singer's overhead, the cost of doing business in the twenty-first century with a band and a road crew of sound and light technicians, costumers, caterers and roustabouts, and a company that included Willie Nelson and his band, John Mellencamp and his band, and their dressers and guitar techs and spear-carriers. Singers had to tour to make money since the advent of digital recording had encouraged piracy and made CDs practically free for anyone who wished to copy a friend's copy of a copy. It was a wonder most musicians made any money at all.

Lady Gaga was doing well that year with her debut single "Just Dance" and her follow-up, "Poker Face," both reaching the top of the Billboard Hot 100. Madonna was the highest-earning entertainer, having grossed $242 million in the past year, mostly from her road show, the "Sticky & Sweet Tour." Elton John and Billy Joel made money with their "Face to Face Tour," and then there was Britney Spears's "Circus Tour." These were exceptions. For most musicians life on the road meant long hours and short pay, and the fact that an old-fashioned rhythm-and-blues band like Dylan's was still doing more than a hundred shows a year in medium-size venues was a tribute to their work ethic and enduring appeal.

The ballpark is forty minutes from my home. I drove the distance alone in the rainy twilight, with no company but a CD I had rather neglected, Dylan's *Modern Times* (2006). I might have brought someone along but I wanted to experience this concert on my own. The only person I really wished was with me was my sister, who had shared with me the epiphany of the Lisner Auditorium concert in 1963 and the historical event of the Madison Square Garden show of the comeback tour in 1974, but my sister was living in England.

Most of all, I didn't want to be with some person who didn't feel the way I did about Bob Dylan, and I couldn't think of anyone else. I didn't want to have to explain him, or apologize for him if he had an off night. I wanted to be alone in the crowd with my thoughts and the singer in view. I drove through thunder and lightning behind the slapping windshield wipers, listening to *Modern Times.*

> *Thunder on the mountain, rolling like a drum*
> *Gonna sleep over there, that's where the music's coming from*
> *I don't need any guide, I already know the way*
> *Remember this, I'm your servant both night and day*

Dylan and his touring band had recorded *Modern Times* in the Clinton Studios in February 2006, after a short rehearsal period at his beloved Bardavon 1869 Opera House in Poughkeepsie, New York. Of the ensemble that had accompanied Dylan on *"Love and Theft"* in 2001 only the bass player, Tony Garnier, remained. With bluesman Denny Freeman playing lead guitar and stolid Stu Kimball playing rhythm, George Receli on drums and Donnie Herron on pedal steel, fiddle, mandolin, and banjo, the new group had a heavier, chunkier sound. The late Mike Seeger liked to call this Dylan's "Howlin' Wolf period," referring to the rough-voiced Chester Burnett, a disciple of Charlie Patton and Robert Johnson who became, as Howlin' Wolf, a master of the electric Chicago blues style with no peer but Muddy Waters.

"Love and Theft" had a light touch and a sense of humor throughout. I missed those qualities in *Modern Times,* a dark album that lacked the gravitas of *Time Out of Mind* and lapsed into nostalgia and redundancy. Five of the songs are well-known blues tunes fitted out with new and apocalyptic lyrics. The other five are foxtrots and parlor tunes, love songs meant to evoke the twilight wistfulness of Stephen Foster and Bing Crosby. The single theme is the struggle to adapt to modern times—the disorientation the country boy feels in the city, the pain of love gone wrong or a ruined idyll.

All my loyal and my much-loved companions
They approve of me and share my code
I practice a faith that's long been abandoned
Ain't no altars on this long and lonesome road.

Ain't talkin', just walkin'
My mule is sick, my horse is blind.
Heart burnin', still yearnin'
Thinkin' 'bout that gal I left behind.

(FROM *"Ain't Talkin'"*)

Dylan was leaning heavily on standard melodies like "Red Sails in the Sunset" (for his own "Beyond the Horizon") and "Rollin' and Tumblin'" (for his own rendition of the same), and if you grew up listening to those songs, Dylan's versions had a leftover taste to them. He had been reading Ovid's *Art of Love* and the *Tristia,* excellent models for any love poet; his lyrics, as usual, were evocative, but he seemed not to have wholly digested his musical or literary influences.

Yet *Rolling Stone* gave *Modern Times* five out of five stars and called it Dylan's "third straight masterwork." Jody Rosen, writing for *Slate* magazine, went so far as to declare that *Modern Times* was better than *"Love and Theft,"* a hyperbole bound to generate a backlash, which came promptly from the *Chicago Sun-Times'* Jim DeRogatis: "With the exception of the closing track 'Ain't Talkin' . . . Dylan disappoints with [an] inexplicable fondness for smarmy '30s and '40s balladry." Masterwork or disappointment, it was Dylan's first number-one album since *Desire* thirty years earlier, also his first record to debut at the top of the Billboard 200, selling nearly two hundred thousand copies the week after it was released in late August. The sixty-five-year-old singer became the oldest person to date to have a record album enter the charts at number one.

No doubt *Modern Times* was a fine album with some excellent songs, but such a degree of success owed something to the aura that

Bob Dylan projected in 2006, as he self-produced his first studio recording in five years. He was riding a wave of personal popularity that few entertainers or poets in America have known: Will Rogers, Carl Sandburg, and Louis Armstrong spring to mind. *Chronicles* had endeared him to a multitude of readers who until then found him remote, if not inaccessible.

Since May 3, 2006, anyone within earshot of a satellite radio could hear his gravelly, precise voice on the *Theme Time Radio Hour* once a week—folksy, humorous, sententious, commenting on the records he was spinning from the 1920s to the present. The mix of tunes each week focused upon a single theme: Mother, Drinking, Marriage, Divorce, Birds, the Devil, Baseball, Cars, a hundred themes in three years. For the first episode the theme was "Weather." Thunder rolled, raindrops pattered over the airwaves, and then you heard the sultry voice of Ellen Barkin: "Nighttime in the big city. The rain is falling. The fog rolls in from the waterfront. A night shift nurse smokes the last cigarette from her pack. It's *Theme Time Radio Hour*, with your host, Bob Dylan."

Bob: "It's time for *Theme Time Radio Hour*—dreams, schemes, and themes. Today's show: all about the weather. Curious about what the weather looks like? Just look out your window and take a walk outside. We're gonna start out with the great Muddy Waters, one of the ancients by now whom all moderns prize . . . one of his early songs on the Chess label called 'Blow Wind Blow' featuring Jimmy Rogers, Otis Spann, and Little Walter. From the Windy City, Chicago, Muddy Waters, 'Blow Wind Blow.' Here's Muddy."

The man who for forty years had been America's greatest mortal enigma had become a "personality." He was a visitor in our living rooms, cars, and workshops, like his fellow Minnesotan Garrison Keillor, a bit rougher around the edges, everybody's favorite eccentric uncle, kindly, garrulous, a walking encyclopedia of old songs, legends, trivia, poems, and jokes. He liked to visit his grandson's kindergarten class in Calabasas and play for the children. In May 2007 some of the youngsters told their parents "a weird man" had come to class and played "scary songs," and the story made the newspapers.

A team of researchers helped to script the *Theme Time Radio Hour*, but Dylan knew more about American music than any of them, and there was never a line out of character.

He sat close to the microphone, sometimes gently popping his *p*'s or speaking in a hoarse whisper, from his mouth to your ear. He had come full circle, this creature of the radio who had spent his childhood hours before sleep listening to disc jockey Frank "Gatemouth" Page on a show out of Shreveport, Louisiana, called *No-Name Jive*. Page had played Muddy Waters and Howlin' Wolf, and rock and roll, the sound of the future, Little Richard, Fats Domino, and Jerry Lee Lewis. The radio had drawn him out of Hibbing into the wide-open spaces of America, prairies, mountains, and cities, a world of possibilities—dreams, schemes, and themes. Now Dylan was on the other side of the microphone, cuing up vintage music, radio ads, and jingles from the 1940s and '50s, reading poems of Emily Dickinson, Walt Whitman, Shakespeare, and Milton, precious sounds of the past he was determined to hand on to the future.

For three years, as Dylan traveled America with the Never Ending Tour, he would steal away for a few hours here or there and hole up in a makeshift studio, in a trailer or hotel room, or in the soundproof cubicle of a local radio station. Leaning into the mike, he recorded his scripted lines for the *Theme Time Radio Hour*, reading them over and over again until there was not a pause, a mistake, or a stammer to be heard in any broadcast.

We could hear the show every Wednesday at 10 A.M. on Deep Tracks, Sirius XM satellite radio until the last episode, titled "Goodbye," was aired on April 15, 2009. A listener called in to tell the old disc jockey he could never really say goodbye. "Well," Dylan replied, gently, "you gotta get over that, or else everything in your life will be half finished."

The last song we heard on *Theme Time Radio Hour* was Woody

Guthrie's "So Long It's Been Good to Know Yuh," and then came the sound of a needle stuck in the spiral runout groove at the end of an old 78-rpm record, clicking again and again, into oblivion.

I stood in the dark infield of Ripken's baseball diamond, somewhere between third and second base, where the shortstop had flourished. Folks of all ages surrounded me, most of them younger than I. Children were free of charge. The thunder and lightning had driven Willie Nelson from the portable stage in center field but by the time I arrived at nine o'clock the storm had passed. The grandstands behind me were not full because many of the fans, like me, wanted to get as close to the stage as possible. Yet there was no pushing or elbowing; there was plenty of room for all.

The crowd of 6,000 started cheering and shouting when they heard the first trumpet blasts of Aaron Copland's "Fanfare for the Common Man." Dylan has used Copland's music, including movements of *Rodeo*, as a prelude to his concerts for many years, stately classical music that is still thoroughly American. Against the dark curtain at the back of the stage loomed a projection of an eye, gray against black, twenty feet high, a stylized eye with a spiral pupil, spidery lashes, and a crown upon it, an emblem to ward off bad spirits.

Copland's fanfare faded and then we heard the circus ringmaster voice of one of the stage crew over the PA system.

Ladies and gentlemen, please welcome the poet laureate of rock and roll. The voice of the promise of the sixties counterculture. The guy who forced folk into bed with rock, who donned makeup in the seventies and disappeared into a haze of substance abuse. Who emerged to find Jesus. Who was written off as a has-been by the end of the eighties and who suddenly shifted gears releasing some of the strongest music of his career beginning in the late nineties. Ladies and gentlemen—Columbia recording artist Bob Dylan!

423

Dylan had approved the script that had been used to introduce his shows since August 15, 2002. Concise, and factually accurate, it was not written by Dylan. The speech was paraphrased from a column that appeared in the *Buffalo News* on August 9, 2002, but he must have believed the words in order to hear them more than a hundred times a year as he strapped on his guitar and turned to face the lions.

Dylan came onstage wearing a dapper white gaucho hat, a pale blue shirt with a glittering embroidered collar, and a sea-green scarf knotted loosely at the neck. He wore a western-style gray frock coat trimmed with little buckles on the breast pockets; his trousers had a white satin stripe running down the seam. His long hair was pulled back over his ears and flowed over the collar, shining in the blue and white spotlights.

He was not overweight but his face had fallen so there was no longer any definition to the famous chin and jawline, and he looked older than his sixty-eight years. The blue eyes, hooded under bushy eyebrows, were bright, piercing. The band members wore uniform suits of pale gray, dark shirts and black fedoras, like chorus extras from *Guys and Dolls*.

George Receli whacked the tom-tom, one, two, three, four; Denny Freeman played a descending blues scale on lead guitar; and the band pushed off into the boogie-woogie bayou of "Leopard-Skin Pill-Box Hat," a twelve-bar, three-chord blues in the manner of Lightnin' Hopkins from *Blonde on Blonde*.

> *Well, you look so pretty in it,*
> *Honey, can I jump on it sometime?*
> *Yes, I just wanna see*
> *If it's really that expensive kind*
> *You know it balances on your head*
> *Just like a mattress balances*
> *On a bottle of wine*

I had forgotten just how good that last couplet is, absurd on the face of it, but then when you think about the way lovers use wine, and a mattress, the subtle logic of the simile begins to dawn upon you.

The pillbox hat was an artifact of the 1960s when Lyndon Johnson was in the White House, an accessory worn most famously by Jackie Kennedy. I looked around me at the youngsters cheering, struggling to make out the lyrics the singer was growling and croaking. It had always been a silly—though picturesque—song, a satire of vanity in a certain place and time. Who would have known the verses would still be funny when the fashion was gone and only the painterly image was left, the leopard-skin pillbox hat, forty years later?

The enduring relevance of the protest songs, on the other hand—especially the lyrics that decried racial prejudice—had become a fact of American history: "Blowin' in the Wind" and "Only a Pawn in Their Game" had influenced generations of voters. Now a black man was in the White House, Barack Hussein Obama, and Dylan had helped to put him there.

The pitched battle between Hillary Clinton and Barack Obama for the Democratic presidential nomination had come to a head in May 2008. Clinton had narrowly escaped defeat in the crucial Indiana primary and Obama won decisively in North Carolina on May 6. The final primaries were to be held on June 3; if Obama gained enough delegates then to clinch the nomination, Clinton would have to endorse her rival.

On May 28, Dylan was in Odense, Denmark, at the beginning of a European tour, but he had been following the tempestuous presidential race with keen interest.

An exhibit of his paintings was scheduled to open at the Halcyon Gallery in London on June 14. As he would be performing in Italy then, he had no plans to attend the opening of his show in England. But he did agree to meet with Alan Jackson of the London *Times* in his hotel room in Odense to talk about artwork and other matters, maybe even the election.

After waiting in a succession of anterooms, the journalist was ushered up a back staircase to a hall. There the road manager pointed toward a door that stood half open, and he went away. Jackson had interviewed the singer in 1997 and 2001. So Bob Dylan opened the door and welcomed his visitor, "with a soft handshake and a volley of courtesies: 'How have you been? What's going on in your life? Are you okay with the dark?'"

There in the hotel room in midday the curtains were drawn shut. Dylan was wearing boots, blue jeans, and a sweatshirt with the sleeves pushed up above the elbows. In the available light Jackson noted that "the famous face is heavily lined and pale, but always warm and quick to smile." Dylan offered the reporter a chair and sat next to him, at right angles.

Jackson placed a large book on the low table between them: the *Drawn Blank Series*, the collection of Dylan's artwork that Halcyon Gallery had published to coincide with the opening in Mayfair. Dylan picked it up and chuckled admiringly. "This is pretty handsome stuff." In 1990 an editor at Random House had given him a drawing book. "I took it away with me and turned it back in again, full, three years later." He sketched whatever caught his eye on the road: train platforms and wharves, taverns and hotel rooms in New York, London, New Orleans, Fargo, Stockholm, or San Francisco. There were portraits of women in various states of undress, whoever would pose for him in studios or in private.

The interviewer asked if there was anything going on in his life in the early nineties that might provide a theme or a backstory to the work. (That was the period of Dylan's second divorce, a half decade when he recorded no new songs.) Dylan shrugged, leaning forward, his hands clasped between his knees, defensive. "Just the usual. I try to live as simply as possible and was just drawing whatever I felt like drawing, whenever I felt like doing it. The idea was always to do it without affectation or self-reference, to provide some kind of panoramic view of the world as I was seeing it." He cited Matisse, Derain, Monet, and above all Gauguin as influences. "I found I could stand in front of any one of [their paintings] for as long as I'd sit at the movies, yet not get tired on my feet."

When *Drawn Blank* came out in 1994 the book got little attention. "The critics didn't want to review it. . . . The publisher told me they couldn't get past the idea of another singer who dabbled. You know, like David Bowie, Joni Mitchell, Paul McCartney . . ." He didn't mind. "I wasn't expecting anything phenomenal to happen. It's not like the drawings were revolutionary. They weren't going to change anyone's way of thinking." For the new show, Dylan had his old drawings scanned, enlarged, and transferred to heavy paper; then he painted over the original images. "And in doing so," he said, "subverted the light. Every picture spoke a different language to me as the various colors were applied."

The art critic for the London *Times*, judging that the show was "reasonably interesting," admired Dylan's enthusiasm as he used different colors upon a single image to create diverse moods. "A long view down a railway track looks threatening and spooky when the sky is orange, but hot and summery when it is blue. . . . With its unrealistic felt-tip colors and a fierce sense of being dashed off, the new art tries to be fauve in too clichéd a way."

No one was taking the exhibit at the Halcyon too seriously, including the artist, but the work was not exactly being dismissed, either. Andrew Motion, the poet laureate, remarked upon "the way in which the works feel at ease through their lack of ease," and Alan Jackson thought the paintings were "consistently technically accomplished and engaging." Asked if he had any plans for future artwork, Dylan said he would like to do some portraits of celebrities who would sit for him—mathematicians, actors, inventors, businesspeople. Even more interesting to him "is the idea of a collection based on historically romantic figures: Napoleon and Josephine, Dante and Beatrice, Captain John Smith and Pocahontas, Brad and Angelina," he concluded, laughing. Would Brangelina sit for him?

He chuckled at the thought. "Maybe, who knows? Whether or not it comes to fruition, time will tell. This [the *Drawn Blank Series*] was easy to do because it didn't clash with any other commitments. If something does, then I simply cannot do it."

Poet, composer, performer, painter, Dylan has his priorities clear in his mind. Dabbling in studio painting must take a backseat to family matters, an arduous touring schedule, song writing, the *Theme Time Radio Hour*, and the second volume of his memoirs, which he claims, to this day, to be working on.

Jackson's time with Dylan had passed pleasantly, as always, and all too quickly. With minutes remaining he mentioned the Pulitzer Prize that Dylan had received in April, a special citation for "his profound impact on popular music and American culture, marked by lyrical compositions of extraordinary poetic power," and all the poet could think of to say is "I hope they don't ask for it back!" The journalist offered that this passage in Dylan's life was proving to be both creative and contented.

"I've always felt that. It's just sometimes I've got more going on than other times." So life is good? "To me," Dylan said, reassuringly, "it's never been otherwise."

The men stood up as the interview drew to a close. But the tape recorder was still running, and the *Times* reporter asked if Dylan had anything to say about the forthcoming U.S. presidential election, only six months away.

"Right now America is in a state of upheaval," Dylan replied. "Poverty is demoralizing. You can't expect people to have the virtue of purity when they are poor. But we've got this guy out there now who is redefining the nature of politics from the ground up . . . Barack Obama. He's redefining what a politician is, so we'll have to see how things play out. Am I hopeful? Yes, I'm hopeful that things might change. Some things are going to have to."

This was perhaps the most surprising thing he had said in forty-five years of talking to journalists. Except for vilifying politicians as a species he had had nothing good or bad to say about any office-holder, candidate, or political cause apart from the War on Poverty. He never mentioned names. He had certainly never endorsed a candidate for high office. So his choosing to speak out the week before Hillary Clinton quit the race for the Democratic nomination and threw her support to Obama was news. The wire services picked up the story, and within hours voters all over America knew that the author of "Blowin' in the Wind" and "The Times They Are A-Changin'" had hopes for political reform and high praise for Barack Obama.

On election night, November 4, 2008, Dylan was performing for a crowd of nearly 5,000 in Northrup Auditorium at the University of Minnesota, the school he had fitfully attended in 1960. Introducing his band members after the first encore, "Like a Rolling Stone," he mentioned the Obama campaign button Tony Garnier was wearing on his lapel. The crowd roared its approval. "Alright!" Dylan continued, "Tony likes to think it's a brand-new time right now. An age of light. Me, I was born in 1941—the year they bombed Pearl Harbor. Been living in darkness ever since. But it looks like things are gonna change now." As he sang the final encore, "Blowin' in the Wind," a few minutes after ten o'clock Central Time, audience members with Palm Pilots and BlackBerrys were confirming that Obama had won the election.

One spectator described Dylan's final moments on the stage as he shared applause and cheers with the president-elect. "He actually danced in the center of the stage as he blew on his harmonica. He looked like a cross between a bandy rooster, a scarecrow, and a grandpa doing a happy dance."

The morning of Dylan's concert in Aberdeen six months later, the biggest news story, dominating talk radio and television, poolside and dinner conversations, concerned the arrest of a black Harvard professor in his Cambridge home by a white police officer called to investigate a break-in. Someone had called 911 to report that two black men were forcing the door open. One was Professor Henry Louis Gates, Jr., home from a trip to China; his door was stuck and his cabdriver was helping him jar it loose.

When Sergeant James Crowley knocked at the door, Gates was irate. According to the police report, when Crowley identified himself and explained he was investigating the report of a break-in, "Gates opened the front door and exclaimed, 'Why, because I'm a black man in America?' Crowley then asked Gates if there was anyone else in the residence. "While yelling, he told me that it was none of my business and accused me of being a racist police officer." When Crowley asked Gates "to provide me with photo identification so that I could verify that he resided at Ware Street . . . Gates initially refused, demanding that I show him identification, but then did supply me with a Harvard University identification card." Gates asked again for Crowley's name but, according to the police report, "Gates began to yell over my spoken words. . . . When Gates asked a third time for my name, I explained that I had provided it at his request two separate times."

Gates claimed that Crowley never identified himself, and that he was incapable of yelling because of a bronchial infection. A *New York Times* reporter commented that "the incident was a disappointing reminder that for all the racial progress the country seemed to have made with the election of President Obama, little has changed in the everyday lives of most people in terms of race relations."

As Dylan rushed through a growling rendition of "Don't Think Twice, It's All Right," I looked around me and saw people of all ages, many of them singing along, and all of them white.

With Dylan on guitar, struggling to sing in a voice that had forsaken melody—a handful of real tones, the rest of the scale only sketched by the singer's shaping of syllables—the group sounded ragged, a straggling ghost of the band I had heard in 1997. I know for a fact that the band can never sound any better than the bandleader, a cardinal rule of Dylan's ensembles for more than thirty years—

since he parted company with Robbie Robertson. He was singing "Don't Think Twice" from 1963 and playing guitar certainly not for his own pleasure but for the audience, young and old, who embraced the lyric as a familiar thing. The original melody requires a vocal range of more than an octave, ten full tones in fact. Dylan no longer had the pipes to deliver the famous tune, or fingers limber enough to pluck the guitar accompaniment. He would talk his way around it, crowding the words into the first measure of every melodic line like a camp counselor leading a sing-along, cuing the group while strumming roughly. We might help him sing the song.

An act of will got him through the bittersweet story of "Don't Think Twice" and at the end there was grateful applause.

Dylan had wisely continued to write new songs so that he could perform them, songs that he could perform. Some of the old songs had become impossible, others, like "Don't Think Twice," a strain. But there was always the blues with its easy six-tone scale, a form where one size fits all and a boy or an old man can get by with four tones or a half dozen. The blues had been with him from the beginning, Blind Lemon's "See That My Grave Is Kept Clean," Bukka White's "Fixin' to Die Blues"; the blues had been a faithful companion and it would see him out.

George Receli pounded out a bright, up-tempo rhythm, eight-to-the-bar; Stu Kimball laid down a boogie-woogie guitar track; and Dylan started singing from a place where he was much more at ease.

If it keep on raining the levee gonna break
If it keep on raining the levee gonna break
Everybody saying this is a day only the Lord could make.

In August 2005 Hurricane Katrina hit New Orleans, Dylan's favorite southern city, and the levee really did break, killing more than a thousand people and leaving tens of thousands more homeless.

Maybe that disaster inspired Dylan to resurrect the blues song by Memphis Minnie and Kansas Joe McCoy "When the Levee Breaks" from 1929, adding some of his own words. After seventy-five years of copyright protection the song had just entered the public domain, so it was fair game at the right moment for Dylan to add his apocalyptic, end-of-times twist to it.

I can't stop here, I ain't ready to unload
Riches and salvation can be waiting behind the next bend in the road.

A topical writer or satirist might have written a fine protest song skewering the government and the Army Corps of Engineers for allowing the flood access to the city over the mud levees and then leaving citizens up to their necks in floodwater, those who did not drown. The poet preferred to hold the glass up to himself:

I look in your eyes I see nobody else but me
I see all that I am and all I hope to be.

At the end of a long two-note guitar solo played by the frugal Denny Freeman (who played most of his guitar solos on no more than three notes), Dylan repeated the first stanza da capo, putting extra passion into the line "Everybody saying this is a day only the Lord could *mayyyaake.*" Scattered applause and a lone wolf whistle met the silence at the end of this number. Then Dylan blew some plaintive notes on the harmonica, and the drummer struck up an easy two-step rhythm with brushes on the snare and cymbals. Dylan was playing the introductory measures to "Spirit on the Water," an old-fashioned love ballad from *Modern Times.*

Spirit on the water
Darkness on the face of the deep
I keep thinking about you baby
I can't hardly sleep

The allusion to Genesis ("the earth was without form, and void; and darkness was upon the face of the deep") prepared us for a love song in the vein of Solomon's, in which the beloved is the sum of all creation, God and the Church embodied in the Bride. The song is very long, for a love ballad, twenty stanzas without narrative development—more than seven minutes on the recording—and Dylan delivered sixteen of them. I say "delivered" because he did not so much sing the simple melody as speak, or growl it, a technique the Germans call *sprechstimme*, speaking the words to the lyric roughly in time to the musical measure. Now and then Dylan's voice would pick up the melody for a phrase, or a line, "I'm wild about you gal," but the effort seemed to be too painful so he would return to *sprechstimme*. The last stanza got a rise out of the audience, as he tossed out a playful challenge with mock fury:

> You think I'm over the hill
> You think I'm past my prime. . . .

Well, I for one was thinking Bob Dylan was well past his prime if he could no longer carry a tune as simple as "Spirit on the Water," which was as sweet and memorable as any melody by Burt Bacharach. However, he continued:

> Let me see what you got
> We can have a whoppin' good time

What did I have? Nearly a half century of memories of Bob Dylan in performance, and ears that this man, perhaps more than any other singer, had educated. I would keep standing here on the baseball field for as long he did. But I have to admit that up until now what I had heard was not inspiring apart from the fact that Dylan was still onstage singing—or trying to sing—in 2009, and several thousand people were watching him.

I recalled that he had once told Bert Kleinman, "I'm usually in a numb state of mind before my shows, and I have to kick in at some place along the line, usually it takes me one or two songs, or some-times it takes much longer. Sometimes it takes me up to the encore!" I was hoping, after the final harmonica notes Dylan blew on "Spirit on the Water," that the singer would "kick in" soon.

Then it happened. Donnie Herron fingered a minor chord on the banjo; Denny Freeman revved up the familiar voodoo engines of "It's Alright, Ma," the repeating Everly Brothers guitar riff, E to G to A, and back again, and Dylan started singing, really singing with all he had, which was more than he had promised.

Darkness at the break of noon
Shadows even the silver spoon
The handmade blade, the child's balloon
Eclipses both the sun and the moon. . . .

Instead of singing the quarter notes evenly four to the bar, Dylan crowded all the syllables into the first measure of each line and then sang the last word for four beats, *noon, spoon*. This was effective, and moving. The crowd showed their appreciation by clapping and cheering louder than before on the familiar lines, and Dylan looked very pleased. He kept grinning at the end of stanzas in a way he would never have done in Madison Square Garden. It was as if he himself was delighted by the invention he had forged forty-five years earlier that was still in perfect working order, even if he was not up to singing all the verses. He sang 80 percent, leaving out the rather abstract fourth section.

"It's Alright, Ma's" satire of religion, sex, and politics had lost none of its relevance or sting since I had heard him play it solo in 1974, and a surprising number of lines had become American prov-erbs: He not busy being born is busy dying; The masters make the rules for the wise men and the fools; Money doesn't talk it swears, etc. Like fugitive lines from Shakespeare or Pope, the maxims of Dylan's most literary composition came to writers of editorials and

Sunday sermons because they expressed, in distilled language, a human truth. They had passed from ear to ear not from the ground up like advertising slogans or nursery rhymes, but from the top down, from Dylan fans who had studied the lyrics and passed them on, quoted them to friends who echoed them until they were ubiquitous.

The Aberdeen concert lacked a clear dramatic structure. The program was divided almost evenly between 1960s classics like "Don't Think Twice" and "Highway 61 Revisited" and songs from the last decade, mostly from *Modern Times*. The tempo regularly alternated from bright to moderately slow, but there was no other logic to the set list.

We could not expect that every one of several thousand performances as different as snowflakes would have the narrative continuity of Lisner Auditorium in 1963, or the thematic unity of Madison Square Garden in 1974. I had been lucky. But it did occur to me that I was feeling a natural entropy that younger fans could not register, the winding down of a well-designed but relentlessly used machine that has not always been properly maintained. In the wake of Denny Freeman's monotonous guitar solos the band contributed little more than a firm rhythm track for Dylan to run on, and the basic melody, the notes his ravaged voice could no longer reach. His harmonica playing was inventive and precise, but his keyboard solos were hardly distinguishable from the pounding of block chords during the choruses.

Yet "It's Alright, Ma" more than lived up to its reputation because Dylan meant every scathing line in his tirade against hypocrisy and injustice; speaking and singing, he commanded every verse, as if he had written it yesterday. There were loud bravos and howls as the drumroll signaled the ending—the first cheers of the night that went beyond deference or flattery to express genuine excitement. Dylan had finally "kicked in," and I had a feeling he would sing not only as well as he could but as well as he needed to.

Instead of building on the momentum, he slowed things down again. It was time to bring us up to date with a song from his newly released album, *Together Through Life*, a slow two-step number called "I Feel a Change Coming On." A languid, last-call love ballad, this one Dylan did not sing; he spoke the lyrics rhythmically to the beat of George Receli's snare drum and a spare guitar accompaniment from Freeman and Kimball.

> *Well now what's the use in dreaming,*
> *You got better things to do.*
> *Dreams never did work for me anyway*
> *Even when they did come true. . . .*
>
> *Everybody got all the flowers*
> *I don't have a single rose*
> *I feel a change coming on*
> *And the fourth part of the day is already gone.*

The fourth part of the day. A day begins at the stroke of midnight. The first quarter is over at dawn and the second at noon. The third quarter goes from noon to twilight, and the fourth part of the day is showtime for musicians, darkness to midnight. *The Ballad of Bob Dylan*: a romance in four parts. How would it all end? How could it end when the hero was still growing and changing?

Dylan had admired the film *La Vie en Rose*, a 2007 biopic about the sad life and death of Edith Piaf. The young director Olivier Dahan was making a new movie about a wheelchair-bound woman traveling America from Kansas City to New Orleans. He wanted "real songs of the American spirit," and what that meant to him was Dylan's music. So he wrote and asked for ten songs for his script. At first Dylan was shocked by the audacity of the request, but then the idea of a movie that used a number of songs for the sound track throughout, instead of the lone song that plays as the credits roll and the audience is walking out, appealed to him.

So he wrote "Life Is Hard" for Dahan, with the help of Robert Hunter, the gifted poet and lyricist for the Grateful Dead, and sent it to the director. Then Hunter and Dylan went on to write another eight songs that became the basis for a new studio album.

Dylan's decision to work with Hunter, or any collaborator at this point in his life, was curious. All he had to say about it was that Hunter was an old buddy, that they had a similar way with words, had cowritten songs before (in 1988, "Silvio" and "The Ugliest Girl in the World"), and would probably write something for a forthcoming play off-Broadway. Nothing is known about their collaborative process. The songs all sound like Dylan songs, as if there was not one that he couldn't have written by himself. In a way, that does indicate a successful collaboration because it is seamless—you can't tell where one poet's work ends and the other begins. On the other hand it makes you wonder why Dylan needed Hunter at all. "Life Is Hard," with its unembarrassed yearnings, is like a tribute to the great 1950s pop singer Jo Stafford, and certainly unlike anything that had ever dripped from Hunter's pen. It is a Dylanesque song that "the little sparrow" Piaf would have savored.

> *The sun is sinking low*
> *I guess it's time to go*
> *I feel a chilly breeze*
> *In place of memories*
>
> *My dreams are locked and barred*
> *Admitting life is hard*
> *Without you near me.*

But Hunter can be funny, and he may have added humor to the runaway favorite on the album, the full-tilt Slim ("Shake Your Hips") Harpo boogie "It's All Good," with its send-up of pop psychologists and their vapid optimism.

A cold-blooded killer stalking the town
Cop cars blinkin', something bad going down
Buildings are crumbling in the neighborhood
But there's nothing to worry about 'cause it's all good
It's all good, I say it's all good, whoo!

This was laugh-out-loud hilarious, and the old man's croaking and cackling was just the right voice for it.

My personal favorite on the record is "If You Ever Go to Houston," which begins and ends with the lines Leadbelly immortalized in "Midnight Special."

If you ever go to Austin, Forth Worth or San Antone
Find the barrooms I got lost in and send my memories home
Put my tears in a bottle, screw the top on tight
If you ever go to Houston, boy you better walk right.

That is a great stanza, whoever wrote it—Dylan, Hunter, or Ledbetter; with the cantina squeeze box slowly droning two-note changes every half-line, like a swinging pendulum above the bass and drum, the song is hypnotic, a hip lecture on how to handle yourself in the hot towns of the Lone Star State. After listening to the tune twice I couldn't get it out of my head.

When Dylan had collaborated with the late Jacques Levy on the album *Desire* back in 1975, Levy's contribution was obvious, if not completely beneficial. He favored a dimension that had been lacking in most of Dylan's work for a decade. A dramatist and psychologist with a Jungian bent, Levy helped to revive the elements of narrative, mythos, and character study in the poet's process after years of intensely personal lyrics.

His employment of Hunter was more mysterious. Because Dylan is economical in all that he does, wasting no movement or resources, if he could have written these songs all by himself, he would have. If he had wanted his friend only to vet the lyrics, Hunter would have been happy to oblige and make suggestions. Evidently Hunter did a lot more than that or he would not be getting credit as a full collaborator.

Writing lyric poetry is a hard and lonely process, and no one can do it forever. Maybe Dylan wanted company? *Together Through Life*: the album was aptly titled in more ways than one.

He had produced his thirty-third studio album himself under the pseudonym Jack Frost, in December 2008, using his road band plus Mike Campbell on guitar and David Hidalgo on accordion.

The official release date was April 29, 2009, but the album was in circulation a month earlier, receiving favorable notices. Ann Powers of the *Los Angeles Times* blog praised "a sound that returns to—and refreshes—the roots of rock and roll," and asserted: "No one should object if the old man just wants to go out to the woodshed and play some blues." That is pretty much what he had done.

One of the most intriguing features of this album was the shift in scene and atmosphere: the wandering minstrel persona of "*Love and Theft*" and *Modern Times* had drifted west, while deepening his connection with the big-city electric blues masters who recorded for Chess Records in the 1950s. The protagonist had left Mississippi and moved to the Texas borderland. Dylan explained his feeling for that part of America to historian Douglas Brinkley, writing for *Rolling Stone*: "Texas may have more independent-thinking people than any other state in the country. And it shows in the music . . . the same type of music that I heard growing up most nights in Minnesota. The languages were just different. It was sung in Spanish there. But where I came from, it was sung in Polish."

Historian Sean Wilentz, writing in the *Daily Beast*, observed that "Dylan's voice, with age, has mellowed (if that's the word) into a blues rasp close to that of yet another Chicago blues great, Howlin' Wolf," and he admired the album's "sunny atmosphere, which comes largely from the Tex-Mex strains from Hidalgo's squeeze box . . . paired with Dylan's current road band regular, Donnie Herron, playing a mariachi trumpet." *Rolling Stone* gave it four stars out of five, and concluded: "Dylan, who turns sixty-eight in May, has never sounded as ravaged, pissed off, and lusty."

That was a sure enough description of the voice Dylan brought to the funky "Honest with Me" in Aberdeen, his only offering from *"Love and Theft."* The number opens with a familiar descending guitar figure from Sly and the Family Stone's "I Want to Take You Higher," and it makes you want to jump and dance. The audience could feel the drumbeat and the throbbing of the rhythm guitar in the ground underfoot as Dylan growled:

> *When I left my home the sky split open wide*
> *I never wanted to go back there—I'd rather have died*
> *I don't understand it—my feelings for you*
> *You'd be honest with me if you only knew*

The high wattage of the song jolted Denny Freeman, and the guitarist punched out his first real guitar solo of the night after the eighth stanza, a soaring cadenza that turned the melody inside out and then folded it up again before Dylan sang the final verses.

A couple of rock songs, "Highway 61 Revisited" and "Thunder on the Mountain," were left in the set list before the encores. But they seemed like lumbering industrial machinery next to the delicate presence of the man standing alone in the spotlight, singing "Forgetful Heart" and the woeful "Nettie Moore." To my surprise, the slow ballads upstaged the sound and fury of rock and roll. When Dylan came out from behind the keyboard, holding the harmonica in one hand and the microphone in the other, the lights dimmed except for the single spotlight where he stood. An acoustic guitar and a bongo drum played softly behind him. He bent one leg toward the other. The stance evoked the gallant chansonniers Charles Aznavour and the late Maurice Chevalier. As the program drew near the end he sang more and more notes, and more tenderly, as if he had been hoarding them all evening, or maybe for his whole life, saving the best for last.

Forgetful heart
Like a walking shadow in my brain
All night long
I lay awake and listen to the sound of pain
The door has closed forever more
If indeed there ever was a door.

The day before the Never Ending Tour buses caravanned down to Aberdeen, Dylan and the band were staying at the Ocean Place Resort and Spa on the Jersey Shore. They were slated to play that night at FirstEnergy Park, a baseball stadium in Lakewood.

Feeling restless, the singer wanted to go out for a walk, and it was pouring down rain. So he pulled on a pair of black sweatpants, a blue sweatshirt with a hood, and tucked the pant legs into his black rain boots. He put on a raincoat, and then another raincoat on top of the first, for good measure. With the schedule he was facing, the last thing he needed was a head cold.

So, dressed for the monsoon, the star left his hotel at 4:30 in the afternoon and walked south with a view of the gray ocean on his left beyond the steakhouses, spas, and taverns of the beachfront. Near Melrose Terrace he turned his back on the Atlantic and walked west on Franklin Avenue, a long block with a grove of trees rising over the rooftops to the south. He didn't really know where he was going and he didn't care much. He just liked the feeling of freedom, walking alone in the rain in a strange town on a day when nobody else was likely to meet him or greet him. He could go "invisible," a word and an idea he relished. Since the age of twenty-three he could not go anywhere where he was not recognized, and he had suffered from the loss of that inalienable right to walk the streets undisturbed by strangers.

The invisible old man dressed in two raincoats, sweatpants, and a hood pulled over his head followed his footsteps into a residential suburb of Long Branch. This was not an affluent area of grand houses with widow's walks and fine cars but a working-class neighborhood with small lawns and fences and clapboard houses, a few blocks from the sea. The biggest home on the block was the Damiano Funeral Home, a rambling old house at the end of Franklin with a gambrel roof and a wraparound porch. In a neighborhood like this, the Boss, Bruce Springsteen, had written "Born to Run" and "Thunder Road," maybe while looking out the window of a house—not like Damiano's but more like this small one across the way, with a FOR SALE sign outside, at Franklin and Third Avenue. (Born in Long Branch, Springsteen grew up in Freehold, New Jersey.)

Curious, the sightseer stepped into the yard, went up to the window, and peered inside. Perhaps it was someone in the house, or a neighbor, who became alarmed by the specter of an "eccentric-looking old man" peeping into the window in "a low income predominately minority neighborhood," and called the police.

"We got a call for a suspicious person," said twenty-four-year-old police officer Kristie Buble. "It was pouring rain outside and I was right around the corner so I responded."

Dylan was walking down the street when Buble pulled up alongside him in the squad car. She stopped and asked him what he was doing in the neighborhood. He said he was looking at a house for sale. He looked at the girl. She had a round face and wide-set dark eyes and a pleasant smile. She looked like a teenager in a police uniform.

She asked him what his name was, and he said, "Bob Dylan."

"Okay, Bob," said the officer, playing along. "What are you doing in Long Branch?"

"Oh, I'm touring the country playing music with Willie Nelson and John Mellencamp," the suspect answered, brightly.

Officer Buble was doubtful. "I did not know what to believe. . . .

We see a lot of people on our beat, and I wasn't sure if he came from one of our hospitals or something." So she asked him for identification. He didn't have any. When she asked him where he was staying he replied vaguely that his tour buses were parked near some big hotel on the ocean. She guessed it was the Ocean Place Resort.

"He was acting very suspicious," Buble reported. "Not delusional, just suspicious. You know, it was pouring rain and all." So she indulged the old man in what she assumed to be a harmless game. "Okay, Bob, why don't you get in the car and we'll drive to the hotel and go verify this?" She opened the back door of the police car, and he quietly got in. "I didn't really believe this was Bob Dylan. It never crossed my mind that this could really be him." Nevertheless, the kind officer tried to make small talk with the man as they rode along Ocean Highway toward the hotel, asking him where he was playing.

"He was really nice though," she remembered, "and he said he understood why I had to verify his identity and why I couldn't let him go." Then he said a disturbing thing: he asked if she would please drive him back to where she had picked him up, that poor neighborhood, after she had verified who he was.

By now she had called for backup, and when she pulled into the parking lot at the hotel her sergeant was waiting there in the downpour near the convoy of tour buses. She got out of the car and told the sergeant, a man a few years older than she, that the old man she had detained in the backseat of the squad car claimed he was Bob Dylan.

He opened the car door, looked at the soaked man in the raincoat and sweatpants, smiling to himself, and shook his head. "That's not Bob Dylan," he decided.

Officer Buble knocked on the door of a tour bus. The door did not open immediately but a voice greeted her. Buble called out, "Are you missing someone?"

"Who's asking?"

"I'm asking! I'm the police!"

So there was some commotion and scrambling. The road manager located Bob Dylan's passport and showed it to the officers of the law, who handed it back before allowing Bob Dylan to return to the world where he would be recognized for who he was, completely and relentlessly known and visible.

For encores at Aberdeen he sang the predictable "Like a Rolling Stone" and "All Along the Watchtower," and sandwiched between them the slow boogie "Jolene" from *Together Through Life*.

"Like a Rolling Stone" he interpreted with something less than his accustomed bravado. He sang with a gruff humility, smiling broadly at references to "the mystery tramp" and "Napoleon in rags," and the image of being invisible with no secrets.

> *How does it feel*
> *To be without a home*
> *Like a complete unknown*
> *Like a rolling stone?*

This famous song began with a snare shot and the words "Once upon a time," like any fairy tale, like the beginning of the ballad of Dylan's life journey. And how would it all end? The Never Ending Tour would end sooner or later, that was certain. Dylan had said so. He also had told us that what unites us all is our mortality, the great and the inglorious, the famous man and the complete unknown.

Tonight the troubadour's caravan would haul off on Interstate 95 south to Norfolk, Virginia, to play a gig the next evening at Harbor Park; then on down to Durham, North Carolina, Simpson, South Carolina, song after song, Georgia, Alabama, Texas, New Mexico, California, show after show. Maybe nothing in this world is never-ending, but for this tour it seems no end is in sight.

Years ago Eric Andersen was visiting Dylan in Woodstock, during his self-imposed retirement from the stage, and the grounded composer kept talking about writing for performance. "If he needed something in a show, you know, like 'it's getting a little slow here, I better pick it up,' then he'd write an up-tempo song. Even then he was always thinking about the show, the *performance*. That was paramount, the live music. I mean, he wants to die onstage. He is one of those people. It happens."

We want blood from our poets, and the greatest of them give a precious share of the transfusion that sustains a life, a culture, a nation: Edgar Allan Poe, Hart Crane, Robert Johnson, Sylvia Plath, Woody Guthrie.

"What more do you want?" asks Nora Guthrie. "There are people who have brought a new spirit to the world. They've really added a spiritual spice to the mix that changes *everybody*. Even if you don't know it you've been affected by these people; their essence trickles through the culture." There are people all over America singing "This Land Is Your Land" who have no idea who Woody Guthrie was; they may have only a faint idea of what the song means, but there is a quality to their lives that would be missing if Woody had never lived. And so there are folks singing "Blowin' in the Wind" halfway around the world whose lives are better for the song even though they do not know who wrote it or the answers to the questions it poses.

And after he dies, no matter when he last performed for a live audience, "once that flow *stops*," Nora continues, "that's when you'll realize that there's not that energy that's going to write those songs anymore." Right now we are all breathing and living it; his spirit is all around us; we turn on the radio and hear his voice; his intelligence is flowing broadly through our culture.

"But once that energy stops, then you'll realize what you had in the time you had it. That's what happened when my dad died in 1967—there was this gasp of recognition. I've been singing this song and this guy's been around." Everything will be different from then on. The world was different in 1960, before Dylan began creating this literature of songs and stories. It will be different the moment he ends his work. Things will have to change.

After midnight, driving west from Aberdeen and south past Gunpowder Falls, heading home, I hear Bob Dylan's voice in my head, not just the voice I have just heard in concert but the voice of a man twenty-one, then thirty-three, then fifty-six years old, nearly my age. And then I imagine an empty stage illuminated by a single work light, and I hear the echoes of music and applause in turn filling the night as it passes over America and around the world, the first part of a new day.

Acknowledgments

I would not have been able to write this book if it had not been for Mike Seeger's example and encouragement for so many years.

I would like to record my gratitude to everyone at Bob Dylan Music Company for their generous support and kind assistance in enabling me to quote from Dylan's songs.

Thanks to my agent, Neil Olson, and my former editor at Harper-Collins, Elisabeth Dyssegaard, for their faith in this project from its inception, and to Jennifer Barth, my present editor, for her advice and support as the manuscript has made its way into print.

Special thanks go to all of my interview subjects, most of whom are named in the text; others were interviewed off the record.

I owe a debt of gratitude to all the previous biographers of Bob Dylan, and especially to the late Robert Shelton, and to Anthony Scaduto, and Larry Sloman. Michael Gray's *The Bob Dylan Encyclopedia* is an extraordinarily rich resource, as are Clinton Heylin's chronology *A Life in Stolen Moments* and his *Behind the Shades Revisited*. No living subject has as vast a historiography as this one, and as it increases in the decades to come scholars will be deeply indebted to these "first generation" biographies.

Some friends here in Baltimore and abroad have provided moral and material support. Above all I want to thank Jack Heyrman, a producer who provided books, tapes, and endless resources and helped with so many connections; Wall Matthews, a collector of Dylan materials and a musician who answered questions; Mac Nachlas, who provided records and discs just when they were needed; Olaf Bjorner and David Beaudouin, who did the same; Terry Kelly, of *The Bridge*, who was so supportive from the beginning, as were John Waters, John Paul Hammond, and Carrie Howland; Happy Traum, who welcomed me to Woodstock; Linda and Bob Hocking, who showed me Hibbing; Greg French, who led me through Dylan's childhood home; and Nancy Riesgraf, curator of the Dylan collection in the Hibbing Library; Murray Horwitz and Ivan Mogull, who helped arrange interviews; Rosemary Knower, who read the manuscript and helped to shape it; and Jason Sack for editorial support.

I want to thank Jennifer Bishop, who kept the home fires burning during the hardest winter.

And then, of course, thank you again, Mr. Dylan, for rescuing my sister, Linda, when she was lost on a winter night in 1963, when all of us were very young.

Notes

Except where cited below, all quotes in the text are from author's interviews.

Chapter 1. LISNER AUDITORIUM, DECEMBER 14, 1963

13   wrote "Blowin' in the Wind": This account comes from David Blue, quoted in Robbie Woliver, *Hoot! A 25-Year History of the Greenwich Village Music Scene* (New York: St. Martin's, 1994), pp. 83–84.

13   In September 1962: Dylan's account of writing "Hard Rain" in the boiler room comes from Bert Kleinman's Westwood One radio interview in 1984. Tom Paxton tells a slightly different story.

Chapter 2. THE NIGHT BOB DYLAN RESCUED MY SISTER

25   The big headlines: "Three Seized in Sinatra Kidnapping," *Evening Star*, December 14, 1963; Warren Unna, "Cambodia Relations Deteriorate," *Washington Post*, December 14, 1963.

26   "multilateral nuclear force": Flora Lewis, "Allies Expected To Skirt Joint Nuclear Issue," ibid.; "U.S., Germany to Push Test for Nuclear Fleet" and "Rusk Arrives in Paris For NATO Conference," ibid.

26   "In other news": Robert C. Hartmann, "Iraq Says Arabs Will Resort to War to Bar Jordan Diversion by Israel," ibid.

27   The Metropolitan Police: Paul Schuette, "Progress Reported in Racial Relations of District Police," ibid.

36   In early July Dylan went down to Greenwood: Robert Shelton, *No Direction Home: The Life and Music of Bob Dylan* (New York: Beech Tree, 1986), pp. 170–79.

36   "the refrain of the song": "Northern Folk Singers Help Out at a Negro Festival in Mississippi," *New York Times*, July 7, 1963.

Chapter 3. THE PAUPER AND THE PRINCE

43   Once upon a time: Dylan made up this tale, which has been elaborated upon by many who have heard bits and pieces of it. Sources for my own pas-

tiche are Izzy Young, "From the Izzy Young Notebooks" (1968), reprinted in *The Bob Dylan Companion*, ed. Carl Benson (New York: Schirmer, 1998), pp. 3–10; Dave Van Ronk with Elijah Wald, *The Mayor of MacDougal Street* (Cambridge, Mass.: Da Capo, 2005), pp. 162–63; Anthony Scaduto, *Dylan: An Intimate Biography* (New York: Grosset & Dunlap, 1973), pp. 81–84; Bob Spitz, *Dylan: A Biography* (New York: Norton, 1989), pp. 153–56.

45   About the same time: Shelton, *No Direction Home*, pp. 28–29. Shelton's biography is the best source concerning Dylan's parents and childhood. He knew and interviewed Abraham and Beatrice Zimmerman. Unless otherwise cited, Shelton's *No Direction Home* (pp. 26–42) is the source of facts for this chapter.

45   Shabtai Zisel Ben Avraham: Howard Sounes, *Down the Highway* (New York: Grove, 2001) p. 14.

45   Robert Zimmerman's father: Shelton, *No Direction Home*, p. 27.

46   Abe Zimmerman fell victim: Ibid., pp. 31–32.

48   There were rules in the home: Ibid., p. 34.

48   "You should have been a girl": Ibid., p. 30.

50   "People would laugh with delight": Ibid. p. 31.

51   Bar Mitzvah: Ibid., pp. 35–36.

51   Camp Herzl: Sounes, *Down the Highway*, p. 25.

51   His IQ: Spitz, *Dylan*, p. 106.

51   Gulbransen spinet: Shelton, *No Direction Home*, p. 36.

53   *No-Name Jive*: Spitz, *Dylan*, pp. 31–33.

54   had his brother David photograph him: Shelton, *No Direction Home*, p. 44.

55   Jacket Jamboree: Sounes, *Down the Highway*, pp. 34–35.

55   "When I put together my early bands": Bob Dylan, *Chronicles: Volume One*, (New York: Simon & Schuster, 2004), p. 42.

55   "Grandma, someday": Shelton, *No Direction Home*, p. 41.

56   "You can't go on and on": Shelton, *No Direction Home*, p. 42.

57   January 31, 1959: Dylan has told the story of seeing Buddy Holly several times, including in his speech at the Grammy Awards in 1998.

57   "When Bob came down here in 1959": Shelton, *No Direction Home*, p. 66.

58   Dave Lee opened the Ten O'Clock Scholar: Scaduto, *Dylan*, pp. 36–37.

59   He allegedly stole: Shelton, *No Direction Home*, p. 73.

60   "It made me want to gasp": Dylan, *Chronicles*, p. 244.

60   "I'll be going away": Ibid. p. 246.

60   In May Bob Dylan made: Clinton Heylin, *A Life in Stolen Moments: Bob Dylan Day by Day 1941–1995* (New York: Schirmer, 1996), pp. 8–9.

61   Following in the footsteps: Spitz, *Dylan*, pp. 102–9.

63   "I was kicked out of Denver": Dylan to Shelton, *No Direction Home*, p. 64.

64   "turning point": Scaduto, *Dylan*, p. 49.

65   "He wanted to be a folksinger": Sounes, *Down the Highway*, p. 68, quoting an interview in *Duluth News Tribune*, n.d.

66   "I'm passing through": This and quotes passim are from Scaduto, *Dylan*, pp. 61–62.

Chapter 4. SPIRITUAL HOMING PIGEON

69   "an extreme sense of destiny": Edna Gundersen, "Dylan Is Positively on Top of His Game," *USA Today*, September 10, 2001.

74   Dylan drove from Madison: Sounes, *Down the Highway*, p. 72.

74   "I was there to find singers": Dylan, *Chronicles*, p. 9.

76   "the scruffiest-looking fugitive": Van Ronk, *The Mayor of MacDougal Street*, p. 158.

76   "I have heard him say": This and quotes passim are from ibid.

78   "He was too raw": Van Ronk to Sounes, *Down the Highway*, p. 84.

78   "unteachable": Ibid.

79   "He had to reinvent the wheel": Ibid.

80   "He also stayed with various friends": Scaduto, *Dylan*, pp. 74–78.

80   Ray Gooch, Chloe Kiel: Efforts to locate these people have failed, including a search of phone books and interviews with Mike Seeger, Tom Paxton, et. al.

81   "The Lost Land": Dylan, *Chronicles*, pp. 25–104.

81   "I was born": This and all Dylan quotes passim are from ibid., pp. 28–45.

86   "Paul didn't get much benefit": Bob Coltman, *Paul Clayton and the Folksong Revival* (Lanham, Md.: Scarecrow, 2008), p. 113.

Chapter 5. FINDING HIS VOICE

87   "might have to change my inner thought patterns": This and other Dylan quotes passim are from Dylan, *Chronicles*, pp. 71–86.

89   Van Ronk's wife, Terri Thal: Suze Rotolo, *A Freewheelin' Time: A Memoir of Greenwich Village in the Sixties* (New York: Broadway, 2008), p. 113; and Scaduto, *Dylan*, pp. 79–90. Scaduto is rich in anecdotes about the early New York years. He interviewed Van Ronk, the Gleasons, Joan Baez, Mike Porco, the Rotolos, and many others in the 1960s, soon after the events occurred.

90   "bouncing from foot to foot": Joan Baez, *And a Voice to Sing With* (New York: Summit, 1987), pp. 83–84.

91   "He had that funny pathetic": Scaduto, *Dylan*, p. 85.

91   "This guitar needs a haircut": Dylan quoted by Suze Rotolo, in turn interviewed by Victoria Balfour, *The Dylan Companion*, ed. Elizabeth Thomson and David Gutman (New York: Delta, 1990), p. 73.

91   "He never stood still": Van Ronk, *The Mayor of MacDougal Street*, p. 161.

92   "It contained all the elements": Scaduto, *Dylan*, p. 94.

92   "I did everything fast": Dylan, *Chronicles*, p. 84.

93   "You said you'd ask me": Scaduto, *Dylan*, p. 107.

94   "the most erotic thing": Dylan, *Chronicles*, p. 265.

94   "funny, engaging, intense": Rotolo, *A Freewheelin' Time*, p. 92.

95   "without parental guidance": This and other Rotolo quotes passim are from ibid., pp. 68–94.

96   "I felt like I was in love": Dylan, *Chronicles*, p. 265.

97   "Maybe we were spiritual soul mates": Ibid., p. 266.

97   "two kids bouncing": Scaduto, *Dylan*, p. 109.

98   "true fortuneteller": Dylan, liner notes for "The Times They Are A-Changin'."

98   "She seemed overshadowed": Shelton, *No Direction Home*, p. 130.

98   "grasping for her own identity": Ibid., p. 131.

99   On September 14, Hester invited: Dylan, *Chronicles*, pp. 277–79.

100   "it seemed too good": Ibid., p. 279.

100   "He was very fussy": Shelton, *No Direction Home*, p. 134.

101   Israel Goodman Young: Dylan, *Chronicles*, pp. 18–21; Van Ronk, *The Mayor of MacDougal Street*, pp. 62–63.

101   So Izzy shelled out: Scaduto, *Dylan*, p. 119.

102   "I watched Bob": Rotolo, *A Freewheelin' Time*, p. 159.

102   "yet I felt insecure": Ibid., p. 95.

103   "paranoid": Thomson and Gutman, eds., *The Dylan Companion*, p. 74.

103   *Brecht on Brecht*: Dylan, *Chronicles*, pp. 272–76.

104   "a song that transcended": Ibid., p. 276.

105   "He was not known": Rotolo, *A Freewheelin' Time*, p. 158.

105   Albert Grossman, thirty-six: Information about Grossman comes from author's interviews and from Shelton, *No Direction Home*; Scaduto, *Dylan*; and Van Ronk, *The Mayor of MacDougal Street*.

105   "the American public": Shelton, *No Direction Home*, p. 88.

109   "the ideas of people being afraid": Turner quoted by Michael Gray, *The Bob Dylan Encyclopedia* (New York: Continuum, 2006), p. 673, transcription of an interview in *Broadside*, May 1962.

110   "I just had it in my mind": Douglas Brinkley, "Bob Dylan's America," *Rolling Stone*, May 14, 2009, p. 76.

112   "I was a mess": Rotolo, *A Freewheelin' Time*, p. 281.

112   "It had to end": Dylan, *Chronicles*, p. 276.

113   "I did not want to be a string": Rotolo, *A Freewheelin' Time*, p. 257.

113   article in *Newsweek*: Andrea Svedberg, "I Am My Words," *Newsweek*, November 4, 1963.

114   "All of us were reinventing": Van Ronk, *The Mayor of MacDougal Street*, p. 162.

118   "I looked down": Nat Hentoff, "The Crackin', Shakin', Breakin' Sounds," *New Yorker*, October 24, 1964, reprinted in *Bob Dylan: The Essential Interviews*, ed. Jonathan Cott (New York: Wenner, 2006), pp. 26–27.

119   "I haven't got any guitar": The text of Dylan's ECLC speech is available at http://www.corliss-lamont.org.

Chapter 6. NEW YORK, 1974

127   "probably written after": liner notes, *Biograph*.

128   "This is a pilgrimage": George Vecsey, "For Dylan Fan, Not Even Rain Can Dampen the 'Pilgrimage,'" *New York Times*, January 29, 1974.

128   "This was somewhat of a surprise": Ibid.

128   "His personal following": Grace Lichtenstein, "For Dylan, The Dollars Are a Changin' for the Better," *New York Times*, January 31, 1974.

128   "His appeal": Ibid.

128   "Mr. Dylan evoked cheers": George Vecsey, "Dylan Sends Garden into Mature Frenzy," *New York Times*, January 31, 1974.

129 "You can't get too close": Shelton, *No Direction Home*, p. 52.

Chapter 7. A SEA CHANGE

147 "A voice that drove out bad spirits": Dylan, *Chronicles*, p. 254.

147 "I was stricken": Scaduto, *Dylan*, p. 170.

147 "I wanted people": Ibid., p. 171.

147 "His eyes were as old": Baez, *And a Voice to Sing With*, p. 85.

148 "I wanted to take care": Scaduto, *Dylan*, p. 171.

149 "Luckily we both had": Ibid., p. 228.

149 "extremely gracious and competent": Gray, *Bob Dylan Encyclopedia*, p. 199.

150 "counterpart": Dylan, *Chronicles*, p. 255.

151 "I'd rather listen to Jimmy Reed": Cott, ed., *Bob Dylan: The Essential Interviews*, pp. 384–40.

152 "in the middle of that": Scaduto, *Dylan*, p. 227.

152 "BEATLES SAY—DYLAN SHOWS": *Melody Maker*, January 9, 1965.

152 "I thought he would do": Scaduto, *Dylan*, p. 227.

152 "I told her while": Shelton, *No Direction Home*, p. 296.

152 "I thought that meant": This and Baez quotes passim are from Scaduto, *Dylan*, pp. 228–30.

Chapter 8. WIRED FOR SOUND

158 "All about my steady hatred": Scaduto, *Dylan*, p. 244.

158 "seeing someone in the pain": Ibid., p. 245.

159 "message to a newborn baby": Shelton, *No Direction Home*, p. 302.

159 "The electric guitar represented capitalism": Sounes, *Down the Highway*, p. 182.

160 "Anyone wishing to portray": Joe Boyd, *White Bicycles* (London: Serpent's Tail, 2005), p. 107.

162 "Ballad of the Long-Legged Bait": Dylan Thomas, *The Collected Poems of Dylan Thomas* (New York: New Directions, 1957), p. 168.

163 "I thought it was great": Cott, ed., *Bob Dylan: The Essential Interviews*, p. 52.

164 "It's very complicated": Ibid., p. 48.

164 "I like what I'm doing": Ibid., pp. 52–53.

166 Robertson told biographer Sounes: Sounes, *Down the Highway*, p. 191.

166 "By God, he didn't change": Ibid., p. 192.

167 a judge married them in a private ceremony: Shelton, *No Direction Home*, p. 325; Sounes, *Down the Highway*, p. 193.

167 "Well, I just don't have": *Chicago Daily News*, November 27, 1965, reprinted in Cott, ed., *Bob Dylan: The Essential Interviews*, pp. 59–60.

169 Meanwhile, he was touring: For Dylan's touring schedule before 1995, I am indebted to Clinton Heylin's excellent chronology, *A Life in Stolen Moments*.

172 "eight miles high" interview: Shelton, *No Direction Home*, pp. 340–62. This is the most valuable interview from the period. All Dylan quotes in this section are from Shelton.

177 a pleasure drive: Dialogue with Lennon and Pennebaker in the limousine is transcribed from Pennebaker footage, outtakes from *Eat the Document*.

178   a later interview: Heylin, *A Life in Stolen Moments*, p. 253, quoting January 24–February 4, 1971, *Rolling Stone* interview with Lennon.

179   "I wanna go home": This footage, included in Martin Scorsese's *No Direction Home*, is believed to have been shot by Pennebaker.

179   "I knew I just couldn't let that stand": Jann Wenner, *"Rolling Stone* Interview," November 29, 1969, reprinted in Cott, ed., *Bob Dylan: The Essential Interviews*, p. 147.

180   Few people now know: Information comes from confidential sources.

181   "How could he do this to me?": Shelton, *No Direction Home*, p. 375.

181   "it wore me down": Cott, ed., *Bob Dylan: The Essential Interviews*, p. 140.

181   "I still didn't sense": Ibid., p. 143.

182   "some ancient poets": Clinton Heylin, *Behind the Scenes Revisited* (New York: William Morrow, 2000), p. 268.

182   "he didn't think Dylan was seriously hurt": Shelton, *No Direction Home*, p. 375.

186   "He would pull these songs": Greil Marcus, *Invisible Republic: Bob Dylan's Basement Tapes* (New York: Henry Holt, 1997), p. xvi.

186   "If they are a map": Ibid., p. xiii.

187   "We were playing with absolute freedom": Ibid., p. xiv.

Chapter 9. THE POET IN THE GARDEN

191   "the first three or four songs": Traum quotes here are from Ben Fong-Torres et al., *Knockin on Dylan's Door: On the Road in '74* (New York: Pocket, 1974), p. 64.

197   "I don't know if Dylan": Interview in *Broadside*, October 1965.

197   "Well, that's the way it goes": Cott, ed., *Bob Dylan: The Essential Interviews*, p. 76.

198   then Abe Zimmerman, his natural father, died: Shelton, *No Direction Home*, pp. 59–61.

199   Archibald MacLeish: The meeting with MacLeish and quotes are from Dylan, *Chronicles*, pp. 107–12.

205   "for gangs of dropouts": Ibid., p. 116.

211   "The ranking Republican": Bill Kovach, "Nixon Faces G.O.P. Move for Data in House Inquiry," *New York Times*, January 30, 1974.

211   JUDGE WILL ORDER NIXON: Steven V. Roberts, "Judge Will Order Nixon to Testify at Ex-Aides' Trial," ibid.

213   "thinking about one of my boys": Liner notes for *Biograph*, 1985.

215   "things can't be measured": Dylan, *Chronicles*, p. 112.

219   "I particularly like the song": John Rockwell, "Tour's Roaring Ovations Leave Dylan Quietly Pleased," *New York Times*, January 8, 1974.

Chapter 10. MIDWINTER: AN INTERLUDE

225   Ellen Bernstein: See interviews with Bernstein in Clinton Heylin, *Behind the Shades Revisited*, pp. 362–63, 366, 371–81.

226   "moments of anger": Christgau quoted in Andy Gill and Kevin Odegard, *A Simple Twist of Fate* (Cambridge, Mass.: Da Capo, 2004), p. 166.

226   "the excruciating cry": Ibid.

227   "Even if *Blood on the Tracks* was literally confessional": Shelton, *No Direction Home*, p. 445.

228   returned to Greenwich village in the spring: Heylin, *A Life in Stolen Moments*, pp. 156–58.

229   Rolling Thunder Revue: The main sources are Larry Sloman, *On the Road with Bob Dylan: Rolling with the Thunder* (New York: Bantam, 1978); Sam Shepard, *The Rolling Thunder Logbook* (Cambridge, Mass.: Da Capo, 2004); and author's interviews.

231   Norman Raeben: Bert Cartright, "The Mysterious Norman Raeban," in *Wanted Man: In Search of Bob Dylan*, ed. John Bauldie (New York: Citadel, 1990), pp. 85–90.

231   "I had met magicians": Pete Oppel, "Enter the Tambourine Man," *Dallas Morning News*, November 22, 1978.

231   "how to see": Interview with Jonathan Cott, *Rolling Stone*, November 16, 1978, in Cott, ed., *Bob Dylan: The Essential Interviews*, p. 260.

234   "What I want": Dylan to Faris Bouhafa, quoted in Spitz, *Dylan*, p. 457.

236   "He revealed his heart": Sloman, *On the Road with Bob Dylan*, p. 113.

236   "He's right out there now": Ibid., p. 114.

237   "Pleasure? I never seek pleasure": Nat Hentoff, "Is It Rolling Zeus?," in Benson, ed., *The Bob Dylan Companion*, p. 134.

238   "Joni Mitchell flies in": Shepard, *The Rolling Thunder Logbook*, p. 115.

239   "We really accomplished something": Spitz, *Dylan*, p. 500.

240   "We're regrouping": Sloman, *On the Road with Bob Dylan*, p. 397.

241   "Everybody did too much": Heylin, *Behind the Shades Revisited*, p. 432.

242   "Bob had a thing": Baez, *And a Voice to Sing With*, p. 242.

244   "unimpressed and bored": Heylin, *A Life in Stolen Moments*, p. 173.

245   "Her skin was white": Baez, *And a Voice to Sing With*, p. 240.

249   "Sara in her deerskins": Ibid., p. 244.

250   "It forces me to extremes": Interview with Neil Hickey, *TV Guide*, September 11, 1976, reprinted in *Younger Than That Now: The Collected Interviews with Bob Dylan* (New York: Thunder's Mouth, 2004), pp. 101–7.

252   "the everyday vices": Interview with Ron Rosenbaum, *Playboy*, March 1978, reprinted in ibid., pp. 109–59.

253   "my current girlfriend": Gray, *The Bob Dylan Encyclopedia*, p. 174.

254   "Someone out in the crowd": *Behind the Shades*, p. 491.

254   "prayed that day": Heylin, *A Life in Stolen Moments*, p. 206.

255   preaching in front of the curtain: Dylan's sermons are from *Saved! The Gospel Speeches of Bob Dylan*, ed. Clinton Heylin (Madras and New York: Hanuman, 1990).

Chapter 11. YOUNG BLOOD

264   "Bob freed your mind": Springsteen speech at Rock and Roll Hall of Fame induction dinner, January 20, 1988, reprinted in Thomson and Gutman, eds., *The Dylan Companion*, p. 287.

266   "I'm just glad to be feeling better": Mark Dowdney, *Mirror* (London), June 4, 1997.

266   "Do you believe in reincarnation": This and quotes passim are from Martin Keller in the *Minneapolis City Pages*, reprinted in *Chicago Tribune*, September 11, 1983.

273   Larry Kegan: Sources include Sounes, *Down the Highway*, pp. 25–28, 48; Gray, *The Bob Dylan Encyclopedia*, pp. 371–73.

278   "Who expects what?": Bert Kleinman and Artie Mogull, Westwood One radio interview, November 17, 1984, transcribed in Cott, ed., *Bob Dylan: The Essential Interviews*, pp. 309–24, and corrected by the author.

278   "whitewashed and wasted out": This and quotes passim are from Dylan, *Chronicles*, p. 147.

281   "It's almost like I heard": David Gates in *Newsweek*, October 6, 1997, reprinted in *Studio A: The Bob Dylan Reader*, ed. Benjamin Hedin (New York: Norton, 2004), p. 235.

282   "I had a revelation": Interview with Robert Hilburn in *Los Angeles Times*, December 14, 1997, reprinted in Cott, ed., *Bob Dylan: The Essential Interviews*, p. 402.

283   "She's always had her own built-in happiness": Dylan, *Chronicles*, p. 201.

284   "in the service of the public": Ibid., p. 154.

284   "It's all the same tour": Heylin, *Behind the Shades Revisited*, p. 648.

285   "There are a lot of people": Peter Wilmoth, *Age* (Melbourne, Australia), April 3, 1992.

285   "There are a lot of times": Robert Hilburn, "On the Never Ending Tour with Rock's Greatest Poet," *Los Angeles Times*, February 9, 1992.

285   "I do it because I'm driven": Interview with John Pareles in *New York Times*, September 28, 1997, reprinted in Cott, ed., *Bob Dylan: The Essential Interviews*, p. 392.

Chapter 12. FINDING THE BEAT

296   Winston Watson: Gray, *The Bob Dylan Encyclopedia*, pp. 692–93.

298   "He could have played blind": Dylan, *Chronicles*, p. 168.

300   "There's no way to measure": Ibid., p. 252.

303   "The band is one tenth as good": Andrew Muir, *Razor's Edge: Bob Dylan & the Never Ending Tour* (London: Helter Skelter, 2001), p. 140.

303   "subverting his own material": Ibid., p. 141.

Chapter 13. TELLING THE STORY

314   "The hero was distinguished": Sam Tanenhaus, "Tiger Woods and the Perils of Modern Celebrity," *New York Times*, December 13, 2009.

Chapter 14. THE GOOD SECRET

331   "The words were hard, were deep": Lanois's acceptance speech at the 1998 Grammy Awards.

331   "That's where we made the demos": Alastair McKay, interview with Lanois in *Uncut* magazine, 2008. Quotes from Lanois passim are from this interview.

332   "the hair on my arms": Damien Love, interview with Howard in *Uncut*, 2008. Quotes from Howard passim are from this interview.

333   He was haunted by the spirit of Buddy Holly: Cott, ed., *Bob Dylan: The Essential Interviews*, p. 405.

333   "And this would happen": Ibid.

333   "I get very meditative": Jon Pareles, *New York Times*, September 28, 1997.

334   "On *Time Out of Mind*, Bob called": Damien Love, interview with Jim Keltner in *Uncut*, 2008. Quotes from Keltner passim are from this interview.

339   "the shining example": www.augiemeyers.com.

340   "It got off the tracks": Mikal Gilmore, *Rolling Stone* interview, December 22, 2001, reprinted in Cott, ed., *Bob Dylan: The Essential Interviews*, p. 414.

343   "he had made dozens": Sounes, *Down the Highway*, pp. 356–57.

Chapter 15. DEATHS AND ENTRANCES

360   "The Pope's idea": *Chicago Tribune*, September 27, 1997.

360   "You say the answer is": Richard Owen, "Why Pope Tried to Stop Dylan," *Sunday Times* (London), March 8, 2007.

361   when President Clinton turned to praise him: Anecdote comes from videographer Helene Haviland, who was covering the event.

361   "I'm proud of his accomplishments": Edna Gundersen, "At the Heart of Dylan," *USA Today*, September 28, 1997.

363   Dresden on May 24: Sources are blog reviews by Sven Lewandowski, Christian Zeiser, and Carsten Wohfold on *Bob Links* website, May 24, 2000.

365   Cagliari: Reviews by Michele Medda and Mr. A., ibid., June 2, 2000.

366   "Bob was very calm": Ibid., Mr. A.

366   "It annoys me": This and quotes passim are from *La Republica*, July 24, 2001, and *Dagens Nyheter*, Sweden, July 23, 2001.

367   "George was a giant": CNN transcript, December 1, 2001.

368   The Australian TV director had arranged: Sources for this are Kemper and Campbell.

372   "On '*Love and Theft*,' Bob really wanted": Quotes from Chris Shaw passim are from Damien Love's interview in *Uncut*, 2008. Other sources for this section are author's interviews with Kemper and Campbell.

375   "I got so frustrated": Gilmore interview, reprinted in Cott, ed., *Bob Dylan: The Essential Interviews*, p. 415.

376   "A lot of lines": Trev Gibb, "Riffing with Larry Charles," *Twenty Years of Isis*, ed. Derek Barker (Surrey, England: Chrome Dreams, 2005), p. 331.

378   "I stopped reading them": Quotes from Dylan passim are from *La Republica*, cited above.

381   "There's a real drive to it": Cott, ed., *Bob Dylan: The Essential Interviews*, p. 414.

382   "the way I really feel about things": Edna Gundersen, "Dylan Is Positively on Top of His Game," *USA Today*, September 10, 2001.

Chapter 16. FACING THE LION

384   "I find myself lingering": Paul Williams, *Bob Dylan, Performing Artist 1986–1990 & Beyond* (London: Omnibus Press, 2004) p. 323.

384   "You're talking to a person": This and Dylan quotes passim are from Gil-

more, *Rolling Stone*, December 22, 2001, reprinted in Cott, ed., *Bob Dylan: The Essential Interviews*, pp. 411–28.

387 "She told you to think globally": Reviews by Jim Bartoo and Jeanne Davis, *Bob Links*, October 19, 2001.

387 "perhaps the funkiest performance": Oliver Trager, *Keys to the Rain: The Definitive Bob Dylan Encyclopedia* (New York: Billboard Books, 2004), p. 120.

387 "There's *nothing* about that girl": Jonathan Lethem, "The Genius of Bob Dylan," *Rolling Stone*, August 21, 2006.

388 "We just wondered": Gray, *The Bob Dylan Encyclopedia*, p. 639.

390 "Bobby, you write so little": Clinton Heylin, *Still on the Road: The Songs of Bob Dylan, 1974–2006* (London: Constable, 2010), p. 148.

392 "wanted to make a Bob Dylan movie": Charles interview with suicidegirls. com.

393 "And the auditorium was half-empty": Roger Ebert, *Chicago Sun-Times*, August 15, 2003.

393 "an unholy, incoherent mess": A. O. Scott, *New York Times*, July 24, 2003.

395 "was transformed by his effort": Reviews on *Bob Links*, April 23, 2003.

396 "Dylan's stroll around": RJ in Houston review, ibid.

397 "You just keep doing your best": Author's interview with Hoikkala.

397 "Lest we forget, while you're writing": David Gates, "The Book of Bob," *Newsweek*, September 28, 2004.

398 "he sometimes slammed": This and quotes following are from J. Weber review, *Bob Links*, July 12, 2003.

398 "He didn't walk anywhere": Randy and Dawn Dilkes review, ibid.

398 "The guys were smiling": J. Weber review, *Bob Links*, July 13, 2003.

399 4:30 sound check: Bob Nilmeier review, *Bob Links*, July 15, 2003.

399 his son Jakob's Little League: Interview with Jakob Dylan by Anthony De-Curtis, "A Different Set of Chronicles," *New York Times*, May 8, 2005.

399 "Larry bought a pig": Bob Nilmeier review, *Bob Links*, July 15, 2003.

400 "I could see visions": Gates, "The Book of Bob."

401 "Johnny was and is the North Star": *Rolling Stone*, October 16, 2003.

402 "people would ask me": Quotes from Young are from the panel discussion at Experience Music Project in New York, November 2004, moderated by Bob Santelli.

405 "If you were going to sell out": Press conference, KQED-TV, San Francisco, December 3, 1965, transcribed in Cott, ed., *Bob Dylan: The Essential Interviews*, p. 75.

410 "After a career of principled coyness": Review of *Chronicles* in *Publishers Weekly*, n.d.

413 "I pray that I can be": Dylan, *Chronicles*, p. 206.

Chapter 17. ABERDEEN: JULY 24, 2009

416 "These guys were standing": Simon Fuller, "Look, Ma, Bob Dylan," *Winnipeg Sun*, November 12, 2008.

416 "He spent ages": "Bob Dylan Visits John Lennon's Home," *Indian Express*, May 12, 2009.

416 Frank Zappa: Frank Zappa with Peter Occhiogrosso, *The Real Frank Zappa Book* (New York: Poseidon, 1989) pp. 20–23; Barry Miles, *Frank Zappa* (London: Atlantic, 2004).

417 "If this wins": Gray, *The Bob Dylan Encyclopedia*, p. 726, citing Greil Marcus interview in *Guardian* (London), May 13, 2005.

417 "I get a lot of weird calls": This and quotes passim are from ibid. Gray cites the Zappa interview with Karl Dallas in Michael Gray, *Mother! The Frank Zappa Story* (London: Plexus, 1993), pp. 185–86.

420 "third straight masterwork": Joe Levy review, *Rolling Stone*, August 29, 2006.

420 Jody Rosen: Jody Rosen, "Bob Dylan's Make-Out Album," *Slate*, August 30, 2006.

420 "With the exception of the closing track": Jim DeRogatis review, *Chicago Sun-Times*, August 27, 2006.

425 An exhibit of his paintings: Alan Jackson, "Bob Dylan: He's got everything he needs, he's an artist," *Times* (London), June 6, 2008. All Dylan quotes passim from this source.

427 "reasonably interesting": Waldemar Januszczak, "Bob Dylan at the Halcyon Gallery," *Times* (London), June 15, 2008.

429 "Alright!": Craig Planting review, *Bob Links*, November 4, 2008.

429 the biggest news story: Susan Saulny and Robbie Brown, "Case Recalls Tightrope Blacks Walk with Police," *New York Times*, July 24, 2009; Abby Goodnough, "Sergeant Who Arrested Professor Defends Actions," ibid.

430 "Gates opened the front door": Cambridge Police Incident Report 9005127.

433 "I'm usually in a numb state": Cott, ed., *Bob Dylan: The Essential Interviews*, p. 321.

436 "real songs of the American spirit": Douglas Brinkley, "Bob Dylan's America," *Rolling Stone*, May 14, 2009, p. 44.

439 "a sound that returns to": Review in *Los Angeles Times*, March 27, 2009.

439 "Texas may have more": Brinkley, "Bob Dylan's America," p. 46.

439 "Dylan's voice, with age": Sean Wilentz review, *Daily Beast*, April 17, 2009.

440 "Dylan, who turns sixty-eight": David Fricke review, *Rolling Stone*, April 24, 2009.

442 "eccentric-looking old man": Wayne Parry, Associated Press, via *SF Gate*, August 19, 2009.

442 "We got a call for a suspicious person": Chris Francescani, *ABC News*, August 14, 2009.

Index

Index

Index

Index

Index

Index

Index

Index

Index

Index

Index

Index

"Oh, Sister"

"Hurricane"

"Sara"

"Maggie's Farm"

"Lay Lady Lay"

"One Too Many Mornings"

"No Time to Think"

"Shot of Love"

"Jokerman"

"Neighborhood Bully"

"Union Sundown"

"I and I"

"Everything Is Broken"

"Ring Them Bells"

About the Author

Daniel Mark Epstein has published more than fifteen books of poetry, biography, and history, including *Nat King Cole*; *Lincoln and Whitman*, which received an Academy Award from the American Academy of Arts and Letters; and *The Lincolns: Portrait of a Marriage*, which was named one of the top ten books of 2008 by the *Wall Street Journal* and the *Chicago Sun-Times*. He lives in Baltimore, Maryland.